Will

FACE
CANCER

John Wilkinson

*Dedicated to my amazing wife Jane, who didn't ask to become
a carer, and to my fantastic children, Max and Lois.
Together they are my raison d'être.*

A CIP record for this title is available from the British Library.

Published by The Self Publishing Studio.

Paperback 9-781999-919658

Designed and created by the author with help from Clere Group Ltd and PAC Copywriting.

Printed and bound by Clere Group Limited in Newbury.
www.clere.uk.com

This book is printed on paper sourced from sustainably managed forests.

CONTENTS

The run up to cancer, medical treatments and beyond to the present day.

1. Nothing to worry about   1
2. Diagnosis   8
3. Building up to surgery   27
4. The eviction of my filthy squatter: first surgery   37
5. The eureka moment   44
6. Over the worst?   53
7. We can rebuild him   63
8. Solitary confinement   75
9. Home again   85
10. Set back and enjoy the ride   93
11. Arise, Gonzalez! Radiotherapy   99
12. Pirates on the starboard bow   112
13. Mission remission   126
14. Recurring nightmare   138

A list of hints and tips for future cancer and surgery patients.

15. My Strategy - Mind, Body & Soul   159
16. Best Laid Plans   174

Written by my wife Jane, aimed to help others who unexpectedly find themselves as a primary carer.

17. Thoughts from Jane   179

The hardwiring of my character: a brief autobiography.

18. Genes and roots   188
19. First memories   191
20. School daze   199
21. Toughen up!   206
22. Let there be rock   216
23. Move down't south   222
24. First rungs   237
25. Not Jonny Wilkinson   254
26. London calling   265
27. Family influence   282
28. Coming home   298

FOREWORD FROM A COUPLE OF FAMOUS SUPPORTERS:

John Wilkinson received a hospital pass in 2017 and set about lining up for a drop goal to win his World Cup of Survival versus Cancer's First XV. Sadly, one in two people in the UK born after 1960 will be diagnosed with some form of cancer during their lifetime. It affects us all though. We all know a handful of people who've had it, got it or will get it - family, friends, ourselves. Cancer doesn't care – it doesn't discriminate.

Phil Tufnell and Matt Dawson MBE

But John was a forward and knew he couldn't kick for toffee, so defaulting to type, he put his head down, tucked the ball under his arm and made a dash for the try line. He knew his future would need a strong mindset and tenacity, both of which he had in spades. Just as well, as he had a huge tumour in his face, leading to some of the most challenging treatments. He endured many gruesome procedures to save him and everyone on the touchline cheered his resolve as he charged through the opposition.

John already considers himself the victor, having outlived most peoples' expectations. Join him at his side throughout these pages, which were written during his illness. As he explores his thinking, find out how he focussed through these challenges and didn't drop the ball.

John describes his approach to this incredible experience and wrote *Face Cancer* to help others who may be facing their own moment of truth. You never know, it could contain a nugget of gold that proves useful for you or a loved one, now, or in the future. As well as raising money for cancer charities, it's also a fantastic read, filled with laughter and tears.

Go for the try line John, right under the posts and win the match. And if you do, it's probably best to let someone else kick for the conversion.

Matt Dawson MBE   **Phil Tufnell**

FOREWORD FROM MY ONCOLOGIST

John and I first met up in the autumn of 2017 and it was clear he was ready to get on with whatever his professionals thought necessary, in order to eradicate the disease.

He's been given a bit of a double whammy in so much as having been diagnosed with a head and neck sarcoma, a very rare form of cancer, which has presented in a critical part of the body which has impacted significantly on his quality of life, both physically and psychologically. Despite the challenges John has faced, he's had to adapt to many treatments that carry a large amount of 'collateral damage' as he calls it.

A patient chooses to deal with cancer in whatever way they wish. I personally feel that their position is helped by making sure they carry on living with an excellent quality of life, rather than waiting for it to overtake them. John doesn't seem to want to stop and I'm delighted he's been documenting his story from the beginning. This will have helped him and I hope *Face Cancer* provides a spark of inspiration or a little gem of knowledge to others who will follow in his shoes.

Best of luck on your chemotherapy, John. The Royal Marsden Hospital Sarcoma Team are with you all the way.

Dr Aisha Miah
Consultant Clinical Oncologist, Sarcoma Unit
BMedSci MBBS MRCP FRCR PhD

AUTHOR'S NOTE

Whilst recovering between maxillofacial cancer surgeries, I found that I couldn't simply rest up and recuperate week after week. Sure, initially I didn't do much else, but the brain that had powered me throughout a very busy former life refused to be left on idle. So out of the blue, one morning at 2am, my mind mutinied.

I woke up in bed with a jolt as thoughts rolled in out of nowhere like freak waves in a storm. Memories from my past crashed on my shore and I wondered why this was occurring. It slowly dawned on me. My mind was sifting through experiences from my life, to get my head prepared for the road ahead. I want to say that a heavenly shaft of light then descended upon me (it didn't) but for me, I had an epiphany of sorts.

Friends and medics had already relayed how inspirational and brave my mindset was up until that point and I wanted to put this to good use. Throughout life's challenges, I found that there's nothing quite like getting advice directly from those who have walked in your shoes.

Perhaps I could help others who might be facing cancer for the first time. Some other poor souls are going to face a brutal cancer type like mine, which involves lots of surgery. Whilst there's plenty of support for more common cancer types, there seemed to be very little out there for maxillofacial cases. It's a shame, as the 'collateral damage' left in the wake of its treatment is quite devastating. How could I help cancer patients and others following the same path as me?

Then it came to me: a book! Within its pages, I could offer some advice, from the patient's point of view.

Could I do it? I managed to scrape an O-level in English at the second attempt, so surely it couldn't be that difficult. Little did I know then! I also thought that by writing events down, I might also get around the medical events I was enduring. When I excitedly discussed the idea with a friend, he said that I'd found the nugget he hoped I'd find: a gift out of adversity.

Within these pages I've used humour, reflecting the manner in which I tend to approach daunting challenges. Yet at other times, I've pondered respectfully over serious issues. I hope you enjoy the balance.

The main objective of my book is to help others with a documented insight. This includes the patients, as well as their carers and supporters. As a by-product, I hope it also raises some funds for cancer charities and provides an entertaining read too.

There will be different reasons for purchasing this book and to give readers direct access to the specific part they want, I've divided *Face Cancer* into four sections:

Chapters 1-14 cover my cancer story: the symptoms, diagnosis, treatments and onwards.

Chapters 15-16 pull together a list of hints and tips gained from the experience.

Chapter 17 is written by my wife Jane and reflects on her role as my primary carer.

Chapters 18–28 offers a brief autobiography - the source of my personality and character.

Writing this book has given me a focus throughout my cancer experience. In its own way it's accompanied me through the tough times and also allowed me to draw a line under some of these. Other memories stay and will always remain raw, they still conjure up a well of emotion within me. These are the mental scars I carry alongside the physical variety. It was challenging to get them down on paper and do them justice. Above all, I hadn't appreciated what a huge cathartic release mechanism it would be. I've enjoyed the experience immensely and can highly recommend it.

Throughout the book, I also invite you to listen to some of my favourite music; it's part of my make-up. These songs sprang to mind as I wrote the book and recalled some of the memories. If *Face Cancer* is ever put to film, at least there'll be an awesome soundtrack! Happy reading, folks :)

1

NOTHING TO WORRY ABOUT

The first signs of the cancer, when life was good and at full throttle

To get the full story, I need to wind the clock back to the end of 2016 and set the scene. It's important to share some of the first signs with you and to reveal what was going on in my life at that time, as I left getting it sorted rather too late. Typical bloke.

You had to pinch yourself really back then, life was good. We'd toiled hard to build a comfortable lifestyle and I was blessed with a fantastic family and very busy, fulfilling life. Yeah, there were ups and downs as with everything, but overall, we were lucky. We were enjoying a purple patch.

We genuinely didn't take any of this for granted though; there were a few health issues in the wider family (which you'll read about later) which gave us some valuable perspective. Jane, my wife, was booked in for an imminent operation, so we were starting to face some headwinds.

Out of the blue, I noticed I had a slight numbness above my top, right-hand side back molars. It wasn't too much of an issue, given there was no pain to speak of. After launching a thorough, week-long flossing and brushing campaign, I was still left with the sensation that something was stuck between my teeth. So I dutifully swung by the dental surgery en route to work one morning for a 15-minute check-up. I sat in the chair, exchanged a few jovial pleasantries with the family dentist, and explained what was up.

"I'll have a look and take an X-ray." In went his dental prodders and mirrors for a gander, my mouth agape. "Can't see anything, you're still grinding, aren't you?" he asked. I nodded and uurrgghhed in agreement.

After the lightning inspection, I relayed that I'd been grinding less than before. Work had calmed down a bit over the past year, so I was feeling less stressed. As promised, the dentist took a side X-ray and I bit down on a tiny plate between my molars. Astonishingly, we looked at the results together some five minutes later. I was convinced we'd find an offending pork scratching but was surprised at the verdict.

"Nothing going on, I can't see anything untoward I'm afraid. Might just be old age, Johnny - take it easy, keep an eye on it and come back if it worsens." Job done, I thought, happy days, let's get out of here.

With a shrug of the shoulders I left - nothing to worry about. Logic said I was approaching my half century so bits of my body were bound to start crumbling away, ache or twinge. It must be the norm, I thought, as I looked at my watch and zoomed off, updating Jane on the way (hands free, of course).

We talked about the far more important, looming medical event: Jane's impending major surgery. In a couple of weeks' time, it would obliterate our daily routine, so it was time to inform work and make some contingency plans.

The following week, Jane went into Basingstoke Hospital to have a rugby ball-sized fibroid removed from the outside of her womb and subsequent hysterectomy. She'd been suffering with symptoms for many months. As a trained body mechanic and fitness professional, she already recognised the knock-on effects this was having on her general health. An uncomfortable gait, pressing bladder, bad breath and backache, to name a few. All the symptoms were worsening by the day. Not ideal when you're running classes and trying to emulate your peak performance. Jane was naturally very much looking forward to getting rid of her poisonous invader. In readiness, she'd organised cover, leaving the small matter of undergoing major surgery and planning for a long recovery.

Ready for Household Duties

Initially, it went pretty smoothly in hospital, but later in the week, she contracted an infection and stayed in a little longer. With elderly parents, we'd already planned that I'd need to take on the domestic duties. I managed to keep on top of work as best I could and heavily used our team's mantra: 'family first.' My boss reminded me that I wasn't expected to do anything except make sure my wife got better. The office sent me a very touching gift set to help me, including marigolds, an apron and duster, together with something for Jane and the kids. I promptly decided to dress up in the outfit to thank everyone and sent a photo in.

♪ I Want To Break Free (Queen) ♪:

I remember the tongue-in-cheek video, made for MTV. The single took off in the UK, but floundered in the US - they couldn't quite get over Freddie's sultry 'heels and moustache' look. Ironic really, given they'd already warmed to Alice Cooper!

To be honest, I found the whole 'house husband' thing quite exhausting. I wasn't used to the speed at which things needed to be done. Prepping breakfast, getting the kids to school, then tidying up the bomb site. Caring for Jane, a bit of lunch, shopping, washing, ironing, hoovering. Squeezing some work in then starting all over again when the kids got back from school. By the end of the day I was punch drunk.

Thankfully though, nobody was poisoned, but I dropped a few balls juggling tasks and keeping up with Jane's exacting standards. My kids, Max and Lois, were fourteen and twelve respectively, and gave me very sympathetic, encouraging hugs, with comments like, "Awww daddy, you're trying your best, I can see that…(sigh)…never mind."

I soon decided to enrol them into looking after themselves a bit more. It was a necessity I said, else things might go off the rails. Hey, here was an opportunity, so I grabbed it! To this day, they continue to do a little more about the house: they tidy their own bedrooms, hang up their own clothes and get the breakfast things out. Up until then, I reckon Jane had over-serviced them. To incentivise them, I introduced a little bit of sibling rivalry and scored them marks out of ten…if all else failed, straight bribery seemed to work.

During these weeks, I consciously acknowledged that I'd gained some special time with my family. I wasn't playing my usual role of disappearing at the crack of dawn and coming back just before the kids' bedtime…every cloud. It was a genuine eye-opener to see what an amazing job my wife did whilst I headed to the office, day after day. Jane has always taken a well-drilled, military discipline to the domestic chores, and organises several weekly classes for her business. She also kept Hubster happy when he came home. A massive 'hats off' to all the home-makers out there who see their partners disappear off to work! It made me think, note to self: I need to assume more of the domestic duties in the future, just as the kids have done.

By the end of Jane's recovery, I'd accumulated loads of brownie points but, as all husbands know, these have a very short shelf life. The whole domestic experience was a nice segue into Christmas. Jane was getting stronger and slowly, normal service resumed. On Christmas Day, we had both sets of parents over, together with separate days for a number of close friends. I got as involved in domestic duties as much as I was allowed and might even have used some of my own initiative now and then. Up to that point, I'd been shooed out of the kitchen as I just got in the way.

In the New Year, work decided to play musical chairs. The leadership team was reduced by a third, as the boss left to take on a new challenge elsewhere, leaving Martin, the other remaining member of the leadership team, and me, to navigate the good ship. Martin's an experienced chap like me and, despite his strange, Yorkshire-derived sense of humour (only kidding), we've always worked well together. Even so, we both knew that we were going to be up against it until our new boss was appointed, which turned out to be nine months later.

About this time, our household got into its usual holiday run-up to the February half-term break and we went skiing as a family. Whilst away, halfway through the holiday, Jane sensed that all was not well with her parents as they hadn't been in touch, so we called them.

Jane's dad eventually gave us the news that Beryl, her mum, had fallen at home. She'd broken her pelvis and arm and was laid up in a ward in Basingstoke & North Hants hospital. Bob said that there was little we could do, so pleaded with us to enjoy the rest of the holiday. With a bit of luck, she'd be back home when we returned. This was clearly a bit of a shocker and we were concerned. We recognised how frail Beryl had become recently after fighting various cancers for over 40 years, but she'd always had an aura of granite about her. Jane's brother, Dean, was on hand to help locally, which alleviated some of the worry and after all, Beryl was in the best place. Tearfully, Jane got her head around it and spoke to her dad on a daily basis.

When we got back home, Jane immediately downed tools to support her dad, so I helped out where I could at home. Beryl was determined to get out of hospital and go home, so Bob set up a bed in the lounge. All went well for a while, but after three weeks, she picked up an infection of sorts and couldn't get out of bed, so was blue-lighted back to hospital. The infection seemed to worsen and we later found out that Beryl had been resuscitated a couple of times within a few days of readmission.

Whilst her mum was in hospital, I made sure that Jane spent as much time there as possible, so I worked from home and once again applied the 'family first' policy. As usual, everybody at work was extremely understanding and supportive.

Unfortunately, the long-term prognosis of sepsis wasn't good. Beryl wasn't enjoying the low quality of life, despite the wonderful nursing she received. After a few weeks, she passed the tipping point of no return. She recognised that she wasn't coming out of hospital and discussed this with Jane, Bob and the doctors when she could. It was a dignified curtain call. All of her family, including her beloved grandchildren, got the chance to say goodbye before she went peacefully on 9th April.

Jane was very close to her mum. They used to natter for hours on the phone every day, so understandably, there was a chasm to fill. Jane and her dad busied themselves by planning a fantastic funeral service and celebration of life party. It was really special and all attendees commented on how uplifting it was. It did Beryl credit and brought the families a little closer because of it. My role was simple: I supported Jane as much as she wanted on a day-to-day basis as she went through the journey of grieving for her very much-loved mother and friend. Over the months, Jane ensured that her dad remained close and, in a way, he started to fill the void left by her doting mum. Life began to take on the structure of a new sort of normality once the dust had settled.

As I slowly drifted back into a normal, frenetic work pattern, my job took an exciting new turn. I was asked to facilitate some risk training. This entailed short but regular trips away from home and, as the timing wasn't perfect, I was conscious of making sure that Jane was supportive and on board. She loved the idea as it would give her some quality time alone with her dad, so I went for it. I eventually ended up taking several slots across the UK, then in June, I went to train our Armenian corporate office.

Numb lip in Armenia, but I looked fine

The months flew by as my diary became extremely busy and pretty unconventional. Weeks were pock-marked with travel. I returned home from Armenia, my final training course, and caught my breath. I realised that the numbness in my jaw had now spread to my top lip and cheek. To be honest, with all the events zooming past me so quickly, I hadn't objectively sat down and assessed my symptoms, which had by now persisted for months. As I wasn't in pain and had been told everything was normal, I didn't see the need to follow anything up, so I shelved the problem to the back of my mind.

To my regret now, I didn't implement 'family first' back then. Instead, I allowed myself to be sucked into the exciting maelstrom of a different work life and juggling snippets of family time. I should have done everyone a favour and got myself fully checked out a lot sooner.

Jane looks back at this period with a huge amount of guilt too. She remembers me complaining about the numbness occasionally and believes that she should have insisted I got it sorted out sooner. I've read that guilt is a common feeling amongst partners of people with illness. So her guilt was natural but at the same time, illogical to my mind.

We often remarked, somewhat tongue-in-cheek, that I had ranked third in Jane's priorities. First place went to the children and second place to Fudge, our much-loved and incredibly spoilt guinea pig. But joking aside, this one lay at my door, not Jane's. I should have taken ownership earlier.

Finally, as the whirlwind of dust settled at work and home, I decided to grasp the nettle and do something about it. I booked two consecutive appointments, one with the doctor and one with the dentist.

Back in July 2017, I had rarely been to the doctor, and didn't even know my doctor's name. So when I visited, I gave a quick overview of my general health and all of my medical history that I could remember. This helped keep within the ten-minute allocated time slot. When I suggested that the symptoms appeared to be nerve-related in my jaw, the doctor agreed that it was likely to be something that the dentist could advise on. She was happy that I was seeing them an hour later and wanted to be kept in the loop. So off I trundled to the dentist.

My family dentist wasn't about at the surgery, so I happily accepted the offer to see one of his colleagues. The dentist saw on the notes that I'd visited in November and, when I mentioned that the symptoms had spread, she said we ought to take a closer look. I was hastily led to a room at the end of the barn corridor with a radioactive sign on the door. Inside, on its own, sat a bigger, better and shinier bit of X-ray kit.

After resting my big Bruce Forsyth chin gently on a platform the size of a tea bag, I was asked to stay very still. The scanning part slowly revolved around my head; this contraption was going to give us a 360-degree picture! After the first dummy run and slight adjustment for my wide shoulders and noggin, we lined up for the final run of images. I held my breath. The staff could sense that I had become a little concerned about their 'urgency' so without further ado, we looked at the pictures.

The dentist declared that she could see a mass of unknown substance in my sinus which needed further investigation, right away. I asked if this might, in her opinion, be something to be concerned about. She said that there was every possibility, but the consultant at the hospital needed to review the findings. 'Houston, we have a problem' rang in my ears.

The dental staff were courteous, efficient and understanding, but at the end of the day, their job was done. An urgent appointment was booked with a Consultant Oral & Maxillofacial Surgeon, Jacob, for 1st August.

At home, we initially tried not to think about it and adopted the approach that it might logically be something innocent. I think the kids lifted their gaze from their phones for a nanosecond and seemed unfazed by it all when we told them. Jane and I didn't see the point in creating worry, so we just checked that they had logged the information. We would find out what was going on after further tests, so there was little point speculating now.

Our respective parents took the sketchy news pretty well. I asked everyone worrying to not worry about it until we had some facts - a bit of an oxymoron, I guess. Jane and I talked a little about some of the possible outcomes, but as emotions were already frayed from that year's rollercoaster, we thought it best to park it until we had some definitive information.

2

DIAGNOSIS

Handling the bombshell of news and driving down the slipway towards the medical motorway

So I rocked up a little nervously at Basingstoke Hospital to the Oral and Maxillofacial Department at 9am. It was a lovely, warm summer's morning, the sun was already beating down and shirt sleeves were on show, but strangely enough, I didn't feel warm at all. I met Jacob bang on time in a consultation room and was surprised to see that he was flanked by a nurse for good measure. Was she there to take notes, be a legal witness or mop me up if I broke down? Anyhow, all of my focus was on Jacob - he was in the hot seat.

Jacob is a petite, gentle, lovely man who possesses the magical gift of a bedside manner suitable for every Tom, Dick or Harriet who might walk in. As with most medical professionals, Jacob exuded confidence and determined pretty quickly how I wanted things delivered. Quick, straight, factual and with time for questions. Straight away he stated that the growth was a tumour. He explained the difference between benign and malignant tumours and indicated that this one was demonstrating signs of being malignant, so yes, it was very likely that I had cancer. I put my hand out to stop the information flow like a nervous school boy, to take a pause and compute this news. Then it registered. BOOM - CANCER.

Instantly something flicked inside of me and I felt a swell of emotion rise within. I had a million and one reasons to live and fight and an image of Jane and the kids came up in my mind. The thought of curling up into a ball or placing two pencils up my nose and finding a corner to rock myself to sleep in didn't enter my head. I could sense my hackles rising - this was war! Despite the turmoil inside my soul, I calmly said, "Bugger."

I then pressed Jacob for a 'best estimate' of my chances of survival. He said my survival chances would be improved as I was relatively fit, strong, a non-smoker and up for it, mentally speaking. He couldn't estimate what my chances were until we knew exactly what we were up against. At that point, I knew there were different types of cancer but my overall knowledge of the disease was shamefully thin. I wanted to understand everything about the enemy.

Jacob stated that he was concerned the tumour was already pretty large and established. When we discussed my story, I revealed that the first signs had presented themselves nine months earlier. He wanted to get things going very quickly. Every now and then, he saw me staring at the desk for a few seconds, and patiently allowed me time for the reality of the facts to sink in. I came back in the room and asked what the next stage was. Jacob squeezed me into a CT head and neck scan there and then, and said he would also organise an MRI scan. Ultimately, he needed to take a biopsy to determine what type of cancer it was, so asked if I could come and see him the following week in Guildford.

I told him that we'd booked a family holiday and, whilst we discussed the benefits of cancelling it, he begrudgingly understood that we needed the break, given the 'annus horribilis' we'd had so far. He tried to persuade me to reconsider, but realising that I wasn't budging, he organised a biopsy for soon after my return. Jacob very kindly provided me with his direct, personal contact details, as he was 'in between' secretaries, and we promised to remain in touch.

I returned to the car, pretty numb, and slumped in the seat. I rang Jane straight away. I didn't want to dilute anything, so repeated every word that I could remember. At the same time, I wanted her to know that I was going to beat this and she didn't have to worry about my mindset. The overall conclusion we reached was that it was quite likely to be a further shitfest year ahead and we would have to take one step at a time. Information would take time to fall into place.

Jane was clearly a little upset with yet another downer on the old rollercoaster of 2017 and asked if we'd pissed off some celestial being in an earlier life. But as we discussed it further, we took stock of the situation. I was fit. The thing was in my face but was not next to a vital soft organ like a heart, kidney, liver or lungs, so it could be a lot worse. Yes, it was next to my brain, but this was encased in a thick skull. I was now engaged with the right medical team and nobody had yet turned around and said, "I'm very sorry, but you have three months to live." Our collective mind-set was as one: sure, one option was to wallow and cry, but there was so much still unknown at the moment and we had a lot to fight for. Yes, *my* fight instantly became *our* fight.

♪ Breakdown (Guns & Roses) ♪

"Remember in this game we call life that no-one said it's fair," taken from their album 'Use your Illusion I and II'. In a documentary on Guns and Roses, frontman Axl stated that he wanted to craft an album with as much impact as Pink Floyd's 'The Wall', one that would be in everybody's record collection. In my

opinion, this was definitely achieved; interestingly, the whole album and tour process on this one was so intense that it broke the band.

I decided to tell Martin at work, there and then, from the car. He and I had been in the thick of it since 1st January. We had adopted a 'watch each other's back,' siege-like mentality and therefore I wanted him kept up to speed. He also knew why I was at the hospital. I decided it was best to keep any further work comms under wraps. At work, people were flat out, and the last thing I wanted to cause was a flash-in-the-pan moment of drama with an incorrect, premature diagnosis.

That night at home, Jane and I told the kids. Nothing was certain, but it was likely that I'd got cancer and that going forward, this would need a treatment plan. We were able to vaguely talk about surgery and also less invasive treatments such as chemotherapy and radiotherapy. Beryl had gone through both of these during her battle with the disease. We also phoned the rest of the family with an update. I kept it brief and, without overplaying it, I gave everyone the sense that the early prognosis was not cookies and cream. I stated that, as there was nothing conclusive, we still had no need to panic. I asked everyone to remain upbeat. Thankfully, no-one questioned why we were going on holiday instead of taking the biopsy. I think I may have glossed over that fact a little, stating that Jacob would fix a date on our return.

The genie was now half way out of the bottle. The excrement had been scooped up and someone was taking aim at the fan.

Early August 2017

So, before the biopsy, we trundled off on our first proper 'do nothing except lounge around the pool if that's all you fancy doing' holiday, in the form of an all-inclusive break to Cyprus.

During the day, Jane and I amused ourselves people-watching whilst the kids did their own stuff. The clientele was mainly Russian, Brits probably made up 25% of the guests, followed by all other European nationalities. The Russian men were easy to spot: bulging bodies in budgie smugglers. The Brits tended to keep to themselves, given we were heavily outnumbered, and the rest of the Europeans made lots of noise.

One thing I bought for everyone before we went away was the latest technology in snorkels. Unfortunately, the fun police intervened, and Jane insisted that I shouldn't try mine as it would aggravate the tumour, so we only ended up taking them for the kids, who loved them! It was their first true scuba experience as they breathed in air around the mask. In the past, I'd thoroughly enjoyed diving in a totally different, colourful world no more than ten metres below the surface of the sea, so it was great to pass on a small glimpse of this to the kids.

♪ Holiday (Scorpions) ♪

"Exchange your troubles for some love, wherever you are"

I spent some quality, individual time with all of my family in Cyprus, where some wonderful memories were made, enabling me to call upon them in the future. I made sure that I had at least one memorable morning swim in the sea with Jane. There were so many early risers at the resort, laying their towels out! It was so refreshing to take a dip in the cool morning air and the sea was warm. After a quick shower, we'd change for brekky at our favourite table in the lovely restaurant.

Max and I had a smashing time on a boat trip; we sat on the top deck with the captain, in the comfy seats. It was interesting that others wanted to squeeze onto the bow, which was a rough ride at times. This reminded me of my first foreign holiday in Corfu as a child. Boat trips were fun, and the best bit was diving off the top when anchored up. Max relived some of my youth for me that day and started to do the same into the crystal-clear water. We snorkelled into caves together and had a good laugh.

Lois and I spent some time in the art studio where we painted rocks and pictures for presents. She loved it and it reminded me of painting the leather jackets for friends in my youth. Lois and I accomplished some real works of art that still hang proudly at home.

There's no doubt that the holiday gave me and the family some thinking and preparation time for what we were about to endure. It was a memory anchor I'd go back to. We also took the time to chat with the kids and underpin what we knew so far - that things were going to get very strange and weird when we got back.

On holiday, the tumour started to make its presence known. Apart from the whole side of my face now being numb, there was accompanying pain too, still manageable with paracetamol to ensure a good night's sleep. I started to massage my face to try and get some sensation back and tapped the sinus area to aggravate the tumour. I wanted the invading parasite to know that I was onto it and wasn't going to let it have any easy ride.

I returned to work mid-week to pick up the baton from Martin who'd admirably held off the Indians at the fort. He was off on his holiday the following week and I said he looked like he needed it. "You don't look so hot yourself, mate!" he replied. I laughed, but on closer inspection, could see that actually, despite my slightly bronzed skin, I was looking pretty dodgy.

The growth in my sinus seemed to be stirring into life and its symptoms were now starting to surface. I had acquired a foul odour creeping down my nose and an acrid taste in my mouth too. The usual dark patches under my eyes were much darker than normal and a new bump in my cheek had appeared where the tumour lurked. Was it going to burst out of my face like the aliens in the movies? Probably not. I noticed that my right eyeball had also started to lift; the right pupil was now higher than the left pupil so it must have reached my eye socket too (deep joy!). I needed to make sure that Jacob was aware of these new developments, so I sent him a text. By now, we were in regular contact.

My work diary had started to show that my hospital activity was ramping up, so I decided to anticipate any interrogations and advised the team of my health situation. It felt fair, given that we were tremendously busy, and they needed to plan ahead as much as possible around my upcoming medical visits.

In Oxford, I simply called everyone around the desk, told the wider open office and phoned colleagues who weren't there that day. I asked Martin to advise colleagues in Reading too. This felt a bit haphazard and unplanned. I realised I'd need to sharpen up my comms going forward, as there were certainly going to be a few more messages to relay.

Despite me sharing the pessimistic, yet realistic, outlook from Jacob's early diagnosis, Martin and our regional director both reacted optimistically. "Nowadays, the NHS needs to paint a bleak picture to ensure it doesn't get people's hopes up for fear of litigation and the like." Nice of them to try to see the bright side but in my heart of hearts, I knew Jacob wasn't covering his arse. He had been fantastic with me, straight with the facts he saw in front of him.

I was in a bit of a glum holding pattern, counting down the days to the biopsy. Work kept me superficially busy but in truth, only temporarily kept me thinking about something else. Being home with the kids was the best distraction. Max and Lois had the uncanny knack of demanding attention like normal teenagers, where some of the most stressful events in their lives were arguments at school or our slow broadband speed.

The road ahead was going to be a tad bumpy to say the least. All I wanted at this point was to understand exactly what I had, get shot of it and return to some kind of normality.

Biopsy Day

There was one young lady in the household who had every right to be grumbling about the forthcoming biopsy and that was Lois, as it was scheduled for her birthday, of all days. To her credit, she didn't moan once. She'd worked out that it wouldn't be so bad spending retail time with Jane and the credit card, without an insanely bored daddy in tow. Early in the morning, Lois opened lots of presents and cards. There were smiles and cuddles, and she was soon looking forward to spending the day with Jane and her friends in town.

A week or so before the biopsy date, I'd convinced Jane that I'd be fine to drive myself. Jacob was in agreement, as long as I had a bit of a rest before the MRI scan, which was scheduled for early afternoon, after the morning's procedure. However, my dad had different ideas and insisted that he'd drive. He phoned and beat me into submission with emotional blackmail. He clearly wanted to help in some way and after we'd dropped the bombshell of news, I could hardly refuse.

As planned, dad was on the driveway waiting just after Lois had opened presents. After I kissed everyone goodbye, we set off. We'd packed well for the day: elevenses, lunch, hot and cold drinks, together with hours of reading material. To be honest, I wasn't looking forward to dad's driving as it wound me up good and proper. He was a very experienced driver, but for some reason, he'd picked up a habit that I thought was bordering on dangerous. When pulling away from a junction, he'd do so in second gear then, as soon as he could, he slipped it into third or fourth gear in low revs. The resulting lurches of the car were grindingly stressful. I later discussed this with mum, who thanked me for mentioning it. Apparently, she'd been remonstrating with him for years about it. I was a little more tactful and suggested to dad that he ought to think about switching to an automatic!

Anyway, I tried to switch off and shut my eyes, whilst staying on high alert. After surviving a few dodgy manoeuvres, we arrived at the Royal Surrey Hospital in one piece, very early for my 9.30am appointment, as we wanted to avoid the traffic. We took our place in the bland, beige waiting area. Plastic plants, dog-eared copies of *Women's Weekly* and *Country Life* scattered the tables. It was a calm environment, in sharp contrast to what I would be facing that day. When my time came, I was called in by Jacob.

He reminded me that he'd need to remove the two back teeth in the top right-hand jaw, as they were already very loose. Hey presto, out they popped without any effort. It showed just how much bone had been eaten away by the cancer. Then followed a series of local anaesthetic injections before he got going on the biopsy.

During the whole procedure, the nurse kept rubbing my shoulder, stating what a brave, little soldier I was being - I hadn't whimpered once. Some of the injections would have been very painful for other people, given the oblique angles at which they were administered and she was surprised I hadn't flinched once. I milked it for as long as I could, then honesty got the better of me. I confessed that my whole jaw was already numb. She gave me a certain look. No more rubby shoulder!

In no time at all, Jacob got cracking with the biopsy. He took deep samples from the holes left by my missing teeth. I kept my eyes half closed but could see Jacob using the full ark of his elbow and hear the surgical instrument crunching and grinding away in my jaw. A stiff push upwards, but thankfully no pain. Whilst performing the procedure, Jacob and the nurse had a normal conversation about work schedules and compared diaries over my chest. In no time at all, the holes were being sewn up to stem the bleeding and I was given a couple of cotton pad bungs to chew on. He explained that he'd decided to take three samples. One for the Royal Surrey, one for an independent laboratory and one for The Royal Marsden, as it was a specialist cancer hospital. Three for the price of one: marvellous.

They then rang the scanning department to see if they could squeeze my MRI in straight away, rather than wait around for the 1.30pm appointment. As luck would have it, they had a 45-minute slot coming up in five minutes. Jacob reminded me that the open wounds in my top jaw could only be sewn as best he could and weren't fully sealed up. As a result, diseased material would now start to trickle from the wound, which wouldn't be pleasant. It was likely to pong and taste foul. Best spit that out, I thought to myself.

In a flash, I was led to the scanning department. I was told to jump onto the bed, make myself comfortable and stay very still. This was my first visit to an MRI scanner. Before I went in, I'd become a little intrigued to find out what the experience was going to be like. At work, Martin had advised me to take a blindfold, as he found it claustrophobic, so I lay back and was slid into the hole. I asked for some rock music on the headphones and, feeling a little apprehensive, I started to try to relax with the breathing exercises that Jane had taught me. These really calmed me and although it didn't exactly fly by, time didn't drag in that confined space as much as I thought it would.

The MRI scanner is a big, very noisy, tube-shaped elongated doughnut. It takes multiple, millimetre by millimetre, bacon slices of photographs on a specific area of the body, from different angles, at 100 decibels. The inside of the machine is whitish plastic (it's not dark) and the roof hovers a few inches from your nose. It could be claustrophobic to some, but I didn't find it too overbearing. Before you are slid inside, you're given ear plugs and headphones and your skull snugly fits into a headrest. The last thing they do is pop a cage over your face. I initially thought it was to stop patients damaging the inside of the machine if they stupidly decided to sit up but was later told that it was an essential part of the kit that took the image. The final cherry on the cake is an injection of contrasting liquid, to help differentiate objects on scan images. In my case, this was administered in the last ten minutes of the scan. The adverse reaction was that it made my core buzz with a warm glow - perhaps I was going nuclear? The whole scan took 45 minutes, but it varies depending on the part of the body being scanned. In comparison, a CT scanner is a large, shallow doughnut, rather than the cave of the MRI machine, and the scanning process only took a maximum of five minutes.

I listened intently for the music and they played some good tunes which I could just hear over the repetitive banging din of the scanner. I later came to realise that each of the scanning departments has the same rock playlist. I got to know this pretty well up to track seven, when the scan ended: *Rocking All Over the World - Status Quo, Waterfall - Stone Roses, Silver Machine - Hawkwind, All Fired Up - Pat Benatar, I'm Bored - Iggy Pop, Fire - Arthur Brown, No More Heroes - The Stranglers.*

It was just as well that my dad drove, as I was in no fit state to, after the double whammy I'd just had. Dad and I were heading back home by 11.30am, three hours ahead of our original ETA. I didn't take any notice of my dad's driving and closed my eyes all the way home. My head was in the clouds and my jaw had begun to ache, so I promptly popped some pills down to meet the inevitable oncoming pain, given that the anaesthetic had started to wear off.

When we got back, the birthday contingent was thankfully still in town, so we sat and watched telly with subtitles. To be honest, there wasn't a lot more I could do. I couldn't face lunch, but just sipped on some soup and spent the rest of the afternoon avoiding pain as best I could. I'd begun a long association with Nurse Ibuprofen and Dr Paracetamol. Now all I could do was wait for the results. It was going to be another week or so but at least I'd get some concrete detail about the enemy.

Diagnosis

Jacob had pre-booked an appointment to discuss the CT, MRI and preliminary test results with me at a local surgery in Crondall, a beautiful Jane Austen country village in the middle of north Hampshire. I could have gone to Basingstoke but elected to go there as I'd been there for a medical a year or so back and loved the drive. Might as well enjoy what you can!

I kept my family updated with the story to date and asked that they allow their positive attitudes to shine through for me. Selfishly, I really didn't want to hear any tears, or 'poor you' language. This would have sapped my emotional energy which I was trying to store up. By all means, if you want and need to have a boo, go ahead and have one, but please try to keep it away from me. I'm trying to hold it together here.

Everyone was primed for Diagnosis Day. Jane, the kids, family, friends, colleagues and me. I'd purposely booked a late afternoon appointment on a Friday, which would buy us some precious thinking time over the week-end if we needed it.

Jane had offered (and probably wanted) to come to all of the previous medical appointments but, given that she was fully informed and enormously busy, I thought it best to deal with the preliminary stuff on my own. No heroics, I just didn't want her to have to deal with the early medical stuff and worry any more than she already was. However, I did ask Jane to attend this appointment as it was likely to be the first time we might get a line of sight to the road ahead and the reality of the situation.

Truth be known, I also wanted Jane there for moral support. I didn't envisage turning into a gibbering blob of tears but who knows what might happen? Jane's got a steely resolve, and this was flashing like the blade of a samurai's sword in the run up to the appointment. In her 'no nonsense' fashion, she instructed me not to drive any more, given that the growth was now making itself more known through sharp pains and hideous odours. Jane drove us to the appointment and was delighted to finally meet the kindly surgeon, Jacob. He received us warmly in his comfy office which looked out onto the stunning, rolling green countryside.

In his typical manner, Jacob summarised what had occurred to date. I noticed he instinctively included Jane within this conversation. Anybody who knows Jane will testify that she likes to talk. To be honest, at times I couldn't get a word in. But I wanted Jane to be satisfied that I was in good hands and that my facts were aligned with Jacob's.

Jane had become very concerned about the effects of the growth on my driving and was determined to discuss this with Jacob. Whilst it hadn't affected my field of vision in the right eye yet, it was now painful, so driving drained my energy. I'd endured a reasonably long commute to and from Oxford, so Jacob advised that I ought to consider not driving if possible. The real danger was that the eye could go into double vision at the drop of a hat and this might not be too clever in the fast lane on the M4 or the windy A34, both very busy roads where you need your wits about you. Much to Jane's delight, this convinced me to stop driving, bar the odd, local journey down the road.

We moved onto the core subject of the diagnosis. As usual, Jacob stated that he didn't want to sugar coat anything and would tell us straight: there was some good news and some bad news. First, the bad news. Whilst it was still subject to further tests, it was extremely likely that the tumour was a rare malignant soft tissue tumour called a sarcoma and this, as we knew, sat in my maxillary sinus.

The good news was that thanks to the 'process of elimination' testing already undertaken at the independent laboratory, they'd established it wasn't a squamous cell carcinoma or lymphoma cancer. Both of these would need immediate, unsympathetic, deep trench JCB-style facial surgery. Every cloud has a silver lining, I thought.

We went through the findings of the MRI report from the biopsy day, some of which is copied here, together with my reactions:

There is a right maxillary mass seen extending posteriorly from right upper fifth tooth extending to a maximum diameter of 6.9cm x 4.6cm x 3.3cm (I quickly calculated that as over 100cm cubed. Wow, quite a large area in the confined area of the face).

Tumour extension can be seen along the course of the infraorbital nerve with extension through the floor of the orbit (I knew it, the bugger had got into the eye socket after all).

Posteromedially extension into the right pterygopalatine fossa is noted (it went further back than I'd originally thought, right into some of the intricate areas of the back of the mouth and was happily chewing up the soft tissue next to the base of my skull).

No encroachment through the foramen rotunda into the skull base is present (Thank god I've got a thick noggin, else it would be in a vital organ).

Biopsy advised, appearances are consistent with malignancy (confirmation that it's cancer).

The independent lab result didn't reveal anything different but pointed out that *'the appearances are those of an aggressive right maxillary sinus tumour that has caused significant bone destruction and tissue damage.'* Jacob confirmed that it had started to munch away at the surrounding soft tissue, for instance, the bone in my jaw that caused the loose teeth.

Although the other two diagnoses were yet to come in, it looked likely that my squatter was a rare version of sarcoma called a Spindle Cell. So it was probable that I had a rare form of a rare cancer - funnily enough, at this point I didn't feel especially lucky or unique.

Thanks to his forward thinking on the biopsy day, the third sample Jacob had taken was already on its way to The Royal Marsden Hospital. As it was a rare variety, they would need to take my case on from here.

Jane was a bit numb and squeezed my hand for a reaction, checking that I was absorbing the gravity of the news. I was numb too, tinged with some disappointment, as I'd been hoping for a conclusive, exact diagnosis and outlook. My delayed return squeeze to Jane was half-hearted.

"Jacob, I don't want to ponder too long on the past, as I want to focus all of my energies on the path ahead, but any ideas what caused this cancer?" I asked. "It's just really bad luck that some cells have decided to mutate this way. You don't smoke, you're fit, you're young (I chuckled and thanked him for that), it's just really bad luck."

We also talked about the likely treatments: the main three were surgery, chemotherapy and radiotherapy. Jacob felt it was likely that the Royal Marsden would want to 'soften' up or reduce the size of the tumour first with chemo or radiotherapy and then operate. It had clearly been lurking around for a while now and was quite large. He was still concerned about the size of the tumour and wasn't certain that it was even operable in its current state. But these decisions would need to be taken by the team at the Royal Marsden.

Jacob mentioned that it might take some time to 'get into the system', probably two to three weeks at most, so the best thing I could do was to continue to let Jane take care of my nutrition, get fitter to face the treatments and be a 'patient' patient. He warned us that we'd need to muster lots of patience as the Royal Marsden was a very busy hospital. The fact is, there's a lot of cancer about and the rare, complicated cases get referred to these specialist centres, so there's a funnelling effect.

Stop and think for a moment here. How many people have been diagnosed with cancer in your direct or extended family alone, not counting friends and colleagues? I can count six! Jesus, this bloody disease is this century's equivalent of cholera or the Black Death, perhaps it's an epidemic, but nobody's saying so.

To be honest, although I'd prepared for the diagnosis and had already been half warned and in some way expected the outcome, I was still a little taken aback by the reality of the situation. In terms of medical conversations, being told you definitively have cancer doesn't get a lot bigger.

The trouble was, I left the meeting feeling frustrated. It felt like I'd just been handed a ticket for a dangerous, unknown mission. Unfortunately, at this stage, nobody could tell me how I was going to get there, what equipment I needed for the journey, what the enemy looked like and importantly, when I was going. And unlike *Mission Impossible*, I didn't get the choice to accept or reject it.

We didn't have a lot to say on the way home, but Jane was compassionate. She asked if I was OK every ten minutes, gave me lots of hugs and looked deeply into my eyes for any sign of worry. I spoke openly about not really knowing enough at this stage, and we both arrived at the same opinion: we just had to take this crap on. Day by day, inch by inch. It's always been a bit of a mantra of mine, only worry about what's in your control, there's little point in getting het up about what 'might or might not' be. Deal with it when it's in front of you.

We decided to tell the children first, and they came home as normal, complaining that the school bus was late, staring into their phones. We sat them down and simply gave them all the news we knew at that time. In Cyprus, we'd prepared them for this point in time and the likely outcome. Despite the huge unknowns and uncertainties, Max and Lois both seemed to absorb the news well; I got special hugs and they both noisily disappeared upstairs. We checked in with them a number of times that afternoon. We then started to share the news with family and friends. I made a number of calls, as did Jane.

Mum put the loud speaker on at home so dad could hear, and I sensed that I just needed to give them the update and let them compute the news in their own way. I could tell that they were clearly upset which in turn created worry and concern for me. Telling my brother was equally hard. At the time, I thought he'd prepared himself for the worst and he came across very strong, but he later relayed that he'd been affected by the cold reality of it all. He became very upset over the week-end and said on the phone that he was prepared to do anything we needed him to do and offered to help us, as and when required.

In fact, both of our families started to offer up lots of help there and then, which was very kind. Although it sounds cruel, we asked for some time to think about what we needed and when we needed it. We couldn't start to plan ahead at that point and had been reacting day to day. Given that the likely medical pathway would involve surgery, we let them all know that there would be lots of opportunities to receive their help further down the road. We weren't wrong - keeping up your support team's momentum is important, so it's best to acknowledge the kind generosity and ask to put it on standby until you really need it.

Telling close friends over the week-end was difficult too. Sometimes it was the first time they'd heard from us in a while and we had to share some crap news. I simply hate passing on bad news to anybody, it's a real downer, even worse when you're calling people out of the blue. "Hey John, how's it going, mate?..." They all commented on how positive and strong-minded I sounded, which was great to hear and I got a real buzz from them. Men don't often show their emotions freely; we don't default to blowing smoke up each other's arses either and would rather take the mickey and have a laugh. But when it came to delivering the levelling news about the cancer, at crunch time, all my mates gave me great vibes. Some questioned me more intensely than others and I could sense frustration in their tone, but at the end of the day, the growing corner of support from family and friends was formidable. I could feel a cloak of invincibility form around me in the fighting ring. I'd already worked out who'd be bellowing support from the sidelines, who'd be ready with a bucket of water and the magic sponge, and who was going to provide some sanguine advice. Everyone had a role.

Exhausted, Jane and I opened a bottle of wine (or two), ate dinner (collected fish and chips to lighten the mood) and sat down in front of the telly. We talked further and I managed to convince Jane that I remained strong and wasn't going to roll over and give in, or have a meltdown.

Later over the week-end, I was left on my own as Jane took Lois to dancing and Max was collected by friends to play football. It still felt surreal and peaceful. I started to personally reflect about the gravity of cancer and the possibility of death again. As I said before, I hadn't yet been given a number of months to live, but the reality of a heightened risk of death had begun to sink in.

Would I be happy to die in the next year or so?

Straight away, my gut reaction was an emphatic and defiant NO. If I died instantly, if heaven existed and I was good enough to enter the pearly gates, then I would be a pretty pissed off angel. There was no way I was 'ready' to die here and now. I didn't want to leave my family. I wanted to fight.

But the question crept back in…it had to. I realised that it's not my call. Death may come to me despite my fighting spirit. I dropped my guard and allowed myself to think about it further - this needed bottoming out.

I got very sad, very quickly, in deep contemplation. If things were out of my control and I faced death in a matter of days, what would I need to do to get happy with the situation?

I was pretty sure that I'd still feel short-changed as I threw off my mortal coil but ultimately, I would have to accept it. The last thing I would want to do is get hung up in the emotion or be angry during my last precious hours. Best think this through.

So I started to think about all the things that I was grateful for in my life. It didn't take long to recognise that, if my time was now up, I'd had a pretty enjoyable, full life during my stint on earth. I measured it by the loved ones I had around me, genuine friends, experiences I've had with them and on my own. It's a bit like the question, what material things would you run in and save if your house was on fire? It would be the photos and videos of those precious memories.

The flip side to this is what would I be missing out on in future years? I'd had a pretty good half century, but health permitting, I estimated I'd miss out on a further 30-40 years or so. I whittled this down to maybe another 20-30 years, given I'd got cancer, but none of it was certain. So the deficit of dying now would be losing out on those future times and experiences with loved ones, such as retirement, seeing my kids progress in life and perhaps even grandchildren.

In crude mathematical terms, with 50 years under my belt, the scales were already tipped in my favour. I'd experienced so much during my life to date in scientific terms too. I'd grown up, become independent, met the love of my life and created offspring. Perhaps I would be going out in my prime, as the next however many years would be played out against a backdrop of health uncertainty. Ageing would see my capabilities diminish gradually over time anyway, it's just that cancer might increase the curve's gradient.

Yes, despite wishing to live longer, on balance, I would accept death if it came any time soon.

I also had a rough idea of what I'd like to do before dying, if there was enough time to organise it. For me, it came down to helping Jane and my children prepare for the absence of a husband and father. Of course, there would inevitably be pain, but I think I'd focus all of my thoughts into building some sort of contingency plan for them. It wouldn't be about me, more about getting them sorted financially as best I could and creating an abiding memory of sorts where they could take some comfort. This might take the form of messages, maybe videos, to be available at certain points in their lives. I'd spend time planning it with Jane, thanking loved ones and saying goodbye - sod sleeping, it would be 24/7.

For the kids, something to play when they went through certain milestones in life. Maybe when they reach a milestone age, like 30, 40 and 50. For Jane, it would be something for the anniversaries we'd shared because that was the choker for her; also a message urging her to carry on with life, meet someone else if she wanted to and be happy.

I'm glad I did exorcise this train of thought there and then, on my own. It was a testament to the gravity of the illness I was facing. Later down the road, things might start to get a little heated, so it was best to do this soul searching in relative calmness.

Then there was a funeral to think about. There would need to be a party too, with a video message. Music is important to me and I felt the urge to listen to a few tracks there and then, with a green tea in my hand. I was in a dark, yet uplifting space that afternoon. I wondered what musical track I'd want played at my funeral.

♪ In My Time of Dying (Led Zeppelin) ♪

In the end I had so many tracks to choose from but plumped for this one – a lovely slide guitar, a tongue-in-cheek nod to passing through the pearly gates and, at the end of the track, a magical accident caught on the original recording which the band decided to keep, so an element of humour too. I played it a few times and acknowledged humour in my armoury.

I didn't share these thoughts with Jane as there was a danger that she'd assume I'd been morbidly fantasising, which is one way to describe what I'd done.

On the following Monday, I was back in the office. Martin and I had been holding the fort whilst we waited for our new boss, Cameron, to join us from Canada. Today was his first day. Over the week-end, I sent Cam a brief note forewarning him that I had some health issues that he needed to be aware of, so the news wouldn't come out of the blue. Imagine that - first day in the new role, bouncing off the walls and your soon-to-be-close colleague relays that he's just been diagnosed with cancer. I felt awful for him and somewhat awkward as I caught the train to work.

We decided to grab some lunch together to discuss, amongst other things, my results and what I might not be able to do going forward. I offered up a solution. An opportunity could be borne from my withdrawal to give some leadership experience to somebody else. This experience would be like gold dust and, as my lighter duties now focussed around risk only, the work streams could be easily defined. This later came to fruition, which was great, as I could see that Martin and Cam would need all the help they could get.

People were chomping at the bit to find out my news, so when we got back from lunch, I quickly surmised that I wouldn't be able to update people on a one-to-one basis.

I'm conscious that not everybody has a work environment that is conducive to the circulation of emails of a personal nature. Also, some people may feel uncomfortable or even horrified about sharing news in this way: it's a personal choice. In my case, I'd benefited from being very open with colleagues over the last few years and am fortunate to have a crowd of well-meaning people around me. I felt it was important to keep people informed in a collective, corralled way so that I could control the frequency and detail of the story. It was exhausting every time I relived it and I wanted to conserve my energy.

I'm also acutely aware that everyone travels on different journeys down the motorway of life and, whilst my little drama was very much centre stage for me, it was likely to only be a 'sideshow' in the lives of most. Fully appreciating that a lot of people would reach for the delete button, it mattered not; by writing an email I could reach supporters and friends who might not have found the time to wish me well to my face.

I sensed that setting the tone of the email was again extremely important, just as it had been when speaking with family and friends over the weekend. In relaying the shitfest of bad news, I wanted to be factual, informative and upbeat, but more importantly, I wanted to give thanks for their support and ask them for more in the future, on my terms. I wanted conversations to remain positive and I needed the banter to continue; having a 'poor you' conversation would only bring me down.

I've shown examples of the messages I sent in the 'Glossary of Sent Messages' section at the end of the book. Hopefully this will give some context to my train of thought at the time they were written.

For the second time, I hadn't anticipated the waves of positive energy that I received from the responses. Every time I got a message back, I felt stronger and more uplifted; it was the best medicine that I could have wished for at that time. I thought there and then that I'd continue to set the tone of future comms and selfishly, I wanted to receive more positive energy. Crikey, I was getting compliments too, and nearly caught myself saying, "I ought to do this more often."

One of the enduring themes within the feedback was that people were impressed with my mindset, attitude and levity. People stated that I'd been inspiring, and to me, that's an immensely powerful word.

This was in stark contrast to feedback I'd received in the past from one of my colleagues, who'll remain nameless. Within a tirade of other abuse, this individual said that they found me completely uninspiring and negative. Thankfully, I recognised this for what it was: a pressure valve blowing for the umpteenth time in their career and a result of their ineptitude in dealing with personal issues. Other such outbursts had arbitrarily littered the team like friendly artillery fire falling on the front line. At the time, I wisely decided to let it go and referred back to it later during my attempts to change this behaviour. They eventually sought medical help on my advice and I think that the problems are still being worked through.

This example highlights how differently people deal with major stuff (in their eyes), depending on their personality and capability. Some will curl up in a ball and need bucketloads of care and attention. Some keep it locked in, some just get on with it and unfortunately, some will lash out. But what's the point of allowing something to eat you up from the inside and turn you into a monster? That's not my style, and not what I want to be remembered for.

At no point though have I ever felt inspiring, brave, superhuman or any of these complimentary superlatives being laid at my feet. I don't think you have an option but to face cancer treatments when you have so much to live for. I wanted to deal with my messaging in a certain way, that didn't bring people down - after all, it's clearly not a fun activity to describe. But it sure felt good to receive these accolades and soak up the positive energy.

And that's the point of it, isn't it? People generally want to encourage you along the marathon from behind the barriers. The human spirit likes a fighter, a trier, an underdog and we all like to cheer on our loved ones and throw them compliments. It shows they care and it's rather nice.

With my diagnosis confirmed, it was now time to advise my regional director, who luckily happened to be in the office too. We had a ten minute chat where we used the analogy of rugby, as it was common ground. He was cheering me on to kick the whole thing into touch, deep into the opposition's 22. Trouble was, I was a second row, not a fly half. Yeah, the chips were down, but no-one's died yet, so crack on! I brought him up to speed with my worsening symptoms and self-imposed worries of reducing office time. He gave me his blessing to do whatever I felt best regarding work in the run up to surgery, offering just the support I needed.

The following weeks

Unfortunately, the symptoms began to worsen after the biopsy. I became conscious of the stench that followed me around and imagined a cartoon of me with dustbin breath, and people wearing clothes pegs on their noses - it was foul. In reality, people were very polite. They said they couldn't smell anything, but I was pretty adept at reading body language and some people found it hard to disguise the kick in the nose I was delivering, despite the ever constant Olbas Oil-infused hankies I was using.

One person clearly hadn't read his emails and bumped into me in the loos. "Bloody hell Wilko, looks like someone's taken a baseball bat to your face, what happened?". I chuckled and explained the situation. Poor Pete, he was absolutely mortified and embarrassed and felt a proper Charlie. Hopefully he took lots of consolation from making my family laugh when I relayed the story to them. Humour is priceless. The fact he wasn't aware underlined one reality. I was a sideshow, and some of them had clearly fallen asleep during the opening night. But I was cool with that.

It was now taking an age to wake up, get ready for work and catch the train due to broken, painful sleep. I initially reduced my office-bound hours and worked when I got back home. It soon became obvious that it was a waste of precious energy hauling myself in and out every day as I was still contributing to work at home too.

The disgusting squatter continued to leak smelly discharge through the holes in my upper jaw from the biopsy and acrid, runny, hot snot started to randomly spew down one nostril over everything it found in its path, often in meetings. Eating my sandwiches was a challenge and didn't make for good viewing. The last thing I wanted to do was swallow the discharge, so I was constantly trying to secretly remove it from my mouth without people seeing. This stinky process became embarrassing and, despite assurances from colleagues, I'm sure nobody liked working within the vicinity of an open, blocked drain.

The negative energies in my head were the last thing I needed at this point, so I decided to call it a day. I reassured myself that for some workers, an office would be archaic; this was the 21st century and lots of friends worked from home permanently. At times I felt like I'd abandoned my post, but Jane, colleagues and friends reminded me that I was very ill and insisted I stop trying to be a martyr.

Looking back, I wish I'd started to listen and take action earlier. My stubbornness caused a lot of frustration to the ones I love - hardly the 'family first' mantra.

3

BUILDING UP TO SURGERY

Meeting the medical team and hatching a plan

Jacob had warned us that it might take some time for the cogs to start turning at the Royal Marsden but, by mid-September, I felt it was getting a little bit silly. Jacob had sent them a biopsy a month ago. I kept the faith but the lack of response felt like they'd lost my referral. This wasn't logical so Jacob chased them on a regular basis.

We were invited to visit Jacob at the Royal Surrey Hospital, out of kindness, where he provided me with a sense of what the squatter looked like. He was happy to go through some of the CT and MRI scans with me and Jane, but we mainly wanted an update from him regarding the referral. He was getting frustrated too and was by now phoning the consultant and asking for an appointment on a daily basis. As a final throw of the dice, he gave me the telephone number of the consultant's PA so that I could chase them directly. He also went on to say how annoyed he was that this whole thing might have been avoided, which took me by surprise.

Jacob was the covering Maxillofacial Consultant for a group of dental surgeries, including mine, and had often reminded the dentists to refer any early signs of gum numbness to him. He expressed how cross he was that this hadn't been referred at the first sign of numbness, as the outcome for the patient was likely to be a lot better. Perhaps all of this drama and large amounts of subsequent collateral damage could have been avoided if I'd have been referred when the first symptoms showed? Makes you think…

The scans were amazing to look at and gave me a great insight into what I'd only read and been told up that point. I fully recommend it to people if you want to get a visual image of the enemy. The only similar experience I'd had was looking at the ultrasound pictures of our children in the womb - clearly a much more welcome sight.

For me, the CT scans were easier to understand than the MRI images. As Jacob adjusted the mouse and moved quickly through slice after slice of imagery, you began to build up a 3D picture, like moving still pictures in the corner of a book.

The black images on the CT scan represented air and clearly, you'd expect to see lots of air around the skull's sinuses. When comparing the two sides of the face, we saw it: the filthy squatter. Lurking, silently filling the pocket of air with diseased stench. It was the first time I'd come face to face with it. Boy, I hadn't appreciated how far back into the skull the sinus, together with its uninvited guest, went. Before then, I naively thought the sinus lay flat, in parallel with the cheek, and was therefore only a shallow air pocket. An anatomy lesson too! I discovered that the tumour filled 90% of the cavity and, true to the character of sarcomas, had started to munch away on surrounding soft tissue - muscle, bone, sinew and cartilage. It was also (worryingly) touching the base of my skull. If it was a self-aware organism, perhaps it had decided to gnaw away on the low-hanging fruit such as my eye orbit, instead of tucking into the skull bone.

Thankfully, I was told, it had not grown too far into the brain stem, the delicate nerve endings at the top of the spine. Thank goodness, or it would have been inoperable and a huge nightmare to treat.

In all of its black and white glory, the macabre visual of my skull, infused with the enemy's invasion, was quite a chilling sight. A proper disgusting, diseased growth. As I said before, I was lucky that it was located in a sinus where the nearest 'essential organ' was the brain, encased in a thick noggin of bone. Had the tumour been located in the abdomen, close to the lungs, heart, kidney or liver, it would have little in its way to munch through the soft connective tissue, so I had to count my blessings.

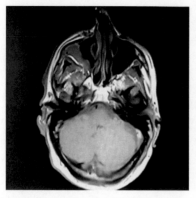

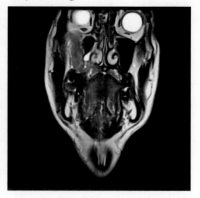

CT scan from above. Black is air, showing the tumour travelling to the back of my eye orbit towards the brain

Face on, showing the height

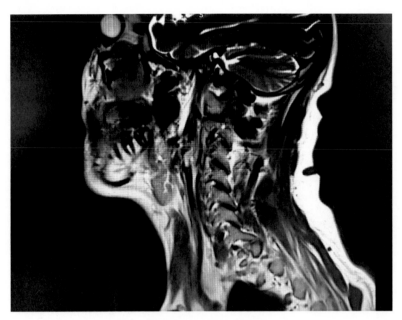

CT profile showing depth

Then, out of the blue, an appointment arrived from the Royal Marsden with an oncologist consultant, set for the end of September. From there on, I focussed on getting fitter, eating healthily and preparing for the road ahead.

Whilst I appreciated that the tumour was pretty well-established, I didn't allow myself to think about it being 'too late'. Jacob hadn't inferred that it might be inoperable, but at the end of the day, these were decisions to be taken by the Royal Marsden. He passed the files across to the new NHS Trust and copied me in. It made for interesting reading.

We met Dr Miah at the Royal Marsden's Sarcoma Clinic for outpatients. She instantly radiated compassion, warmth, intelligence and experience, and thankfully, also had a straight-talking style. She was very apologetic about the time it had taken to get me into the Royal Marsden system; even by their standards, it had been an extremely long wait. At this initial meeting, we quickly established that this was a rare type of sarcoma, which in itself was a rare classification for a cancer. The *Understanding Sarcomas* leaflet we'd read listed thirteen different types of sarcomas. The Spindle Cell variety wasn't even listed.

She went on to say that sarcomas were nasty little blighters and, as such, medical procedures would need to be immediate, decisive and invasive.

These would cause some collateral damage. Initially, whipping it out through surgery was recommended, followed by other treatments such as chemotherapy or radiotherapy.

Given that it had invaded the fatty area below my eye orbit, Dr Miah was sure that I'd lose the whole eye, which was extremely common in paranasal cases, despite my eyesight not yet being affected. To be honest, I'd already come to that conclusion myself. I'd recognised it was an unwelcome, but probably necessary, procedure. You don't want the squatter's little brother popping up later because you were too light-footed and soft at surgery.

Nevertheless, since I didn't possess a medical background, I reckoned that I was allowed to ask a few 'numpty' questions, so I fired away. I naively asked whether it would be possible in some way to hold on to the eye for a while, maybe 'put it on ice' whilst the squatter got scraped out, then 'pop it back in' during the rebuild part of the surgery? Looking back, I didn't just want to simply acquiesce, throw in the towel, and lose dual vision. If there was a glimmer of hope, I'd rather keep it. Dr Miah laughed, loved the silly question and said she'd put it to the surgeon. I discovered that all of the key people like the surgeons, oncologists and radiographers met up on a weekly basis to discuss cases, and my case was being debated the following week.

We talked about the location of the sarcoma. As a soft tissue tumour, they were more commonly found in limbs and the abdomen, and it was very rare to find one in a face. This was usually the domain of a squamous cell carcinoma, so I was a bit of an abnormality on this front.

We left clutching grimly onto various leaflets. All cancer types are vile, hideous forms of disease. Some cause more worry than others and some are extremely deadly. I tried to get my head around what was lurking inside me.

The most obvious thing I was aware of, when compared to other cancers, was its location. Quite a site. Right slap bang under my eye, around my upper jaw. Surgery was definitely going to change my appearance. Probably not for the better either, but the policy of get rid, then worry about the consequences, was the sensible one. But afterwards there'd be no hiding it. If you're unfortunate to get cancer and it's out of sight, I guess you might not have to worry about its visibility, you can cover stuff up. Not for me: it would be pretty obvious to everyone that something wasn't right.

Also, the sarcoma's location was pretty much dead in the middle of most of the senses. Sight, smell, hearing and taste: they were all going to get a shock to the system one way or another.

Everything in your head is compacted together with different types of tissue, bone, cartilage, enamel and sensory nerves. It's a box of tightly-packed magic, quite an amazing, complex control centre of your being when you consider what your head supports. Most things that send signals back to your brain seem to be in there somewhere. The procedures would be like simultaneously being attacked with a baseball bat and chainsaw which might, in the long run, knock some common sense into me.

Cancers can be in lots of less accessible areas and near some pretty major organs which makes them very difficult to treat. Mine was located in the 'let's tread carefully, so as not to damage more than we have to' camp. Treatments are life-changing. "We need it all out, with a surrounding margin of healthy tissue," kept replaying in my mind. This wasn't going to be pretty, but then again, I never was!

That week-end, I reviewed the information I'd taken home and trawled the internet for facts. Frustratingly, there was very little written about undifferentiated spindle cell sarcomas in the maxillary sinus. I scratched around trying to find a needle in a haystack and came up with a couple of pin heads.

Head and neck cancers only account for 4% of diagnosed cancers in the UK (according to a charity, around 11,600 cases per annum), nowhere near the top ten types, according to the NHS. I couldn't find any statistics on the number of UK paranasal cancer diagnoses. Without this, I'd have to do some rough calculations and make some assumptions. The internet stated that 2,000 people in the US were diagnosed with nasal or paranasal cavity cancer, so halve that to 1,000 as I had the paranasal variety. Then divide by, say ten, given the population difference with the UK (let's say 700 million vs 70 million). You could be looking at as little as maybe a few hundred cases of paranasal cancer in the UK per annum. With that kind of rarity, no wonder funds and research were diverted to other more common forms of cancer. Funding would get more 'bang for its buck' and help more sufferers.

The sarcoma leaflet stated that only 1% of cancer diagnoses were sarcomas, a rare one for sure. As my type wasn't even listed, there was very little precedent to go on. There was no "Well, the last 200 cases of your type suggest that X then Y is the best course of action." I got the distinct impression that we were in uncharted territory. Wikipedia (not a tested medical research site) suggested that spindle cells naturally occur in response to injury, which sometimes mutate into cancerous cells. That was food for thought. If you read the later chapters of my brief autobiography, you'll understand what I think the likely cause of my cancer is.

When we got back, I updated family, and jotted a message to friends. I widened the audience further so as to pick up anybody who might not have heard the news yet. I'm glad I did as a number of friends were still finding out. Again, I wanted to keep the tone upbeat and on my terms. I used humour to diffuse the intensity of the information. Once again, this can be found in the 'Glossary of Sent Messages' section at the end of the book.

Again, I enjoyed a renewing, fresh wave of positive energy woven into the responses. This was most welcome as things were becoming pretty daunting when you looked at the facts.

From this point on, things started to speed up; it was as if my health team at the Royal Marsden had dropped a gear and were accelerating hard. Further scans were hurriedly booked and somehow, I was squeezed into a number of medics' already-busy schedules. A friend of Jane's family, Jeff, had gone through a number of treatments for thyroid cancer some months previously. He'd predicted that the conveyer belt would suddenly jolt into action, in a flurry of activity. How right he was.

Once the scan results came back, we went to review them with Dr Miah. Immediately, she gave us the great news that the cancer had not spread. Quite often a sarcoma is metastatic, in other words, it spreads to other areas of the body. It was common for sarcomas to jump to the lungs which dramatically reduces a patient's survival chances. Phew, we took a pause to allow the good news to slowly wash over us. Jane openly burst into tears and cried with joy. After a few months of negativity, it was refreshingly different to get anything positive back from the medical team, like getting a lollipop at the dentist when you were a kid.

It sounds rather blasé looking back now, but I'd naturally assumed that it hadn't transferred anywhere else, given my overall health, although you can never be 100% sure. I wanted to know what was happening next, but before I was told, we had some further news to absorb.

Oddly, the filthy squatter had hardly grown since last being measured by Jacob's scans a month or two earlier. Dr Miah commented that there was no rhyme or reason for this slow down, but slowed down it had! Whilst nothing could be proven, Dr Miah commented that my mindset, healthier diet and life-style would not have hindered this. I think this double negative meant a positive, in other words, a nod to our approach, especially the diet. Dr Miah confirmed my sarcoma type was indeed a little different to her usual cases, but we'd treat it like the other sarcomas, in a logical fashion. Hold on to your seats.

Jane and I had focussed on 'cancer-tackling' ingredients within a number of supplements and foods. We were happy with this non-endorsement from the medical fraternity and felt that our efforts had been worthwhile.

I asked about the next steps as I just wanted to crack on and remove the disgusting, parasitic slug from my body as soon as possible, before it suddenly had another growth spurt. Dr Miah told us that the surgeon still needed to establish whether it was operable or not, given that it went way back to the base of my skull, near the stem cell. I was confident that it would be, as Jacob had outlined what surgery might entail, but now I was told in no uncertain terms that it might not be. I left with a little nagging doubt.

I say a little nagging doubt - I meant a large one. In my questioning, I'd ascertained that my survival chances would be hugely compromised if it was inoperable. Splitting the tumour and leaving a portion buried deep inside would increase the risk of it spreading further. The ideal scenario was to remove it and a 'healthy margin of tissue' as a whole.

Sarcomas are graded in two ways. The first is its growth rate, which ranges between Low, Intermediate and High Grade. Low Grade is synonymous with slow growth, High Grade is very abnormal and nastily aggressive. The next grading determines how large it is and whether it's spread to other parts of the body; this ranges between Stage 1 and 4, Stage 1 being Low Grade, relatively small (less than 5cm) and not spread to other parts of the body. Stage 2 is any grade, larger than Stage 1, but not spread to any other part of the body. Stage 3 means high grade, but not spread, and Stage 4 means a cancer of any grade that has transferred to any other part of the body. I was grateful to be diagnosed with an Intermediate Stage 2, borderline Stage 3. It could have been a lot worse, especially as it had been festering away in my head for almost a year!

When we got home, I updated family and friends and sent another message. Wow, it was great to convey some good news for a change, even though we'd yet to hear whether surgery was possible. The responses were equally positive and, in a strange way, had started to become an antidote to any train of negative thought that might have crept in.

We finally met my surgeon, Cyrus Kerawala, on 1st October. He quickly confirmed that he was happy to operate and immediately filled the room with calm and purpose as he talked through his proposed procedures. It almost felt like I'd willed it to be so, but in fact, it was a close call. If I had been told that it was inoperable, I would have probably gone down the recommended road of trying to shrink it with radiotherapy, then surgery. It would have been a body blow, but I was always mindful to put my wellbeing in the hands of the professionals and follow their advice.

Cyrus and Dr Miah had a fantastic working relationship and it was evident that they had known each other for a number of years. After researching his profile, you could tell that Cyrus was a leading expert in his field. All I needed to do was nod, go with the flow, ask a few initial numpty questions and comply with whatever he suggested. Simple really. Some people may be tempted to research and second guess the next stages, but quite frankly, I don't see the point. In my mind, this would have been a complete waste of energy and fraught with the danger of inaccuracies and false fact.

Cyrus then pulled a white rabbit out of his hat and gave us a surprise we weren't expecting. He described the forthcoming surgery as a game of two halves. Given that I was fit, mentally strong and young (thank you, again), Cyrus wanted to see what he could do to preserve the right eye, rather than remove it.

Nothing was guaranteed, as he needed to analyse the removed tumour to ensure the mass of tissue contained a suitable margin of surrounding, healthy tissue. But he reckoned with a fair prevailing wind, he might be able to keep the eye relatively intact. Up to this point, I'd written my eye off and was delighted to be given a chance to keep it. This was amazing news and clearly the preferred cosmetic choice when compared to a flap of skin over the socket, a glass eye or prosthetic one. Another advantage to keeping it was that less tissue would be required from the donor site. All great then, right? But - there was a drawback.

In order to go down this path, I'd need two separate surgeries. The first would evict the vile parasite - a resection - then the second would be a longer reconstruction surgical procedure, taking tissue and bone from a donor site somewhere else in my body. The choices were the shoulder blade, the hip or lower leg. Cyrus paused to allow me to take this wave of news on board.

I smiled and said, "Let's go for it." After all, in my mind, the worst that could happen was that I'd lose the eye in the second reconstruction surgery if tests confirmed it was infected, so I'd be back to where I'd thought I was anyway. Heads you win, tails you don't lose.

At this point, I was even more glad that I'd raised the numpty question at Dr Miah's first consultation, as it had clearly been tabled in the medical team's discussions. He'd gone away, put his thinking hat on, reviewed the case and came up with a cunning plan.

My understanding about which parts of my face I needed to wave goodbye to was a little hazy, given I couldn't work out what would be captured by the 'margin of healthy tissue'. Until this point, I'd assumed that the facial skin, part of my nose and possibly my tongue were going to be consigned to the hospital incinerator. So I simply went down the list, hoping for the best - fingers crossed, squeaky bum time.

1) Will I lose any of my facial skin? No - great, I could grow my beard back!

2) Would I lose any of my nose? No - great, I could still wear glasses.

3) Would I lose any of my tongue? No - thank god. I think this would have made speaking, eating and drinking extremely difficult, all the basic things I wanted to preserve in later life.

Being emboldened by playing the numpty question card before, and gaining some confidence from the positive responses, I asked for the left lower leg to be the donor site. My logic, as discussed with Jane, was that it would have the least impact on my recovery plans, which would entail going to the gym. "OK, we'll see," Cyrus said. Jane and I left with the knowledge that surgery was going to happen about mid-October, given that it would take a few weeks to line up the team of surgeons. Wow! The Royal Marsden was now in fifth gear, building up the revs and moving into the fast lane.

We told family and friends as soon as we were home, clearly chuffed by the news of potentially saving the eye. This was another bout of good karma and I wrote another message, spicing up the words with an image of the opening battle scene from the movie *Gladiator*, which I love. (See Glossary of Sent Messages). Finally, we were launching an attack on the enemy and I was delighted…unleash hell!

Over the next few weeks, I continued to focus on mind, body and soul. I was going in for an awful double header, a home game, then a trickier away fixture was to be played out, so I needed to prepare as best I could. I reached out again to the friends who'd undergone cancer surgery, in order to get some advice, especially to tap into their mindset; this proved helpful.

Naturally, everyone's mental preparation is going to be different. There was little that Jane, my family, friends or colleagues could offer apart from tremendous encouragement from the sidelines. I could only resonate with people who'd actually gone through it, or something similar. In this regard, the advice from my friend Anja was fantastic. At the end of the day, it was going to be me under the knife in theatre, so I needed to get my head completely around it.

I started to visualise the 'before and after' look of my face as best I could. Cyrus had gone through where the incisions were going to be. Whilst I was looking forward to some war wounds for my troubles, it was more than I'd bargained for. The long scar would go through the middle of my top lip, splitting it in two up to my nose. It would then follow around under my nostril, hug the side of the nose all the way to the inside corner of my eye. Then it would travel under the eyelid to the outside corner of the eye. The face would then be hauled back like a peeled fruit so most of the material below my eye socket and upper jaw could be removed by surgical saw. I was under no illusion. A good amount of teeth, muscle and flesh was going to be lost, along with some of my senses. I thought that there was every chance that eventually this wouldn't be noticeable to the casual observer after the swelling had died down, given that the damage beneath could be covered back up by the original facial skin and I'd grow a beard.

I felt it only fair after the surgeries that I would have a trophy scar or two to chat about, but it sounded like I'd have more stitches than I'd first envisaged.

Over the next couple of weeks, I kept calm, showed Jane that I was in control and kept reminding my uninvited guest (yes, I talked to the offending area of my face in the mirror) that its days were numbered. How much was I looking forward to hearing that it'd been removed and was on the chopping board in the pathology lab.

A full-on attack was to be launched, no prisoners were going to be taken and all this was done under the command of an expert medical general. Bring it on.

♪ Damage inc (Metallica) ♪

This full-on, powerful track raises the hackles for battle: "Charging hard and no-one's gonna give in, sight and smell of this, it gets me going." I'd play music a lot before playing a rugby match to psyche me up; before you get on the park, you need your head to be tuned in. Attitude, focus and aggression are the staple diet in the forwards. If you're short on any of these, the opposition will sniff it out and get the upper hand. The backs tended to do their hair.

4

THE EVICTION OF MY FILTHY SQUATTER, FIRST SURGERY

The introduction of a different look

The morning of the first operation came around. I gave the kids a huge cuddle as I lay in bed before they dashed off to school. I assured them that everything would be fine and I'd be getting better from this point. I took the last photo of my old face with them for posterity.

Last photo before a new level of handsomeness

Jane drove me up to London and her brother Dean came along for moral support. Despite the planned onslaught of surgery, humour in the car was buoyant. The sun shone through the grey clouds and I was happy that sister and brother were going to enjoy the rest of the day at the V & A and various cafés.

At times of hardship, family members got closer; like a squeeze in a scrum, it makes the unit stronger. Both sides of our families had different, individual challenges to face but, despite this, when we needed it, their support came through.

Another friend who was taking a great interest in me was Jeff (the one who'd warned us about the conveyor belt). He's a family friend of Dean and Jane's who'd known them since they were teenagers. Jeff was texting from his home in Patagonia and wished me well.

Chilled out, relaxed and excited, I was in the pre-op room at the Royal Marsden, sizing up the small, anti-DVT socks left with the brown paisley gown to change into. "They're not going to fit me," I declared. However, the nurse insisted that the size was determined by my narrow ankles and didn't take into consideration my large calf muscles. A wafer of a curtain separated me from the room's nursing staff, who kept on asking me my name and date of birth, just to make sure I wasn't somebody who'd just walked in off the street for a laugh.

Once changed, there wasn't much else to do, so I decided to do a sudoku. I couldn't find anything to write with so I crept outside the curtain to ask if I could borrow a pen. On the desk sat three doctors, already dressed for theatre, huddled around the screen, looking intently at images of my scans. When I asked for the pen, one beamed a smile and gave me his biro. I quickly scuttled back to my booth knowing that they'd come knocking soon. The best news that morning was that I could wear underpants under the gown, which was the size of a tent with obligatory gaping holes at the back. I didn't fancy getting a draught around my undercarriage.

No sooner had I sat down, the three smiling assassins came in to introduce themselves, each one appearing in a line like a stage act. We chatted through the procedure and I signed the consent forms about the various risks. The three amigos were Francesco, who seemed to be the lead, John and Owain. I didn't know it then, but I was going to see them regularly afterwards. Cyrus was still scrubbing up in theatre.

Ever since being first diagnosed, I'd been very much looking forward to Eviction Day, imagining this to be the first and decisive medical attack. Over the last few weeks, the squatter had ramped up its activity and there and then, it made one final volley of shots down my nostril. I felt one last putrid discharge run onto the arm of my nice, crisp, freshly laundered dressing gown. I apologised as usual but needn't have bothered; the three amigos didn't care. They'd seen it all before.

Then we mustered to go. Showtime. I was escorted down to theatre by the nurse to the basement where all the operating theatres seemed to be. Cyrus was waiting in the corridor just outside the anaesthetic room, leaning casually against the wall. It was good of him to say a few words of encouragement, we shook hands and he said all would be fine. That air of confidence again put me at ease and any lingering doubts evaporated.

So, into the anaesthetist's den I went. Blimey, they were packed in tight! I could see the three amigos and also half a dozen or so others who were concentrating on getting me to sleep. I eagerly hopped onto the bed and clocked that it was 1.55 pm. Clearly they were aiming to wheel me into theatre for a two o'clock procedure. They inserted the cannula, injected the sleeping potion and asked me to count down from 100. I was great until 89 and remember feeling fuzzy at 86.

♪ Comfortably Numb (Pink Floyd) ♪

An all-time classic from the boys in pink: "Just a little pin prick, you'll feel no pain." Fantastic couple of Gilmour guitar solos, the second one being my favourite.

Text from Jane to Jeff: *Heard from the surgeon at 6.30pm, all went as planned – 'a very uneventful' surgery. Cyrus is pleased and is hopeful that John will keep his eye. He's in the recovery room now and I'm popping in soon to see him on the ward. Deano and I were both momentarily very happy, thanks for all of your support.*

When I came to on the ward, I didn't feel any immediate pain and was aware that I would still have heaps of anaesthetic racing around my body. I took a selfie and reviewed my face. I looked shocked in the photo (see below), but this was because I rarely used the camera. Jane came in and had a wobbly-kneed, weepy moment when she saw my face; she was clearly shocked. The stitches were thick and black, also there was an abundantly vivid, puffy scar which followed the long route described earlier. I thought at the time that it was a bit of a monster, given that I counted thirty or so stitches (little did I know then). Due to the swelling, my facial features were a little off centre, but you could see that when things settled down, it was going to be spot on.

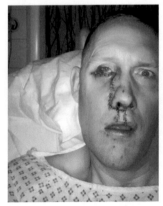

The selfie to review the new level of handsomeness

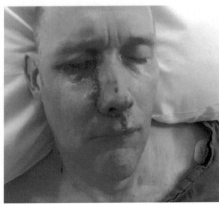

Jane took a less horrific photo

I couldn't feel anything where the tumour used to be, in fact the whole of my face was completely cold and numb. Cyrus had said they'd temporarily backfill the space left with some kind of medical Polyfilla.

Jane started to convince herself that everything was going to be fine; after all, I was still here. She needed to get home as it was 8pm, so we had a cuddle (a snog was out of the question) and she left. I was feeling pretty awake and raring to go, so when the menu came round, I ordered a soft food dinner. I noticed that my small-sized DVT socks were round my ankles; they hadn't managed to stay halfway up my calves as I predicted – surprise, surprise. I asked the nurse for a larger pair. These ended up being a snug fit and I lay back, happy and calm. Little did I know then, but it was one of my nurse's first days at work. Nicole had recently graduated and I was one of her first patients. I didn't sense any nerves and she melted in nicely with the other professional staff who were there. Nicole told me this when caring for me again after my second operation; it was nice to have some continuity.

When the steaming food arrived, it filled the room with appetising aromas. I was starving hungry and ready to wolf it down as best I could. Unfortunately, my stomach had different ideas and I started to feel very queasy. Thankfully, the nurses were on hand and I started to bring up a lot of liquid, which happened a few times. My mind told me that I was hungry but my body was having quite the opposite sensation. Apparently during surgery, I'd lost 1.5 litres of blood. The theatre team couldn't find it, they looked behind my tongue and it hadn't turned up in their drainage machinery - I'd clearly guzzled the lot down.

Text from Jane to Jeff: Was a bit of a shock seeing John, he's so strong and not on morphine, but chatting away. He's maybe out on Friday night. Yes, quite agree it's a project, it's a bloody rollercoaster.

During the night, I woke up several times, which wasn't surprising following the sickness incident. The nurses kept a close eye on me, and I began to explore the inside of my new mouth with my tongue. Weeks before the operation, I'd visited a dentist at the Royal Marsden who'd taken a mould of the inside of my mouth, so I was expecting the temporary prosthetic plate in place of the roof of my mouth to be a reasonably snug fit.

Chuffing hell! The whole roof of my mouth was now smooth plastic, not just half of my palate. Unbeknown to me at the time, I did keep half intact, for ease of sewing on the plastic version that was to cover the whole of the roof of my mouth. I could feel at least two bolts holding it in position (later I discovered there were a further four) and these went up somewhere into the bone of my surrounding skull. The plate also had clasps around the left-hand top row of teeth to keep it fixed in one place and the right side of my top teeth was now a temporary denture from the canine back, with the tiniest teeth set in it. These didn't meet the natural teeth below in my lower jaw and it was purely for show - a bit pointless as I couldn't lift my top lip to show them off. My bottom right-hand jaw was considerably swollen and felt like it had been hit by a sledgehammer and the rest of the right-hand side of my face was a mixture of numb or achy.

I started to try to drink some water. Hilarious, as I couldn't close my mouth and it just simply ran down my chin and front. The nurses dived to the rescue, so I quickly adopted a strategy of leaning over to the left and chucking my head back to swallow. The running water in my mouth found holes that weren't there before, so I clearly needed to adopt a new tactic to get food and drink down. It was going to be a bit messy, but nothing a hundred serviettes couldn't mop up.

In the morning, during the usual early doctor's rounds, and despite my lack of sleep, Cyrus said he wanted to see me go home as soon as possible, preferably today. Even I thought this was quite optimistic, so didn't commit to anything, just nodded and produced a reassuring grunt. The next wave of medical visitors included the anaesthetist and I confided that I'd like to probably stay in another day at least. He gave me a wink - no problem.

I was by now even hungrier so I ordered some breakfast. Once I had slurped my way through some porridge and stuffed some soft bread inside me, I felt my body becoming a little more energised and in need of certain bodily functions, so I opted to visit the loo and take a shower.

The nurses were understandably a little nervous about sending a 6 foot 2 inch giddy lummox on his first solo, post-op flight, but equally, I didn't want them in the bathroom looming over me when checking that certain things were still in working order. I felt I was strong enough to do what I needed to do on my own, so a compromise was agreed. I'd keep the door unlocked and pull the emergency cord if I got into trouble whilst they'd wait nervously nearby. All went well.

I was exhausted after chomping, dribbling and burping through lunch and dinner and zoned into some Netflix for the evening. I called Jane to let her know that I'd be coming home tomorrow and was looking forward to it. Jane was surprised it was so soon, but equally happy for my return. After all, it was a good thing to be going home, where recovery can improve further.

Thoughts of my own comfy bed, the cuddles from Jane and the kids and my own creature comforts warmed me. What could possibly go wrong?

♪ Sweet Home Alabama (Lynyrd Skynyrd) ♪

"Big wheels keep on turning carry me home to see my kin…where the skies are so blue, Lord, I'm coming home to you." A superb, Southern Boogie, fuzzy-feeling kind of song that says, it ain't perfect, but I love home. The Van Zandt brothers had such a laid-back style and Billy Powell weaved his licks on keyboard which set up the dreamy rhythm for me. I first heard it in my parent's back garden when I was twelve, trying to impress two older teenage girls, sisters from next door, who were sunbathing. I spotted them through the deep conifer trees and thought I'd impress them by blasting out some AC/DC on my ghetto blaster. They yelled, "Too loud, got any Skynyrd?" They tossed a cassette through the fence and asked me to listen to Freebird and this track. My first introduction to the band, from two beauties through the bushes. It's also a favourite with my kids too, driving back from the beach or airport after a holiday, as the song puts you in the mood for walking through your front door. Even Jane lets me play this one in the car, which doesn't happen very often.

On D-Day, mum and Jane came up to collect me. I left the room, thanked the nursing team and wandered down the corridors to the pre-organised pick-up point. I still felt pretty strong in my legs as I'd only been lolling around in bed for a couple of days. Despite my face looking like someone had left a messy scribble on a partly-inflated football, nobody batted an eyelid; they'd seen it all before.

The reception area at the Royal Marsden is a light and airy environment, ubiquitous with the sense of health and hope. On a wall is a mural full of well-wishing 'special dates' to patients and ex-patients. The whole area is a bubbling hotpot of people from all creeds, visiting for the same thing: cancer treatment.

I sat in the reception area and watched the world go by. It was a fantastic multi-cultural mélange. In the ten minutes I waited, a large group of orthodox jews bustled in, a number of muslim groups with women in full niqabs and hijabs silently floated by and an entourage of brightly coloured, African-costumed visitors noisily made their presence known. The building's entrance is quite old-fashioned with a Victorian 'In and Out' entrance which makes things easy for drop offs and pick-ups. A wide, stone staircase takes you down to road level from the revolving hospital door. Jane pulled up in the front, as planned, and I slowly walked down the steps. I felt a sense of escape as we pulled away from the gates.

The traffic home was pretty light, but I noticed every judder and cats-eye in the road. By the time we arrived home, I had to use every ounce of energy within me to scrape myself out of the passenger seat, walk inside and collapse onto the sofa. Plonk. Jane fussed about me and gave me a huge hug, which warmly relaxed me again.

I decided to have some chewable food for lunch to give my mouth a further test drive. Ironically, the single 'chewing point' where my teeth came together on the left-hand side of my mouth had a metal clasp across it, helping to hold the plastic plate in place. Every time I chewed, I tasted metal and the clasp gave off an irritating 'squeak' like a wonky shopping trolley wheel. What with that, the leaky mouth and lack of taste, eating was clearly going to be different.

The kids came in from school and we had lots of cuddles - it was lovely to be home.

5

EUREKA

A nerve-wracking first recovery and the genesis of my book

On that first night home, I only managed to grab five hours' sleep, given the pain and discomfort in my head, so I woke up feeling pretty exhausted. I'd decided to keep up the dosage of ibuprofen and paracetamol, as a large amount of pain had started to hit the side of my head at the jaw socket, where one of the wires holding the plastic palate was bolted on. The side of my forehead was also very sensitive and the inside of my mouth felt grim. "It wasn't like this in hospital," I thought. So I also took a dose of codeine for the first time too. I guessed it was all to be expected given that the anaesthetic was still wearing off.

I absorbed a little more Netflix that morning for distraction purposes and caught up a little with my sleep but the pain now seemed to worsen around my mouth and eye. My right bottom eyelid hung below its normal position due to swelling, and this exposed the conjunctiva, which was understandably bright red with anger - it wasn't used to being on show in this manner at all! During the day, it started to swell up like a mini, pink airbag in front of my eye. Over the same period, my mouth, which had a few new holes carved into it, started to tighten and fur up. Also nodules of white stuff gathered around the wounds. We weren't prepared for these side effects, so presumed I'd picked up a couple of infections.

The swelling peaked the next day; the conjunctiva was now in front of the eyeball and it felt like I was chewing razors in my mouth. Given the pain, I only wanted to consume liquid food and Lois set me up with a whiteboard to communicate as I didn't want to aggravate my mouth by talking.

Daren't talk, with Bob and Jane

We decided to call the Royal Marsden helpline for some advice. Their recommendation was to go to the local A & E (not likely!) or phone a doctor. As it was the week-end, we rang the doctor's telephone service, 111. I'd barely made it downstairs when the doctor arrived and he sat down to have a look. As he'd arrived without any medical background on me, he was clearly a little shocked at what sat in front of him. I looked like I'd gone fifteen rounds with Anthony Joshua. As soon as my story had been explained, he prescribed a dose of antibiotics for the inflamed eye.

We kept a photo diary of the growing swelling.

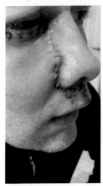 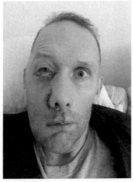

Puffing up nicely

♪ Get in the Ring (Guns & Roses) ♪

A cheerful little ditty from Axl and the boys about their misrepresentation in the press and inviting the perpetrators to a fight. There's a line that rang in my head: "Crush your head, put it in my vice, Paaaiiinnnn... yeh!"

I continued to try and distract myself as much as possible from the pain, wanting to rest, vegetate and chill out as best I could. But the mind is a funny thing. I started to think about the past, seeking answers to certain situations that I'd experienced in life that might have been subconsciously important to me. We all might naturally review these at times. For some reason, during recovery, my mind went into memory overdrive. Maybe it's a reaction to the anaesthetic, perhaps it was a reaction to the body's trauma and shock, or it could simply be what some minds do when left in neutral. Either way, I'd never experienced such an intense period of reflection, so I started to capture these on paper.

It felt good to have some extra medicine for the eye, so I grabbed two hours' sleep. That afternoon, the build-up of white stuff and pain in my throat had become unbearable, even with codeine, so we planned to phone 111 again the following morning. I was on the third day of codeine now and it was making me drowsy and dizzy. Given the further cocktail of medicine I was now popping, I decided to stop taking them.

The next morning, my mouth and throat felt like I'd been gargling barbed wire. We rang 111 but had a devil of a job getting through to anybody who could talk sense. Jane got upset by the changed tick-box style of interrogation. Mum tried too but, despite a stern matron-like tone, got nowhere. They wanted to speak directly with me, so eventually the phone was passed over. I could hardly talk. The health worker at the other end of the line clearly disregarded every word we'd relayed and seemed to think I needed to be rushed into A & E to clear my airway, which wasn't the case. My airway wasn't blocked, but my voice was in meltdown. I took a deep breath and asked her to get her supervisor to call us back.

Thankfully, we got a call back from one within the hour who'd listened to the taped conversation. Clearly all sorts of alarm bells had gone off there, as this was our second call in as many days. After sprinkling a little common sense into proceedings and further re-telling my whole story, a visit by a doctor was organised. The second 111 doctor visit was as quick as the first. After the initial shock of seeing me for the first time, we recounted the story again and the doctor prescribed a second wave of antibiotics for the mouth, together with some protein drinks. Blimey, if I felt like I was on Mars in the morning, I'd soon be on Saturn by the afternoon - strap me in 'cos I was going on the trip of a lifetime!

Having dropped the opiate codeine from my pill collection, I actually started to feel much better the next day. In fact, good enough to go out for a walk in the sun with Jane. We didn't go far but it was a refreshing change, and nice to feel a breeze whistling around, even if only half of my face could sense it.

The following part of the week whizzed by in a bit of a blur while my crack nursing team looked after me. I tried to stop sleeping during the day to ensure that I'd go out like a light when I went to bed, which duly occurred as soon as my head hit the pillow. The next thing that happened on the Wednesday night was nothing short of surreal.

I woke up at 2.30am but not in pain: my mind had started to race away with itself again for some reason. I tried to get back to sleep using all the methods I knew. Breathing exercises, meditation, watching the anaesthetic picture show in my eye and reading a book - nothing worked. I was wide awake. What was going on? I sat bolt upright, determined to work out what was happening and began to contemplate.

I had a feeling inside of me. On the surface, it was a strong urge to thank everyone in some way. I wanted to thank my triangle of support: my family, my medical team and my friends, for all of the motivation they were giving me. I remembered the fun people had enjoyed when we partied in honour of Beryl's long and extremely full life at her celebration party, so started to think how I could emulate this.

I started to think of a 'thank you-cum-50th birthday party' - that's it, a Half Century Survival Party! It was still very early in the morning and instead of falling back to sleep, my mind went up a gear in terms of creativity and reflection. No sooner had I sketched through some speeches, I started to delve further into the core of the feeling that was still keeping me awake.

It started to unwind in my head. I also wanted to help first-time cancer sufferers or surgery goers like me, by giving some insights from my experience. So often I'd had such positive compliments from family, friends and medical staff about my mindset. If I could help just one person, I would be very happy. Through life, I found it ever so helpful speaking to people who'd had a similar experience, but I didn't know anyone. How could I reach out and provide this help to others?

After thinking it through, I decided that this could best be achieved in the form of a book. It would be nice to raise money for charity too. I would clearly need some help, as this sounded like a social media quagmire. Until recently, I thought a tablet was what Moses wrote God's Ten Commandments on and a 'tweet' was a Spanish idiot!

So, as you do at 4am, I started to draft out some broad ideas. I jotted down several key 'learns' which I felt could help others on a similar path. Then my mind went off-road again into my history and childhood. It felt like my subconscious was providing me with references from the past, to arm me for the path ahead. You know what, I could also make this an autobiography. After all, it might be nice to leave some memories for the kids to read when they're older.

That, folks, was the very genesis of this book. A sweaty, tired, lonely, dark corner of my bedroom in the early wee hours one morning.

♪ I Just Can't Slow Down (Joe Satriani) ♪

From his 'Flying in a Blue Dream' album, a fast-paced song which seems to relay the pace of my mind at the time. I couldn't take the keys out of the ignition. This motor wasn't coming to a stop any time soon and each night my mind was racing with ideas and memories for the book.

The next morning, Jane found me slumped up in bed, snoring, mouth wide open, surrounded by my iPad, tissues, pills, towels, scribbles and bottles of water. I'd fallen asleep on the job! As soon as I de-welded my tongue from my mouth plate, I blurted out what I'd been up to. Pausing for breath, I looked at the 'to do' list I'd scribbled down. I'd now got lots to get on with. Sister Jane left her patient with raised eyebrows and calmly said, "Yes John, whatever," which translated as "WTF, you should be thinking about getting better first!"

We discussed it further over liquid brekky and recalled how Richard had warned us that something like this might occur - he wasn't the first one who'd spotted a creative streak within me.

Brothers Grimm

Later that morning, a crack commando garden team in the shape of Steve arrived to mow the lawn and trim an offending pine tree. What a star - no fuss, excellent job. We spent some good time outside, just enjoying the fresh air, chatting about our childhood and families. Another positive, seeing more of my brother.

I've always been a little in awe of Steve. He spent several years studying architecture at Cardiff and unfortunately graduated at the height of the recession in the early nineties. That must have been tough, to be newly-qualified, primed, ready to go out in the world and live your vocation. But there were no jobs to be had. Construction was on its knees and the Civil Engineering sector was taking a battering. Architects were being laid off, not recruited. Undeterred though, Steve cracked on, got a job at Vodafone pretty easily and quickly rose up the ranks, clearly showing some natural skill in Corporate Services. Well as we all know, yo-yo UK recessions don't last forever and as soon as he could, Steve took a pay cut to join a firm of architects to pursue his dream. He always knew what he wanted to be when he grew up.

In comparison, I joined the bank at seventeen years old because it had an office and was something to do with the word 'business', whatever that meant.

It was Friday! I was feeling great - always do on a Friday. Mum came over and we walked down through the woods onto the common where I showed her the highland cattle that roamed in the trees, due to ancient local grazing rights. We chatted further about my regurgitated childhood memories. I was seeing Cyrus in the afternoon and the appointment soon came round.

The magician and I

Within his surgery, Cyrus was in a cheeky mood, but with his serious hat on, he confirmed that everything was absolutely OK, there wasn't an infection after all!

My mouth was full of slough (as in the town, but pronounced sluff), produced naturally by my body during the healing process. This is a gathering of dead cells that are the pre-cursor to new fresh living cells underneath. The eye's swelling was also very normal and it was healing well. I was advised to quit the antibiotics there and then, which was a relief. This was the best news we'd had all week! Chatting further, it was clearly impossible for the local surgery or 111 doctors to advise on post-operation symptoms like mine. Cyrus invited us to contact him directly in future if we had any worries. Simply send a photo and he'd respond. This put our minds at rest instantly, but now I had to deal with the removal of the stitches from my face - marvellous.

I was taken to a side room and left with a nurse called Herman. I got straight into the breathing exercises as he went through the 'lift and cut' procedure with each of the stitches. Basically there are two knots: the first needs to be lifted out of the skin, so the stitch can be cut. This wasn't without a certain amount of discomfort, but I kept my nerve and put up with what I could.

We got through each one of the little blighters on my long face scar. I did pretty well, but there was a particularly sensitive one right on the inside of my upper right eyelid, next to my nose. Surprisingly, I'd managed to absorb the pain when he took the stitches out of my upper lip, under my nose, alongside the length of my nose and underneath my eye, but Herman's attempts on this last one were proving unbearably painful for a lightweight like me. The air had started to turn a shade of blue courtesy of yours truly on the fourth attempt, so we summoned Cyrus back.

As a surgeon, he alone had access to a special, extra-long, thin-bladed knife locked away in the corner of a nearby cupboard. It was over within a minute, without a whimper from the soft lad. Elation.

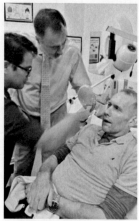

Jane and I got home, bouncing off the walls with joy. Cyrus had completely deflated the drama of the so-called infections like taking a pin to a balloon. I was advised to eat, drink, talk and be merry once again. He also recommended that I get down the gym soon - clearly I was wasting away. Why not? It made me feel better, didn't it? Sister Jane and Matron Mum held a party in my honour, a knees-up, and decided to tuck into the

"I have a cunning plan," declared Cyrus

champagne that work had kindly brought around before the operation. But it wasn't long before we faced the next major medical incident...

Chef Lois was preparing her usual tortilla delicacies for the oven when, in all the excitement, she dropped a bowl and cut three fingers. There was at least a thimbleful of blood spilt, so the half-inebriated nursing team were thrown into medical action, alongside 'scar face' daddy. Calmly, I was immediately thrust into medical duties, applying pressure and checking the patient's vital statistics. In an instant, I was giving, not receiving care. It was refreshing. I enjoyed nursing Lois through her dramatic injuries and thankfully, no amputations were required, but there were some jolly painful cuts!

Matron, Nursey and new patient Lois

The next morning, Jane came in with a sports bottle of ginger, turmeric and lemon to do the daily de-weld of my mouth. Mum, who'd stayed a few nights to be on hand, came by the bedroom door to say 'Hi'. Lois gave me a cuddle and waved to show me that her fingers were getting much better, so all was good.

Although we were sleeping separately, Jane and I had started to sip tea together first thing in the morning in bed to regroup. I explained to Jane that I'd worked out why I'd started to read some pretty heavy-going material in the run up to the procedures. My subconscious mind had gone into automatic and started to prepare for my horrendous treatments. I started to reflect on the enormity of the cancer experience I'd had to date.

Then out of nowhere, it happened...I started to cry uncontrollably, floods of tears, shoulders-a-heaving. Blubbing like a baby in my wife's arms for a good few minutes. Gazza at the Italian World Cup, the Rivers of Babylon, two of us as one. In joy, yes, tears of relief initially, and more joy as it went on - it was electric! Maybe it was PTSD or an aftershock from the surgery, perhaps it was relief at being given the thumbs-up from Cyrus and hearing that the squatter had been evicted...it matters not - it was lovely. Jane closed the door gently to allow us some privacy and said I ought to think about stopping as she was worried a little about flooding my dodgy eye.

Clearly I had changed, physically and psychologically. I was now more emotionally unstable, or is that more in touch with my emotions? Openly crying with Jane was such a new experience. I'd always assumed the Steady Eddy, rock-solid role to Jane's emotional roller coaster, as we call it. Jane was far more in touch with this stuff than me. To date, she was the ying to my yang, and vice versa.

It was such an enriching, natural, cleansing wash of emotion. It was like taking a shower in the purest, most refreshing waterfall of happiness. Admittedly, I'm writing this now, a little worried that I'll be seen as a bit of a soft touch, but hey, it's part of the story and it's a change for the better.

♪ Sweet Emotion (Aerosmith) ♪

The song starts off with a velvety smooth voice box guitar effect, courtesy of Mr Perry with percussion, then slowly gives way to some edgier power, thumped out by Mr Tyler and the boys. I first came across this track on Axe Attack, one of my first albums. This led me to delve a bit deeper into the band and their back catalogue, when I had the money. I was primed and ready when Aerosmith's renaissance came, thanks to MTV, their dally with RunDMC and the gargantuan FINE album (Fucked Up, Insecure, Neurotic and Emotional).

Later on, mum came into the room later and we compared notes - she hadn't slept either. She was worried that dad was tucking into too much beer at home without her supervision.

I dusted myself down and asked Jane to come back to our bed going forwards, to see if we could break the new habit of waking up at 2am to write the book. We decided I should have a non-liquid breakfast, to take in more calories and put on some weight. Wilko's American Diner rustled up a breakfast of waffles with manuka honey, poached eggs with flack seeds sprinkled on top, together with a side of ginger, lemon, apple and pepper drink. Bibbed up as usual, with a tea towel to catch any fall-out, I wolfed the lot down in under an hour; it was good to get back on solids again.

Jane and I went for a walk in the sun in search of my arse, which seemed to have fallen off somewhere. We probably did a mile or so and on the way back, I popped into Paul and Lana's, who live just around the corner. Paul sadly lost a brother to leukemia before we first met, so I knew I was bringing back some sensitive memories for them and wanted to show how positively it was going.

Paul and I first chatted and sipped coffee; he was impressed with the surgery. Lana wears her emotions on her sleeve; she'd already given me a wet shoulder when I sat down and sensitively told her about my diagnosis and treatment plan. Seeing her reaction to my new appearance was going to be a litmus test for my current 'dribbling, rabid, scarred, bulldog with a hint of Marty Feldman' look. Lana held it together really well and said it was far better than she'd anticipated. Happy days, so perhaps I wasn't super mega fugly. Vanity is overrated anyway. As another friend said, you can't polish a turd, but you can sprinkle a bit of sparkly glitter on it, and my scar looked fantastic!

To help me achieve more sleep, Jane returned to our bed that night. We also removed any electronic gadgetry, so if my mind sprang into creative mode, there'd be nowhere to log it. It worked: I slept well and my medical log book noted that I notched up 6.75 hours, with a cheeky ibuprofen fix at 3.30am - not bad.

6

OVER THE WORST?

Over the initial hump, feeling a little more human and the changing plans of reconstruction

The weight loss from surgery and laying around for prolonged periods was a bit of an eye-opener. Muscle wastage was rapid in my case.

After being home for a week or so, I started to feel stronger and more independent. I wanted to get into the cycle of building weight through exercise and started to go back to the gym.

♪ Kickstart My Heart (Mötley Crüe) ♪

This is a song about being resuscitated from a heroin overdose. It carries a medical theme in parallel to my story, but I love it as it's packed with energy. It's one of the songs that gets your blood flowing; if you listen to it before you have to do something physical, you get an added adrenaline rush.

I've always been prone to get a little carried away at the gym and clearly I couldn't go mad now. Understandably, Jane wanted to keep me in check, so she came too and reigned me in.

Before all this started, I didn't really pay much attention to my weight, I was more interested in my fitness, strength and body shape. We don't even have any weighing scales at home. It was now important for me to focus on this as I would be facing further surgeries. Cyrus had said to expect 10% weight loss through surgery, so as I faced at least one other, I needed to 'rebuild' weight before losing even more.

Although the weighing scales were probably inaccurate, they were a constant barometer that I'd use to assess my weight going forward. According to the scales, I weighed 88kg, so had lost 7kg (15lbs) since building my fitness and trimming down to 95kg from 105kg, before the first operation. I'd lost over a stone again!

My middle-aged doughnut and beer-induced midriff had vanished, as had a considerable amount of muscle tone, especially around my rear and legs. When I looked at the BMI chart on the internet, I was just in the 'Overweight' territory for my 6 foot 2 inch frame but I looked thin.

The workout was light, shorter than my usual 80 minutes, but great. When I got back home, I felt fantastic. My body buzzed again with endorphins and dopamine which raced around for the first time in ages - oh how I'd missed the gym. I always knew that this had to be a core part of my recovery. Given the exertion, I knew I'd sleep well and that this should build appetite too, so all in all, a good routine to get into.

I'd been a gym goer since my mid-twenties whilst playing rugby. Throwing weights around and jumping on various bits of CV and resistance machinery is my escape, my punchbag if required. Some like to run, some like to cycle, but my 'me' time is the gym, clunking about sweatily on rubber mats. When I don't go for a week or so, I get grumpy and stiffen up. As anyone will tell you, it's twice as hard getting back into it after having a break.

At the gym with Dan - Park Health Club

Before I'd been diagnosed, I'd managed to weave a visit or two in to the weekly work schedule, so had a reasonable level of fitness. This was something I intended to maintain when I got back to work. Without stating the obvious, it's good to try and break down the sedentary office environment as much as possible. I used to feel guilty about not getting to the office very early, but lately recognised that this feeling was a personal insecurity. An office is a better place with happier, fitter people. Exercise and working out is also said to improve your mental wellbeing, especially with neurological disorders such as dementia.

With the help of my 'feel good' body, I sent an update message to friends. Again, I wanted to pen something humorous and informative about the current position, next surgery procedures and the book idea. See 'Glossary of Sent Messages.' The feedback I received was electric. Everyone thought the book idea was great and some offered to help get in touch with publishers. Some dark-humoured messages made me laugh out loud, just how I wanted it.

I also tested out my slurring speech on some other people and phoned the speech therapist at the Royal Marsden. I got some great feedback; people could understand me. I later phoned Matron and was advised to slow up a bit (I think mum could sense me getting a little carried away).

I also enjoyed a nice call with my mate, Ewan, who was understandably proud as punch. He and Serene had just welcomed their second child into the world. Happy news.

I spent a good deal of time resting in front of the news and became fascinated with the thought of death coming at you out of the blue. One day you're healthy and minding your own business, then in a split second, you're not. It's not like you have time to do anything about it, but weirdly enough, I began to feel a little grateful about my experience. If death was to come, at least I'd had time to see it coming and accept it.

Back at home, Jane had been dreading her birthday for weeks. It was bound to bring back memories of Beryl as it was her first birthday without her mum about. Jane really needed a lift and I arranged it for her in the bedroom, first thing in the morning.

The kids had accumulated presents and cards that had secretly been deposited with us over the last week and were buzzing with excitement when they came into our room, ten minutes before they needed to get ready for school. Jane brought me the usual pint of De-Weld juice, alongside buckets of builder's tea, and it was great to see that Beryl had entered the room too. A fraction of her ashes were kept in a lovely, small phial at home. We watched as Jane opened cards and gifts from us all. If Jane hadn't been looking forward to this day, it wasn't showing, as she was clearly lifted by all the well-wishers.

Jane is so well-loved by family and friends and if you make it into the inner sanctum of her trust, you will not find a more loyal, supportive ally. She doesn't suffer fools lightly though and like me, can't stand double standards and two-faced operators. All of her supporters knew that she was still enduring a horrible year and her family and friends made an extra effort for her birthday.

The kids had independently chosen and paid for their own presents to Jane, which made us both very proud. Clearly, a lot of thought had gone into these. I reminded her that things were not as grim as they might appear and made her favourite breakfast, of special-recipe poached eggs with freshly ground coffee, which she adored. Seeing me 'doing it' was also a vital sign that I was in better shape. It was my first coffee for a month or so and it gave me a mini rush too. Jane made and received a handful of lovely calls before dashing off to her classes and left the house on a real high.

Jane was still racing around, running her business, and I felt that she was putting unnecessary pressure on herself. She knew that she was probably going to do less later in the year when a few classes would dissolve due to an expired lease, but this seemed a long way off. After chatting it through, we concluded that, for her sanity, she needed to take a break from some of her classes.

I've always liked talking with Jane about her business. Over the years, I'd often offered up advice or an opinion when asked. I'd even helped coin the business' name and provided a sounding board when thinking about pricing and communication. Jane had built up a fantastic local reputation, providing a first-class, high-tempo exercise and free-style yoga business, coupled with a personal body coaching service. She wasn't coping well with the burden of yours truly and eventually took a break from the business for about three months. This would allow her to focus on me, which she wanted to, I may add, through the worst parts which were probably yet to come. It was like taking a plug out of an inflatable; all the pressure heaping up on her seemed to seep away to the tune of a high-pitched raspberry. Needless to say, all of her loyal clients were very understanding and knew that, all things being equal, she would return in a few months.

Tension had started to build up in Jane's neck, so I started to provide her with some massage treatments. I've always been told I had healing hands and the pain eased after a few sessions. For me, it just felt great to get back to a semblance of normality for a little while, me helping my wife. We had always supported each other, but I felt it had been all me, me, me since the diagnosis.

Reviewing the medical log, I noted that I'd started to have a regular eight hours' sleep, without taking painkillers in the wee hours. Jane commented that my body was looking reasonably better, apart from my lack of arse, which still seemed to elude me. She seemed to have accepted my Marti Feldman eye and the slanted, dribbling mouth.

Halloween came round and understandably there was a natural build-up of jokes directed at me. It's a bit mad every year in our neighbourhood; some people like ourselves put a lot of effort in and dress up their homes with all sorts of sinister, spooky stuff. People drive from miles around to trick or treat on our streets. This year was an unusually quiet one; we had lots of visitors as usual but had to put a notice outside to say that we weren't participating this year due to illness.

I began to push out the envelope as much as I dared in terms of pain relief by reducing the daily pill count, especially later in the day when I became tired. It was trial and error, so sometimes I misjudged it and got a rap over the knuckles from Jane for being Mr Grumpy. Slowly though, I whittled it down from seven to two doses over 24 hours. I was really chuffed with this. The side effect was that I became more tired in the evening and Jane complained that the snoring walrus had returned to the bedroom! To get some sleep, Jane quietly began to creep off to the spare room in the middle of the night.

In mid-November, we went to see Cyrus at his afternoon clinic. He was as laid back as usual and declared that he was 99.9% certain that the 'reconstruction' operation would be on 21st November. I was excited to hear that I'd be getting a titanium mesh to hold up my eye. Bullet-proofing was clearly a key consideration here and I started to think about Steve Austin, the six million-dollar man: 'we can rebuild him' echoed in my head. I enquired if there was any chance that the operation could leave a more distinct scar. I certainly wanted a war wound to show off and the first operation's scar was so good, it was now difficult to see. Cyrus slowly crossed his arms and looked me in my one good remaining eye, before saying, "John, I hope you're not asking me to do a crap job!". Yet again, we returned from Cyrus' surgery in a buoyant mood.

We noted how well the kids seemed to be coping with my condition. Max was in a good space, he appeared to be making the right decisions whilst growing up and was putting some effort into his studies, seeing the benefit in better results. At the outset, we set out our stall by stating that he didn't need to worry about dad, but we wanted to worry less about him and his schoolwork. Emotional blackmail maybe, but when coaching kids in sport, you move from a 'tell' style to a 'self-coach' style. Max got it and in the main, he cracked on where he needed to. Notwithstanding this, he was still a loud, energetic, sometimes stroppy teenage boy, totally adored by us, his two proud parents. Lois seemed to be coping well too, stating, "I don't care if daddy has scars and is more ugly, he's still my daddy and I love him." Talk about kids just telling it like it is!

My good mate Chris helped us out a lot. He takes his godfather duties to Max seriously and grasped the opportunity to cart Max to his U15 footy matches whilst I was incapacitated. Out of the blue, he also got some shopping in to help Jane out. This was well-received. Jane told me that Chris had also been inspired by my fitness regime in dealing with the cancer and had decided to jack in cigars and vape cigarettes, at least for a while.

Chris mucking in

My illness clearly had a ripple effect on friends and family as they started to assess their own lifestyle. Steve is now far more conscious about what he eats for breakfast, how many coffees he has a day and has started going to a local gym. He has even started the regular exercise of cycling. Mind you, he still enjoys walking into town on a week-end, meeting up with mates in the pub and, in his own words, 'getting battered' - some habits will probably never die. Dean also changed his coffee-drinking habits and focusses on remaining hydrated.

As days went by, I could sense that my sleeping patterns were improving and I was eating more. So with increased energy levels, I slowly started to build up the gym visits and notched up the weights. Now and then, for a change of scenery more than anything, Jane and I would drive over to Newbury and go to the spa gym complex, Donnington Valley, used by my father-in-law. It was lovely to get into the pool, steam room and even the sauna after a workout and we often stayed for lunch afterwards. These little excursions made me feel more human, even though the roof of my mouth felt like the inside of a plastic spoon and the medical Polyfilla that had temporary filled in the gaps left by the removed mass of the tumour was aching a tad.

Getting out and about

Having the kids around, whilst noisy and draining, was a great motivator and provided lots of joy as I got to see them more. I was able to help with homework now and experience the daily dilemmas from school such as feisty friends and teachers' feedback. It felt good, I was helping.

Mum was still visiting reasonably frequently and one afternoon she rang to say that she'd had a fall. Thankfully it had only shaken, not broken her, so we asked her to rest up, and not come over for a week or so until she was ready. It highlighted that Jane too, as a carer, needed to make sure that she looked after herself.

Over the weeks leading up to the second surgery, I felt the urge to reach out to people I'd lost touch with and had some visitors too. I wanted to make the most of my time before going into surgery once more, recognising that I would probably have to lie low again once I came out.

Visits from friends

59

With time now on my hands and some memories of my past still vivid in my mind, I wanted to pick up from where I left off with some family and friends.

One side of the family I felt I needed to speak to was my dad's, especially his brother Mick's family. Although we didn't see much of him, I was always fond of Mick. He was very welcoming when we were last in touch, at a family reunion in 1998, where Steve and I introduced our soon-to-be wives, Anne and Jane. He'd clearly done well in business, building it up over decades, and his sons now ran it.

Unfortunately, Mick passed away over ten years ago and I'd always felt guilty about not attending his funeral. I should have carved out time to go. I was travelling frequently with work, living in Beckenham, Max was very young – excuses, excuses. Sometimes you need to step off the carousel to go to something important like that, otherwise you regret not doing so later in life. I don't intend to make the same mistakes any longer: life is literally too short and my outlook had been rebalanced.

I had a LinkedIn connection with his youngest son David, my cousin, so I penned an email apologising for the lack of contact and relayed my news too. I was also interested to hear about Mick's illnesses before he passed away. Dad had mentioned that he'd been diagnosed with a sarcoma. Thankfully, David replied and passed on my well wishes to his mum and brother. Mick had indeed had a sarcoma in his arm and this spread to the bone, so he had to have his arm amputated. This must have frustrated the hell out of him as he, his wife and kids were all keen golfers. It was great to be in touch again and exchanging messages. I've no doubt they'll swing by if they're in the vicinity; I certainly will see them if I find myself near Cheshire.

As time wore on, various things started to irritate me more. The holding pattern of the temporary false mouth roof and Polyfilla face didn't help. After some stitches came loose in my mouth, the false, plastic palate began to flap around and was unpleasant to deal with. I allowed my frustration to magnify my annoyance at certain things. Victor Meldrew had entered the building!

I felt miffed about some of the news on the TV and perhaps I allowed myself to get grumpy about various things that came across the airwaves. A *Panorama* documentary had tried to sensationalise the known practice of tax efficiency provided by offshore islands such as the Isle of Man. The journalist seemed to be hounding the wrong target; if the whole world wanted to change the well-known corporate practice of tax efficiency, then it needs to make this a massive issue for its elected bodies and aim the debate of change to the powers that be: the G7, G10, United Nations, law-makers etc., so it could be done on an international, fair basis. A lot of voters indirectly benefit from tax efficiencies from within their pension holdings and the like, so if the rule book needed changing, there would have to be a wide, serious culture change in the world of capitalism. Maybe it's now due - the rich seem to be getting wealthier at the cost of the common man.

Clearly there were shady characters behind the cloak of secrecy that some offshoring facilitated, and these players need to be hunted down. But to aggressively interview some poor sod who happened to work in an offshore office in the past missed the whole point and was nothing better than journalistic bullying. Aim your guns higher up the food chain, where the rules are made, if you want change! If you read my brief autobiography, you'll understand why I empathised with the journalist's target a bit.

Clearly grumpiness was starting to set in and appeared outwardly too. I got more and more irritated with the fixed roof of my mouth and shamefully snapped at Jane in the gym one day. She wasn't doing anything wrong, just fussing over me with care. I'd dropped my locker key and quickly ducked down to get it, when a woman gawped at my damaged face. In reaction, I half shouted at Jane, "I'm OK, let me be." Clearly I was becoming more of an ogre and Jane quite rightly had a long overdue word with me on the naughty step. I apologised, felt like a prat and carried on to do a 45-minute workout, vowing that I would check in with my brain before venting fury in future.

I attended an outpatient appointment at Cyrus' clinic with mum. It was great to introduce her to Cyrus and she was very excited to meet such a celebrity in our lives. He was as positive and practical as usual and answered all the questions I'd prepared, and a few off the cuff ones which mum threw in for good measure. There were still no pathology results to discuss, so I just clarified a few things with him in terms of the aftercare and eye physiotherapy. The surgery was almost certainly going to be on the planned date of 21st November, after which, Dr Miah was likely to organise some radiotherapy. Seeing the path ahead gave me a good boost and, coupled with the post-gym dopamine racing through my body, I drove home dribbling down my front (I still hadn't worked out how to seal my mouth when trying to smile).

A couple of days ahead of the second operation, I needed to get in touch with Cyrus. Unfortunately, the skin under my dodgy eye had burst during a sneeze, after the build-up of an abscess. I worried that infections might be taking hold. He wasn't concerned and explained it was minor; he'd fix it with a skin graft during the operation. He had some more important matters to discuss.

Abscess about to blow

Cyrus explained that he'd just received the pathology report, but it hadn't conclusively given him the evidence he'd asked for. He was quite rightly (and thankfully) a perfectionist by nature and needed the lab to work on it further. The knock-on effect was likely to be a postponement of the operation. He asked if I could put up with the temporary mouth roof for a further fortnight. I boldly said that if the long-term outcome was better, then I could. Cyrus would keep me updated.

In truth, I was really suffering at this stage. Eating had become an issue and the pain in my jaw was significant. Looking back, I hadn't paid enough attention to the jaw exercises. I'd wrongly figured that it didn't matter, given I was going back into surgery and everything would be 'reset' at the next surgery. I should have paid far more attention to the physiotherapy of my jaw as it later came back to haunt me, big time.

On the day before surgery, we went to the gym in the morning. I figured that if I was going to be lying around in bed for ages, I might as well get a workout in beforehand. Whilst we were out, Cyrus left a voice message. The tables had turned. He was now 99.9% certain that the surgery needed to be postponed. He went on to say that I didn't need to bother turning up tomorrow, he was standing down the surgical team. The rollercoaster had turned a corner and was now heading for the ground. Our hearts sank. We'd have to get through a couple of more weeks somehow. If I needed to go onto a liquid diet, I would.

Thankfully, the gods must have been listening, as later that afternoon we got another message from his secretary. "Cyrus says ignore his previous message, the pathology department have just come up trumps and we're set to receive you for surgery tomorrow as originally planned." As the rollercoaster sped through the bottom of the dip, it now started to climb towards the heavens. I don't think anyone could have been happier than me to be going into a planned ten-hour operation. Jane and I were excited and smiling once again. Bring it on.

7

WE CAN REBUILD HIM,
SECOND SURGERY

Getting more than I bargained for and a timely, god-sent experience

Jane and I had agreed that I'd just be dropped off at the steps so she could zoom straight home. The traffic had been light and we arrived much earlier than planned. As I walked down the corridors, I dodged cleaners who were still buffing the floors in readiness for the day ahead. Eventually I waited in the comfy seats for the pre-surgery area to open. Everyone who saw me must have thought, "He's keen." I was. Chomping at the bit, wide awake and ready to go.

Looking thoughtful at RMH

The reception eventually opened up and ushered me in to the familiar, curtained surroundings of a paisley-gowned waiting cubicle. This time, they even had the correct-sized DVT socks waiting for me! In no time at all, Cyrus popped his head around the curtain, and we went through what was going to happen. This all seemed to be water off a duck's back for him and his calmness was again infectious, so I relaxed.

We talked briefly about the lower leg donor site. Approximately 20cm of bone was to be taken from my fibula and recreated as an upper jaw and cheek bone. Also, lots of skin with blood vessels would be used for the skin graft, free flap to replace the medical Polyfilla. I showed him that I'd shaved my leg in preparation, along with my forearms. I'd learnt that for me, the most painful thing in hospital to date was the removal of plasters and cannulas from hairy skin. They always seemed to be glued in place by dissolved hair, skin and welding fluid. I know women wax their legs and get used to the pain but most blokes choose to remain hairy. It's an agonising pain that I've never got used to. Stitches, wounds and removed bones - just bring on the usual painkillers and a bit of paracetamol for afterwards, no problemo!

By now, the other surgeons had joined Cyrus in the cubicle. I asked them to use the same leg to find what they needed if the lower leg was not forthcoming; that way, I'd still have one fully working (stronger) leg. We went through the paperwork and consent forms again. It was the big one on paper: a marathon 9-10 hour procedure. One of the three amigos from my first surgery, Francesco, would work on my leg whilst Cyrus cracked on with the maxillofacial area. Given the time in theatre, afterwards I'd be sent to the Critical Care Unit, CCU (Intensive Care, in old money) as a precaution, which was normal protocol, for at least one night's observation. Then I could expect to be on the ward for five or six more days. I didn't hover on the fact that this was major surgery as I just wanted it completed, but was also aware that it always carried a slim chance of going wrong.

After completing the paperwork, everyone was happy, so I trundled down to the side room next to the theatre to be put to sleep. I noted that the clock said 8.58am and the team had no problem knocking me out. I counted backwards from 100 and got to 87. Everything had gone like clockwork as I drifted off. With a bit of luck, I'd be cosily tucked up in a bed that evening.

Jane waited for the normal call that evening to confirm that I was out of theatre, but it didn't come until 4.15am the next morning - it had been a sleepless night. The operation had taken a tad longer than expected and the team had to deal with some issues. The kids were packed off to school as usual and Jane travelled to London to see me in CCU.

Once there, she came into my room with two doctors to wake the sleeping beauty from his anaesthetic-induced slumber. My audience all looked at each other, waiting for someone to make the first move. Then one of the doctors rolled up his sleeves and said, "Let's see if we can pull the tube away from his mouth for a start." As if resurrected, I stirred, my eyes slowly opened and I was surrounded by three gently smiling celestial beings in a very bright, large, white room. I couldn't talk so gestured for something to write with. "Let's get him a pen and whiteboard." After a few indecipherable scribbles like a spider with three broken legs, I managed to communicate. "Am I in hospital?" I asked, just checking that I wasn't beyond the pearly gates. I clearly hadn't got my bearings.

Jane softly explained that the surgery had taken a lot longer than planned, due to unforeseen complications, and gave me a warm cuddle as best she could in the circumstances. After fifteen minutes, I was happily slurring my words, but talking again. Cyrus and Francesco phoned Jane to say they'd like to pop up to see the patient; when they arrived, it gave me a boost of energy from out of nowhere.

They explained that the procedure had almost doubled in time to nineteen hours. It was Cyrus' second longest and Francesco's longest surgery to date. Apparently, to maintain their focus, the team took turns on some Japanese and Korean karaoke. I'm sure there were times where they needed to lighten the mood or shake things up, for the sake of the team's sanity. The surgeons had taken 20cm of healthy bone from the fibula in my left lower leg, but were unable to find an appropriate area of skin from the same site because they couldn't find any blood vessels. They explained that every patient is different beneath the skin, nobody is text book, and it's not until you get in there that you see how an individual's anatomy is mapped out. So undeterred, they travelled up to my upper thigh in search of the skin with healthy blood vessels. This tissue replaced the temporary medical Polyfilla which filled the hole above my palate, up to my eye socket, following the removal of the tumour. En route, they also found lots of indicators of deep vein thrombosis, which figured, as my dad has suffered with this hereditary disease. Something for Steve and me to chat with the kids about later on as they'd be susceptible too. This meant that I would need to take regular blood thinning injections whilst in hospital - yay!

With all the excitement of hearing about the surgery, I experienced an initial release of joy after getting through the ordeal and couldn't believe what I'd heard.

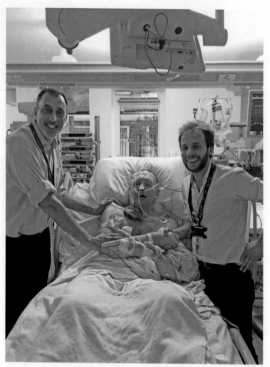

The sorcerer and his apprentice, Francesco

In a way, I was oblivious to what the surgical team had been through in theatre, as I was clearly unconscious throughout the whole ordeal, but think about it for a moment. Nineteen hours, on your feet, keeping your wits about you, making life-changing decisions that affect the patient, concentrating on everything that's going on within a major complicated surgery. I have total respect for them: I've never worked a nineteen-hour shift and the risks associated in my profession don't come close to life or death. I didn't know what to say, but tried as best I could to say a heart-felt thank you, with special effect dribble for show. Cyrus gave a nod to my fitness and mental attitude, but also reminded me that even if the patient is unconscious, they are not simply sleeping through the procedure. Despite being asleep, the patient endures the anaesthetic, being sawn, cut up and rearranged. Even though you're not awake, your body lives through it.

The surgeons had rebuilt the six million-dollar man's face. I now had a bullet-proof titanium mesh bolted into the bottom of my eye socket to hold up my eye. Somewhere under the swelling, my fibula had provided a new upper jaw and cheekbone and upper thigh skin was used as a 'filler'. As I spoke, I felt a mass of hair resting on my tongue which I took as a good sign; at least my tongue had maintained its sensitivity. I think we all got quite excited with relief, but I was incomprehensible. Clearly it was going to take a while for things to settle down, or up, in the case of the hanging flap in my mouth. Then we were asked to keep the noise down as another patient was wheeled into the room on the other side of the curtain (I was in a two-bed room).

Steve arrived later and leant over when Jane went to get a coffee. He confided, "I'm jealous of that scar on your neck, mate, well cool, looks like you've been in a knife fight." After nodding off a bit, I started to come round again. Jane said, "You ought to have a look at your leg." I peeked under the sheet that covered my body. I think I muttered, "Fuck." In glorious, thick black knots, the stitching ran from just below the level of my hip, down the side of my leg and split into a funky two-pronged fork shape above the knee. The upper leg was now a lot thinner than usual, given that they'd had to squeeze the same thigh contents back into a smaller container of skin. I also

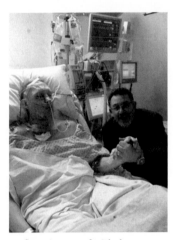

Steve impressed with the scars

had what looked like a peculiar small, bulging hillock atop the moat of the fork of the stitches. The lower leg's stitching went from below my knee, right down to my ankle in matching, thick, criss-crossed black. It too had some curves, like a fast chicane in a race track.

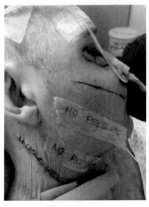

The neck scar

Time for a mirror to inspect my face. They had indeed recut along the original scar from the resection and for good measure, also replaced the blown hole area under my eye with a new patch of skin. I noticed two strips of masking tape over my swollen cheek area with the words 'No Pressure' written on it in biro. Either people would think twice before using my face as somewhere to rest a mug of tea or it was a joke from the surgical team. Perhaps a reference to how my frame of mind may have been whilst out cold, compared to the labouring, focussed medical team during the long surgery?

Moving around in bed was a little constricted as I was hooked up to various medical instruments. I'll try to give you a sense of what I was wired up to, by travelling down my body from head to toe.

I had an oxygen tube up one nostril, a feeding tube up the other which went down the back of my throat and a Doppfler machine attached to a tube in my neck. This sounded like a baby's heart beat in a womb when listening to ultrasound and monitored the blood flow going through the flap. Next to that hung a drain tube out of my chin area called a pendular, protruding down my neck like a used condom. This encouraged gunk to drain directly from deep inside my upper jaw. On my chest were several ECG pads which monitored heartbeat, blood pressure and other vital statistics. On my arms there were cannulas hooking me up to bloods and saline. For good measure, in my undercarriage, I had the joy of a catheter (thank god I was anaesthetised for this insertion!). Given the heavy surgery area, sticking out perpendicular to my leg were four drain tubes, three at the top and one at the lower leg donor site wound. Here, further gunk would collect in bottles placed on the floor. I wasn't about to leap out of bed anytime soon!

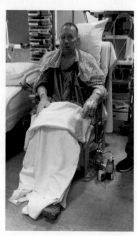

Sitting down - check out the drainage bottles!

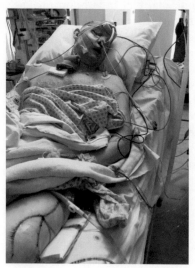

Straight after 19 hour operation, wired up

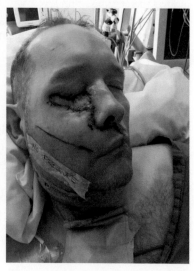

Close up, reopened previous stitches and a new flap under my eye

The CCU environment was vastly different from the ward where I'd been before. The nursing ratio was 1:1 for a start, so if you are inclined and able, you can spend more time talking to the staff. What an international set they were! I had a fantastic array of nurses from the UK, European continent, the Middle East, Far East and beyond. All very personable and focussed on the patient's care, making sure you took your meds and were as comfortable as possible.

I chatted with them and asked why they went into healthcare, how they came to get the job there and how many years' experience they'd had. There were varying answers: some had a calling because they simply wanted to take care of people, some saw the profession as a way to explore the world and some simply ended up there because of their experience. Each had different styles and attention levels. One had OCD and spent an age making the sheets on the bed straight, the wires tidy and paid an immense amount of time monitoring and logging information. Each would write up notes and complete a comprehensive handover when their shift was taken over by a new nurse.

CCU beds are situated beneath a gantry of machines which hover like a huge, illuminated halo. Various screens show your oxygen rate, heart beat and all sorts of other measurements. I hadn't noticed how bright it was until I asked the team to swing my bed to face the window for a change of view one night. It was like being in front of the advertising lights at Piccadilly Circus. I didn't get much sleep that night and soon realised it was best to have the screens behind you.

I felt some tingling and sharp pain in my swelling leg. I'd been self-administering minute doses of fentanyl (more potent than morphine) from my hand-held PDA. This allowed a tiny amount of potent painkiller to seep into my body every five minutes. When it lit up, I depressed the button. After a while, the side effects of the continuous drugs became evident to everyone except me. My brother said I didn't stop talking and Jane said I slowly became quite ratty. I remember seeing the kids on day two, who promptly redesigned the nurses' whiteboard for them.

During the day, the small hillock in Thighville started to grow. The peculiar, moat-like scar and the river that ran through the shire showed signs of cellulitis, an infection where the flesh around the stitches went a deep shade of pink. The skin started to seep serum and the leg began to inflate; something was bubbling inside. My leg soon resembled a roasted red suckling pig that chef Heston might have prepared for a medieval banquet. I wondered if they'd ever had an exploding leg on the ward?

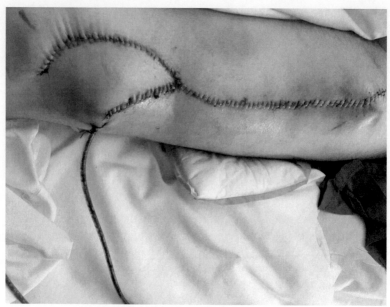

Heston's suckling pig roasting nicely

The whole medical team seemed to visit me throughout the day. The surgeons started to infer that I might need to top up the nineteen hours in theatre with a 'quickie' two-hour procedure, to clean out the infections going on inside the leg. To double check their suspicions, I was whisked off to the ultrasound department, which confirmed I was indeed growing large infections as well as two huge clots in my thigh. The doctor in ultrasound had a go at sucking them out with a large, wide-bore syringe but the clot was too congealed to get the down the needle. Not wishing to hold back on examinations that day, I also received a chest X-ray for good measure, to ensure that no DVTs had crept into my lungs - all clear upstairs, thank chuff.

Francesco broke the news that I was definitely going to theatre and explained a new procedure. Now that I had a flap inside my mouth, the anaesthetic process and setting up for the induced coma was going to be a little different this time around. They would need to observe the position of the ventilation tube via a camera, to check it went to my lungs not my stomach: nobody needed a ballooning belly in theatre. Thankfully, the camera would be on the end of an optic cable that had to go up my nose and down my throat. Ordinarily they would just move your tongue to one side and look into the back of your throat. "Hey ho," I thought, "Let's just get this thing over with. If I survived nineteen hours, two hours will be a cinch."

In no time at all, I was in the side room to the theatre and a dozen of the team were around me. I looked at the optic tube. "It's wider than my nostril." I muttered. To be honest, they probably couldn't understand what I'd said; as a matter of fact, everyone had begun to look puzzled when I spoke to them. So we cracked on. I'd be back in bed for tea and biscuits in no time!

After a spray of green local anaesthetic up the nostril, the tube was unceremoniously rammed up. I couldn't feel any pain, but recognised the sensation of flesh being ripped from the inside of my nose and throat. We just had to get it into position now, past the vocal cord.

At this point I froze. I could neither inhale nor exhale and I started to panic. I turned to Francesco and mimed that I couldn't breathe. We had eye contact, but he looked at another colleague behind his mask and I think said, "Don't worry, it might take some time." I wasn't getting any help from him so I turned to the person holding the anaesthetic and mimed vigorously that I couldn't breathe. My lungs started to slowly burn and my toes began to tingle.

I'd experienced suffocation before during a diving accident in Malaysia. I was buddied up with Jane and we were 25m deep. I had stupidly wandered off from my buddy to explore and the gauge on my poorly-filled air tank malfunctioned. My regulator's air flow rapidly seized up and I knew I needed to take some action. I turned to find Jane and she was about 10m away from me. Given that I was trying to gulp what air I had down at that point, I had to make a split-second decision. Do I try to race over to Jane and grab her reserve regulator or go for the surface? I decided to go up rapidly, rather than risk rushing over to Jane, panicking her, and fumbling with a reserve regulator that might also be faulty. As I sped towards the surface, exhaling as I went, to ensure that there was no effect from the bends, it felt like the journey would never end. My legs were strongly pumping away, but the surface didn't seem to get any closer and I began to experience the tunnel vision of passing out as I sucked the last morsels of air out of the restricted airway.

Back in the anaesthetic room, I started to experience this same sensation. I was now sitting up and miming very expressively. The team didn't come near me but seemed to buzz busily around. They seemed unfazed by my frantic actions. Everyone kept their calm except me, thinking I was going to suffocate! Mind you, I've no doubt I'd have been resuscitated - there were plenty of medically-trained people about!

I don't know how it happened but I thought, "Sod it, they'll just have to get this thing out of my lungs." I took the deepest, strongest inhalation I could muster and something at the back of my throat gave way. There was a rush of air, I collapsed back flat on the bed and didn't need to try to beat 87 on the countdown. I was out cold as they simultaneously applied the sleeping juice.

This was one of the most terrifying parts of my whole cancer story and it shook me to the core. I think it triggered a new sense of vulnerability and self-preservation when I got back to CCU. It affected me deeply over the next day or so as I woke up with nightmares, feeling short of breath.

The surgical team were chuffed with the results: they'd removed 1.5 litres of serum from the gooey leg, both haemotomas and had given the insides of my thigh a good wash down. I quizzed them about the suffocation method and they just confirmed that I had looked 'a bit puzzled'. Puzzled? Clearly my charade skills were extremely rusty! In hindsight, over a year later, I realise that I should have perhaps asked for a relaxant or pre-med to chill me out.

Although I was eating and drinking by now (albeit like a six-month old, messing up a bib every time), the fantastic nurses now had to put up with a proper sulky drawers.

I told them to stop fiddling with me, stop waking me up, just let me be and leave me alone. I'd reached a low point. Battered, broken and fed up with the whole situation, I was clearly feeling the side effects of the drugs and surgery. I was experiencing delirium, a known behaviour recognised in CCU wards that I'd read about.

They say everything happens for a reason…the next event will remain vividly with me forever.

The next morning, I woke up to find myself being stared at by a stern-looking woman from the edge of the curtain which separated the two beds in the room. She'd obviously been there for a few minutes as she didn't initially realise that I'd clocked her. I was clearly quite a sight. "Nosy cow," I thought. She jumped with surprise when our eyes met and disappeared back to the assembled party around next door's bed, muttering something in a hushed, American accent. " Y'all should see the state of him next door!"

Breakfast came around and I found myself staring forlornly at an unopened yoghurt. I was sizing it up, wondering how best to get it down my cake hole rather than down my chest. My radar picked up movement next door. It was eerily quiet, the patient was now awake.

Jane had informed me the night before that he was a 30+ year old man. I hadn't heard him arrive from surgery overnight. I'd worked out from the ensuing conversations that he was surrounded by his wife, parents and relatives from the USA, including the steely-eyed lady. His much younger kids were at home. My neighbour seemed like a chirpy chap.

His medical team entered his side of the curtain on their morning rounds and stood around the bed. He welcomed the surgeon like a family friend, and clearly enjoyed the same level of familiarity I'd felt with my surgical team. This was his first meeting post-surgery.

"Hi, how did it go?" he asked. "I'm feeling good and hopefully, following the recent chemo, you were able to take the rest of it away?" he cheerily enquired.

There was a poignant pause. The surgeon's tone was instantly very flat and factual.

"I'm afraid it didn't go as we both hoped it would. When we opened you up, we were expecting it to have receded and, as you know, we were prepared for a resection. Unfortunately, we quickly found that it has aggressively grown further into other areas." There was now more compassion in the surgeon's voice. "My colleagues and I consulted with others whilst you were unconscious and felt that the best thing we could do in this inoperable situation was to sew you back up and speak with you as soon as possible. I am very sorry but there was nothing we could do in theatre."

I held my breath out of respect. I didn't want my neighbour to know that I was listening in to what was an extremely sensitive conversation, and hoped he assumed that I was asleep again.

The surgeon continued, "We recommend that you get discharged as soon as possible and spend some time at home with your family." It went quiet for what felt like a whole minute's silence.

Pleasantries were exchanged and the medical team left, followed by some of his family. Clearly all of them were still absorbing the news.

I felt my emotions rise. Christ, poor bloke. What would I do now in his situation? Clearly his cancer was far worse than mine and there I was, getting grumpy about my poxy leg and some yoghurt! It was so sad, so very difficult to listen to, let alone be a part of it. My tears welled up, and I wanted to go and give him a hug, or at least say how very sorry I was for him, but clearly this wasn't going to happen.

The remaining family members clumsily started to try to change the subject and get the patient to engage in other conversation, which he bravely did. Such a low situation, such a British reaction, no screaming mothers, no shouting at God or pleading for divine intervention. Within ten minutes, the conversation was all very matter of fact again and focussed on getting the discharge papers organised and the patient packed up to go home.

About half an hour later, Jane walked in looking radiant and bubbling with energy. I quickly mimed in charades that she needed to be silent and beckoned her to quickly come over to me so I could whisper what had happened. Jane and I sat in silence and the nurse, who was covering both beds, was clearly aware of the situation. He recognised that we were keeping quiet, given the circumstances, and in one look and arm gesture, relayed that there wasn't such a brave face next door now.

Slowly the family peeled off in couples to get a coffee, I guess to let the emotion off outside of view and the nurse went to console the anonymous patient quietly. He was discharged very quickly that morning.

The playing out of the excruciatingly personal drama next door delivered a renewed perspective to me. I was provided with a stark reminder of how lucky I still was. My spirit needed a well-deserved kick up the arse and by golly it got one, the timing was perfect. When I think about this even now, I'm still very emotional. It was meant to be, it was a message, a sign. God bless him.

8

SOLITARY CONFINEMENT

Reaching my septic turning point

Avoid looking at the photo below if you're squeamish!

Given my loss of blood, I'd been hooked up with the first of three blood transfusions during my stay in CCU. Whilst it was seeping into my body, all I could smell was shepherd's pie - weird. The flap in my mouth had started to bleed and I could taste raw meat at the back of my throat, where something resembling fresh road kill dangled menacingly. The camera had clearly done some damage and I wondered if this was my epiglottis in tatters. I could feel raw flesh further up in my shredded nasal passage too.

I asked for a mirror to inspect the damage and was rewarded by the sight of a hanging glob of blood at the back of my throat. I tried to snort it out or cough it up but it wouldn't shift. Jane wasn't too comfortable with the guttural sounds I was summonsing, so we called the nurse. A doctor inspected the clot and I widened my mouth as best I could and tried to say ARRRRR - it came out as NNNNNNG. Enough for the doctor to grab and rip it out with forceps. We took a photo of the grotesque lump, the size of a sausage, in the doctor's gloved hand. Hopefully, the last side effect from the third operation was now on its way to the incinerator.

The offending dangler at the back of my throat. Nice

The CCU doctors became increasingly worried about my still 'fit to burst' leg. Despite the last clean up from surgery, it continued to expand and seep serum from its stitching like a ticking time bomb. The surgeons were a little more chilled with the situation and were happy to adopt a 'try, wait and see' approach with various antibiotics, to treat the infections. As a back stop, if they or I thought it was worsening at any point, they would whisk me off for an ultrasound to check it out.

Further surgery at this point was the last option. They explained that the body has many bacteria roaming around within it. For some reason, my upper left leg seemed to contain more than the average amount of mucky buggers for a human. Maybe it was all of that squatting down in the scrum I did in the second row. I'd often got cut, swollen knees and simply showered as normal, knowing that it would heal after several pints of Guinness, a well-known medicinal cure of the day.

So I was hooked up to a carousel of different antibiotics and regular blood tests were run to analyse my body's response. With a bit of luck and a downhill slope, we might hit the jackpot, get a positive response and deflate the suckling pig. The trouble was, unbeknown to me at the time, I was 'becoming septic' and the CCU wanted me transferred to a single room for fear of cross infection.

The next morning, the new CCU doctor was a little more forthright. She was determined to sort out the infection problems and said I would need to go into surgery once more to remove these. I politely declined the offer and explained that the surgeons had recommended I continue with antibiotics under observation. Beneath my genial manner lay a person in absolute fear of undergoing the suffocating camera procedure once more. I'd do anything to avoid this until it was the absolute life-or-death last option available.

She became very persistent and started to engage with other doctors on the ward to get their opinion and support. I was visited by an array of prodders and thinkers. Whilst I was delighted to know that she had my best interests at heart, I was less than happy that she'd tried to force the agenda.

I asked her to sit down next to me so I could calmly explain my situation, face-to-face. I went through my journey to date: the resection in October, the 19-hour operation and the follow-up two hour suffocating, camera-gate episode that I was still reeling from. I asked her to listen very carefully.

"The surgeons are keeping a watching brief and we're hoping that the antibiotics will start to kick in. Please let me be clear, there is no way I want to have a further surgical procedure. Just so there's no misunderstanding, I'm not signing any fucking consent form until all of my medical team is on the same page." To be fair, I may have been overly blunt, but I'd thought I'd given enough clues when her idea was first aired. The doctor slowly absorbed my response, which I don't think she expected. She went off to find those surgeons.

My emotions were running very high at this point; my hackles were up and I was high on painkillers. I was very assertive and stupidly felt like that part of the medical team was conspiring to work against my wishes. I felt alone, my back up against the wall.

As I started to reflect on the hissy fit I'd just had, I began to feel a little sorry for myself. Then the phone behind me rang, so the nurse passed it to me. Until that point, I hadn't even realised that there was a phone there, or that the nurse was present throughout all of this. Shows how wrapped up in myself I'd become.

It was Jane. "When do you want to see me, John?" she asked cheerfully, like a ray of sunshine cutting through the gloom. Tearfully, I asked her to come straight away to back me up. It felt like 'they' were trying to get me back into theatre. Within half an hour, Jane was there at my side, reassuring me in the trench, ready and armed to repel the perceived enemy.

Thankfully, the surgeons confirmed later on that they'd spoken with the doctor and everyone agreed to continue with the 'antibiotics and observe' option. They were now all on the same page. A wave of relief consumed me. I lay back surrounded in peace and tucked into some breakfast as best I could, which was still mainly precipitating over my chin and chest.

As luck would have it, my parents were also visiting that day. I appreciated how difficult this was for my dad as he has what can only be described as a phobia of hospitals. I don't think my conversation was up to much and I was drifting in and out of sleep. I was still struggling with sleep at night and the knock-on effect was that I frequently passed out during the day for a cat nap.

Given that we'd found that I was a serial clotter (I was still on blood-thinning injections), the drain tubes inserted in my leg were now blocked with goo. The nurses told me that they would need to remove the tubes to minimise infection. It would be good to remove some of the spaghetti network that surrounded me in bed. Also when I was up to it, I didn't fancy trying to walk with four bottles clanking around my ankles.

During the day, mum and dad had played tag team between the visitors' coffee room and my bedside. In that day's game of musical chairs, it was poor dad who drew the short straw as he was present when they took the first two drains out. I said I'd understand if he wanted to duck out but I think he wanted to stay and give me some moral support.

Cutting the stitches around the entry wound stung, but no drama there, as I was punctured like a pin cushion at least eight times a day with cannulas, blood tests and blood-thinning injections. Once finished, the nurse excitedly grabbed the first bunged-up drain which went into the lower end of my upper thigh, to the side of the moated hillock, where the infections were. She softly whispered that we'd do this 'slowly and surely' and calmly started to pull. Oh, how those dulcet tones lured me into a false sense of security! At first, I expected it to smoothly pop out, as did dad, who seemed very interested, given this was happening right in front of his eyes.

"Are we there yet?" I winced, as the pain built, seeing we'd already pulled out a few inches or so.

I then sensed how deeply the tubes went into my leg; clearly they needed to reach the area they'd been draining. This was several inches away from the entry point, in my thigh. I could feel every millimetre of retraction as the pipe seemed to unfurl within a highly sensitive area ever so painfully, and I started to scream louder as the pain escalated. The air turned blue with profanities and all went very quiet on the other side of the curtain (which by now had another patient in) as I effed and jeffed against the whole world in a deep, gutteral, animal growl. It finally came out and I turned to dad, who was by now very white. The nurse waved the offending tube triumphantly, covered in several inches of blood and goo - "Ta da!"

"Crikey, that was a long one," announced my torturer. I resisted the obvious smut joke as I was concerned about dad; he was now right in the middle of his worst nightmare, staring into space. Thankfully, we both calmed down from the drama and chuckled together, probably more out of shock than humour. I gripped the bed for the removal of the second drain. Compared to the first one, this was a bit of a let down, as the end was closer to the entry point in the lower leg. The other two came out relatively quickly too.

That afternoon, Mr BioHazard was wheeled down the corridor to his own room in CCU. To my delight, there wasn't a toxic tent or gas-masked nurse in a nuke suit and respirator to receive me. In fact, I was pleasantly surprised when I was warmly welcomed by the smiling Eva, a nurse from Spain, who stayed with me in my CCU cell for the remainder of my stay. Having my own room meant less disturbance for me, so I was very happy. I'd heard a handful of patients noisily come and go in the two-bed room and, after each visit, the area underwent a very noisy, deep clean which disturbed any rest I was trying to grab. For everyone else, it meant that my now infectious body could be isolated, which was important.

I wasn't advised at the time, but later, when reading my doctor's notes, I discovered that I'd contracted the killer blood infection, septicaemia, and had started to show signs of sepsis. It was just as well that this wasn't mentioned as it may have been difficult for Jane to deal with, given that her dear mum had succumbed to sepsis six months earlier. No wonder they were giving me a cocktail of drugs and testing my blood three times a day!

Given these complications, there was an inevitable knock-on delay to my departure from CCU, and we were now well beyond the anticipated 'one night'. We started to receive lots of emails and calls from concerned friends and supporters, who had expected me to be home by now. It was lovely to know that people genuinely cared, and we couldn't just ignore the messages, but fielding the well-wishers was becoming unmanageable. As soon as one person got to know, another would ask, then you'd be asked for an update from both the next day, and so on. I thought about how I'd controlled the comms and suggested Jane send a round robin email to everyone, to give them a quick update of the situation and within this, say that we were going on radio silence for a bit. We needed to focus on the matters in hand - I needed to get out of the deep, dark woods as there was a wolf tracking me down. The message seemed to do the trick and we were able to aim our energies purely on getting my health better.

Over the next few days, my body became more infected as I slid up the danger curve of the sepsis spectrum. I was assured that the antibiotics had started to do their job, but it didn't feel like it. By now, I'd had a week's worth of food inside me accumulating in my gut, so clearly it wasn't just the leg infection causing my body to go septic. My temperature was rocketing, my blood pressure fell dramatically and, as a consequence, I experienced something called the 'rigors' a few times.

I started to feel very cold, when in fact my body was overheating. Then I sweated profusely and each of my muscles would periodically go into violent spasms and seizures. At one point, Jane and mum each held on to a foot to stop my legs jumping about and Eva advised me to wedge my shoulder against the top of the bed, to hold my body rigid against the shaking attack. Jane calmly advised me to visualise cuddling Lois under my arm, where a pillow lay.

Everyone told me to concentrate on controlling my breathing, as it was very shallow. I deeply inhaled for ten, held it for ten, then slowly exhaled through my nose in a steady, firm manner for ten. After a while, I fought the temptation to gasp and began to starve my body of air a little through these breathing exercises. After forty minutes, my breathing and rigid position seemed to overcome the seizures. As I began to recognise the warning signs of an oncoming rigor attack, I would start to use breathing techniques to counteract them and felt a little more in control. It was a battle for me and obviously quite stressful for Jane and mum to witness me like this.

I'd been fed laxatives for a handful of days and my bowels began to feel like they'd have something to offer in my body's out-pipe department. My tummy started to rumble in a familiar way, signalling that there might be some imminent action.

Eva explained that in CCU, they used bedpans; patients who couldn't get out of bed would sit on them in bed and do their business. This was going to be an interesting balancing exercise as I hadn't managed to get out of bed yet. Every time I'd tried with the physiotherapists, I had passed out due to low blood pressure, and eventually I became too ill to try. But I was up for a bit of balancing bowel movement!

I was expecting a solid, plastic potty-looking thing and was somewhat surprised when Eva passed me what looked like a disposable cardboard coffee tray that you might find in Starbucks. She proudly said, "You're a big guy, so I've strengthened it by placing one inside the other." She was a fantastic double bagger. Without wishing to burst the bubble of optimism in the room, I gently suggested, "This isn't going to work: it's too shallow for a start and it just doesn't look strong enough."

Eva convinced me to give it a go and left the room out of courtesy. I climbed aboard for a magical ride atop a tray which was no deeper than a box of tissues. I won't go into details, but I passed the empty, crushed cardboard tray back to Eva. "I think I've gone off the idea now, let's try again to-morrow."

The next day started with me keenly trying to work out what alternatives there might be. Short of getting a wheelchair or dragging myself into a nearby loo on my hands, I reckoned there must be a viable option. "Have you got a, you know, a commode?" I innocently enquired, fully expecting the answer to be a no. "Oh yes," said Eva. "Then why didn't you offer me this straight away?" I asked.

She looked repentant and quietly said, "If I'd offered it at first, you'd have never tried the bedpan." I could have lost it there and then. There was no logic in keeping its existence a secret, but instead, I opted to simply laugh at my predicament. "I think we need it as soon as possible," I blurted, through gritted teeth. "I've been backing up more overnight and I'm going to burst if I don't go soon." My insides felt like they contained a convoy of juggernauts.

Eva located an available sanitary throne lurking in the corridor and secretly snaffled it for my use. Within a minute, it was proudly wheeled into the room. It looked strong, robust and most importantly, had a deep pan. I was definitely up for the job ('scuse the pun) and there was a shimmering, inviting glow radiating from it, beckoning me. I was going to get on that commode even if it killed me! Eagerly, I staggered out to the edge of the bed and climbed aboard. Eva left the room. She and I were united in one belief: there would be a result here.

I don't normally find the need to relay details of my bodily functions, but I believe this is an exceptional case and an occasion worth noting. Let's just say that it felt like my bowels passed the equivalent of a fleet of double-decker buses. Very satisfied, after the second pan, and considerably lighter in load, I slowly climbed back into bed. My face was numb, swollen and frozen, but inside I was smiling like a very satisfied Cheshire cat.

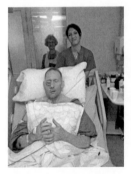

Eva and Mum, locked in my cell

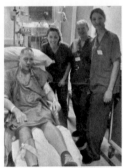

Visiting nurses from the CCU ward with Eva

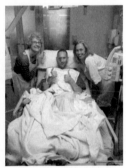

Clearly a lot lighter and better afterwards!

From that very point on, everything started to feel much, much better. This was clearly the turning point of my long second hospital stay. Funny how everything came down to a basic bodily function. I was told it would still take a while for my temperature to come down, given the leg infection, but I was now ready for the removal of my catheter, which took place on the same day. By now, I'd stopped using the PDA and to my surprise, could not feel much pain. Alternative pain relief was regular paracetamol, together with oral morphine if the pain got too much.

News got around to the others in the medical team in CCU and, with a burst of renewed energy, I was able to stand up and show the physiotherapists how fast I could scuttle down the corridor on a zimmer frame. It came as no surprise when I was told that I'd been going back to the ward in the morning. Happy days, I was high with relief to be leaving CCU. Not even the removal of alternate stitches (leave one, miss one) around my face and neck dampened my spirits.

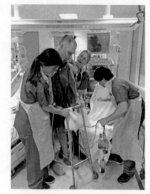

I'd been in CCU for a total of nine nights when the plan was to stay only one. I knew I'd survived a mini medical ordeal of its own whilst there, in terms of the infections. Although I couldn't remember large chunks of it, I can safely say that I was very well looked after and enjoyed the company of the

Just about to pass out

nursing staff. In a strange way, I was going to miss the intimacy of the friendships made with the 1:1 care. However, given the choice, I wouldn't want to stay for a lock in again if you paid me.

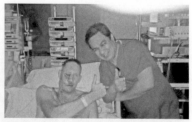

The amazing people at CCU

My bed on the normal ward looked a lot smaller, but it didn't matter. I had a telly that worked well, a few creature comforts and I started to order larger meals with double helpings. Jane, mum and Steve were delighted that I was out of CCU. When we talked about the recent days, we found that our memories were still pretty raw; clearly we'd all gone through the wringer and emotions were pretty frazzled. We focussed conversations on the way forward and what lay in front of us. It was a case of making important decisions like what to watch: *Homes under the Hammer* or *American Pickers?* A better alternative to worrying about what drama might unfold next with my leg and high temperature.

Daily visits from the surgeons ensured that the suckling pig's infection gradually reduced in size. As well as juggling different strains of antibiotics to battle the infection, they physically removed what they could. Several of them took turns on their individual rounds to simply squeeze down hard on the inflamed area around the swollen leg scar, which caused loads of gunky serum to spew out. Better out than in! Despite sounding horrifically painful, it wasn't, just mildly uncomfortable, like pushing on a numb bruise. Still, I looked the other way, so as not to be put off breakfast or lunch.

Early on during my stay on the ward, my facial stitches were completely removed and stitches were also taken from different areas of my leg when it looked healthy enough to hold together. I was beginning to be weaned off the antibiotics as my temperature eventually stabilised to a normal range after a few nights.

As soon as I could, I showed the physiotherapists, nurses, Jane and mum that I was now capable of stairs, visiting the loo and showering unassisted. Clearly things were improving and after five days (and checking in with Jane), I confidently asked everyone to target 8th December as a discharge date. Mindful of the early, nerve-racking return from the first bout of surgery, I didn't want there to be any unnecessary complications at home.

Cyrus visited on the penultimate day. "You survived then? Well done. Too many don't." This was a nod to the gravity of the infections I'd endured and my underlying level of fitness, health and mindset. I'd clearly been close to the wire.

Family visits

By the time discharge day came around, I was just taking iron tablets and paracetamol. The wound which ran the length of my whole lower leg had healed completely, but my upper leg would need further time and a little bit of help. I was given a vacuum dressing called a 'pico'. This had its own tiny, battery-driven motor to suck out any gunky remnants from the open holes. It had a long battery life and was designed to stay in place for seven days in ordinary cases. At the time of discharge, I was filling up one pico dressing every two days, so I became a bit of an expert in changing them.

On discharge day, Steve had gently, but firmly, insisted he come up with Jane to collect me and again, it was planned like a military exercise. Jane, as driver, sat with the motor running on yellow lines between the ambulances outside the side entrance of the hospital, above my ward. Meanwhile, Steve collected me and took my belongings downstairs whilst I said a deep and heart-felt, but a little rushed, thanks and goodbye to the staff on duty.

I climbed into our old jalopy for the journey home. Jane had insisted she drove the old car up as its passenger seat was like an armchair: larger and I could stretch my leg out. Thank goodness, as my limb wasn't flexible and stuck out straight in front of me with the pico on. Feeling over the moon, but consciously feebler, I sat and watched the world go by through the drizzle-filled windscreen, like a gormless, dribbling ghost. Any passer-by catching a glimpse of me must have thought that someone had escaped from the funny farm.

9

HOME AGAIN

Putting the last sixteen days behind me: recovery, take two

As I walked through the front door, I instantly felt like a huge weight had been lifted from my now skinny shoulders. I was awash with cherished memories that had been created within its walls and gave Jane a huge, warm hug. In no time at all, I was bombarded with cuddles from the kids who noisily returned from school as usual and rushed in to see me. They were over the moon that I was finally home.

Back home, squeeze tight

Having recuperated once before, I quickly got back into the groove, but it was a tad different this time. I had the double challenge of learning to walk, as well as talk again. During the last few days in hospital, I'd been seen by the Oral Speech Therapy team who helped me form words with my new, chunky flap in my palette.

One of the biggest worries was a medical condition called trismus (also known as lockjaw) and I had it - bad. It's a massive, untreatable condition, a pain (literally) in the jaw area which tries to force your jaw to seize up after surgery. I learned that it worsens through radiotherapy, which I knew was my next treatment. Triple whammy then: not only was it bad, but it was going to get worse. I had to deal with it there and then.

At the time, I saw this as one of the biggest, long-term challenges to my wellbeing and lifestyle, bar a return of cancer. It had the potential of ruining the basic tasks of getting calories down my throat and talking. I wasn't wrong.

I was initially given a state-of-the-art mechanical solution to combat this: twenty large, wooden lollipop sticks. I was taught to stack the sticks in my mouth, forcing one after another into the middle of the stack, so as its height grew, my jaw got forced wider and wider. The muscles creaked as they stretched with pain, but repetitive physiotherapy like this was the only known way to combat the condition. The exercises needed to be frequent and became (and have become) part of my daily routine. I pounded away seven times a day with seven sets of seven seconds. After a while, the sticks became less usable as they got soggy and splintered in the tight grip of my left enamelled jaw. I couldn't use them near to the seizing jaw as there were no teeth and the gum was swollen from surgery. I got to the heady heights of eighteen splintering sticks before I asked for an alternative solution.

This came in the shape of a blue monster. The Therabite. This plastic machine emulated what the sticks did. It had a hand trigger that would force the mouth open whilst your teeth sat on small pads and the range of the movement was adjustable. It was clearly a huge money spinner for the manufacturer as they knew that patients had to reorder many pads, given that they soon lost their grip on the machine due to the wet environment of the mouth. I asked the supplier, who maintained direct contact with the user, how much they charged the NHS for the four mouth pads. Over £10.50, and these lost their grip after a couple of uses - daylight robbery! During the course of writing this book, I broke two therabites, trying to force my jaw open wider, and these weren't cheap at £250 each.

To learn to walk, I initially did very short, local ones outside as I stumbled even on the flattest of surfaces. In trying to build up my weak ankle and wonky knee, I included some gentle inclines after a couple of weeks. Well, I had to find my arse, which had gone missing, yet again.

I'd come home during the run up to Christmas and guessed that putting on weight wouldn't be a problem with the abundance of calorific food about. Jane wanted to satisfy my appetite for large breakfasts, so purchased a whole black pudding which was consumed over the course of a month. She feared I'd pig out and adopt a horizontal, sofa-surfing recuperation strategy for too long but, despite the appeal of slobbing out in front of the telly with a tub of Quality Street, I only gave my body a rest-up when it demanded it. I was determined to stay mobile.

Back home, there was plenty of domestic routine to be getting on with, so I plunged in where I felt I would not get in the way. I loved helping out with the decorations and also dived into other seasonal duties such as present ordering to Santa, who now lived in the Amazon. Writing the cards gave me an excuse to get in touch with some friends once again and update some on my circumstances, which then led to a number of visits in the following year. In the build-up to the 25th, we were determined to have a great time, and we did, but this year we needed to take it a little easier and planned to visit family, instead of our usual role of hosting.

Resting up petered out after the initial couple of weeks and, in the run-up to Christmas, I felt sufficiently strong to get down the gym, even if it was initially only for twenty minutes. It was clear that I'd lost a lot of muscle whilst lolling about in the hospital bed, so there was plenty to do. On the day before discharge from hospital, I was weighed in by the dietician staff at 81kg, a mere featherweight. They were genuinely concerned and talked about inserting a feeding tube in my neck. I thought to myself, "You can fuck right off with that idea, thank you," and explained that I'd simply lost muscle weight around my legs and rear again. I had the benefit of Jane at my side, who would be a driving force of knowledge and said they needn't worry. Thankfully, they had some faith and gave me lots of protein shakes to take home.

The gym again provided a welcome change of scenery and a bit of routine in terms of building up strength with weights and time monitored on the machines. By mid-January, I was visiting every other day. The pico dressing had been worn for a month now and it certainly got some strange looks at the gym, but I didn't care. Quite a few times during the day, its electric motor would kick into action with an audible squeaky, purring drone, like a phone vibrating loudly on silent or someone breaking wind in a high pitched manner. After a while, this began to get on our nerves, especially in the middle of the night, forcing me to turn the motor off. At times, it seemed to completely have a mind of its own.

We couldn't work out why the pico started to go off randomly and guessed that the seal might be leaking as a result of some staples of cat gut used to hold the two edges of the upper leg wound together. Perhaps it kept getting a slow puncture.

On our first outpatient catch-up with Cyrus, we asked him to have a look at the leg wound. He happily pronounced that it needed air to heal, the dressing had done its job in the first few weeks, but the wound was building up with slough now. We gladly dispensed with the pico dressings that afternoon and never looked back. These are not cheap contraptions at c. £120 each and I had four unused ones. We offered to return the fully sealed, unused dressings back into the NHS, but were told that they would be destroyed as they had been dispensed - it was policy. What a waste of resources! Surely for expensive, unused items, there could be a central depository to check that the items had not been tampered with and return them to stock, saving the NHS millions? Nope.

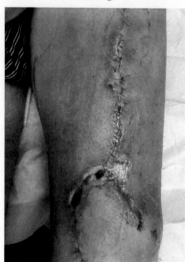 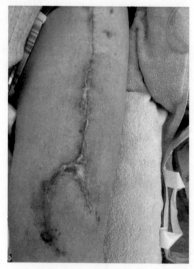

| Leg before pico, stitches selectively being removed | Leg after pico, healing up in the fresh air |

To assist healing the now 'open to the air' wound, I applied tamanu balm, which worked a treat. This was a Christmas gift for Lois, who'd suffered slightly with eczema, but she was happy to donate it to the cause. I also regularly applied olive oil to the lower and upper leg to keep the skin moisturised, as it was susceptible to sores in the early days.

The swelling in my face didn't seem to want to dissipate and Jane mentioned that it could take months if unaided. So she got in touch with a friend she'd made on a fitness course. Dawn ran a local lymphoedema unit and I was booked on to a course of manual lymphatic drainage (MLD).

MLD shifts built-up liquid in the swollen upper layers of the skin and guides this to the nearest lymph nodes where it naturally drains away into the lymphatic system. It's a very effective technique. Jane was really interested in seeing Dawn work her magic and asked to come along to my first session, so she could copy some of the moves. Picture this…

On the lower half of my body, I'm stripped to my snug-fitting underpants, lying face up on the surgical table, feeling chilled and relaxed. Dawn decides to massage upwards on my left upper leg. To emulate Dawn, Jane does the same on my right upper leg. The nearest lymph nodes are in the groin area and Dawn, while talking through the process, seems to be making a beeline for my tackle. Jane is trying to symmetrically follow on the other leg, but is slower, so only at mid-thigh.

Men 'dress' a certain way, and I was conscious that Dawn was on collision course with a certain part of my anatomy. To allow Dawn to finish at the lymph node, next to my pant line, I had to surreptitiously manhandle my little chap out of the way whilst she chatted with Jane. Of course Jane spotted this and started to giggle. Dawn, the utter professional, finished the job and helped Jane get there too.

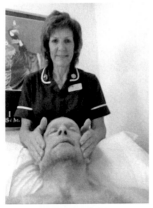

Dawn, a fantastic adviser and one of the MLD experts

Back to the science. I found the session very relaxing and afterwards, I could feel the relief of dissipated pressure. Dawn was very experienced and attended international conferences on the subject. She rightly identified that radiotherapy was going to increase the swelling and I booked up some sessions that weaved into the 30-day radiotherapy timetable. She had worked with Sue at the clinic for years, so I alternated between the two of them. Both were on top of their game and, being ex-nurses, were able to provide comment on anything that came to my mind in the whole gambit of the medical world I was exploring; it was therapy too! Every time we met up, they made me feel better, gave me positive energy and over time, reduced my swelling. I felt that they went the extra mile for my benefit.

Dawn also introduced me to some strange medical hosiery which, to the untrained eye, might be mistaken as a garment worn in a bondage dungeon. In the brochure, under the heading of 'head masks,' were different types, each tailored for swelling in various areas of the head. She went straight for the mother of them all, the most-hardcore-in-the-brochure headpiece with all the bells and whistles. This compression mask would completely envelop my head, so as to constantly apply pressure to the lymphedema in my eye, cheek and upper jaw. I sighed. Really? It was the most horrific-looking one, like something out of a chainsaw movie. Dawn measured my face to fit the exact contours of my facial features, even my Bruce Forsyth chin.

The nylon garment was manufactured and shipped in from the USA; it looked rather menacing in black. Somehow, fuchsia pink, skin tone or royal blue wasn't going to cut it. I do have a reputation to maintain, you know! I named it the Mexican Wrestler Mask in a message to friends.

Yours truly, the gimp without a choke ball

Dawn and I laughed out loud as I put it on for the first time. When we composed ourselves, we recognised that I couldn't wear it in public, else I'd be mistaken for an armed robber or terrorist, and surrounded by a police SWAT team in no time at all. I am wearing it now as I write this: it's comfortably tight and is helping enormously to keep the swelling at bay. Boy, I look very odd, nonchalantly walking around at home - like I have a secret, little fetish, and a dungeon.

In consultation later in the month, Dr Miah and I discussed the two 'belt and braces' follow-up treatments. Radiotherapy and chemotherapy. I was advised that sarcomas displayed a low response rate to chemotherapy, so coupled with the fact that it had not been deemed a fast-growing tumour, I decided to duck it, for now. This wasn't a decision taken lightly, mind you. Some people opt to throw everything and the kitchen sink at it. But in my case, the medical team were happy that the radiotherapy would yield good results alone. Besides, I wanted to keep something in reserve if it were to later recur.

When asked, the radiographers and the speech and oral teams at the Royal Marsden didn't think MLD was a great idea during radiotherapy, but to be honest, they didn't seem informed about it; they thought it was a deep tissue massage. So, it was with Dr Miah's blessing that I continued to go. I'm glad I followed my gut instinct. Whilst I questioned the opinion of some of my team, I deferred, as always, to my oncologist who is the purveyor of all things.

Dr Miah also agreed that it would be good to get an expert to assess the extent of the damage to my right eye, as I'd lost a lot of sight, probably 90% of my vision. If the ophthalmologist believed that there was a chance for my eyesight to recover, then the radiotherapy dosage administered (units of measurement are called greys) to the sensitive area at the back of the eye would be set at a level to ensure it would not irreparably damage the tissue. If, however, the eye was already defunct, then they would, with my authority, zap away merrily at the highest level of greys permitted to human beings.

My radiotherapy was going to be a full-on course of 30 days over six weeks, focussing on the original tissue that still remained within my face, that had sat next to the removed tumour and mostly focussed around the fatty areas of my eye orbit. The aim was to kill any other unseen mutinous, mutating cells that had decided to start up. You wouldn't catch these potential new, little buggers on the CT and MRI scans, so best to carpet bomb the area. Having been there a number of times by now, I was so relaxed about the scans this time round and I actually fell asleep in the MRI.

A new experience in the run up to radiotherapy was the building of the mask - my death mask, as I called it. Everyone I spoke to warned me that the moulding process was horrendous, but I genuinely loved it. Perhaps the MLD had already got me used to my face being manhandled. A warm sheet of plastic mesh was placed over my face and shoulders and I was firmly bolted to the table. Then three nurses moulded it to the exact contours of my face and shoulders whilst the mesh cooled. The mask was then ready to fix me in place within the radiotherapy room so that I remained absolutely still whilst they accurately aimed and zapped. Visions of the laser scene in the James Bond movie *Goldfinger* rushed into my head. Horrendous? Nah - it felt like I was being fitted out with my own suit of armour! (See 'Glossary of Sent Messages').

Bizarrely at that time, I watched a programme on BBC2 *Surgeons: At The Edge of Life* which showed a very similar surgical procedure to mine. The patient underwent removal of the tumour and reconstruction in a 10-hour operation and lost her eye. She had an amazing prosthetic mould built for her orbit area, together with a life-like eye. It was deemed to be groundbreaking stuff.

I had a think about what had been achieved with my surgeries. Overall, I counted my blessings that I still had my eye and felt like a bit of a pioneer, or a medical guinea pig.

Whilst visiting for the mask-making, Dr Miah popped in to tell me that the CT scans were fine, and she was awaiting the MRI scans. I wished her a Happy New Year and got the dates for my 30 sessions of radiotherapy sorted out.

Then, out of the blue, we were asked to see Dr Miah and Cyrus on the following Monday, just before the ophthalmic surgeon's appointment. Jane and I instinctively knew something was up.

10

SET BACK... AND ENJOY THE RIDE

Dealing with further headwinds of bad news

Cyrus was perched on the edge of a table as Dr Miah sat in front of the computer screens; they both looked serious. It was strange seeing them less chirpy than usual. They both clearly had their 'concerned' heads on. It was a somber atmosphere.

After some preliminary warm-up questions, we jumped straight into the meat of the detail. They'd found something puzzling on the latest MRI scan. The recent scan had picked up a spherical blob of unknown substance underneath my right eye. Jane and I looked at the image intensely. Yep, there was no disputing it, it looked like a squash ball had been left in by one of the surgical team for a giggle. This probably explained some of the stubborn swelling and pressure in the area. Boy, looking at the image, you could also see how much swelling I still had at the side of my ballooning face, but this new substance was weird.

Cyrus said he couldn't work it out. He'd opened up and rebuilt that area of my face during the second surgery but hadn't come across anything. Not even a marble, let alone a squash ball. It was located near the new titanium mesh that held up my eye, in a fold of muscle. He was perplexed.

If this was a new tumour, it must be super aggressive to have grown so quickly, off the scale of reality in fact. I asked whether this might be a haematoma or infection. Let's be honest, my body seemed to have a habit of producing these random little monsters.

A good old biopsy was the only way to determine exactly what it was, but given its position, this meant taking the mesh apart within a lengthy, tricky operation and undoing all of the good work completed to date. It was also too inaccessible for the 'smash and grab - needle in and suck method', which I naively suggested (I was still playing the odd numpty question card). Also, if we concluded that a biopsy was the only option, this would put the radiotherapy back a couple of months. Everyone, including me, was keen to get zapping ASAP.

So I, or we, had a decision to make. Press pause and go for a biopsy or go forward as planned into radiotherapy. My gut told me to carry on and start radiotherapy: we could focus our guns onto the unknown ball and, in doing so, it might reduce in size. If it showed signs of being cancerous later on, we could go down the surgery route again and perhaps chuck the kitchen sink of chemotherapy at it as well. By pursuing the radiotherapy route soon, at least the other areas of the high risk, fatty eye tissue would be zapped too. After canvassing further thoughts and information, I said that I wanted to crack on with radiotherapy, together with further MRI scans and CT scans during the radiotherapy sessions to monitor the squash ball's growth. You could see they were relieved.

Jane and I were a little numb coming out of the room. It had been drilled into us that this indeed could be cancerous. Nothing could be certain without a biopsy. Dr Miah explained that it was her role to be objective and plan for the worst - I understood this. We went across the road to a tatty Italian café for lunch, which was frequented by most of the hospital staff (everyone seemed to be wearing a pass except us). Jane, mum and Steve had used it as a food base whilst I was in CCU. We got a table by the window and, whilst waiting for the coffee and food, I looked at the busy street outside. Life is full of ups and downs and whilst your personal drama might be vividly playing out, everything around you carries on regardless - which is kind of comforting. Taxis dodged pedestrians in the busy street, people stopped at shop displays to ponder buying a £20,000 bath for their Chelsea pad and cyclists sped nonchalantly through zebra crossings and red traffic lights without a care in the world. Life goes on. We chatted through the logic of proceeding with radiotherapy, despite the risks, and updated the families when we got home.

It wasn't long before we were up at hospital again seeing Rodger Whitelocke, an Ophthalmic Surgeon at the Royal Marsden. We needed to understand whether the loss in eyesight was temporary or not, which would determine the dosage at radiotherapy around the delicate optical area. He was a very pleasant, 'old school' gentleman who liked things done a certain way; he reminded me of a school headmaster. You knew you had to allow him to finish what he was saying as he wouldn't appreciate you cutting in with a further question, if you know what I mean. His equipment looked like it had been with him since the start of his long career - he'd been a consultant for 37 years. I reckoned he knew a thing or two about eyes.

I was invited to rest my chin on an ageing, but precise, German-engineered eye measurement device, for closer inspection. As soon as I popped my large chin on the pad, the right-hand light went out unexpectedly. The bulb had gone. Was this an omen, I thought? Rodger had clearly been a scout in his youth. He was prepared for every eventuality and proudly produced a new bulb from a drawer and proceeded to change the dud one. "Only happens once every two years," he muttered. "These bulbs cost £125, you know." "Probably more now, post-Brexit referendum," I volunteered. I don't think I caught a returning smile.

Anyway, after a big fumble trying to get the contraption going again, we restarted the inspection of both eyes.

Being inspected by Rodger, after the bulb change

"You have great eyesight," he said positively, then declared, "Your left eye functions very well, but as you know, your right eye is severely under-performing in its duties. The eyeball and surrounding tissue is very healthy, but unfortunately, the optic nerve at the back has an established atrophy. In other words, the eye's wiring to the brain isn't working." Apparently, it's like owning the most modern, largest, clearest TV in the neighbourhood, but not having an aerial or Wi-Fi. He went on to relay, "The optic nerve is about 1mm wide and carries about a million stem cell nerve fibres within it. Regrettably, there is no way medical way of repairing this, and in my experience, it will not repair itself." In layman's terms, my right eye was a gonner.

Even though I'd initially prepared myself for the loss of the eye at my first consultation with Dr Miah, I couldn't help feeling a pang of deflation in my heart. Keeping my eye would have been the cherry on the cake, so to speak, or at the very least, made the two sets of surgeries seem even more worthwhile. I didn't initially show much disappointment and said, " It's about surviving the cancer, not retaining my right eye's sight." My disappointment grew as it dawned on me that my blind spot was permanently all the bigger now.

Rodger's experience told him that pressure from the tumour on the optic nerve had caused the damage, but I reminded him that I could remember having great eyesight in my right eye, up to the first surgery in October.

Yes, for a while I allowed the negative thoughts in, it's unavoidable. After all, it's not every day you get told that the cancer might have come back and that you'll be virtually blind in one eye for the rest of your life.

♪ Kicked in the teeth again (AC/DC) ♪

From the brilliant Powerage album, this song is actually about being dumped by a girl, but I often have it playing in my mind when something doesn't go well at work or home. 'Sometimes you lose, Sometimes you win'. I was getting a little sick of the bad news we were getting but when I put things into perspective, it wasn't the end of the world.

Jane and I understandably felt a bit bruised by the double whammy of crap news, but to steady the ship, we reminded ourselves how fortunate I'd been to date, compared to others. I'm convinced that my eyesight was collateral damage from the surgery and, whilst this made me a tad annoyed, I started to think of the bigger picture.

It was necessary to save my life and with it came with risks that I'd signed off to. Although sight wasn't maintained in one eye, I still had the body of the eye intact in my socket, which in the long run, should be cosmetically better than a hole or a false eye. It also seemed to move in conjunction with the other eye when looking left and right. So I decided to accept how the cards had been dealt and counted myself lucky to still be in the game. The conversation I'd heard through the CCU curtain was still a raw, vivid reminder of how things could have turned out. I needed to keep a positive mindset for radiotherapy.

I relayed the news to Dr Miah on the phone and asked her to increase the zapping dosage around the eye to the maximum level. I thought, if the sight's damaged a little more from radiotherapy, then so be it, the bigger picture is about eradicating any evidence of the filthy squatter and any litter it may have left behind. We discussed the squash ball again and Dr Miah had organised an MRI scan to be taken on the first day of radiotherapy to assess its growth. Again, she was never prepared to say that it was a bruise, but after a while, I found myself stating it was one. I didn't want a gloomy cloud following me in radiotherapy and taking residence above my head. At the same time, I was conscious that there was a chance it was something more sinister, but I didn't want to dwell and waste energy worrying about a 'what might be' until I had to. I'd cross that bridge when and if I got to it. I'd need to summon every ounce of energy if it turned out to be cancerous, and this was probably way more than I currently had in my tank.

Yes, inevitably, parcels of bad news come in a set of three. The third didn't concern my health though, which probably made it all the worse as it truly was out of my control. In 2002, my dad had gone into hospital with a prostrate complication; although this wasn't deemed cancerous on a routine wider check-up, they discovered he had cancer in his bladder lining. Thankfully, they picked it up early and he was given treatment of keyhole surgery and a chemotherapy-type chemical wash, which seemed to cure the disease. He'd been having regular check-ups thereafter.

Mum brought me up to speed with dad's current health issues. In a recent check-up, they'd found a cancerous lump again, marking the return of the disease. He was booked in to have it removed, but worryingly, he needed scans to see if it had spread to the bladder wall and beyond, to other surrounding organs. He was also suffering with stomach pains under his ribs.

This all came out after I phoned mum and caught her in a bit of a teary state. Unbeknown to me, she'd driven dad 20 miles to A & E in the early hours one morning, a route which isn't kind when you're not the most confident of drivers in a torrential gale. My parents were putting a brave face on it for me and hadn't mentioned it at the time because we were going through the latest twist in my little drama.

Clearly, they were worried about the outcome of dad's scans, and we discussed what was familiar ground - having to patiently await the scan results and consultations. Mum's experience through my story to date had hardened her mindset. They were now more stoic and made sure they kept physically fit with swimming and activities as normal. In 2002, they seemed to put everything on hold. It was great to see their current attitude - perhaps I was rubbing off on them?

Mind you, dad had been in the wars over the last few years too. He was once clearing leaves on his back lawn with the petrol lawn mower. Given he was in his late seventies, and an engineer by trade, he designed and made a home-made clamp out of string to keep the throttle open. Starting the thing had become exhausting for him.

Inevitably, given the wet weather, the mower's passage between the blades and the bag became clogged. So using his problem-solving mind, he envisaged the mechanical schematics of the machinery and confidently reached down to clear this out with his hand, without stopping and having to restart the engine. Unfortunately, as he did so, his fingers hit the rotating blade, travelling at 3000 rpm. He remembers the next few minutes quite vividly, as I imagine they are seared into his memory. The mangled remains of two fingers were hanging from the hand and he started to shout up to mum for help. Mum is a keen artist and couldn't hear any of the pandemonium outside, as she had the radio playing loudly as she painted away. Dad made it upstairs, decorating the hallway stairs and walls with blood like in a slasher movie. They eventually called for an ambulance.

Now he is without parts of his middle two digits on one hand, so his grandkids call him Spock. He can easily perform the 'live long and prosper' sign at a moment's notice.

Bizarrely enough, he also recently had a squamous cell tumour on the tip of one ear removed, so for a brief period, took on some further features of the Vulcan.

Back to the story. I tried to support my parents as much as possible and buoyed their spirits as best I could. It made me feel useful whilst preparing for the next stage of my treatment that awaited: radiotherapy.

11

ARISE, GONZALEZ THE GIMP! RADIOTHERAPY

The slow realisation of its enormity and impact

Before I started the long, 30-day course of radiotherapy, I made enquiries about getting the treatment done locally. I was exhausted just thinking of travelling up to London on a daily basis. But Jane, mum and Steve poo-pooed this idea pretty early on and stated that I should keep all the treatments under one roof at the Royal Marsden.

I weighed up the pros and cons.

When I sat down and logically thought about it, it was in my interest to make it as easy as possible for all of my medical team. If required, they could quickly pick up the phone with other team members they were familiar with in their own radiotherapy department, and didn't need the barriers of different IT systems and different NHS trusts to get in the way. Also, I ran the risk of delaying the treatment if I transferred the RT to another trust as they'd need to 'sort out the admin'. This, I knew from personal experience, could take months. Not ideal when you need a zap ASAP. Crazy, but that's how our national service has evolved over the years.

Most importantly, if I went to another hospital, I'd lose the key advantage of the Royal Marsden: teamwork.

The nearest alternatives were either the Royal Berkshire in Reading or the Royal Surrey in Guildford. The traffic around my way is always rubbish, so I estimated that I'd only save about an hour of daily journey time at most if I got decent appointment times at the Royal Marsden. On balance, I opted to carry on at the Royal Marsden.

To pacify Jane, and for safety reasons, we needed to organise a driver to take me up to the Royal Marsden for the daily treatments. I was forewarned that the course was gruelling, so there was no way I could drive and I definitely didn't want Jane's world to be impacted further by weaving in a daily return trip to Chelsea. This was not going to be without considerable cost. In the immortal words of Cheryl Cole's make-up advert, I pronounced in my best Geordie accent "Because I'm worth it!"

We looked at a number of cab firms and I know that they have profit margins to make and mouths to feed, but the quotes were astronomically high. At this point, my parents stepped in out of the blue and gave me some money to cover the cost; this was so very kind and unexpected. They insisted I use their money and genuinely wanted it to be put to this use. It was another way of showing their love and support and it was gratefully received. Without a doubt, I was very fortunate. If people didn't have this type of support, I was advised that Macmillan would consider funding some of the transport cost.

I was resigned to shelling out a small fortune when Dawn, my MLD guru, mentioned that she knew a chap who had done some volunteer driving, whisking people to and from hospital. He might be interested in my plight. Peter and I got in touch and I couldn't have asked for a finer gentlemen to help me. I paid mileage, wear and tear and a contribution to his 'wine fund', as he put it. We met up before it started and hit it off there and then. Thanks to Dawn, I was sorted.

Peter loved rugby; he'd played open side flanker for London Welsh in his day and the topic was often discussed. England had recently beaten Wales 12 - 6 at Twickenham during the Six Nations and he still picked me up! Mind you, I did feel obliged to mention that they were robbed of a certain try by the TMO.

He'd enjoyed a varied career path, starting originally as a teacher, then worked at Lloyds Bank, before ending up at IBM selling software to NHS trusts. He'd recently been given a golden goodbye handshake and was at a loose end. Aside from volunteering for the Citizens Advice Bureau, I was his main employment for six weeks. I started to plan the parking around our trips, but we soon binned that costly idea for some more fluid arrangements.

In no time at all, my first day of radiotherapy came around and, as planned, an MRI scan was organised to compare the new lump now from a month or so back. I fell asleep in the scanner again and kept my fingers crossed for the result, which I'd pick up at the weekly clinics with Dr Miah.

Within a few days, Peter and I got into the swing of turning up early at the Royal Marsden, hoping on the off-chance for an early finish. I'd jump out as the car screeched to a halt in the busy side street, then Peter would find a residents' parking bay to use for an hour or so. Once my session was finished, I'd give Peter a buzz, he'd pick me up a minute later at the same corner and whisk me off to face the M4, M25 and M3 home. He

had a Jaguar car and it reminded me of The Sweeney. He'd be Jack Regan, pulling up with a screech at the entrance, and I'd do my best as George Carter to make a hasty getaway. Cor blimey, Guvnor!

As a primary cancer treatment centre, the radiotherapy department at The Royal Marsden Hospital is a very busy hub. Despite this, I was warmly welcomed by the receptionists who quickly got to know my name. In addition, the staff in the various treatment rooms were very kind, informative and understanding.

Treating Jack Regan, aka Peter, to a nice brekky

They have five radiotherapy machines at the Chelsea site and the facilities are at the leading edge of technology. But it's the people that make a difference.

In the several waiting areas dotted around the department, people usually sat silent and nervous, deeply wrapped up in their own personal battles whilst waiting for treatment. I tried to make conversation most of the time, but also respected people's feelings, testing out my body language-reading skills.

Some people clearly just wanted to be left alone, to deal with the treatments in their own way and behaved like a tube or train passenger, closed off with their head buried in a newspaper. I loved chatting with the women in full burqas; I don't think they were expecting someone to approach them. Perhaps it's not done in their home country? Anyhow, no diplomatic incidents were reported. The Royal Marsden clearly marketed its services overseas. All of the Middle Eastern ladies I spoke to were from Kuwait; they often travelled in an entourage, with sisters or daughters, if they needed language help. I found that they were surprisingly open about the cancer treatment they were undergoing, more forthcoming than I'd expect as they described the parts of their bodies that were afflicted. "We are very wealthy in Kuwait and will pay for the best" - this just goes to show what a gem our National Health Service is.

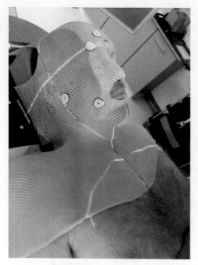

In *Goldfinger's* clutches The death mask, in all its glory

My treatment was going to be the maximum possible dosage allowed for human beings. No holds barred, no softly does it. It was going to be full on. Unfortunately, I'd learned that radiotherapy rays don't just stop at the targeted area; they travel along the trajectory until they're harmlessly absorbed by the lead walls. Not only could I expect some side effects to the concentrated area of my face, mouth and eye, other parts of my head, including my brain, would be zapped too. Some more collateral damage. Nice.

Initially, the machine whizzes and whirrs into place for 30 seconds or so, then there is a buzzing whilst it zaps you with high-energy X-rays for 10-20 seconds. This cycle is repeated five times and the whole treatment, from lying down to leaving the room, only lasts a maximum of fifteen minutes. You can't feel anything in the room, but I noticed the metallic smell of static electricity, similar to when you pull a jumper off over your head.

At the end of the first week, I received the good news from Dr Miah. The unidentified squash ball mass hadn't grown over the last month or so, and it was behaving like a bruise. She said she'd keep a check on it and would run a CT scan in week three to see if it had changed.

Radiotherapy side effects are cumulative and ordinarily start to slowly emerge in the last two weeks or so of a six-week course. I was advised to expect a lack of taste, hair loss, facial burning, eye irritation, worsened sight in the right eye, a further tightening of the jaw and tiredness. Before I went in, I found myself preparing in a similar way that I'd tackled the

With Dr Miah   Midway through radiotherapy

surgery, by building up my fitness in the gym, except this time my leg was still healing. So I tackled two birds with one stone and tried to eat like a monster. Thankfully, my weight built to about 90kg, so if it was to fall back, I would have less to rebuild afterwards. I was pretty confident, given that I was making a good recovery from surgery. Bring it on, do your worst.

Unfortunately, all of the above side effects started to kick in during the third week. Oh shit, it would only get worse over the next three weeks, I thought - deep joy. The radiotherapy nurses said that the side effects were early and more profound, given it was my head and face getting zapped. Nobody had mentioned that one until now.

I hadn't anticipated how my nose would react. The nostrils began to run constantly and became full of sores. Nosebleeds were frequent, especially during the morning when I'd clear them out. Huge black lumps of tar-like mucus lay in the tissue after a good blow. Mmmm, just the appetiser I needed for breakfast.

I adjusted my diet to softer food as time went on, given the pain in my mouth, but I ensured I got plenty of food down me. For breakfast, I'd have whizzed-up porridge, whey protein, Manuka honey and an almond milk shake. I'd also have two vegetable shakes a day which would have tasted foul, but for the added fruit like pineapple. For lunch, poached eggs were a favourite as they're soft and full of protein.

At the end of week three, we had some great news from my parents. Dad's cancer hadn't passed beyond the walls of his bladder. He now had the unenviable task of deciding whether to keep the bladder or have it removed. Either way, dad now faced a course of chemotherapy and additionally, radiotherapy, if he chose to keep it. Given that this marked the second return of the cancer, its removal wouldn't affect his lifestyle too much, so he decided to have it whipped out.

Due to the pain whilst eating, my brain kept telling me I wasn't hungry. I had to override this and instinctively carried on eating, despite feeling a little nauseous. The mind does like to play tricks on you!

I needed a pick-me-up and a cheer from my corner of the ring, so instinctively sent a message to the growing distribution list, describing my new head garment as the Mexican Wrestler mask. I gave a nod to how lucky I felt to be alive and how great it was that the squash ball was proving to be innocent. See 'Glossary of Sent Messages.'

In the fourth week, the surface of my tongue felt like it had been grilled for several minutes and the inside of my mouth now began to get raw with sores. Thank goodness I couldn't feel half of my mouth, including the roof. On the flip side though, one positive was the loss of the hair from the hanging flap in my mouth, which was skin from my thigh. It was still rather swollen, but actually started to feel smooth and a little more normal in there.

Jane and I bought my parents a Nutribullet, which we thought would help them during dad's recovery. This was as much for mum's benefit as dad's. We figured we needed to keep mum fit and healthy too as she would be dad's primary carer from now on.

This point could be missed. Healthcare is naturally directed at the patient's wellbeing, but you've also got to ensure the carer is 100% fit too. So now, all of our parents had access to a Nutribullet and the delights of green, grass-odoured gunk.

One afternoon, whilst convalescing, I sat watching the Calcutta Cup, where Scotland wiped the floor with England, and started to listen in on the conversation Jane was having with my parents. Dad's outlook really pleased us; he was openly saying how he was inspired by my bulldog spirit and wanted to live on for many more years. He was motivated by the wish to see his grandchildren get married. This was great to hear, streets ahead of where he'd been in the past, and I'm sure this type of visual target kept Jane's mum, Beryl, alive for so many years too.

After a typical low, groggy radiotherapy day, I tried to summon energy from deep inside. And so it began. A debate amongst friends, following the last message, gave birth to an alter ego that I later came to rely on. He was a Mexican wrestler, of course, his headgear gave that away. But now he needed a ring name. And then it came to pass, from herein he would be known as…Gonzalez the Gimp. A true representation of a black-masked, psychotic alter ego who would take on anything. He'd spit in the face of radiotherapy's side effects, rip its head off and piss down its throat.

The debilitating pain from the inside of my mouth seemed to have peaked for now and, whilst everything remained blistered and dry, I managed the occasional solid food meal. It's good to chew to ensure your digestive tract operates well. I was now dozing off a lot during the day, especially during the car journeys. Peter kept things quiet and smooth in the Jag, and I would retire early to bed at the end of the day.

First thing in the morning had become the groggiest part of my day during all of my treatments, when the painkillers taken to aid a good night's sleep had worn off. This feeling was amplified by radiotherapy as my mouth, face and eye reacted to the daily beating it had taken. My scorched mouth, which was as dry as a camel's hump, was extremely painful and my eye had started to weld up with gunk. It was as if the slugs from the garden had decided to go racing around my eyelids overnight. Jane and I just routinely ploughed on, getting through each day, dealing with what was in front of us. I continued to drink the lemon and ginger-infused water to open the mouth, two mugs of tea and a green nasty from the Nutribullet. And to help keep the swelling down, I started to wear the gimp mask overnight and inserted a dressing soaked with saline solution over the eye.

The Beast from the East welcomed in week five of radiotherapy, a Siberian, sub-zero delight which wreaked havoc across the UK. We ill-prepared Brits love to make a drama out of the weather and, with ten sessions to go, I didn't want to get anxious about the possibility of not being able to make it to a number of sessions, so I asked what would occur if I couldn't get to London. Essentially, they would be added to the end of the six weeks or, subject to the doctor's approval, could be administered alongside other sessions, as long as there was a six-hour gap in between. The radiotherapy department seemed to be running late every day as people struggled to make it in, and occasionally an urgent case landed in their laps from the hospital which caused knock-on delays. But you've just got to roll with it and take each day as it's served up; no point getting wound up about something that is well outside of your control.

Text from Chris: *How's your boat race (face)? Have you set off any geiger counters*

My response: *Melting snow at 20 paces, they've got me on standby to clear Heathrow's runway and the M25 over the next few days*

The final week of radiotherapy went reasonably OK. I'd got used to the odd delay and there weren't too many glitches. I had the two snow days tagged on to the following week for good measure too. I'd got to know a few regulars at the 'Carlisle Club' (named after our radiotherapy machine) and was delighted to hear that I wasn't the only one coming in from outside of London. Barry and Sue were a retired couple who lived in 'the middle of nowhere', near Dover, and Bob came in from Selsey, in Sussex. On my last day, the nurses were happy to receive my chocolates, by way of a thank you. They really did look after us as best they could in that department and everybody I spoke to was very complimentary about the staff.

After the last Tuesday session, I sat down on the settee with relief and decided to go for a walk to try and clear my head. Symptoms at the time were just about bearable and I thought that this boded well for the week-end ahead. A friend at work, Tim, was a steward at Twickenham and had very kindly arranged to take me to the last match of the Six Nations championship - England vs Ireland beckoned. Whilst walking, I gave Tim a call and said how very much I was looking forward to going and catching up with him. The birds were tweeting in the air around me and the hazy sun was warm on my skin; it was quite spring-like, even though patchy snow lay around.

I got a little ahead of myself because when I woke up the following morning, I started to feel the pain build. Over the next few days, the side effects worsened a great deal. Gonzalez couldn't be summoned as my face was too tender to wear the mask, so I had to ride the pain out with pain-killers, cream and sprays. The inside of my mouth resembled a microwave meal as my lips, tongue and roof of my mouth continued to cook well after the power had been turned off. My face and eye felt like they were glowing in the dark; a bag of frozen peas helped a little, before thawing out in under five minutes.

Unfortunately, I couldn't make it to the game in the end, and this was a sign. The next few months were going to be a challenge.

♪ Burnin' Alive (AC/DC) ♪

A much later track from the Young brothers, from their Ballbreaker album. Sums up the feeling in my head at the time, a blistering song which energised me and installed resolve. They've always been one of my favourite bands and became a global monster of one, whose success can be attributed to sticking to their musical formula - everything at 100%, no ballads. Just blues-based rock, and what they record is equally awesome live.

I've seen many bands in my time and it never ceases to amaze me how much energy is created on stage by the best. AC/DC are no exception: it flows easily into the crowd if the band is any good and seeing this lot is a tiring business! You spend hours screaming, punching the air and jumping up and down with the rest. If you want evidence, watch the YouTube video of 'Thunderstruck' from their 2012 concert at River Plate. Pay attention to the crowd when the song gets going; it makes my hair stand on end with excitement every time, and reminds me of my experiences.

My dad started his course of chemotherapy, so we began to compare notes. He seemed to have loads more energy than me and I applauded his desire for long walks. His nine-week treatment involved a double dose, single dose, then a rest week, in three blocks. He was glad he'd elected to have his bladder removed, as it minimised the risk of the cancer returning.

Unfortunately, his white cell blood count wasn't high enough to go straight into the second set of injections, so he had to undertake a transfusion and a number of injections to stimulate the bone marrow in his bones. The side effects were very painful and this kept him awake, so I suggested (Jane's suggestion really) that he take the injection earlier on in the day so as to keep mobile, rather than lie in pain at night. We were both going through the mangle.

During the Easter break, we were visited by Grant and Shelley. Unfortunately, Shelley's father had passed away in the last week, but despite this, the whole family came over to see us. It was just like taking up where we left off. Some friends just seem to 'slot in' and before long, we were killing ourselves laughing at Grant's crap jokes, no matter how bad they were. Shelly gave me a crash course in social media and urged me to get cracking on raising awareness of the book.

Jane and I visited the Royal Marsden again for an MRI and later, at the appointment with Dr Miah, we were able to look at the image alongside the previous one, to check the status of the squash ball. It was great news -

the unknown matter under my dodgy eye had reduced in size, so we were all chuffed.

That week-end, Chris came around for a catch-up. The weather was in full spring mode, evidenced by birds in song and a growing lawn. Unfortunately, you couldn't plan for my demeanour and I had a little setback. At the time, the only thing I could put it down to was that the MRI rays had aggravated my healing head, which was still hugely sensitive, puffy and red, following radiotherapy. My cheek, eye and jaw swelled up and my lethargy returned by the bucket load.

I was what they technically call 'zonked out' and sat through a lot of the week-end on the sofa. I wasn't much company for Chris or anybody else. Thank god I had booked in three MLD appointments the following week; these and the gimp mask would reign the swelling back under control over the next week or so. Gonzalez had to get back in the ring again.

Over the week-end, I realised that I hadn't updated my friends for ages, so I wrote an email on Sunday night. People would read it first thing on Monday morning. I'd subconsciously reached out to my corner for a cheer of support to lift me through this setback-cum-wobble…the mind works in mysterious ways. Given my fuzzy head, it took ages to write (clearly my brain had been cooked a little too).

I recognised that, at that precise moment, there might not be a lot of day-to-day stuff going on in my life, but people were still racing around at 150mph in theirs. Again, it was fantastic to receive lots of well wishes of encouragement from friends. I didn't want to come across as a moaner, so didn't mention the heightened side effects. Instead, I acknowledged the good news of the bigger picture and likened the delayed, heightened side effects of radiotherapy as having a microwaved meal for a head, still cooking despite being out of the oven.

Armed with the wave of positive vibes, I set about starting up on Facebook and set up a JustGiving site, as well as updating my LinkedIn profile. It took me ages, but I did it. I also sent a new message - see 'Glossary of Sent Messages.'

It occurred to me that I needed to go public with my story and, as a result, I would have to openly share my changed appearance too. In a way, I was embracing my new face - pushing the scars, swelling and disfigurement out there was a one-way step forward. I couldn't put the genie back in the bottle once it had been released. My exposure to social media had been encouraged by friends to help with the book and aided by my more technologically-enabled wife. But I was the one who still had a moment's pause before I nervously hit the 'publish' button.

I've never been first in line for new technology. Social media evaded me for some time and, to be honest, in the past, I questioned why people would want to put a picture of a plate of food or some other mundane thing on a page, but I think I missed the point. It doesn't really matter what the content is, it gets people connected and builds a forum to share feelings. Initially, I was a lumbering dinosaur caught in the headlights of technology, trying to create content and work out how to make effective, interesting posts. On the third day, I was astounded.

My pages had followers, hits, traction and bizarrely, donations came in as a result. I'd only set up the JustGiving page to bank some cash that had already been generously given to me for the Royal Marsden Cancer Charity, but was amazed that I'd raised over £1,000 in less than a week, and was still writing the book. I take my hat off to these platforms! I was connecting with people I hadn't spoken to for ages and was soon receiving donations from friends, their friends and complete strangers, who'd never even met me. I don't regret investing this time and made a mental note to self to circulate updates through these channels.

I reconnected with many friends too who I'd lost contact with and one of my new Facebook friends included an ex-girlfriend, which was initially a little embarrassing. In the early days, Jane was helping me out by frequently logging in to accept friend requests to the *Face Cancer Book* page and innocently accepted her without knowing. Jane and I were touched by her kind comments though. She went out of her way to give me an update on what she'd done since we parted over twenty-five years ago. She even apologised for treating me the way she did, but to be honest, it wasn't necessary, as neither of us were perfect and were both finding our way at the time. She now had four kids, was soon to be an unexpected grandma and did a lot of good charitable things back in New Zealand's North Island where she bred horses and cattle with her husband on their farm. Fair play I thought, sounds like you're having a cracking time. A much less miserable one than when we dated!

One funny Facebook incident involved a lady who said she knew me. To be honest, in the early days when numbers were building, there were several people whose names I didn't personally recognise, but they knew people who went to school with me, so I accepted them. Petra sent some lovely messages of support and was clearly shocked hearing about my news. It wasn't until a couple of weeks later that she started to infer that she was an old neighbour of mine. At this point, I had a dilemma. I realised then that she must have got me mixed up with another John Wilkinson (who I found out, after some research, had bizarrely been to the same school - who would have thought it!). I fessed up. I didn't want her to start worrying about a complete stranger she didn't know. Thankfully, she saw the funny side and we still remain friends, on Facebook at least.

A wave of friend requests also came in from my old rugby club in Hungerford. I also knew I had to start planning my Half Century Survival Party and, although I had hoped to visit the club at an annual memorial game at the end of March, sadly I wasn't well enough to go. Thanks to Facebook, I was invited to one of my old mucker's 50th birthday party and reconnected with many old club mates.

Shani, a colleague who'd gone on to do great things in the marketing and media department, also helped me by putting me in touch with a number of employee and ex-employee networks. Not only did I reconnect with loads of colleagues, but on a couple of occasions, some also shared their radiotherapy stories with me. One senior manager's story resonated.

He'd been afflicted with a brain tumour and also underwent 30 sessions of radiotherapy, administered to his head. He had, like me, always possessed a good work ethic. He confided in me and talked privately about his experience. He could see that I was anxious about when to return to work. He stated that he'd rushed back to work far too early and deeply regretted doing so. In the long run, it made things worse for him, his family and colleagues. He strongly recommended that I didn't make the same mistake. It helped me enormously to underpin what everyone was telling me. Having heard it from the horse's mouth, I'd need to stop feeling guilty about possibly returning in months, maybe years, rather than weeks. I would only go back when I was properly ready to do so.

My medical team kept reminding me that the recovery from radiotherapy is a long, brutal road, not something that I could simply brush off and bounce back from. Dr Miah indicated a full recovery would take a lot longer than I might want it to and the MLD nurses, Dawn and Sue, were also pretty direct with their feedback. The reason I was having relapse days with no energy was because I wasn't providing my body the rest it needed, in other words, I was overdoing it. At times, I should have listened to my body more. When I ignored its demands, it took control and laid me out of action a number of times.

I completely underestimated the time it took to overcome the side effects of radiotherapy and assumed that it would be a 'bounce back' recovery curve like I had from surgery. Instead, it is a glacial, grinding, low gradient curve. Side effects were wildly amplified as the doses had targeted highly sensitive areas around my eye, mouth and face.

As the swelling slowly receded, the true, hitherto unforeseen but permanent, ravages of my radiotherapy began to emerge. Some of my surgeons' great work had been decimated. It had targeted areas in my head, hitting tissue that was still healing or adjusting to its new home like friendly fire. Some stitches inside my mouth started to rip away from the new hanging flap.

All of this could start to get you down, and I must confess that I was initially angry about it. Why didn't they advise me to start with radiotherapy, then go on to surgery? However, when I thought about it rationally, it was logical. Surgery can't be undertaken for at least nine months after radiotherapy because the skin wouldn't survive. I just had to accept the picture and look at the long game.

I naively hoped that some of the new side effects might only be temporary, so that when the dust settled, my new level of normality would be better, albeit not as great as it was before this all began.

12

PIRATES ON THE STARBOARD BOW

*Routines of my new daily life, stepping out into the public eye
and fulfilling a dream*

Unfortunately, radiotherapy then claimed another permanent casualty. Droopy Drawers - my bottom right eyelid disappeared without trace. The shrinking of the skin graft beneath the eye was assessed by Cyrus, who confirmed it was yet another side effect of radiotherapy and, without a lower eyelid, my eyeball had become exposed. It felt precariously perched in the socket and seemed to defy gravity as I walked around. Sue at MLD said that the eye would probably fall out if I got a swift knock to the back of my head. I'd be a human version of Swingball!

The body is an amazing thing and instantly, the conjunctiva formed a protective film over the lower eye. I guess it did so to keep any nasties out and also anchored the eyeball into the socket more firmly at the same time.

Throughout this period, there were weeks of inactivity where my energy was sapped and quite often it felt like I was back to square one, like I'd just been discharged from hospital. At first, we'd put this down to overdoing it again in the gym, coupled with the cyclical effects of radiotherapy, then Jane said, "You know what? Your breath stinks, so let's try and get to the bottom of this." We altered my diet, cleansed my mouth more regularly, but after no change, looked at the clues and researched the symptoms. It all pointed to an infection, maybe sinusitis, so with Dr Miah's blessing and encouragement, we went to the local surgery, took swabs, got the bacteria diagnosed and were prescribed antibiotics.

The clues were there. As the radiotherapy had created holes in the roof of my mouth, remnants of food would end up in my nasal cavity where it would fester, causing a bacterial infection. At some point, my body would be strong enough to fight the infections unaided by antibiotics, but in its dilapidated state, it currently needed all the help it could get. I'd also need to start cleaning myself more thoroughly after mealtimes and this couldn't be achieved by simply brushing my teeth. I needed to wash out the smeg from my nasal cavity too.

Jane introduced me to a 'netipot' which we had knocking around at home. After eating, I'd fill the pot with warm brine, suck this up through my nose into my nasal cavity where I would snort and gargle like I was trying to summon up a lot of snot. Then in a flash I would blow each nostril out. Redundant mucus and more importantly, old bits of food, would ricochet off the inside of the sink into the plughole. Better out than in! The only problem was this guttural action made you sound like a dying elephant seal being throttled to death - not one for dinner party entertainment. Best done behind closed doors!

A new necessary tool, the netipot   The old tool, the dreaded Therabite

The drowning intake of salty water up into my nose meant that I had constantly wet, runny nostrils and we reckoned we needed to do something about this infection hotspot too. My right nostril had collapsed thanks to the surgery, so we needed to open it up in some way. Jane had another brainwave and we purchased some nasal strips, often worn by professional athletes and available over the counter as a snoring cure.

So at night, I started to wear these. Under the gimp mask across my swollen nose, alongside the dampened eye dressing. What a picture I must have looked. But it worked and I could breathe so much better. This allowed me to sleep much more deeply, which would help with recovery. Happier days.

♪ Breathe (Pink Floyd) ♪

A beautiful piece of Pink music: every time I hear the song, it asks me to lay back and relax.

After a while, the infections became the norm and, following the kick start of antibiotics, my energy levels rose once more. I got into the cycle of taking swabs from my nostril and eye at the doctor's surgery to determine what bacterial infection I'd contracted this time, and this would in turn be tackled by differing antibiotics. After four weeks on various drugs, we decided I ought to give my body a chance to build up strength naturally and elected to come off them. This was done with the agreement of the medical team, on the strict understanding that as soon as I noticed my energy levels start to wobble, I would jump back on the medication. It seemed to work.

At the same time, Jane and I concentrated on my diet and I began to take in lots of healing foods and also got introduced to essential oils and their healing properties.

I researched eyepatches as I fancied becoming a full-blown pirate and my exposed eye became sore. The usual disposable ones seemed far too large for the job and, given the elastic band, were dreadfully uncomfortable, aggravating the titanium nut in my eyebrow which had become prominent as swelling receded. I found a great site online in Canada, measured myself up and put in an order. It came through a few weeks later and was very dapper indeed.

Max went on a week-long school trip, so we decided to throw caution to the wind and flew to Toulouse for a long week-end in the spa resort of Bagnères de Luchon, in the French Pyrenees. We needed a change of scenery and the town offered a complex of ancient natural springs, set deep within the mountains. These were said to be excellent for people who had post-radiotherapy and respiratory difficulties. It felt like we'd hit the bullseye and Luchon didn't disappoint.

We endured a little health incident just after landing though. Jane and Lois had gone into a motorway café we'd stopped at to get some food, leaving me to do my usual mouth-stretching exercises on the therobite, before joining them. After I completed these, I looked in the mirror and noticed something near to the corner of my eye. It looked like an innocent bit of phlegm, left over from a sneeze. I brushed it away and more of the gunk started to pour out of a hole.

The skin graft under my eye had formed a leaking abscess, so I quickly got some saline solution from the medical bag that accompanied me everywhere and continued to gently apply pressure to draw as much of this out as possible. Half an hour later, Jane found me walking to the café, a little drained.

When I told her, she cursed the stupid of idea of travelling so soon. But we were there and had five further days ahead of us. We surmised that the cabin pressure must have caused the build-up and again, it was better to get this stuff out of your body than leave it lurking inside. For all we knew, it might have been remnants of the squash ball picked up on previous scans. I was still getting my strength back, so rested every day. Cyrus confirmed that it sounded fine on an email, so we relaxed and enjoyed the rest of the holiday.

We also made some lovely friends, the owners of the B & B, Au Delà Du Temps, Maison d'Hôtes à Bagnères de Luchon (thoroughly recommended). François had recovered from a major heart attack and endured a significant heart bypass. We had an instant rapport with them and they totally understood why I still needed to take a nap and convalesce. They set up and went on to run their own vineyard in Cognac, but life was stressful. After their health scare, they opted for an easier second life, and just did it. François was now as fit as a fiddle and they were kindred spirits, a kind couple. Food for thought. We shall return!

| On flight, mask to protect me from airborne germs | The spa and healing natural waters of Luchon | Frederique and François. I'm on orange juice! |

Back at home, fundraising was fun and Jane's colleagues at Bikram Yoga decided to dedicate their closing night to raising money for the charity. Over 60 Yogis attended a packed studio for two healthy sessions, then went down the pub to celebrate. In a single evening, they raised over £1,000, which was amazing.

All of this goodwill and generosity kept my spirits high. I was glad to have started broadcasting more. When visiting to watch a World Cup football match, Chris commented that I ought to find something to do other than going to the gym. I responded that I was taking time to get better and felt pretty busy with all that was going on. Fundraising, Facebook, writing and now organising my Half Century Survival Party. All without exhausting myself and taking the occasional daytime nap - I felt busy enough.

On the door at the yoga fundraiser

Dad faced up to his cancer battle admirably and, at the sprightly age of 79, went into major surgery to have his bladder, prostrate and some groin lymph nodes removed. They reconfigured his plumbing and, at the end of the procedure, he was left with a urine bag which would fit onto a stoma, essentially a tap at the side of his abdomen. I felt a little guilty about not visiting him in hospital, but they understood that I had to remain selfishly healthy: the last thing I needed was to pick up a bug, or give dad one of mine.

My dad and his younger, more handsome, pirate version

To be honest, I had my worries about his operation, as I'm sure mum did too, given that he's not had a great track record with hospital surgery. But he came through pretty much according to plan, weakened, but unscathed by any follow-on infections. By the fifth day post-discharge, he was up and about, increasing his mobility as instructed.

One of dad's oldest friends was Ian, who happened to be my godfather too. Having just one eyepatch had become annoying but I didn't fancy

A veritable selection of patches

ordering some more before fully exploring a home-grown alternative. I soon realised that I needed a couple of modifications to the design. The wind would whistle through gaps and cause the eye to scab over, which was very painful. Although I couldn't find a UK manufacturer, Dawn gave me the idea of asking Ian if he'd be happy to manufacture a couple of new ones. He was part-owner at a well-known saddlers and I was delighted with the results. He generously waived any idea of payment, but I promised to take him and my dad out to lunch when dad was fully fit again. I think he liked this idea a lot.

The UK enjoyed a balmy summer. The heat and long, light nights felt like we were abroad. I found that I couldn't do much so just relaxed, which helped. When the kids broke up from school, life revved up a tad, but they were out most days seeing their friends. In July, I went to the hospital for the first of the regular, three-monthly MRI and CT scans, by way of a check-up, and cockily, wasn't surprised to hear that I'd been given the all clear. In my head, I'd already assumed that there'd be no recurrence. Dr Miah and Cyrus' professional manner made me sit up and take note that I couldn't take anything for granted. It brought me back down to earth again.

We discussed the state of the smouldering, ravaged battlefield in my mouth and face. In particular, the surgery sites that radiotherapy had napalmed. Cyrus wasn't a happy bunny. You could sense his frustration: part of his diligent work had been left in ruins.

He confirmed that I'd need surgery to fix the new problems that now presented themselves, but I'd have to be patient as the skin wouldn't be receptive until November at the earliest. Undeterred, we prepared a wish list of four things I'd liked fixed.

Trismus was at the top, but couldn't be treated by surgery, so I'd probably have to carry this affliction as long as it lasted. This was likely to be for the rest of my life. The holes in my mouth and eyelid could be fixed by surgery, but in their opinion, I'd need to continue to naturally recover for as long as possible. The Frankenstein nut, which was now becoming very pronounced at the side of my eye socket, could be whipped out any time under a local anaesthetic. Given that I wanted to minimise the number of visits to theatre, it was best that we looked to do all of these procedures in one go. We chatted about false teeth too, as I was still missing many teeth in my new, upper right jaw, including canine, pre-molars and molars. Would the trismus improve if a denture plate could be fitted with some false teeth attached? Would we be able to get it into my mouth?

I also built up a relationship with a wellbeing network at work called *Ability*, whose members came together on a periodic conference call, to discuss various health matters. I was invited to speak about my story and take questions from the floor. The organiser had seen some of the emails I'd sent to friends and had already published a brief one-pager of my story in their newsletter. I set myself up at home for the call and spoke for about 30 minutes or so. It was a bit surreal re-living the story again and I was worried that I'd just drone on, but I got some interesting questions back. I was very pleased that I was clearly coherent for a long, sustained period. Talking was now quite difficult as my voice had become incredibly nasal, given the holes in my mouth.

After speaking at the *Ability* forum, someone who worked in another office called me out of the blue and we spent half an hour or so chatting about his diagnosis. He'd already undergone surgery to remove a tumour on his lip and was essentially seeking guidance as to whether to go into radiotherapy around the area. He was understandably nervous. I felt that our discussion helped him reach his ultimate decision. I also recommended he dig out his critical illness plan to see if he was eligible to claim. This went down well, as it hadn't even occurred to him. He left our call itching to go and find out. I stepped back for a moment and took note. It was already happening - I'd actually helped someone else by talking about my story. It felt electric, natural and very positive. I was buzzing for days.

On Facebook, I posted a video that I'd compiled with my technologically-gifted twelve-year old daughter, which only lasted a minute or so. It was a light-hearted, news-flash style montage of photos and clips. Its aim was to increase the number of followers to my *Face Cancer Book* page and it ultimately reached about 18,000 people after I promoted it with some free funds from Facebook. But it didn't seem to make any difference to the number of followers. "Ho hum," I thought, "worth trying, but clearly not much use in trying to recruit followers." But then, out of the blue, I was contacted by a stranger called Chris. He'd undergone similar surgery two years ago.

When we met up at a local garden centre, we spent all morning chatting and comparing notes. I found this very grounding as I'd finally met somebody who could immediately relate to my predicament. Although he wasn't able to provide any clues to my short-term recovery, it was wonderful to have someone in the same boat, and great to hear it from the horse's mouth. Despite being fifteen years my senior, he shared my daft sense of humour. We decided to keep in touch, and still do.

Hearing Chris' story also gave me some perspective. He'd endured a far more aggressive tumour and, at the tender age of 63, underwent some of the same procedures as me, under Jacob, as his maxillofacial surgeon. Chris had elected to remove his eye as the disease had wreaked more damage to the surrounding tissue around his orbit. He openly volunteered that he'd had a tough time getting used to his new looks. My description of his handsomeness is that he's 'similarly different'.

Body dysmorphia is a mental illness where you feel embarrassed or ashamed about the appearance of a part of your body. Take a minute to imagine having to deal with emotional and physical scars because you've had maxillofacial surgery following cancer. You don't really have a choice and it's pretty brutal.

It's automatic to notice the visible, physical differences in people. It's a natural function of the brain as your mind instantly assesses someone's physical appearance and makes a decision on them as a person. Crikey, she's gorgeous, he's handsome, don't fancy yours much.

The face is a major part of this information taken in that snapshot decision. In films, baddies, monsters and villains often have facial disfigurement, be it a scar, a dysfunctional eye or an eyepatch. Chris and I had the complete set.

Additionally, when you engage with somebody, it's the face that's the first thing you look at to see whether the person is free to talk and you try and establish eye contact. No escaping it, when you've had maxillofacial surgery, it's a game changer to the way people react to you. Other disfigurements can be hidden. When your face changes, you can hardly wander around with a paper bag on your head to hide.

I had already noticed a difference in the way I was treated whilst mixing it up with the great general public. I stick out like a sore thumb, I'm different. Some people gawp, some look away and some make an extra effort. I don't mind people looking out of curiosity, as I said, it's a logical human reaction. When being served at say a shop, there's always a pause as the person serving you computes what they are seeing. I then generally benefit as they try to cover up their clumsiness with a better service - bonus! I genuinely love it when a few people find the courage to ask what's happened, though this is rare. It gives me the option to explain fully, or just say I'm a trainee pirate, to break the ice. You need some stock answers.

When people repeatedly stare and I sense their discomfort, I do get mildly irritated. I initially refuse to take any notice of them as I don't want them to project their problems on to me. Their discomfort is their problem, not mine. I've got enough of my own! If they persist and gawp, I find it rude. I sometimes give them a one-eyed, grumpy Paddington Bear stare back to embarrass them and, if this doesn't work, I'll say something like, "Haven't you ever seen an eyepatch before?", hoping that they might think about their actions. But thankfully, this doesn't happen too often.

I accepted my new looks early on, in much the same way as enduring the cancer. You either embrace it or pointlessly hide away, hoping it will change. It won't. I'd also add that, dare I say it, I kind of revel in the mystery of it. There's part of my character that's always wanted to be different from the crowd, and now I am. Although given the choice, I would have chosen a different reason.

I'm probably making a wild assumption here, but I believe that it's probably far more difficult for the average woman to accept than the average bloke. I say this because so much of a woman's identity seems to be derived from their looks; you only need to review the make-up industry to see that. Whilst writing this book, I saw a programme where a young (compared to me) lady had undergone some invasive maxillofacial surgery treating an upper jaw tumour. Jen Taylor chronicled a blog and photoblog of her face changes post-surgery. I'm going to heap the words 'brave' and 'inspirational' on her, here and now. Wow, I'm sure her public actions have gone on to help others, so I tip my hat to her. I got to meet Jen later - read on.

Anyhow, back to my story. I was very happy with the news of my scan results and, feeling like I'd genuinely started to help some people myself, I sent out a message (see 'Glossary of Sent Messages').

We travelled to France (via ferry this time) for a week in August to celebrate my 50th birthday with my brother and his family, catching the last of the super-hot weather. I loved the house we rented and the nearby town of Jocelyn. Going out was easy and wandering its medieval streets was a superb tonic; a huge change of scenery for Jane and me. I'd become quite confident again driving and undertook a fair amount whilst abroad. Steve's family hadn't spent that long with us before and it just underpinned how much closer we'd become. My sister-in-law was fantastically organised like Jane and yet it seemed the time spent together was an eye-opener for

Two tribes descend on Jocelyn

them. Anne commented how, until then, she hadn't realised how much the disease had affected my day-to-day life.

She got to witness the multiple grind around mealtimes, for one thing. My daily routine involved fighting the trismus with very painful exercises (which still plagues me to this day). Eating was notably slower as I had to cut up little morsels that could fit in the tiny gap between my teeth and was only able to chew on one side. After eating, I'd need to follow up with the usual deep cleansing of the mouth and nasal cavity, courtesy of the netipot, and further mouthwash to fight infections. The discomfort in my jaw and face was also very clear.

On top of the obvious day-to-day differences, which also included altered speech, Anne commented how much quieter, fatigued, slower and careful I'd generally become. It was the first time I'd heard this reaction from somebody who'd known me for a long time. It was because we'd spent a long time together, not just a flying visit. Usually when we go out for a short while with friends, I'd save energy in advance, prepare myself for the event, in terms of jaw exercises, and clean myself properly when I got home. The only thing that would be noticeably different is the time it took me to eat and my sometimes incomprehensible voice. But friends would always politely skim over this and say, "You're looking great."

I think my new demeanour surprised Anne - to be fair, I think it would surprise most people who'd spent a lot of time with me before the treatments. I jotted a message to friends which gave some further news.

On my 50th birthday

When we returned to Blighty, I also completed an abseil of the 262-foot Arcellor Mittal Orbit at the Olympic Park, in aid of charity, together with several colleagues. It had been postponed for a couple of months due to high winds, so the build-up to the event seemed a little more intensive. They were very kind to let me go first and I was surprised by how easy I found it. I'd become more emboldened. In the past, heights had given me wobbly knees, but I just strolled up, took the instructions in and got it done. Perhaps thanks to having endured so much more over the last year.

Hanging   Dangling   Relieved

As noted earlier, I had some sort of epiphany soon after my first surgery. Within this was a deep-rooted need to say thank you to everyone for their support and, at the same time, I wanted to celebrate my 50th birthday. I'd never really been one for big self-celebrations, but this milestone was important. Much more so as I'd survived a point of my life that I'd targeted at the outset of my treatments. I was determined to bring the idea to life.

As the date loomed closer, we began organising. We created colourful table decorations with illuminated, empty, decorated bottles and constructed a photo wall and display table showing off my paraphernalia. Lois and I created a four-minute video to show the guests at the speech slot. None of this could have been achieved on my own. It was great seeing Lois' and

Jane's creative skills fizzing with energy and it gave our family something to pull together around, after the great break in France.

In the end, over 90 family and friends turned up, and 40 or so stayed on at the hotel. Anja, Klaus and Ben came over by train all the way from Berlin, Derek flew in from Edinburgh and mates came from far and wide. Buddies from my earlier years I'd recently reacquainted with, work friends and members of the rugby club came too. I said to Jane, it was like a wedding party, but much better, as there were no odd family members you'd rather avoid.

I asked everyone to watch the video, which chronicled my life through photographs and poignantly reflected on my last year or so through various treatments. We wanted it to be visually strong and thoughtful. Yet at the same time, it had to be reflective, fun and show how the audience's support had helped me. I don't think there was a dry eye when we showed it, mixed with simultaneous roars of laughter.

♪ Purple Sky (Kid Rock) ♪

The video was set to a piece of music that had been playing in my mind throughout my recovery as I planned the party. "But if I'm gonna live until I'm fifty, I'm gonna need you be my side." It embodied my yearning to get back to normal and live life well, and it's a damn good song too. "I just wanna drink 'til I'm not thirsty, I just wanna sleep 'til I'm not tired, I just wanna drive 'til I run out of highway. Into the purple sky."

I gave a short speech and to my surprise, remained comprehensible with a microphone. Perhaps my speech wasn't as bad as it sounded inside my head? The venue kindly provided me with a chair to rest on and Lois popped a reserved sign on it for me, but I looked on it as merely a backup if I got too drunk too early. On the night I didn't use it, no chance, I partied hard and didn't go to bed until about 3am.

The event was everything I'd hoped for, and more. In truth, the reality blew my expectations away and I'd like to think that it left a legacy of memories with those who came. It certainly did for me, but it was also more than that. It drew a line in the sand by celebrating getting through the 'worst of it' and seeing through a promise I'd made to myself during my eureka moment - much like the book in your hands now.

And that's why it felt appropriate to end the cancer story part of this book here, on a high. I'd achieved something I'd set myself to do a little under a year ago, so it kind of felt like the closing of a circle.

Jane and I at the Half Century Survival Party

Max getting led astray

With Anja, Klaus and Ben   Watching the video   Perrier, Johnny, old times

When I initially did so, a number of my friends who had read the draft commented that they felt it had ended abruptly. Oh!

I didn't want to 'pad' things out for the sake of it, but then my story fortunately (or unfortunately, from another viewpoint) took a twist which justified further coverage.

13

MISSION REMISSION

Frustrations, further twists in the road and the fourth operation

It was October 2018. The collateral damage from surgery and radiotherapy meant that I had to keep up the grinding routine. Painful exercises, an age to eat and post-meal washes of my nasal cavity. I also had to endure a very sore area around my eye which still openly weeped for its long-lost bottom eyelid.

I'd accepted that some of the symptoms were likely to be life-long hindrances, but equally, I wanted to explore what was possible in terms of mending any of these. The meeting about my July scans had highlighted my bugbears and I sensed that, since then, I'd merely drifted down the stream and was heading towards Christmas, when I'd have further scans and a follow-up conversation. Sod that, I wanted to crack on.

By chance, I'd reached out to my first consultant, Jacob, and he invited me to pop in for a catch-up. I wanted to at least get a photo with him for the book and Facebook page as I'd had my epiphany after meeting him. We talked generally about my state of limbo and he persuaded me to give the hospital a gentle nudge: what was there to lose? The nine-month clock of leaving the radiotherapy skin tissue lapsed in December, so wouldn't it be nice to get on the front foot a bit?

Jacob, who remains in touch

I visited Cyrus and he agreed, "Yes, sometimes we need a push." On reflection, they're so busy dealing with the conveyer belt of new cases and treatments, sometimes 'follow-up' procedures might find themselves on the back burner. He got on it straight away and started to research the possibility of implants for my new upper right jaw bone and seeing a new eye specialist, with a view to rebuilding a new lower eye lid. Oh, and whilst we were there, we could sew up the holes in the roof of my mouth and remove the titanium nut from my eyebrow that was wreaking havoc with the eye patches. Not life-saving, more like life-enhancing surgery.

I'm glad I called in when I did because I was hoping to get these procedures done in January: no point trying to jam it into December when all the medical staff were looking forward to a very well-earned break, and I didn't fancy recovering over Christmas. Cyrus said he'd make enquiries with a local dental practice and got in touch with a new eye guy, as Rodger had retired.

I felt like I was in the best shape I'd been in for ages. My weight floated between 87-90kg, depending on which set of scales I hopped on, the pain was as low as it had ever been and I was getting stronger in the gym. The long summer had clearly helped my recovery, so Chris and I took a few days' holiday to Majorca. Jolly boys on tour.

We ate well, walked for miles, rested and enjoyed the last of the warm sun kissing the Mediterranean island. We'd promised each other in 2017 that we'd get off on a short boy's holiday when I was well enough, and it

Trying to beast it in the gym

was good to deliver on that. I was feeling in the best condition I'd been in since radiotherapy. Sure, some of it was still buried in my body and I wasn't anywhere 100%, but I reckon I was 80% of where I used to be before cancer dropped into my life. My highlight in Majorca was Palma. I was surprised how beautiful and interesting it was. We explored many cobbled streets, walking between buildings steeped in history. The break passed without major incident and I reckon it gave Jane a brief rest from me and her worry too. On the plane back, I noticed a little air bubble in the corner of my eye skin when I blew down my nose to equalise the pressure, but felt it was minor. Flying still clearly played havoc with my eye area; I needed to be aware of this for the future.

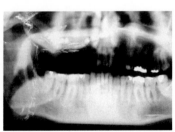

X-ray of my mouth - look at the staples holding the flap together

On my return, Cyrus had been busy getting the ball rolling. Jamie, at Guinea Court Dental Practice, and Richard, the eyelid specialist, were new faces who again told me straight, just how I liked it. Jamie was delighted to have a 'special' case for a change, something a little different and a challenge, given my trismus. Implants meant at least two operations in theatre with other stages, over several months.

Palma in the distance on a nine-mile walk with the Jolly Boys

Richard was far less committal. It was like I'd taken my second-hand car into a garage to investigate a knocking noise under the bonnet. "This is very complicated and I can't say now that we'll be able to help." The trouble was, my body had merrily consumed my eyelid through the radiotherapy healing process and the skin graft under my eye would be like working with rubber, not lovely, elastic, healthy, receptive skin. If it could be done at all, I had two options. The first was to take a two-inch wide piece of skin from my forehead and, with its blood supply already attached, reposition it as the lower eyelid. The second option was to take a free flap from the inside of my wrist and replumb its blood supply into my neck, where there was already a build-up of scar tissue from the previous surgery. The former choice was the simpler option, but as far as I was concerned, a non-starter. I didn't fancy bearing a gaping scar down my forehead as well. I'd start to look more like a Klingon.

The eyelid rebuild plan wasn't yet a write-off, but it was definitely in the 'needs a lot more thought and a whole new team on this' box. Any thoughts of Richard popping into theatre in January at the same time with Cyrus were blown well and truly out of the water. Oh well, at least I could get on and improve my mouth area.

Maybe it was psychological, but after visiting the new dental practice and the eyelid specialist, it felt like my conditions started to worsen. Had

Majorca been too early? This was in total opposition to the feeling of joy I had, that we'd finally got things moving again. My face and jaw area became far more painful and the dodgy eye area was now hyper-sensitive.

I went back for scans at the Royal Marsden at the end of November. Jane and I were happy to revisit familiar territory and had a bite to eat locally. Yet again, I fell asleep in the MRI scanner, so relaxed I'd become to the process. It all passed uneventfully.

In early December, Jane and I had a week-end away with friends in Uppingham and I also popped in to see Perrier. It was lovely to get out. I started to experience headaches at night so had to duck out of a couple of planned Christmas events. I didn't want to overdo it but needed to get to the bottom of my current ailments.

My GP changed the surgery where she worked and I had to make a formal request to follow her, stressing that it was important for me to have continuity in my healthcare. It was 'unnecessary admin,' declined initially by the programmed receptionist. "Computer says no!" Thankfully, common sense prevailed and my appeal was approved. I visited the doctor and we got some swabs analysed.

The results came back: I was carrying a new load of infections. The trouble was, I was probably always carrying an infection of some sort. But my current condition seemed different. It was now disturbing my sleep, pain pulsated back and forth along what felt like the optic nerve behind my dodgy eye. It had the knock-on effect of zapping my energy and demeanour the next day. Paracetamol and ibuprofen didn't touch it. To be honest, I was initially worried it might be a strain of meningitis, but talked myself out of this as I wasn't experiencing some of its symptoms. My GP confirmed that I had a myriad of some standard infections in my nose and eye area, so I jumped on a course of antibiotics.

Soon, I was back up to the Royal Marsden for the mid-December scan review meeting. Dr Miah first asked how I was feeling. I gave her an update and mentioned the infections and pulsating headaches. "Mmmmm, I don't want to set hares running, but the scans have picked up a swelling around your cranial nerves, behind your affected eye." There are thirteen cranial nerves under the back of your brain and the area is effectively the junction box before the wires go into your brain. "We're worried that it might be the return of the disease." Pause. Absorb. "But, given your current condition, it could be related to the infections you mentioned, so take the course of antibiotics, get rid of those and let's re-scan in late January to compare."

Dr Miah caught my unpatched eye racing around the room in thought. "I can see you're worried," she observed. I was still taking in the news and trying to draw parallels with my headache position. At least I knew why I might be getting them, I just didn't know whether it was a recurrence or an infection causing them. It didn't feel like I was grasping at straws, but given my history, I was happy to think that it could indeed be infection-related. Dr Miah repeated that it was a possibility, but clearly couldn't be certain. We went on to analyse the symptoms and deduced that it heightened when I lay down, so to ease the symptoms, I should try sleeping upright as much as possible and needed to take it easy. Cyrus would need to determine whether the planned surgery for 12th January 2019 could still go ahead.

In her view, Dr Miah was convinced that the sooner we sewed up the holes in my mouth, the more likely we were to stave off these recurring infections. Even if it was cancer, we couldn't tell now. So best employ some PMA and get my mouth fixed. In effect, I'd been carrying open wounds in my face for about nine months now. It took a while to fully absorb the news as I'd stupidly convinced myself that everything was fine and dandy again. I was even going to ask whether it might be possible to do post-scan meetings over the phone, to reduce logistics. "You'll notice I didn't ask that one," I said to Jane on the way back home. "I'd have kicked you under the table if you had," Jane said sternly. Daft bugger - I'd incorrectly pre-empted the result once more. Kicked in the teeth again.

The stone-cold reality was that I couldn't be given the three-month all-clear. In hindsight, I was still absorbing the news when I phoned mum and my brother later to provide an update. We chirpily told the kids that we suspected it was the result of an infection, but again, stated that it might not be. Fingers crossed. They took it pretty well but the eyes gave it away. Their worry had heightened.

As the facts sank in, I went to a quiet corner to contemplate. I started to explore the worst case scenario again, away from prying eyes. Inevitably, I revisited earlier thoughts of meeting the Grim Reaper. I was once more saddened very quickly. Seeing the pain in Jane, Max and Lois' eyes was tough. But like before, through my thought process, I felt, on balance, OK with it. If I received a tap on the shoulder from the Angel of Death and had to cash my chips in at the roulette table, I might come away feeling a little short-changed, but overall, I still had plenty of winnings.

Jane took a while to lift back too; clearly the body blow of the scan results was taking its toll on both of us. I asked that we both snap ourselves out of it. What will be, will be, and Santa wasn't going to visit a grumpy house.

Not that it mattered - it was clear that my own Christmas wasn't going to be quite as healthy compared to past ones, but I didn't want to spoil it for everyone else. I certainly needed to avoid alcohol and ducked my favourite seasonal indulgence, cheese and crackers. I'd started to avoid dairy where possible as I found it clung around far too long in my nasal cavity and created a pong.

I'd planned to send a message on Facebook, wishing everyone well and confirming the all-clear. There was nothing for it: I relayed the full news and anchored on the possibility of it being down to infections. This 'dodgy scan results' message created a tsunami of responses wishing me luck, and my positivity counter went up a few notches.

The kids were forthcoming with their present list and, to be honest, we didn't hold back. It was the least we could do after they'd been through a pretty strange year. We spoiled them rotten and felt glad that we were able to, and see how much it meant to them.

We'd planned to go and visit our friends in Berlin between Christmas and New Year, but given my condition and the aggravation that flights seemed to cause, we felt it best that I stay at home. There was no way I could travel, I simply didn't have the energy. But I made sure that Jane and the kids jumped on the flight. I'd had a jolly to Majorca and now it was their turn. This gave me four days at home to stew, relax and get my head in the right place for the upcoming operation, which was still subject to final approval.

By all accounts, they had an amazing time seeing the sights with our family friends, Anja and Klaus. I had a number of visitors too, just to make sure I was keeping my chin up. Steve hoovered up most of our leftover chocolate biscuits, Ewan popped in for a breather from his young family and my mate Richard took me out for a long, local walk. The balance of peace, plenty of food, the gym and long rests was just what I needed.

The next thing to focus on was the appointment with Cyrus before the planned surgery, to get his sign-off. After finishing the antibiotics, things were slightly better and I'd become accustomed to pain-induced, broken sleep from the headaches. I'd worked out that I'd just have to sit up when they came at night and deal with it; breathing exercises also helped. It meant I was doing less during daylight hours, but I still squeezed in a session at the gym every other day. More for my sanity and to maintain my appetite, than going full-on with the weights.

In what seemed like no time at all, I was in front of Cyrus, who'd not yet heard the news. He shrugged his shoulders and said I looked fine, so was happy to proceed. We cantered through the procedures. Fix holes, whack in implants, remove nut and, on Jamie's request, shave some of the hanging flab from the gum to make it easier for the implants. It sounded excruciatingly painful, but in truth, I wouldn't feel much of it as a lot of my mouth had no feeling. The news of the go-ahead and the responses received from the subsequent message update made me feel far more positive. I was ready for further surgery and began counting down the days.

In the week running up to the operation, I'd started to reign in my energy. I thinned out activity, notched down the weights and reduced the gym time. Conserve. As usual, Jane didn't miss a thing and noted that I'd been much quieter as I'd withdrawn a little into myself. I'd be happy to emerge from under my shell and show some outward confidence, but I didn't seem to want to come out to play. In truth, I was still worried about the choking anaesthetic process and, given the continued thumping headaches, I lacked sleep and clarity. This caused a cloud to hang over me longer than I wanted. Yes, I was still conscious of the cranial nerve shenanigans too.

The pre-op appointment went without a hitch and, although I was feeling lousy, it seemed to pass with a thumbs-up for my ECG reading. As a precaution, I was sent home with a body wash and nasal ointment to quell any MRSA that might be lurking, given that it'd been picked up back in 2017. I paused for thought. The bout of monster surgeries I'd endured were now over a year ago but the memories were still very vivid.

We rocked up to hospital early on Saturday 12th January, this time more locally. Logistics meant that life at home was far more chilled and relaxed than if we'd been trekking up to the Royal Marsden. As it was the week-end, we assumed I would be the only case and Cyrus would be itching to get back home for lunch. That illusion was quickly shattered in the waiting area. We were the first to arrive but after twenty minutes, there were five groups of people. We were led to our allocated room. Jane helped me get my head around the choking thoughts. We reflected that it had occurred when I was in a right state, reeling from the car crash of a 19-hour surgical procedure, horrendous infections and panic. I was reminded that I'd been very grumpy and had shouted and yelled at everyone before the incident as I thought the procedure hadn't been authorised. Logically, taking the emotion out of it, no wonder I was a tad uptight back then. Not so now - I was quite calm.

I was fifth into theatre. Bugger. Nurse Melissa said not to worry, the preceding ones were very quick procedures. In fact, one had already been discharged. Sit back, relax and enjoy the ambience of the room (magnolia seventies decor overlooking the vista of the aircon unit and boiler facilities – yes, the Royal Marsden has its benefits!) and, most importantly, remain calm.

Good news! The pre-op tests confirmed that I no longer carried the MRSA bug: a nod to my new washing regime. Head, shoulders, legs, pits, chest, bits, back, sack and always last…crack. Bloods taken also showed good levels of minerals and stuff, a tip of the hat to the diet I was on, thanks to Jane.

Cyrus bounced in. He went through the procedures once more and I signed the forms. He asked me to draw a diagram to show him where I thought the holes were in the roof of my mouth. I thought we'd established this already?

In came the anaesthetist confidently. I'd sensibly mentioned my fears to Cyrus and the pre-op team and I wanted a pre-med to chill me out. "We'll let them know," I was told. The anaesthetist looked puzzled and said, "But you'll be unconscious when we check your air passage." They hadn't been told. Her body language said it all before she spoke. "Oh, I don't think you're in the right place to do that procedure, it's not something I'm familiar with here, I'm going to have to chat with Cyrus." Our hearts sank. We didn't utter a word, just quietly checked out where my belongings were. It looked like I was going to have to get changed out of the ill-fitting gown and go home.

Thankfully, in strode another doctor with the anaesthetist. "All sorted, sorry to give you any concerns," she said. "We found a doctor who happens to be familiar with the procedure. He's well aware of what needs to be done, so Thunderbirds are still go." And breathe - that was lucky, then! I'd be given a dose of temazepam to send me into orbit, a drop of something to 'dry me up' and here's the new one: a couple of injections into my voice box so the camera tube would smoothly slip down like a spoonful of treacle. Nice.

I was bumpily wheeled into theatre, but it mattered not. I was in my very own sleepy space rocket, well chilled out, the silver surfer riding the milky way, dude. Injections given, noting it was two minutes to midday. A spray of local anaesthetic up the nose, a jimmy with the optical cable and, as quick as you like, the anaesthetist declared, "All done." I don't remember anything else. I didn't even get to start counting down from 100, but I didn't feel cheated.

I came to with Cyrus in the room. "All good," he said, which was as much detail as I could absorb at the time. I ran my tongue gingerly into the roof of my mouth: stitches everywhere, but not around one of the holes at the side of the flap. Apparently, I started arguing again. Cyrus asked me to let it settle for a couple of days as it might change when it sealed up. When I came round again, I'd moved rooms and Jane came in. I immediately said, "I don't think he's sewn up the big hole. There aren't any stitches there and I can still feel it - I can't believe it." Out of all of the procedures that day, getting the holes sewn up was the one that would deliver greater benefits. Jane had the sensible, non-drug-riddled head on. "Stay calm, give it time, it might seal up above the hole." She gave Cyrus a call who said he was sure it was fixed, just give it time.

Given that large parts of the inside of my mouth had been imported from my leg, sure enough, I couldn't feel any pain from my new jaw. No nerves. It tasted raw and I knew it should have been hurting like a bastard, but funnily enough, I didn't miss it. I was so delighted to lose the extremely uncomfortable 'nut' in my eyebrow. Strangely, this turned out to be a screwed up bit of the titanium mesh (you may remember this had been put in to the base of my orbit to hold my eye up). Weird, how did it get up there? Anyhow, it was sorted and out. Yay.

I showed the nurse I was capable of taking a wee, walked unaided to the bathroom and asked to go home. I was home in front of the telly by 8pm and sent out a Facebook message. So many people had wished me well, which felt like an army of support, and I wanted to share my news.

Max and Lois had written me a lip-trembling card to take into hospital. I was delighted that they were able to show their emotions in such a manner. Back home, I was sat up in bed when Max and Lois both came back from their visits to friends. It was lovely to get massive hugs and cuddles before I went to sleep. Lois spilled over several times; it was evident they'd both been a little worried. We talked for some time about the latest episode of Cancer Coronation Street. Totally unprompted, they stated that they'd taken a lot of positives from this time - we were kind of on the same page. I squeezed them both tightly and pride swirled around my heart. Totally unprompted, they said that the curved ball thrown at them in life would give them perspective for their lives. I reminded them that whatever happened, I was a part of them, my blood raced around their bodies, I was, in fact, always with them. Couldn't get rid of me, poor buggers.

I slept well, laying down that night with no pulsating headache, due to all of the drugs racing around my body. In the morning, I responded to the many well-wishers. What fantastic support! Harnessing a small part of this was ammunition for my fight. All in all, this latest hospital visit had been a quick in and out, a ram raid compared to my last visit. Phew.

Lights, Camera, Action

Cyrus emailed to check how the patient was getting on, yes - on a Sunday! He confirmed that he'd left the hole as the stitching was causing the skin to blanche. But he'd sewn it up further inside, where the stitches took. We'd have another look in a follow-up visit and would also get the chance for another bash at it when I went in again for stage two of the implant surgeries. I thanked him for his magical work and that of the anaesthetists, which he passed on. I cracked a smile with my now swollen, dribbling mouth. The rabid St Bernard had returned so I'd need to get a drip tray for my chin.

Six days into recovery, Jane took me to Hackney Studios for a video shoot of a campaign being organised by Macmillan. On paper, it was the last thing I needed so soon after surgery, but I'd committed to them that I'd be available and was really honoured to be asked. On the day, I met up with the lovely Jen Taylor. She was as bubbly in life as she came across on film. I also did some joint filming with Adam, a fantastic guy who'd fallen ill whilst on business in New York, and had been forced to remain there to be treated for brain tumours they'd discovered. Jen was in remission and coping very well on the face of it. Adam was coping well too, but was looking at immunotherapy as he was experiencing recurrence.

The shoot took an hour and the finished video lasted 2.5 minutes. It included several people with cancer discussing the language used by the general public when talking to us. In my view, we're all different and therefore have an individual story to tell. Whilst one person's concern on film was wondering when her hair was going to grow back, another's concern was living day-by-day as she'd been diagnosed with terminal breast cancer. It was a real eye-opener for me and again, something that gave me perspective. They were kind enough to use subtitles in the film, which was definitely required when I spoke. The holes in the roof of my mouth continued to play havoc with my voice.

The campaign was aired on the BBC , ITV and a number of news websites. I was advised that it had been viewed 28 million times within ten days! It was great sharing it on Facebook with my supporters.

My 15 seconds of fame, on the BBC News

At a follow-up consultation, Cyrus reviewed his handiwork and concluded that we'd indeed need another bash at the mouth holes during stage two of the implant work. Meanwhile, my dissolvable stitches continued to undo like a straining zip, as the swelling in the roof of my mouth destroyed them. It was very irritating as this was what I really wanted to get sorted, but there wasn't a great deal that could be done.

During a Facebook campaign to build up the numbers of followers to my page, I was contacted by Kelly, a lady in Newbury, whose dad had undergone something similar to me, a decade or so ago. We eventually met up and compared war stories. Dave was now the fourth other person I knew of who'd undergone similar surgery for face cancer and he'd had a tough time of it. Dave had contracted squamous cell carcinoma in his front sinus above his right eye and the condition first appeared in his neck. Like Chris, he'd lost an eye and was amazed that I'd kept mine because of the recurrence risk.

We agreed that there is nothing more powerful than connecting with others in the same boat and would have benefitted from this connection during the treatments. With each of their consents, I put Dave and Chris in touch with each other and I became even more determined to start up a support group for face cancer sufferers. I'd mentioned it to Cyrus at the earlier consultation and he was minded to put me in touch with a colleague who was looking to build this too. Dave and Kelly were extremely close and really appreciated me making contact. It was equally rewarding for me, as it gave me the opportunity to weigh up some potential future decisions, in terms of keeping or removing the eye.

I was on a high from these events, despite the continued broken sleep due to the returning horrendous headaches. Logic dictated that clearly something wasn't right, as I had at some point been infection-free and still experiencing the excruciating pain. As the weeks passed running up to the scan review with Dr Miah, I started to believe that the suspicious swelling wasn't infection-related after all. Jane had noted earlier that I had become a little withdrawn, quieter than usual. I had now started to contemplate what Dr Miah had also objectively warned me of when we last met.

I was mentally preparing for more bad news.

14

RECURRING NIGHTMARE

The second diagnosis and further treatments

February 4th was, ironically, World Cancer Day, and we arrived at the Royal Marsden for a 9am appointment, after a two-hour rainy, traffic-ridden journey. Just. I bailed out of the car at the side entrance to be on time at the 'Cyberknife' reception whilst Jane parked up. I was just getting the seat warm when Dr Miah led me to a consulting room. "I'm very sorry, but we think it's recurrence after all." I'd already prepared for this news and had been thinking as much over the last few weeks, so I had a raft of questions. I asked how certain they were, what my survival chances looked like and what treatments were available. I'd already got my head around the emotion and wanted to crack on with whatever was the next stage.

At that point, Jane came into the room and sat down as we brought her up to speed. I squeezed her hand as the gravity of the situation fell into focus for her. Jane had clearly not let herself think of the worst scenario until now. She burst into floods of tears and my heart heaved seeing her deal with so much anguish. We cuddled and composed ourselves.

Dr Miah went on to compare the two MRI images, one from November and one from January. "If it was an infection, it would have disappeared by now." She wouldn't get drawn into conversation about my chances as she wanted to take another scan to get three time points, but the medical language used wasn't 'long-term' and the tone of her conversation wasn't 'optimistic'. I clarified whether this was secondary cancer as this remained in my head. It wasn't officially considered to be, but in reality, as it had spread to new parts in my head, it could be deemed so. The cancer had tracked along the optic nerve into the base of the skull towards the pituitary gland and most worryingly for me, had reached the dura lining of my brain, inside my skull.

Despite the whole area behind the eye being carpet bombed by the maximum amount of radiotherapy allowed to human beings, some stubborn cancer cells had taken refuge in a fall-out shelter and were now retaliating. "It's indolent, stubborn and therefore aggressive. But thankfully, slow growing and not rampant." Dr Miah also confirmed the obvious: the area was inoperable and no more radiotherapy could be administered, as my head would start to melt if any more was given. I also discovered that sarcomas were unresponsive to immunotherapy (I'd taken an interest in this whilst chatting with Adam at the Macmillan shoot).

She would organise further scans at the end of the month, and we'd come back to review this third time point and build a plan. In the meantime, any further reconstructive eye surgery would have to be put on hold, given this development, but Dr Miah wanted me to continue to undertake surgeries that would improve the quality of my life, such as sewing up my eyelid. I have to say that Dr Miah was fantastic in dealing very sympathetically with Jane and answering my demanding questions, when half the time, she had no answers.

As we spilled out of the room into the full waiting area, Jane and I clearly looked like we'd been through the wringer. Out of courtesy, people looked away; they had their own dramas to play out that morning and were hoping that it was policy to deal with the bad news patients first.

I gave my sobbing, beautiful, caring wife a hug in the corridor as busy nurses flitted by. I reminded her that it wasn't over and I would fight on. 30% was six times better than 0.5% and my now distant friend and fellow author, Liam Ryan, had won through those odds. Liam needs a mention here: he'd been part of my own story since I recovered from the first set of operations and was a kind of kindred spirit to me. Liam and I had started corresponding when I began writing the book you now hold in your hand. Halfway through my two initial surgeries, I stumbled across his name and learnt that he'd written a book about his similar condition in a leaflet from *Swallows*, a head and neck cancer charity based in Blackpool. I reached out to him to see if he could give me some advice, since his masterpiece, *Cancer 4 Me 5 (after extra time)*, had been a very successful self-publication. At the time, I was researching all possibilities for my story and what the process was for getting it to print and ultimately, published.

More to the point, Liam was afflicted with a face cancer and endured some similarly comparable brutal surgeries and treatments. He was the first 'other person' I knew who'd walked in my shoes. He's been warm, gracious and extremely helpful at all times. He even read an initial draft of *Face Cancer*, whilst struck down with an infection in hospital, and provided me with a valuable amount of fantastic encouragement and feedback. He was very taken by the read and filled my heart with resolve to get the book out there. His story is nothing short of a huge success, both in terms of his life before cancer and winning through, well beyond the five-year remission mark.

Jane initially read his book and got a great deal from it, as a carer, but I had shelved it for later. I didn't want his story to influence mine in any way. I decided to read it now. This was the first time I'd truly felt up against it and I needed to tap into the resolve of somebody who'd endured this section of the path, faced chemotherapy as the last roll of the dice and left cancer in the rear-view mirror. It's a fantastic read. His storytelling style is very different yet it's spooky how similar our path and thoughts have been. I thoroughly recommend it as a 'must read' too. I messaged Liam to give him a heads up and, true to form, he came back with, "You've got this John, I was you….and that was seventeen years ago." Just the medicine I needed.

Back to the day's events. As luck would have it, that day we also had an appointment with Richard, the ophthalmologist, booked at the Chelsea and Westminster Hospital, down the road, so we got the car and parked up there. As we had an hour to kill, we got our bearings within the maze-like, modern hospital and went outside for a coffee. Like before, we stared out of the window, looking at the world carrying on as normal, whilst our planet had come to an abrupt stop. In the waiting room, we were seen quickly, but were told that Richard was on holiday. His colleague, Anna, took some notes in his absence and was very compassionate, as emotions boiled over again. She promised to call him personally to find out what was going on, and delivered on that promise.

By the time we were downstairs, we received a call from Richard who was actually working at the Royal Marsden that day, not on the beach, so we arranged to see him in the afternoon. With further time on our hands, we found a snazzy café and had some lunch. Chicken pie for yours truly - sod it, I was going to eat whatever took my fancy from hereon in. In no time at all, we walked along the bustling Fulham Road back to the Royal Marsden to see Richard, having had time to clear our heads and reset.

He was up to speed with the recent results and, although he couldn't proceed with a reconstructive operation for the eyelid, he was happy to sew the upper eyelid down, to seal the area. It felt like we came away with at least a grain of positive news from the Royal Marsden that day, but clearly this was outweighed by the nightmare of recurrence.

On the way home, we discussed how we'd break the news and decided to keep it from the kids until they returned from their pre-planned holidays after half-term. Max was going skiing with the school and Lois was going abroad with friends. They needed a break away from Cancerville and were so looking forward to their respective breaks. In stalling this news from the kids, we figured that we couldn't tell friends either and of course, couldn't go public. To provide some air cover over this time, we'd tell people that the scans remained inconclusive, if they asked. We planned to reveal all after the next scans, which were being scheduled for the end of February.

This meant that we would be armed with a lot more information from the scans and could also provide some detail about treatments too. It would be better than dropping the bombshell and sending people into a holding pattern, without knowing what was being done about it.

Meanwhile, we would tell immediate family; we couldn't cheat them of the full truth and felt like we needed some release mechanism to get us through the next few weeks. Rather than making an emotional call in the car or in earshot of our radar-eared kids at home, I sent a brief text and stated that we'd follow-up with a chat or visit. We asked them to keep it top secret, as both brothers had kids who were in contact with ours.

At home, it took a while for Jane to tearfully absorb and digest the news. I remained focussed and calm and this gave her some comfort. My earlier self-preparation had already seen me through the emotion and I was now concentrating on the facts and the job in hand. It's not that Jane had been in denial before, but it was the first time my mortality had been openly debated between us.

Now we have a further battle ahead. I still have so much to live for, that hasn't changed one iota. By the grace of god, I might well survive a good number of further years, but it didn't feel like it was going to be anywhere near decades. Chemotherapy initially looked like it was going to be a path of further horrific hassle and side effects and, in the end, it felt like I was like rolling a dice, which wasn't loaded in my favour.

To help, we kept on discussing perspective and compared my position with a recent local news event, where healthy people had been killed in a freak car accident in the next village. This assisted, as always. Jane slowly came onto my already thought-out page. Together we concluded that I'd actually had quite a good innings at the cricket pitch of life and our kids had grown up to know me very well, possibly unlike my poor neighbour behind the curtain, back in the CCU ward.

We discussed the situation frequently behind closed doors to help Jane come to terms with it. The kids, especially Max, knew that something was up, but seemed happy that it was a natural reaction to the black cloud of 'inconclusive scans' hanging over our heads. It felt absolutely right to keep it from them at this stage. The build-up to their holidays was getting exciting whilst in complete contrast, the pressure cooker heightened as we kept our secret away from the kids and friends.

As painful as this was, we knew that my demise was a distinct possibility, so it helped for us to talk in practical terms. We arranged to update our will and set up a power of attorney. I knew that Jane had managed to gain control of the tailspin when she asked me calmly to write down what I wanted for a funeral, which I already had mapped out in my head. At this point, we recognised that the shock of the news had left the building and we both started to focus on the future once more.

At home, I visited the doctor to obtain a more effective, nerve-blocking medicine that Dr Miah had recommended, amitriptylene. I also started to visit a local osteopath, Louise Sanders. Over a couple of weeks, the drugs made me dizzy as they started to seep into my bloodstream, and Louise's treatment began to improve the throbbing pain at night and relieved me of some neck spasms I'd picked up.

About a week later, I noticed that the right hand top quadrant of my head, above my dodgy eye, had become numb and the eye was now fully blind and no longer moving within its limited range. Living with the creeping symptoms meant I began to take things one day at a time. I couldn't tell if I was going to have a great night's sleep, or be drained from the drowsiness of the medication, so we planned my day in the morning around what I felt I could cope with.

I was emotionally strong whilst bringing my parents and brother up to speed when I met up with them, but again, they got the better of me when I started to talk about how Jane was coping. Thankfully, Anne, my sister-in-law, threw Jane a lifeline and offered her an independent shoulder to cry on. Steve and I knew she'd need this going forward.

A few days later, Dr Miah rang out of the blue to confirm that her colleagues in the medical team had recommended that I jump on the wide-based chemo, not the narrow-focussed, take-the-pill at-home variety. Domestos would be administered once every three weeks, six times, and my white blood cell count would need to be monitored closely. Regular six-weekly scans would measure the treatment's effectiveness, so there was clearly going to be multiple trips to London on the cards. Double bugger. The drug was a 40-year old, tried and tested variety called *Doxorubicin*. The *Macmillan Cancer Support* information sheet gave lots of detail on side effects, treatment procedure and pointed to me needing to keep a close eye out for infections. I'd need to undertake regular temperature checks, something I didn't tend to bother with as a matter of course. Part of the collateral damage caused by chemotherapy is wiping out your immune system, so untreated infections can be deadly. I was a serial infection carrier, given the holes in my mouth and eye, so I'd need to understand whether I could keep taking antibiotics as a form of protection throughout the chemo.

Dr Miah and Jane felt it was important that I grab enjoyable moments in life wherever I could, and insisted that I aim to go on a cheeky, pre-planned ski trip with my buddies towards the end of March. So Dr Miah initially suggested we start treatment a few days after my return. It felt important to ring fence this precious break. It meant I still had a lust for life, and a short-term personal goal to aim for. I'd certainly become more mindful of experiencing the small things in my daily routine and had been smelling the roses over the last month or so.

In all honesty though, I was internally debating whether I should think of going skiing. I wanted to get cracking with the chemotherapy as soon as possible. I needed to have it confirmed that the growth hadn't started to ramp up, so insisted we carry on with the planned scans at the end of February, and not delay them, as Dr Miah had suggested.

If they showed that the cancer's growth had continued, then we'd need to get started ASAP. The last thing I wanted to do was to leave it for a further month whilst the filthy disease munched deeper and deeper. Every millimetre of lost ground could have significant implications to my quality of life. Also, with the continued headache-ridden, broken sleep and sapped energy, half of me felt like a couple of days with my mates on the piste and short-haul flying could be a disaster waiting to happen. Not least because I'd be blind in one eye and weak in one leg on the ski runs.

The glass-half-full side of me still wanted to go very much. I'd missed out last year and some of my ski buddies were especially going this year because I was, or at least they had used my attendance as a bargaining chip with their wives. I didn't want to let anybody down and felt 'life's for living'. Trips in the past had been excellent fun. There's nothing quite like getting a pass from home and pratting about on the mountains amongst a group of hilarious blokes. Now and then we'd ski too.

We'd already devised a cunning plan to overcome my disabilities which would have been inconspicuous beneath the ski outfit and helmet. I'd already ordered a fluorescent bib with 'BLIND ON RIGHT' printed on the back, the theory being to prevent random skiers going into my (now much larger) blind spot. Additionally, my mates would take it in turns to ski behind my right-hand side like fighter escorts in a bombing formation, to provide me with some cover. They were also planning on wearing fluorescent bibs and regaled me with the messages they were going to have printed on their backs: "BODYGUARD", "KEEPING AN EYE OUT FOR HIM" or "PIRATE'S MATE" came to mind.

On balance, I resolved that I'd be minded to go, but I'd need to review it day-to-day as the time approached. I'd carry on taking the medicine, improve my sleep, eat more and get stronger at the gym. This would also help to prepare me for the bouts of chemotherapy – killing two birds with one stone!

Once the kids had flown out on their holidays, Jane and I stayed at the Donnington Valley Hotel in Newbury for a night, for a change of scenery and to take a necessary pause in proceedings before the week ahead which entailed surgery, more scans and another visit to Dr Miah. It did us both the world of good. Steve and Anne had dinner with us, where I drank over three pints of Guinness for the first time in months. I sneaked off to bed early and Steve made sure I got to my room where we hugged. It had been a fantastic night and he got emotional at my door. I hugged him tighter before he wandered back to the bar for another round of drinks with Anne and Jane. Jane's dad joined us for breakfast and my parents later had coffee with us before we went home. The break was a great idea and worked a treat.

On the following Monday, 18th February, I went in to have my top eyelid temporarily sewn down to see what it felt like. We arrived at the Chelsea & Westminster Hospital at 7.20am, having got up at an ungodly hour to miss the traffic. We pitched up at the treatment reception at 8am, just to make them aware we were there. No sooner had I logged my name, a nurse came in from behind closed doors and asked me to follow her - she'd been waiting for me to turn up! I was quickly ushered into a changing facility and then took a seat in the male waiting area, alongside four other blokes. Two of us were clearly booked in for eye surgery and the other half were awaiting procedures to their hands. The other eye patient was a large, Irish gentlemen in his fifties. He'd had cancer on an eyelid and showed me his rebuilt one; it looked pretty good, I must say, but remained half-closed. Unfortunately, my dreams of a working eye had well and truly been put on the sword: my strategy was now to 'lock it up and leave it.'

It was decidedly chilly in that holding pen; even the nurses with jumpers, scarves and hats on said so. I was given a blanket to mill about in. So there I was, gowned-up in my underpants, sporting DVT tights and a dinky pair of beige grippy socks. I probably looked like a dishevelled pirate who'd been plucked from a shipwreck in the sea, wandering around with an eye patch on, trying to keep warm with a blanket around my shoulders.

I was told that mine was the second of the procedures that morning and was initially lulled into a false sense of optimism. Unfortunately, this turned out to be wishful thinking on their part as I ended up being fifth in line, again. Why they ask everyone to get changed first thing is beyond me, but I was finally summonsed to theatre for sedation at 11.30am. This was administered in a side room using an IV drip. In went the drug, and out to space launched my consciousness, before I was wheeled into theatre to see Richard. I can't remember much of the procedure, except his administering drops in each eye. I later found out that Anna was there too. I was wheeled into the recovery room awake, but drowsy. I wanting us to miss the traffic and asked to be discharged as soon as possible. After showing that I could pass some urine, within an hour, I was discharged and we were on our way. I left the treatment centre clutching some eye drops, feeling like somebody had just used my eye for the opening shot in a game of snooker. We were home by 3.30pm; aside from the wait, a very efficient NHS experience.

As the swelling went down over the next few days, I quickly regained my strength. I noticed how I could no longer feel the eye painfully drying out in the wind whilst walking. It was also nice to be freed from constantly applying damp gauzes to it, especially in the middle of the night. This was definitely the way to go. Sealing it up gave me relief from the constant nagging sensitivity of the eye, a small but welcome improvement in the quality of my life. As the swelling reduced further, I noticed that the nerve medicine had started to work its trick and sleeping gradually improved. Jane commented that I was eating more, and I began to go to the gym and exercise more regularly, even if it only involved a quick walk around the block. I was definitely on the mend, so to speak.

A few days later, I went up to the Royal Marsden for more scans and popped in to see Dr Miah the next day to review the results. In short, there was no further spreading, the contagion remained in the cranial nerve and dura lining of the brain, but it had continued to grow, very slightly, which in the confined space, spelt further danger. The report noted an increase in volume within the soft tissue in the right skull base, the right side of the face and right orbit. It went on to list a dozen delicate structures involved in that tight, compact area of my head, some of which were now encased by the disease. We reviewed the paperwork given to us. On the first page, it reminded us that chemotherapy treatment was not curative, but is administered to improve symptoms, maintain quality of life and prolong life. Well, my friend Liam is now seventeen years in remission, so it worked for him!

No escaping it though, chemotherapy needed to be issued ASAP, not after the ski holiday. Dr Miah was still determined that I remained focussed on going, so wanted to start the course of treatment on 7th March. If all went to plan, then I might feel up to going on the third week after the dose, but of course this couldn't be guaranteed. I was now up for it and didn't feel like I was in limbo any longer. My health had enjoyed an uplift so I was now minded to grab the ski holiday.

With the third set of scans now done, Jane and I could set about broadcasting the news, but first we needed to break it delicately to the kids. They'd had a fantastic time on holiday and, so as not to make a big drama out of it, I tried to subtly drop the hand grenade during Sunday breakfast, after Max had got over the long coach journey back home. We'd prearranged that Jane wouldn't be in the room as she might crack.

I gently gave them some of the facts that we felt we should share and sweetened the overall news with the 'relative' good disclosure - it hadn't spread elsewhere in my body. They questioned why we hadn't told them earlier and soon realised that it was for their benefit, to ensure that they'd enjoy their holidays more. They were pleased that there was chemotherapy available and said, "If anyone can do it, you can, dad." On first impressions, they'd taken the news pretty well, which made us proud. Sure, we knew that we'd need to remain close to them and check in frequently, without spooking them further. Just as well, as it turned out that there were some inevitable wobbles later on.

I started to feel anger at the disease now; I'd kept this at bay to help Jane. She had always hated seeing me get cross as I became a short-tempered, heavy-handed, nonchalant bear with a sore head. This would have deepened her sorrow further, so as best I could, I kept a lid on it. But now this disgusting disease was further affecting my children. I guess this triggered a protective instinct in me. Thank goodness I was going to the gym regularly so I could physically burn off some of this emotion. After a while, like in my sporting days, I started to harness this unbridled energy and channelled it into spirit for the road ahead.

It helped. I started to recollect that Dr Miah had said that my specific diagnosis of an undifferentiated spindle cell sarcoma was unprecedented. So I began to apply an optimistic logic and viewed chemotherapy as the one treatment that would defy the odds and work in my case. No wonder the cancer had survived maxillofacial surgery and radiotherapy: it was chemotherapy that was the golden ticket all the time!

At home, I turned the music up when I was on my own; my playlist had become more hardcore now as this felt good for the soul. I hated this thing with every fibre of my body and used the anger to dig deep and find more resolve. Once again, I was looking to survive, except this time, the odds were clearly stacked against me. If it wasn't ultimately to be, I didn't want to leave anything on the field of play. If cancer was to eventually get the upper hand, I'd already accepted my fate with grace, so in one way, cancer was never really going to win over my mindset. I wasn't going to be taken prisoner, I'd rather die fighting with a smile on my face. It didn't have a hold on me, I had nothing to fear personally if I were to pop my clogs, but would need to soften the blow for my loved ones.

♪ Ronnie Rising Medley (Metallica - a tribute to Ronnie James Dio) ♪

The chaps from San Francisco's global-dominating band put their own 'gentle' twist on four original classic Rainbow songs, which were all co-written by the legendary RJD. The track, recorded in 2012, was cut to celebrate the life of Dio, who succumbed to stomach cancer in 2010. It features: Light in the Black, Tarot Woman, Stargazer and Kill The King. In my opinion, the last two were some of the best written by Messrs Blackmore, Dio (& Powell) and deserve a separate listening of the originals on their own merit.

Now that the genie of the news was out of the bottle, I told a number of friends face-to-face or over the phone and out of courtesy updated my line of management at work. Everyone seemed to respond in a similar manner. Initially curses, followed by words of encouragement – "remain strong," "if there's anyone who can do it, it's you, John." There was heartfelt crying too, which was such a lovely show of emotion. Despite their uncontrolled flow of tears, I held it together pretty well and found myself consoling some friends - "Don't worry, I've got this, I'm gonna kick its arse." It was so great to be reminded how much people cared.

Jane and I were relieved to get the monkey of news off our backs. It was a release just before breaking point as we'd become quite exhausted over the last few weeks - keeping secrets is hard work!

The conversations full of positive energy added to my strength and armoury once again. In a sense, it patched me up and gave me some ammo - sweet on the soul and fuel for my resolve. A couple of days later, we both went public, sending messages and using social media. The kids did too with some of their friends. Again, a huge wash of positivity helped buoy up my spirits further.

Unfortunately, Jane didn't feel the same way when she received similar messages of support. Friends and clients were quite rightly saying, "Make sure you look after yourself," but she tearfully reminded me that since she had prioritised me at the top of her list, then the kids, then the other multitude of stuff to keep the house running like clockwork, she simply couldn't get down to the bottom of her 'to do' list where she lay.

It was heart-breaking. I might had been revelling in the fight, but it was crushing my wife. I suggested that Jane try to minimise looking at the messages, but she couldn't, they were heartfelt and from people close to her. Anyway, this wouldn't have addressed the issue: we needed to find a way to give her time to meet her needs. Over time, the problem unwound. Jane dropped a couple of classes in the week and started to accept small offers of help: a lift for the kids here, a few prepared meals there (thanks, Janette). This helped take some of the burden away.

Then Jane decided to use a different tactic to retrain her thoughts; she was sick of waking up in the middle of the night with worry. She met up with 'different' people who could relate to her position, people who had walked in her shoes, so to speak. In essence, she independently did what I had done by reaching out to Liam and picking up his book - how great minds think alike!

A fellow fitness professional's husband had sadly passed away recently from chronic bowel cancer and indicated that it was timely for her to talk too. Jane also attended Reiki treatments which helped, not least because the practitioner was a trained counsellor and Jane liked to talk. Another lady, Greta, was a cancer nurse, who had been suggested by Jane's friend, Carmen. Both ideal candidates, so what was the worst that could happen? This new input helped enormously and gave Jane a much more positive spin on my position, which I've tried to summarise here.

She was told to overhaul her thought process. At the end of the day, John's life (that's me, folks) contained many things that kept him energised. A busy family life, the excitement of nearly completing the book and planning its launch, improving stamina at the gym, and maintaining many friendships. Cancer was only a small part of his life. Jane didn't own me and I independently operated my life as I chose fit. She had to 'let me go', allow me to crack on with the job in hand and concentrate on herself. She reflected that my 'busyness' reminded her of her mum, Beryl, when she endured cancer. Beryl kept working on the finance and admin of the time-consuming family business, whilst rearing two children and looking after various other family and friends. Instead of allowing her illness to take over her life, she just got on with what kept her busy and marginalised the impact of the disease in her life. This applied logic allowed Jane to worry less and allowed me to build on my bloody-mindedness. Things started to get easier.

Additionally, Greta left us both some material to explore the power of the mind, which had proven a number of times in scientific experiments that it actually healed the body, not the medicine. This sounded a bit 'out there', but in fact the research stated that if somebody completely believed in something and was inclined to do so, let's say that the chemotherapy was going to be an easy treatment and 100% successful, then their mind would create various chemicals and programme itself to deliver the said outcome. In short, this underpinned where my thoughts were now heading, so I eagerly delved into the pages of the book, *You Are The Placebo* by Dr Joe Dispenza. I recommend this too.

Meanwhile, Jane gave me some new exercises to stimulate new pathways in my brain, which in turn would enable me to finalise my mindset. This theory already sat well with me and other friends she spoke to who had a scientific background. In my view, I had always applied the same sort of 'mix it up' logic in the gym, to ensure that my body didn't get 'stuck in a rut' with the same body movements. What happens if you constantly train a certain way, day after day, is that your body becomes conditioned and you stop receiving benefit from that exercise. I always juggled my routine to keep my fitness on its toes.

Back to the story…my chemotherapy was delayed by a week, to allow me to undergo another visit to the Chelsea & Westminster Hospital for my sixth operation, to permanently sew up my eyelid. Well, you might as well squeeze another op in and this would underpin a little improvement to the quality of life. No problem I thought, my mind was now convinced that all would be fine. I'd hardly be affected by chemo and I knew the eyelid would settle down in readiness for the ski trip.

As I waited around for the chemo to start, things hotted up on the book front. Pru, a local mum and professional copywriter, had been recommended to me by a friend. She proofread the book in double quick time and fell in love with the content and its aims. *Face Cancer* wasn't the only book she'd been involved with and she wanted to introduce me to another author, so took me to meet James Ketchell, the day before my chemotherapy started.

Over the last few weeks, my mindset had been stirring up from the depths of my mind's ocean to a huge breaker rolling in towards the beach. Meeting James and absorbing some of his energy seemed to lift it out of the sea further; the crescendo had started to break towards the shore now in readiness for the journey ahead.

James had climbed Mount Everest, rowed the Atlantic and cycled 18,000 miles around the world. His book, *The Ultimate Triathlon*, is a worthy read.

He was now in his run up to departing on a new round-the-world epic adventure in a gyrocopter and, whilst we couldn't take a spin on the day, he invited me to his farewell party and promised me a trip on his return. Here was somebody whose bloody-mindedness had kept him going through some failed missions and a serious motorcycle crash. More to the point for me though, James credits his mindset and brain getting him through some hair-raising moments on his adventures, so much more than his physical body did. He's driven by his mission to inspire people to believe that they can do anything they put their mind to, it's infectious. He's living for the moment, pursuing a passion and successfully managing to broadcast his inspiring message to thousands of followers through speaking events and social media. Food for thought for me!

Me and the ultimate adventurer,
James Ketchell

We were now in familiar territory at the Chelsea & Westminster Hospital on Monday 11th March 2019. They advised me to rock up a little later as I was to be the last of the eye procedures. This time, I was a little more prepared for the wait and took some thermal socks (learn from your mistakes). I wasn't surprised that the ETA of my procedure was put back by a couple of hours, but at least I was warmer.

For this procedure, the anaesthetic was lighter, to overcome the hurdle of receiving a local anaesthetic in the eyelid area. Consequently, I didn't go too far into orbit and was totally aware of what was happening. I didn't feel pain, which was no surprise anyway, given my general numbness on the right-hand side of my head, but I did feel the scrunch of the cutting and tug of the stitches. To enable the two lids to 'seal,' they removed a layer of the eyelid. Ouch! Just as well I couldn't feel a thing.

In the recovery room, I was welcomed with, "Hello, you again? You were only here a few weeks back, weren't you?". One of the nurses recognised me as I held my eyepatch, determined not to lose it. In no time at all, I showed them that I was drinking, eating and passing wee. So I was dispatched with my eyedrops in very little time and got home in the early evening to be greeted with warm hugs from the kids.

Over the next few days, I kept my eyepatch off, as was now the norm indoors. I felt confident that getting air to the wound would help its healing. It was likely to remain scabbed for a while as both lids had been cut, so I was careful to use sterile wipes when gently washing it. Knowing that I needed to conserve energy, I avoided the gym, but took in a couple of walks.

I became tremendously excited when I had confirmation that my forewords for the book were coming to fruition, and rather emotional too - tears of joy, endorsement and accomplishment, all in one. Our great friend, Tricky, had introduced us a week or so earlier via email to Phil Tuffnell and his lovely wife Dawn, after I texted Tricky to relay that they had kindly donated to my JustGiving page. It doesn't usually happen to ordinary blokes like me, I thought, and I was just staggered by their support and willingness to help. Phil kindly agreed to endorse the book, along with Matt Dawson. It was meant to be. I also asked Dr Miah when we met up later and all was good.

Later in the week, we arrived at the Royal Marsden for my first dose of chemotherapy. They were happy to rely on my blood results taken a week earlier, so I just had to wait around for the medicine. For some reason, the waiting room was absolutely jam packed with people, so Jane and I were lucky to find a chair. I would say that 95% of people there - fellow patients and carers - were from the Middle East, which created a different atmosphere to the one I was expecting.

In the chemo room, all patients had a special, spongy, electric chair and the privacy of a curtain, although nobody used it. Their loved ones sat around for hours whilst the medicine went in. Thankfully, I was already aware that mine would take only fifteen minutes to inject intravenously by hand. I wasn't prepared for a three-hour wait for the meds to be 'made up' in the pharmacy though. During this time, Dr Miah came to visit: a proper ray of sunshine. She could see that I was up for it and that both Jane and I were in a very positive space. I was gonna nail it! She also advised me to stay on the antibiotics during the first three-week cycle and arrange a further blood test, as a precautionary measure, just before I was due to leave for the ski week-end. She was very determined to make sure that I still went and complimented our mindset and attitude: life's for living, not sitting around waiting to die. This was an important mantra for Jane and I, giving us both positive reinforcement when our minds started to wander into dark areas.

Within an hour, we texted my brilliant doctor at the local surgery and she had sent the prescription in and arranged for the blood tests.

To kill two further hours, Jane and I went outside for some fresh air and grabbed a bite to eat. We ended up in a very recognisably-American-branded sandwich joint opposite High Street Ken tube station. Jane was a little worried about how her pirate might cope with the crowds and constant

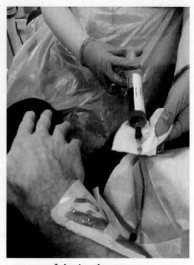

On the steps, going for chemo at
The Royal Marsden

Injecting the venom

noise and bustle, so I showed her. It didn't faze me one bit. I procured some seats, set out my space, got my home-prepped food out of my bag (rebelling against the establishment's policy) and slowly munched away. Eye patch on, lots of curious stares, but so what? I was going for chemo later, so this was laughable.

Back in the comfy chair, I waited for the medicine to arrive. In walked Marie-Rose, a lovely Irish nurse, who came with a shiny hostess trolley full of syringes. We chatted a bit, and she told me that she was expecting a baby boy around my birthday, and was amazed when I asked her permission to take a photograph or two. I explained about the book and she loved the idea. She warmed to me when I said I was rooting for Ireland in the Six Nation's match in Cardiff the following day. Perhaps it didn't dawn on her that my heart would actually be in Twickenham where England faced Scotland, and needed Ireland to beat Wales, in order for us win the competition!

I was already hooked up to a saline drip on a pump, which was administered via a two-way cannula in my right arm. On top of this, over the next twenty minutes went a further saline wash before and in between the administered doses: anti-sickness, steroids (to keep my pecker up) and then two syringes of the bright red medicine. I was already familiar with the possible side effects and Mary Rose added, "Did they tell you that it might make your pee red too?". That would be interesting, something to mention on Facebook! I was sent home with a couple of boxes of anti-sickness medication, mouth-wash and a gritted smile of determination. Instead of wondering what would happen next, I was more bothered about getting home and cracking on with social media, finalising the book and watching the rugby.

Jane collected me from the In/Out pick-up point outside the hospital and we were home by around 5pm. My chemo cocktail, including steroids and anti-sickness drugs, seemed to do their job very well. I felt no worse, ate well, completed posts on social media and went to bed happy, where a decent night's sleep lay ahead. I was awake in bed writing about the past week's events you've just read the next morning. Still buzzing then!

The next day, Chris came over and we chatted, whilst Wales showed themselves to be worthy winners of the Grand Slam. I then went to the pub to watch England throw away the Calcutta Cup to Scotland, in what was the highest ever points scored draw in international rugby - what a rollercoaster of a match! More importantly, I was out enjoying myself, having a few beers with Richard and Paul, later joined by Jane and Lana.

In the week, I spoke to Louise, my osteopath, during treatment about my book and she kindly put me in touch with her husband, Paul, as he'd written a few in his time and was now offering advice to authors on publishing. Talk about timely intervention! When we met up, he too was bowled over by the project and was happy to work on it with me. Another case of 'meant to be.'

Life's for living, and it was looking like I would be going skiing after all.

But now I need to bring my cancer story to a close. In ending it here, I recognise that you, the reader, might feel deprived of some closure. This isn't done lightly, I promise. Please allow me to try to explain my logic.

Think about the book's core objective: to help even just one further person to deal with this repulsive disease. I now need to receive the satisfaction of achieving this goal as many times as possible. In seeing *Face Cancer* come to life, I will get one hell of a turbo injection which will take me through the next few months, perhaps when I need it most.

I also want to ensure that the publishing and promotion is focussed on areas where the book's core objectives can be fully met, and hopefully, exceeded.

Please don't feel cheated. By purchasing and reading it, you've actually helped bring the story and the aims of the book to life, and I thank you for that. Please spread the word and pass this on to anyone else who might find it helpful. If you want to, please give feedback on the website, or my *Face Cancer Book* page on Facebook. I'd love it.

In return, I make a commitment to you. When I officially become cancer-free, I promise to inflict a sequel on you!

Conclusion

To bring you some closure though, I think it's worth exploring where my head is as I finish writing the book. In a way, I believe it's a fitting cessation of the story so far.

I wouldn't wish cancer on anybody and wish it had never gate-crashed my life. I'd love to wave a magic wand, roll back the clock and have ducked the disease. Period. But unfortunately this is the real world and I'm not Harry Potter. If I had a choice, it would be heavily loaded in favour of avoiding cancer at all costs! Obviously. But it's indiscriminate and not in your control, it doesn't care, pays no attention to age, gender, creed, race and frequently, one's overall good health. Sure, you can live a cleaner life and take care of your health and I advocate the benefits this will bring you mentally and physically. But it doesn't give you a Get Out of Jail Free card where cancer's concerned. For whatever reason, one day you're told you've got cancer and you need to deal with it in your life. Just don't allow it to take over your thoughts forever.

There's plenty of wishes in my tank that fuel my desire to live on and prosper, much to do with supporting and enjoying our children progress through their lives. At some point, it would be lovely to plan and enjoy a long retirement with Jane. I'm going to survive this. I'll endeavour to remain strong and bloody-minded and take on whatever's put in my path. Of course, I accept the reality of odds with a gritty smile on my face (albeit a bit lob-sided and prone to dribbling, thanks to the surgery). At the same time, I am not submitting to any sort of inevitability.

Let's all assume that the medicine unlocks the enigma code, I fully recover and step onto the magic carpet ride of normal life again. Visualisation. What does my new, second life after, or with, cancer look like? Despite the elation of kicking the monster into touch, there are still certain things that are gone forever that I miss.

The sight in my right eye and the vastly reduced span of my bite – boy, do I miss biting large chunks out of food. The lack of sensation in my face and leg means I so miss the ability to kiss my wife, talk eloquently, run in straight lines or expend full energy. The collateral damage of maxillofacial treatments has left deep scars, both physical and emotional, and some form of pain will always be present too. I'm not going to win any beauty contests (nothing new there) but as I've already eluded to, I've grown to accept my differentiation and secretly like it.

There are clearly many downsides to having succumbed to the grip of cancer, not least my predicted, shortened lifespan, but I think it's also important to weigh it up against some positives as I notch up each day as a victory.

I've received gifts that I would never have had, because of the repulsive disease: it's like Christmas (not). Imagine for a minute that cancer had a modus operandi: infiltrate, breed, multiply, invade, destroy, create havoc, and cause indiscriminate pain to a patient and their loved ones. Not really a nice being, is it? I bet it hates that some of its victims can also revel in the benefits it brings to them. In your face cancer, up yours! Here goes:

I'm now in closer touch with my emotions and will always remain so. This experience seismically reprogrammed me as a human being. I'm a better husband, father, brother, son and friend for it.

I've also spent a good deal of quality time amongst those I love, at critical times in their lives. The kids are in their teens. When I was their age, I felt disconnected from my parents and just wanted to get on and move out at the earliest opportunity. My kids began to draw on us as parents more and more as they became young adults, and I was there to help. The unusual experience of having an ill father about has also given them a healthy perspective to take into their own independent lives. Sure, a bit of a tough gig, but they'll be stronger for it.

Time has been the surprise present I found in my stocking, something I had in short supply in the past. I have spent this wisely and fully where I could. I'm now in touch with many more people from my past and have made some fantastic new friends too. In all honesty, that probably wouldn't have happened if I continued on the trajectory before my illness kicked in.

Now, because of cancer, I've become a doer, not just a donor. I found a new gear in my engine, to do something special. I hadn't appreciated it was lurking there, but I reckon we all have it invisibly within us. Some go and do it anyway, without being triggered by a health event: climb Everest, row the Atlantic, fly around the world. I'd assumed I had a plain 1.6 litre engine under my bonnet, but a side effect of contracting the disease and having time to burn kick-started something inside of me.

Another gift I now possess is a huge amount of perspective. Minutiae doesn't matter anymore and I refuse to give a shit about some of the trivial stuff that used to wind me up in the past. Nowadays, when I find myself cursing in a queue or swearing when the internet connection has a wobble, I'm quicker to row back and let it go. Why do I still initially get wound up? I guess I'm now quite possessive over time and the quality of it, despite having more of it at my disposal on a daily basis. But my initial frustration now quickly evaporates, whereas it might have snowballed in the past. Long-term illness is a great leveller: you definitely start to see things in a different light.

Mindfulness is a pressie too. I've slowed down the speed at which I operate so that I smell the roses, observe more and appreciate the wider picture. What once might have been a chore, like washing the car, has now become an experience of sorts.

I'll not be thanking cancer for these gifts though, despite being inherently polite. In my view, something of its nature doesn't deserve any gratitude, it wasn't asked in and I wish it had never come. On balance though, survival, plus the positives, far outweigh the negatives of living on with the side effects of the disease.

When I pass the five year mark of remission (when you are officially declared as 'cancer free') then fantastic, let's party again. I'll continue to live with all the deficits and benefits mentioned above. There will be many things I might miss, but the depth at which I now swim is a much richer experience.

Let's now logically think through another scenario: my time on earth is short and I pop my clogs. I know I'll be missed and the pain of loss will be hard for those I leave. I've already discussed my exit plans with you and will try to put these into action. As you know, overall, despite it being against my wishes, I will get comfortable if this is the route forced upon me. This is about getting my head around the other outcome. Here, cancer doesn't have a hold on me in terms of fear, worry or regret. Sure, I'll still feel short-changed, but overall I will be satisfied with my pile of chips to cash in at the roulette wheel of life.

If there are pearly gates, then I reckon they're open for me. I've not done anything I can remember that might put my entry at risk and, in general, I think being 'nice' is in my DNA. My being, my spirit and my memory will stay with my family forever. My blood races through the veins of my children, so in a way, I will never leave my family's side.

I'll survive. If the unexpected happens, then cancer still hasn't beaten me. Hah! Heads you win, tails you don't lose.

Facing any cancer is a levelling situation - it doesn't get a lot bigger in the scheme of medical experiences. It's an unwelcome, uninvited guest in your life. At the end of the day, only you choose how you wish to engage with the situation. Rather than hide behind the sofa, I decided to face cancer at all times and everything that came charging down the path with it. I'm glad I did.

If you're reading this facing your own challenges, I sincerely recommend you do the same. I wish you well from the bottom of my heart. Stay on the high road - you'll see light a lot sooner than if you were in a tunnel.

THE END (OF MY CANCER STORY)

15

MY STRATEGY - MIND, BODY & SOUL

For those who may be seeking some quick, accessible tips.

As I've already said, the main objective of this book is to help others who may be facing similar challenges with cancer, surgery, or a mixture of both. I'm very conscious that everyone will approach this experience in their own way, but you never know, you might find a nugget of gold in here. I do hope so.

A support network is essential. I picture this as a triangle. All of your medical team are in one corner; in the other corner are your family and friends and finally, in the last corner is you. You're not in the middle of the triangle, you're part of it. I firmly believe you need to help yourself too. When it comes down to it, it will be you, in your bubble, who will have to face up to it.

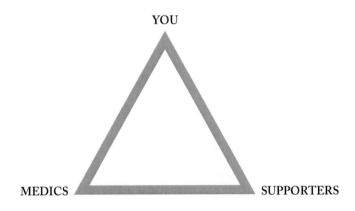

The approach any corner of the triangle adopts to whatever is in front of them will impact on the other two corners of the triangle too. Your actions don't have consequences for you alone.

To help you in your corner, I've split the tips into three camps: Mind, Body and Soul. Each one is fundamentally an action that I adopted that helped me as I travelled down the road. The insights may unsurprisingly reveal that I had more of a mental challenge - it certainly felt like it.

As they say on X-Factor....in no particular order.

Find your motivation. It's a personal thing for everybody and people will find different sources. I can only write about my experience. I think a lot of it is self-motivation, driven by a survival instinct, but I was also plugging away on behalf of my loved ones who have a lot of emotional capital invested in me. They bloody well expected me to fight too. You need to find a motivation to endure the road: perhaps the harder the journey looks, the more valuable this needs to be to you. Facing cancer may not be a battle in everyone's mind, perhaps it's just an adjustment or an acceptance, but either way, there has to be something, or somewhere, you aim for in the distance.

As I reflect on my situation, I'm blessed with so much to live for. I unashamedly want to grow old, retire and see my children grow up and make their way in life. I'll move heaven and earth for my family, so going head to head with this disgusting disease is what I instinctively chose to do. I didn't ever contemplate surrendering in a flood of tears - what's the point? It's a complete waste of energy and a slippery, poisonous slope.

Over the last forty or so years, Jane witnessed her mum fight various cancers, and herself endured life-changing surgeries, following a major road traffic accident. Consequently, Mrs W doesn't have a lot of patience for moaners or ditherers and won't stand by whilst loved ones have a wallow in the pool of self-pity.

After many battles and relapses, Jane's mum, Beryl, eventually called it a day when she was ready to go, but that was after doggedly coping with the treatments and pain. Beryl squeezed the pips of a further twenty or so extra years of life from her body, so that she could witness her kids prosper and start their families; and she held on to be fondly remembered by all of her grandchildren. Her fight for life was an inspiration.

Think about the positives. One way that helps my mindset to deal with the considerable downsides of cancer is to concentrate on as many positives it provides as possible. It's been an enriching wash of emotions, both good and bad, and I'd like to think I'm a better person for it. I certainly now have a few stories to tell. I've also grown closer to my family, friends and reacquainted with a few key figures from my past life, which has been fantastic. It's also changed the way our family sees each other; I appreciate them much more now and I'd like to think that we're now a little bit more grateful, patient and tolerant with each other.

Think positively. There's a lot of scientific evidence which points to patients having better health outcomes when they believe a treatment will work. This is also explored in a good number of debates where the power of the mind, which creates various chemical sequences, actually triggers the body in preparing and curing itself. I don't have the medical capacity or space to explain it fully here, but wholeheartedly recommend you explore this further. In the book, *You Are The Placebo* by Dr Joe Dispenza, there are some pretty breathtaking experiments that walk you through. The science is easy enough to understand, even for me! Fully recommend this, it came in when I needed it the most.

Think through the negatives logically. Supporters want to see a fighter. When I'd bump into people, they'd encourage me to stay positive and remind me how 'inspirational' I was being. This all comes from their heart, it's good, it makes them feel like they're helping and sometimes, it gave me ammunition to fight.

The reality is somewhat different - you can't be positive 100% of the time. Negative thoughts will hover and you will have to process them. It's absolutely healthy to think, "What if this treatment or that operation doesn't go to plan?". Embrace it: you may initially get rather emotional. It's a process, grieving for your possible demise. I found that once I pushed through the anguish, I focussed on the facts. I started to think ahead and devised various contingency plans. If the angel of death were to tap me on the shoulder, and perhaps give me an ultimatum of a few weeks, I would be prepared. Dealing with those negative thoughts was actually helpful.

Time, your gift. Having the merry-go-round slow down for a while gave me back one thing: time. Instead of racing around trying to catch snippets of it, I found I had time in abundance during recovery, so I tried to make the best use of it where I could. It was a gift and had a massive positive effect on me. When I was up for it, I made sure I did things that I never 'normally' had time to do. I wrote a book, created an active Facebook account, reconnected with many friends from the past and made new friends too.

Conserve energy. The treatments can seem daunting and are endured by you alone. Sure, your loved ones go through their own drama (in some ways, a worse position, as they're a passenger of fate), but it's you in the hot seat at the end of the day.

Early on, try to let go of the small stuff and bank your emotional energy for when it matters, if possible. Learn to say 'so what' to minutiae, it's the start of a perspective you'll carry forward in your new cancer life. Jane commented that I always slowed up in the last week running up to surgery; I didn't want to expend mental energy analysing the 'what ifs' of the future and she hated a couple of stock phrases I'd use: "What will be, will be," or, "It is what it is." It wasn't that I didn't care about outcomes, but it was a trigger that would diffuse any angst-ridden conversations that were building up inside of me or her. I'd also clear as much out of the diary in the weeks before a procedure. Doing nothing but focussing on my physical health was in its own way therapeutic.

I might be lucky in this regard. It's just not in my nature to get worked up and excited about forthcoming events, say a holiday. Jane is the polar opposite and probably enjoys the build-up as much as the thing itself. I'm much more compartmentalised. "Got to get through X, do Y and sort out Z before I can let myself go." I literally don't start to enjoy the holiday until I'm in the departure gate, by which time, Jane and the kids are exhausted! Sure, going on a holiday is very different to surgery, but it felt like I was defaulting to my personal modus operandi.

Be a 'patient' patient. During the diagnosis stage, I quickly sought advice from friends who'd directly suffered with cancer. Jeff and Anja get a special mention here - thanks for your sanguine advice. One of the gems they both relayed was to consciously slow the pace of your life right down and summon an incredible amount of patience. Conjuring up patience is probably one of the most challenging things when you're very ill, as your head is screaming out for the immediate delivery of facts, diagnoses and cures. The methodical medical pathway can take months. When you transfer between different NHS trusts there seems to be an obligatory long delay, but it simply takes time for a new 'healthcare machine' to get warmed up and running.

Where I live, the yellow brick road for rare, specialist cancer cases like mine leads to the Emerald City - The Royal Marsden Hospital - so it becomes a centre of excellence and research. As a consequence, we switched NHS trusts. Jacob started to send them biopsy results in mid-July and referred me after diagnosis, but my initial meeting with one of the Wizards of Oz took what seemed months to come through. Why so long? The Royal Marsden is simply inundated with work. As we waited week after week for news of an appointment, it became frustrating for all of us, but you have to be patient. Sometimes frustrations of a loved one would bubble over on the telephone with me. All I could ask them to do was to park it, as I didn't want to lose energy on stress. My advice is to measure expectations, get your support network used to the idea of the big picture and keep your fingers crossed.

Plan support. I'm blessed with family and friends who offered up their help at the first whiff of my bad news. My advice is to spend some time prepping the parents of your kids' friends. Take up offers of lifts etc. People make genuine offers of help and love to be involved in a small or large way. The England Rugby Team has match starters and finishers from the bench. We made sure that we didn't overload people at the beginning of my treatment, if we knew that we might heavily rely on them at the end. One example was my mum: she kindly offered a starter pack of help within days of the news, in the shape of ironing and washing, to help Jane out. This would have helped, but would also have left us with less to occupy our minds whilst we were waiting around for the wheels of the healthcare machine to start turning. We also reckoned (rightly, as it turned out) that we might need some help from mum when I underwent various surgeries. So we asked her to keep her powder dry.

Own the comms. Ensure that all of your family and friends are on the same wavelength as you. You have the opportunity to determine how you want people to engage with you about any sensitive subjects. In my case, I reckoned it would be an energy-sapping experience if I'd have to delicately tip-toe around various people's unstable emotions - second rows don't do nimble footwork in size eleven boots. I quickly identified people who were likely to have a wobble and took control. I asked them at the outset what I needed their support to look like: I wanted upbeat, supportive banter, with no gloom and tears. I also decided to send updates to many people in one group message on email and social media, rather than go through the gory, unfolding drama many times bilaterally - another energy-saving device, folks!

In advising everyone that I wanted to communicate, I opened up the gates and received many responses. It was just the tonic I needed at times and allowed people to pour out their support uninhibited. I received lots of emails relaying how I was admired for my approach to the problem and how they loved the writing style. This became a source of inspiration for me to write this book. I also stumbled across a number of colleagues who'd had similar experiences and listened to their advice – there's nothing like hearing it from the horse's mouth.

Although, dealing with a high volume of responses can be draining. I felt it courteous to respond to all well-wishers as they'd made the time to send me some good vibes, so I would do them in a couple of sittings where possible, rather like only attending to your email inbox a couple of times a day, rather than checking it every fifteen minutes. It helped me avoid becoming a busy fool, or at least less of one.

Humour. You're not likely to receive a more earth-shattering piece of personal news than being told you've got cancer and could die. After all, you don't get told that you're alive and healthy when you're born. I think humour is a perfect sweetener for the negative news as it takes the edge off things and for me, it's better to laugh in the face of adversity than to cry. I appreciate that others may wish to adopt a different style; in deferring to humour on occasion, at no point am I belittling the gravity of the situation. I am simply taking control and doing it my way.

Telling the kids. Every parent will naturally make their own mind up as to how they want to deal with advising their kids. In our case, we decided to keep them up to speed completely but didn't hover on the negatives. Max and Lois were fourteen and twelve respectively when I was first diagnosed, old enough to understand. We got them to ask any silly questions and if we didn't know the answer, we said so. This was a great tactic as more than once, it led to a question that we hadn't considered asking the medical team. We also asked the kids to think about what they might tell their friends and allowed them to determine how they wanted to do this. I simply asked for a little discretion at times - Max and Lois were never going to announce it on social media, but I asked them not to send any photos - that was my job on social media.

Prepare for the killer 'totes emoshe' question. This one's the giant kahuna of them all and would certainly be an emotional trigger for me if I was ambushed with it out of the blue. They say children ask the best questions, as they get straight to the point and don't dress them up. Lois, my twelve-year old daughter, came up with the big one: "Are you going to die, daddy?". Thankfully, I'd already worked out what I was going to say to this. My answer was inspired by the ITV series of *Doc Martin*, "Yes, I will die eventually, we all do, but I'm not planning to do so any time soon. If things change, I'll tell you." Careful here, as children need to be aware of the dangers of surgery, so we reminded them when the procedures came about what the likely outcome might be and made them aware that it could go Pete Tong. I still got hit broadside by some questions though; one in particular wasn't about me it. Martin asked, "How's Jane coping?". This one opened me up - I knew Jane was under so much pressure, and had been on the receiving end of a crap year. Despite all of this, she was being resilient as a rock for me. I was unable to speak for a while, then fought back tears as I croaked, "Amazingly."

The power of the numpty question. Similar to a child's bombshell technique, you should be very comfortable to ask as many questions as possible during consultation with health professionals. I never felt stupid and was glad that they were well-received, which often gave me a greater understanding of the situation. The medical team do not expect you to have any medical knowledge and genuinely want as many questions to come out as possible, no matter how stupid. This was affirmed by Dr Miah when I asked whether I might be able to keep the eye. She said that often the best questions are the numpty questions from the patient or their relatives, as they make the professionals sit up and think. The numpty questions are like gold dust! Don't be bashful, write them down and blurt them out with pride

Don't be shy to chase. I found that I had to maintain the momentum of my medical team from time to time and set out the dates of procedures that suited me. Don't get me wrong - they were brilliant, but often they seemed happy to let sleeping dogs lie. I believe they are just so damn busy with new cases that they don't see the wood for the trees, and sometimes people don't have a good day when they're dealing with you. You need to keep them engaged with your long-term goals and push for the delivery of planned procedures when you feel timescales are slipping.

Hear it from the horse's mouth. I found talking to various people who'd actually undergone similar treatments was a great source of information. There's nothing like meeting someone who's walked some way in your shoes. Their candid views carried gravity and insight that weren't always covered in a pamphlet or book. Advice like that is priceless. If you're unable to find people, Macmillan run a community hub on their website and are accessible to speak to on the phone for any questions. I joined one of the groups and engaged a little. Soon I found I was also offering some advice to people who later joined too. What goes around comes around - it was good karma.

I'd like to be able to somehow pull experiences together from people who've suffered similar maxillofacial surgery and, in a way, this book might just be a catalyst or starting point.

Inform work ASAP. Of course you might have shared one or two snippets of news with some colleagues, but tell the boss quickly. It's their business that's going to be affected by your absence, so you owe it to them to be expedient with news and updates. In my case, I relayed that, as the symptoms worsened, I'd need to slow down, work from home a lot and finally sign off sick near surgery time. They were great. If an employer doesn't allow you to adjust your work schedule, or makes life difficult for you when you are suffering a major illness, you've most probably got grounds for a legal discrimination case.

Check the HR policy. Whilst we are on the subject of planning work stuff, I'd advise you to check your HR policy regarding sick leave, benefits and pay. Ask for clarification on anything that is concerning you. I couldn't ask for a more supportive stakeholder in my line management and employer, but at the same time, policy kicks in, sick pay expires and bills don't stop coming. Many employers are genuinely crying out to be able to demonstrate support in the workplace, so give them the opportunity to make corporate phrases like 'flexibility in the workplace' a reality. Clearly, this is very much dependent on the tone at the top. If they don't display compassion, you have policy to fall back on.

Visualisation. In amateur sport, our coaches prepared our minds for the matches ahead, especially where they were relatively significant fixtures for the club. I'd close my eyes and visualise what it felt like winning, how my loved ones would feel and what they'd say. Visualise photographs of yourself in your mind of what the victory celebrations would look like. It's a well-trodden path in sport and it has also served me well in business, to overcome nerves at vital presentations, pitches and meetings.

As I'd no experience of facial surgery before, I talked at length with the surgeon about what the visual effects of surgery throughout the various procedures were, and what changes to expect over the course of recuperation. I started to imagine what it would be like without the symptoms of the filthy squatter and allowed myself to excitedly visualise my face after the second operation, fully recovered. This did me no harm. Instead of being wracked with nerves about the immediate impact of various surgeries, visualising the end result kept my focus on the long game.

Organise logistics. Sounds like a small thing, but the Royal Marsden has very limited parking facilities, so plan your logistics. We used an online app *JustPark* for trips. It would generally cost £16 for a whole day's parking within a six-minute walk from the hospital - not bad for central London!

Track performance. When you first get home from hospital, your head will be all over the place, so prepare a rough medical log to track your health performance. My mum's nursing experience came into force here and we devised a simple one-pager in an A5 book. Rows included titles such as pain relief, sleep, food eaten, temperature, probiotics, exercise and bowel movement. The columns were then completed with the detail. That way, I could check whether I'd taken certain medicines (believe me, you forget) and after a while, I'd analyse the trends over the days by flicking through the book. I could pinpoint when I first started to eat solids, noticed when my pain relief began to get under control and subconsciously made a mental target to improve the trend. It felt like it was giving me some control.

Financial planning. Check if you're entitled to income protection or critical illness with current policies - you might need them. Also update your will or write one if you haven't done so already. Also consider a power of attorney or living will. Very importantly, show your partner where all of the important policy documents are, what cover is available and leave the contact details of the boss at home, should anything go wrong.

Give the enemy an identity. I'd read somewhere that it helped to give your cancer a name, rather than calling it a tumour, growth or another medical term. Apparently, it's 'healthy' to think of it as a third party so you can ask it to leave your body. Well, I had no plans to call it Tarquin the Tumour or Sid the Sarcoma - the last thing I wanted to do was give it a sign of affection.

I started to think of it as a useless, filthy parasite. After all, what do tumours contribute to their host? There are similarities with parasites such as ticks or tapeworms, they merely feed off the host's energy and don't give back. But in the case of cancer, it's clearly worse than that; its growth often results in deadly consequences as the thing takes over. My uninvited guest had taken residence in a roomy sinus air pocket within my face so I started to think of it in terms of a 'squatter' nobody had invited in. It suddenly appeared out of nowhere and was making one hell of a mess.

I think anger is an underrated emotion, and there are so many examples in history and sport where it is a fantastic motivator. So, against liberal tree-hugging advice, I openly despised every nanometre of my squatter's existence. I visualised it being burnt alive at some hospital incinerator, or better still, cut up and examined whilst conscious. This very unwelcome guest didn't give a damn about the mess it was making of my face, my nose, hankies, life and my family's emotions. Cancer is indiscriminate, it doesn't care. I called it the 'filthy squatter' to conjure up something you'd probably want to evict with more than your regular bailiff. Surgery would be its eviction and keeping another one out would require the napalm of follow-up procedures such as radiotherapy.

Dealing with differing levels of interest. Observing how differently some friends reacted during the path of recovery was amusing at times. Let's face it, people are very different: some want to converse deeply about your psychological state and explore the intricate details of your recovery. Others quickly want to know that you're simply fine, brush it aside and disengage from any of the detail you may wish to share. They drive the conversation of wellbeing, stating, "You're looking great, John, just like you were." Whilst underneath the bonnet, your engine might be far from fine and yearning to share why you're not well. You know that some people's reaction will annoy you but the trick is not to let them. Get selfish and tune into selective hearing. As a bloke, it's probably in my DNA already! At the end of the day, everyone will have an opinion, it's just sod's law now and then that you'll hear one you don't want to.

BODY

Improve your fitness. Get your motor running, head off to the highway.... if you're facing surgery, it's important to be as fit as possible. Naturally, people have differing levels, so if you're not fit, take in a few walks and get the old ticker going, but clearly first ensure that you don't have contradicting medical advice.

My medical team saw that I was relatively fit and strong, so encouraged me to get as fit as I could, as I'd initially be facing two consecutive major surgeries (which turned out to be three!). When I was first diagnosed, I weighed 16.5 stone. Given my work was often sedentary for many hours of the day, I would have been more overweight had it not been for my relatively healthy diet and regular exercise. Being office-based also had its culinary temptations. There was the occasional overeating episode with pork pies, home-made scotch eggs (Tracie, they're amazing!) and custard doughnuts thrown in, plus plenty of alcohol at the week-ends. I was already going to the gym twice a week, so carried a fair bit of muscle, together with a middle-aged Chubby Checker tyre around my waist.

I wanted to keep up my end of the bargain and make it as easy as possible for the medical team - remember the Triangle Of Support. My diet needed to change and I knew I needed to get fitter. At the gym, my weights notched up and I undertook more cardiovascular work. I started to eat more healthily and took daily long walks too. The effect was positive. Before I went into my first surgery, my fighting weight was fifteen stone: I'd lost a whole stone and a half, so was a lot trimmer. Jane has a machine called a Body Stat which measures the water, fat and lean weight percentage in your body. We started to track this and watched my fat weight fall; simultaneously, my hydration levels and lean weight percentages improved.

Get advice on nutrition. Jane focused a lot on my diet. I'm blessed that Jane is a fitness guru and to top off her own knowledge, she tapped into a network of experts who chipped in to aid my wellbeing and recovery.

I was advised to think beyond having the tumour and also ensure my body's systems were in tip-top shape. For instance, don't just think of your digestive system, get your kidneys and liver in shape to make sure they can get rid of the inevitable wash of medicines from procedures.

In the run up to surgery, we decided to reduce red meat and cut out alcohol. We also researched the benefits of certain supplements and natural ingredients. These were either anti-cancer, anti-inflammatory, pro-digestive or anti-oxidant. For those interested, my list of daily intake includes the following:

- Food Supplements: Magical D- Magnesium, Vitamin D, Core Minerals, Proflavanol C100

- Vita-AntiOxidant, Glutamine mixed with water. Clean, plant based protein drinks - I avoided dairy and sugary concoctions as they created gooey saliva.

- Probiotic: twice a day (keeps you regular)

- Homeopathic: Echinacea D5, Lachesis D12 and Pyrogenium D30

- Essential oils: frankincense , tea tree oil and peppermint (through a diffuser, to aid breathing or place in mouth to cleanse and freshen the breath when battling an infection)

I also ingested oregano which acted like an antibiotic after a couple of weeks and was a great cleanser. You only need a drop in a pint of water as it's very potent.

Naturally, you need to speak to the medical team about taking any of these, especially when treatments such are radiotherapy or chemotherapy are offered up.

Liquidise healthy food. Sometimes it was too painful to chew and eat solid food, so we liquidised meals to ensure I got the goodness. We have a Nutribullet (other food blenders are available) and on a daily basis, I drank at least one garlic/ginger/lemon-infused smoothie, laced with spinach, kale/beetroot and spirulina. Initially, these tasted hideous, but after a few days, I found that I got used to it, and even began to get a little buzz as I gulped it down, knowing the flask's contents were helping me. I genuinely think that the attacking properties within these ingredients gave the tumour something to think about. I wasn't going to let the filthy little squatter have free reign in my face.

I'm in no position to medically prove this, but my oncologist did mention that the tumour had stopped growing at one point. At the very least, it couldn't have done any harm.

Jane also frequently made bone broth from chicken carcasses and this was either added to food or drank as a soup. It's said to have great cell regeneration properties, much-needed in recovery.

Manuka honey. This gets a mention on its own. It's very pricey, but is a pure form of honey that is naturally created over a long process by busy super bees. Worth investigating, as it holds anti-bacterial properties. I added this to foods where I could and it was my 'spread of choice.'

Spice up your life. I cut down the daily intake of regular tea and coffee and replaced it with en-vogue alternative teas such as turmeric, chamomile, mint, green and ginger, again to absorb as many anti-oxidants into my system as possible. Although I maintained my 'treat' of two mugs of builders' tea in the morning, I soon got used to these concoctions and the girls in the office would compare notes with me. One of the ladies, Eksha, came back from a holiday in Kerala and fed me some amazing, spice-infused natural coffee which could probably fuel a space shuttle launch.

Lymphatic drainage. Another thing I was asked to keep a regular check on was my lymphatic drainage system. Lymph nodes can get really clogged up with post-operative swellings and it's best to help them along with an expertly administered massage to drain them. Initially, I adopted a daily shower routine which involved a wash down, massage and slapping of the key areas: it certainly wakes you up in the morning! In the lead up to surgery, I was prescribed Hydrex as I had been diagnosed as one of the 10% of people who have MRSA, a bug that increases the risk of infection. The label states that one of its ingredients is 'industrial methylated spirit' - it's not what you'd buy your Grandmama for Christmas. More like something that would be used to clear up a nuclear spillage; Chernobyl's probably covered in the stuff.

It's important to note the right order to lather up your body parts; after all, you don't want to be cleaning your face with some lather from your backside. Apologies for being graphic here, but I think this became more important when using a medical solution that looked like it might burn your skin, rather than cleanse it.

After the vigorous cleansing, I'd stimulate my lymph nodes further by slapping my armpits, kidneys, groin and backs of my knees. Given my facial surgery, I also gave the node areas under my chin a daily brush upwards in an ark, to the back of my neck, then swept down to the shoulder blade.

I was very fortunate to receive the medical services of nurses who administered Manual Lymphatic Drainage (MLD) at the Hampshire Lymphoedema Clinic. This was the main weapon in my arsenal to tackle the huge amounts of facial swelling incurred post-surgery and through radiotherapy. Lymphoedema is liquid that the body generates between cells in trauma as a natural protection mechanism for the damaged area.

I generally went twice a week to the clinic and found MLD extremely effective. They introduced me to some frightening hosiery, my gimp mask, and the clinic became a special sanctuary. I've no doubt that MLD enabled the best recovery of my facial features. Looking back at the 'before and after' shots, you can genuinely see the difference it made.

Pain relief. Last but not least, manage your pain relief effectively. You'll be advised by the medical staff as to what's on offer and they'll constantly ask you to rate your pain out of ten. Being a bloke, I've not experienced the pleasure of childbirth, but I know what a gruesome man-flu feels like. With this in mind, I never went above a seven. Initially I wanted to be reliant on just paracetamol and ibuprofen at home, but kept a cheeky couple of boxes of codeine phosphate (an opiate) in reserve. My codeine intake was limited to just three days after the first surgery. I found this really powerful stuff - it made me dizzy and caused my alimentary canal to clog up. Later on, when the cranial nerves kicked off, I went to a nerve blocking medicine called amitriptyline. It took a while for it to 'settle in' and do its job, but eventually it helped.

The key for me was to keep the maximum dosage topped up in the early days, then reduce the dosage over time, when I could face it. My medical log I kept demonstrated the trend and sometimes I'd inadvertently miss a pill time slot, so cut the dosage by accident. A key breakthrough for me, two weeks after surgery, was not waking in the middle of the night to top up the dose, as it meant my sleep became undisturbed.

Also, if you are a cancer patient, you can get an exemption card which pays for your NHS prescriptions for the next five years - every little helps!

I found the tactic of distraction really useful in the early days. Find something to occupy your mind when you're in a lot of pain and you'll find it relieving to be thinking of something else. I spoon-fed myself TV box sets in the early days of recovery - anything that took me away from the reality of the situation.

SOUL

Visualisation (again). Another pearl of wisdom given to me by a previous sufferer was to make a vivid mental picture of your most happy space at home. Sense it in your bones, smell it, be mindful of what images and emotions it conjures up, take a mind photograph of you in the space and remember how you feel there. Use this when the chips are down or you're in a space you don't like. My favourite spot is sat up in bed after waking up, next to Jane, as the kids come in for a cuddle before scuttling off to school. I'd conjure this image up during early MRI scans, painful nights and sleepless early mornings in hospital.

Meditation. Before I started the treatment, I hadn't had the time, or to be honest, the inclination, to give meditation a go, but I'm a believer that you can't knock something until you've tried it. I opened my mind to meditation after friends relayed what help it gave them during some of their medical challenges. I used *Headspace.com*, which provides a great ten-day free trial and got me in the zone. It helped me set up a basic level, but I didn't go on to explore it further. My advice is, don't dismiss it.

Yoga. Even a knackered old second row forward like me got into yoga and, despite some of the body limitations (very tight hamstrings), I received value from it. I used *udaya.com*, which provides a variety of yoga lessons ranging from 10-40 minutes, covered all the main body areas, and was available in beginner to advanced classes. Some mornings, after scraping myself out of bed, I found yoga fantastically refreshing and it felt like I'd had an all-in-one mini workout and stretch. If some of the stuff is beyond your body's limitations, just wait for the next move.

Breathing. My two gurus, Jane and Richard, talked about the value of breathing properly. It's an often over-looked foundation block of wellbeing and is said to aid cell regeneration. Sounds basic, but it's said that if it's done properly, it can be a relaxant, stimulant and aids cell regeneration. For me, it weaved in nicely with the meditation and I learned to slowly breathe in, hold the breath, then exhale. I was encouraged to count during each of these three actions. I started on four, but before long, I was inhaling for ten, holding, and then slowly exhaling for ten too. Jeepers - at first, my lungs felt like they were bursting out of my chest, but after some time, I reaped the benefits of persistence. It centred my focus and helped enormously when I needed to break through a pain barrier.

Purify listening. Make sure your ears are listening above the noise when the medics are talking. I chose not to blur my limited knowledge with a deep trawl of internet research. I don't necessarily trust what's written on various websites and wanted to put all my faith in my medical team. After all, they're the experts, and the Royal Marsden is the centre of excellence. I didn't want to waste precious time and energy debating some threads of unsubstantiated 'facts' on Wikipedia.

There's always someone worse off than you. It might sound a little chilling or cut-throat and I'm not suggesting you gawp and point at those less fortunate than you, but within the daily news, there are plenty of examples of people who don't have some of the freedoms, comforts and life that we enjoy. This reminded me that, despite being inflicted with a grim disease, my prognosis was relatively bright, compared to some in the world. I'd honestly take my place over someone who had experienced the horrors of Syria. Of course, in hospitals, I was also abundantly aware that there were many around me inflicted with worse, more aggressive illnesses, and some would not return home. You might call it a bit of perspective.

16

BEST LAID PLANS...

They say that the best laid plans of mice and men often go awry. I don't sense that my plans ever went completely off the rails, but down the path, various unexpected things flew in from left-field. Here's some I never saw coming.

Post-surgery symptoms. One of the most important bits of advice I can give is to ask your medical team what is likely to happen in terms of the healing process. I learnt this lesson after being discharged from the first operation, when the filthy squatter was evicted. It's a bit like NCT classes I attended, in that all the information provided by the experts had been geared up around the procedure of operation day (the birth). In reality, we were ill-prepared for the post-discharge symptoms (bringing your newborn baby home) and experienced a few unnecessary, stressful wobbles.

When I first came home, I thought I'd contracted a couple of horrible infections, together with unannounced swellings on the side of my face which, annoyingly, hadn't reared up in hospital. The exposed conjunctiva in my eye decided to inflate like a small party balloon.

Days later, the inside of my lacerated mouth was coated with what can only be described as a white sticky goo, which welded itself lumpily to all the raw flesh. In a bit of a panic, we got hold of the Royal Marsden week-end helpline, who advised us that we had two options: to phone the 111 NHS local mobile doctor service or go to A & E at Basingstoke. Clearly the latter was a non-starter in my state, so we called 111 twice, when each of the separate symptoms heightened. The different doctors arrived in turn, one to look at my mouth and the other to look at my eye. They each quickly deduced that I had contracted a grim infection and each prescribed a course of antibiotics. Following a sweep by from our district nurses, who had been dispatched from the local doctor's surgery, we were told that, despite these drugs carrying bowel-cementing side effects, we had done the right thing. By the next week, my mouth was so sore, I'd decided to stop talking and changed to a liquid-only diet, so as to not aggravate the mouth, and merrily carried on like this for a week or so.

We weren't told anything to the contrary until we met up with my surgeon, Cyrus. After inspection, he gently explained that everything looked fantastic. All of the swelling and furring up was part of the ordinary post-surgery healing process, summoned to action by our magical human bodies. It was evident that the local medical teams were not used to post-surgery symptoms and they followed their training, dutifully dispensing an appropriate course of drugs for infections.

Clearly, when we left the hospital, if we had been armed with information on what to expect, then we would probably have been confident enough to ride it out.

The mind slips into autopilot. My mind prepared itself for the tough mental journey ahead without me consciously knowing it. When I first started to get an inkling that I was facing a shitfest of cancer treatments, I started to read books that hitherto hadn't interested me. I suddenly became fascinated in military stories which emulated resolve, attitude and a struggle behind enemy lines. These included *Legionnaire* by Simon Murray, *SAS Rogue Heroes* by Ben Macintyre and *Nazi Hunters* by Damien Lewis. It wasn't until I started the treatment that it dawned on me that my noggin had independently started to prepare for the mental battle ahead. It had gathered its ammunition on personal hardship from the pages within the books. I've always admired the life and death decisions made by our armed services or emergency services, and wondered how you get to possess this steely focus. Some of this was rubbing off on yours truly. When recurrence occurred I found myself reaching for books that talked about long term survival and the power of the mind.

Patience. Despite being warned, I totally underestimated the amount of patience required in the early weeks, but quickly worked out that sometimes pushing doesn't help anybody. It's best to conserve your energy; everyone at the Royal Marsden was great, doing their best, but incredibly busy. Waiting to get into the system took a long time. Take your turn in the queue, let the professionals exercise their judgement in terms of whether to push harder for a response (which Jacob did) but do ask for regular updates.

The NHS is not joined up. When you are discharged home, the local surgery won't call you to relay that you're on their radar. I was little naive to imagine this might occur and I just assumed that any local surgery would want this information about someone on their patch. After all, we all have an individual NHS number, so it can't be that difficult, can it? It does happen, but often I'd receive a copy of a letter from The Royal Marsden dated months after a meeting with the consultant - it's not a priority of theirs. I recommend you proactively take control, give your surgery a call and speak with your doctor. If you require their services, you'll find yourself in good hands, bar their lack of post-surgery experience, as explained already. The local doctor's surgery and district nurses valued being included. Later on down the path, when I actually faced infections, they rightly made sure that my oncologist and surgeon were brought into decisions about antibiotics. As a consequence, be prepared to relay the story from the beginning, time and time again - there doesn't appear to be a common set of notes against your NHS number that everyone can refer to. On my second discharge from the Royal Marsden, nurses hooked up in advance with the surgery and district nurses to ensure that I'd get help with my leg dressing.

Family first. I question whether I truly practiced what I preached. Initially, I felt guilty about leaving work and surmised that I was not quite ill enough to take time away from work. Jacob was happy for me to keep going into the office as it was a healthy distraction, but looking back, I overcooked it. When I eventually started to listen to advice from friends, family and colleagues and slowed down, I saw the unnecessary compounded worry I'd caused them by being stubborn. They, better than I, could see how ill I actually was.

Lingering anaesthetic. In my right eye, I was experiencing hallucinations of sorts for a couple of weeks. This may have been stirred up with the few doses of codeine, but they started in the hospital. I had a vivid, golden-green kaleidoscope of moving images playing in my mind. They resembled pictures, humans, aliens, men, women, tattoos, and seemed to last a minute or so before changing. Shame there was no soundtrack as it looked to be quite a show! I think they were random as they didn't stir up any particular memories, they just seemed to be created out of nowhere - it was bizarre.

Embrace the upsides. You will spend more time with loved ones and you need to feed off the positive energy they unconditionally give. Take advantage of this time at home, get an extra cuddle in now and then, help with normal post-school parental chats, even though you might end up dribbling. I'm closer to my family than I was before and I take this as a huge positive.

Park the grumbling. Try to keep a lid on any negative moans and contain any frustration as much as possible, as it brings those around you down. They're probably at the end of their tether too, putting on a brave face for you! Loved ones want to see you getting better, so park the grumbles and hissy fits. It's just going to turn people off and creates a circle of negative energy. I was told firmly by my daughter on my first outburst that I was a right grump, grumpier that Mr Grump from Grumpville, winner of last year's grumpy competition. Broadcasting grief doesn't help anybody, so if you need to get things off your chest, try and find a way to release it out of sight. Or harness the anger for your fight - easier said than done though!

Heightened emotions. If you don't show your emotions naturally before your journey, you're likely to find that your inner, vulnerable child comes out to play on this rollercoaster. I'm a better man for it and embrace this reintroduced richness to my life.

Delirium. I was in CCU (intensive care) for several nights after the second wave of surgeries. My PDA provided me with self-administered doses of fentanyl (more potent than morphine apparently) and the nursing staff encouraged me to keep my pain relief topped up. This I dutifully did every five minutes, when the green light allowed me to. After a while, I must have been near Saturn, but had also become despondent and grumpy. Before admission, I'd read up about the effects of being in CCU for prolonged periods, but hadn't expected to show any signs of delirium. My advice is to read up on it, use your pain relief as you want to, but be mindful of the effects and make sure your family are aware too.

Differing medical opinions. During the second wave of surgery, after consecutive nineteen-hour and two-hour operations, the CCU doctor was very concerned about a second bout of infections in my upper left thigh and recommended a third surgery. The surgeons had visited earlier and, whilst sharing these concerns, wanted to adopt a 'sit and wait' tactic, with an ultrasound check if needed. My advice is to push back and ask them to get on the same page.

Sudocrem. It isn't just for babies with nappy rash. Also if you have prolonged periods of sitting and lying down, wear trunk underpants rather than boxer shorts. Parts of my lower undercarriage resembled a lacerated haggis on a butcher's block: enough said.

Radiotherapy side-effects are long-term. I went into radiotherapy thinking that it would be a case of several weeks of treatment, followed by a couple of weeks of recovery, soon returning back to fighting fit level again. Recovery from radiotherapy is nothing like recovery from surgery. It lingers in the body for a long time and, when venting my frustration about the glacial recovery, I was told to measure recovery in months, not weeks. I massively underestimated this and its brutality. The clues were there: I'd had it administered to my eye, face and brain.

Given this, the *Head & Neck Cancer Symptoms* brochure from Macmillan warned to expect a more prolonged recovery and worsened side effects.

If you have radiotherapy to tissue that has also received surgery, like a skin graft or flap, then be prepared for setbacks. In my case, radiotherapy annihilated some of the excellent work done by my surgeon and turned fleshy, reception skin grafts to the consistency of burnt rubber. I was left with holes in my mouth where healed stitching opened up and my right eyelid disappeared into the skin graft of my cheek, leaving an exposed, very sore eye. That then had knock-on effects on the quality of my life, post-surgery.

17

THOUGHTS FROM JANE

I asked Jane to give her perspective, as a primary carer

I remember the day John told me he was going to write a book. I listened to his reasoning and felt an inner strength almost exude out of him. I also remember my thoughts as I left his bedroom: doubt, disbelief, fear and a sense of angst, as I wondered how he could rise to a challenge such as that whilst convalescing from such a horrendous ordeal. Honestly, I just nodded and congratulated him on his bravery, his fortitude, his essence and all the other synonyms that could be associated with the word 'hero'.

John is so gracious, I like to think of him as a warrior. I never thought he would actually even start it, let alone finish it. His battle scars are prominent and bring with them daily limitations and require constant care. How would he have the time and the mindset to be able to write it all down, whilst struggling through his recovery? You know the answer.

A while back, John suggested that I write a short piece for his book. I immediately slammed him down, insisting that my account would be completely different. Six months later, having read most of the book, I realised that *my* side of the story could also help or assist someone.

It began to dawn on me some weeks after the initial 'bang' that as well as John's wife, I would soon be his carer.....a distinct contrast altogether. "Why?" you may ask. "Isn't that what you signed up for when you got married?". To some degree, yes, but the weeks turned into months and it's now been almost two years. Our daily lives have changed somewhat.

First and foremost, I am John's wife. I love him dearly, his pain is also my pain, but he now needs constant daily help. Whether it be in the form of preparing food and drinks, cleaning our home, driving him to doctor's appointments or MRI scans, researching health supplements, essential oils and massage treatments - the list is endless. Although I never tire of helping, it is much like a full-time job in itself. I play my role as part of the team, because that is how we've had to tackle our new life with cancer.

In the months leading up to his first operation, John and I seemed to 'gel' together in mind, if not so much in words. Our minds were moving in the similar direction, but at different paces. We both thought about the individual role we had to play and allowed each other time to think this through. When we sorted it out in our own minds, we came together to talk – our way of dealing with the shock and enormity of what we would need to endure.

Anxiety was a huge part of my initial process. On waking in the morning, it seemed to move from the soles of my feet up through the muscles in my legs, take over my pelvis, swiftly rise to my throat and finally the crown of my head. It was an all-encompassing feeling that left me in a type of stupor. I moved in a daze, through the fog that plagued my mind. After a week or so, I realised that I couldn't let it 'get me'. Like John, I had no option. So I had to re-group and reassess: a diplomatic way of saying, "Jane, just get on with it!". But it just wasn't that easy.

As a health and fitness professional, I understand the importance of nutrition, movement, wellbeing and mindfulness. I had lots of information and contacts but, at that moment in time, my head was like an extremely messy filing cabinet. Segments labelled John, House, Children, Job, Money, Death, My life, Friends, all lay on the floor in a twisted heap of papers. I needed to organise them in order of importance and assemble some kind of system, if this knowledge was going to be of any use. I needed to adopt a Code of Conduct.

My suggestions below define the process I have followed which then enabled me to take control and bring order to what was an overwhelming chaos.

NO. 1: WELLBEING

Look After Yourself is my top tip to any carer or family member. It's not just the patient who has to endure this, it's the entire family. My health, as well as John's health, was of utmost importance. How could I look after him and our children if my health took a decline?

It takes time, love, understanding, consideration, compassion and strength to plough on through the minefield that is cancer, with its diagnosis and treatment dropping like bombshells. At first, it seems an impossible task, but as time moves slowly forward, so do you. Take baby steps at first.

It's not going to happen overnight, but try to allow your mind to take a break from the worry. Let yourself be free for at least part of your day, giving you time to re-evaluate and subconsciously think. Decide what you enjoy most and find something that fits in to your schedule, whether it's going for a facial, a swim, a walk, a haircut or a drink with mates. Use any free time wisely and enjoy it! A natural reaction to this is a feeling of guilt - why should you be enjoying yourself if they are in such pain and discomfort? It's only with time that you will get used to the idea of the mantra 'look after the carer too'.

Gradually, using all my knowledge of nutrition and wellbeing, I began to boost John's health by increasing all of our healthy habits and making them a regular occurrence, three times a day. Not only did John consume smoothies containing raw garlic, ginger, lemon, celery, beetroot and pine-apple, so did I. To be fair, I had already changed my daily routine a few years ago to include more of these, together with supplements. So I guess you could say I was lucky that I already knew 'what to do'. But that doesn't make it any less time-consuming!

If you search the web and social media sites on health and wellbeing, it's not difficult to work out what foods and drinks are most beneficial to your diet. You could always invest in a private session with a holistic practitioner or nutritionist to give you an idea of what and how to prepare food and drinks.

Taking a more healthy approach to your (and your patient's) daily routine and diet will give you a feeling of control. This in turn feels like a positive amount of authority over the illness.

I replenish John's body with the fuel it requires to repair, and this gives me a purpose and a role in the recovery that I'm proud of - a sense of worth. Together with this innate pleasure, I am also feeding my body and mind with a wealth of goodness which gives me the motivation to keep on going.

NO. 2 COMMUNICATION & MINDFULNESS

After diagnosis comes the gloomy task of relaying the same story to family, friends and then work. When leaving the safety net of an oncologist or consultant's office, you're not advised on how to handle this part of the journey. Little do you know how tiresome, and occasionally, how astonishingly awkward, peoples' reactions will be. I am still amazed today, eighteen months later, that some experienced, intelligent, grown adults have the ignorance to speak to me with such a lack of sensitivity.

Without describing any single episode, I just need to point out the damming effect they often have on me. John is quite thick-skinned and always tries to weigh up a situation before he speaks. I, on the other hand, have always worn my heart on my sleeve and, to my detriment, I find it heart-breaking when anyone speaks out of turn.

My advice is to be mindful, of yourself and your situation. Again, it takes time to realise this and to act upon it. Perhaps enrol in a mindfulness course (once a week, for a six-week period)? Luckily, I did just that about four years ago and still draw on these techniques today.

I began to sense when I needed to refrain from engaging in conversation with someone. I protected myself from falling too deep into communication and instead, politely moved on. Through making initial mistakes, I now feel stronger, and more in control of my actions and feelings.

NO. 3 EMOTIONAL SUPPORT

Emotions need nurturing, just like growing flowers from a seed. There's more to gardening than just planting. You need to watch plants carefully for the first signs of pest or disease and then take preventative action if the weeds grow.

Treat your emotions like seeds and use those special family members or friends to monitor and look out for you.

Who do you turn to for support? In my case, I have a few to choose from depending on how I'm feeling. Our children have been our constant saviours throughout this whole ordeal.

Unlike some, I've never displayed too much adoration for my children in public, but now is the time for me to do so. Without them, I truly believe that John and I would not have found the energy or our zest for life.

Max and Lois intuitively provide care, respect, love and humour at the right time. Their ability to provide a cherished, precious answer or feeling does not even have to be spoken, they just know. I call them our saviours, because they are.

Although I am perceived as a gregarious, happy person, I do relish my own company and privacy. During John's illness, my personality has taken a large knock. I no longer feel content. A deep, internal melancholy resides in my heart and mind, however, that does not mean I can't and don't enjoy life.

There is a balance in every part of this world, within our bodies and soul. So I use my children, close friends and companions for those times when I need to reflect and enjoy myself, to talk and listen. Those special people know when I need them and are always there for me. **Find your supporters** and use their time wisely. They have a life too.

CONCLUSION

Memories are remarkable and bizarre. They become suppressed over the years but they all have a purpose. Hopefully, once your filing cabinet becomes a systemised catalogue of events, you may just start opening them up for reference.

At the age of eleven, whilst on holiday in America, my wonderful mum was taken ill with a blood clot on the lung. I will never forget her instruction to me whilst lying on her hospital bed: "Jane, you must do all the washing-up, cleaning and look after daddy and Dean" (my brother).

Luckily for us, she survived and continued to live a life bursting with excitement and love for her family. Ten years later, she was diagnosed with Non-Hodgkins Lymphoma. She told me via the telephone that she'd been given between three and six months to live! She passed away almost thirty years later, a few months before John was diagnosed with cancer.

Hers is an outstanding story of mind over matter. She was a fighter and lived life to the full. It's only now that I have relived some of those younger memories and realised that they have had a lasting effect on my subconscious.

At the age of 25, I broke my legs and arms in a major road traffic accident. Life had literally 'flashed' before my eyes when the brakes on my car failed, as it launched down a hill to a main road. I honestly thought I would die.

Now suddenly, my mum - the cancer patient - had to change her focus as I needed full-time care for over a year. How situations change and force us into a completely different psyche.

I have never been a devout religious being, but I am respectful of the role that religion plays in peoples' lives. Now, in my time of need, I do find myself enjoying time to reflect and be at peace with the spirit in my head.

I remember school days at church, reciting the Lord's Prayer, and can hear an echo of the phrase 'Lead us not into temptation'. I do wonder if we all worry too much about indulging in 'temptation', often thinking negative thoughts and worrying about the what ifs, without seeking out the good moments? There was a strong sense of irony about my accident. I'd spent much of my life until that point constantly worrying about mum, when in fact, I turned out to be the one who needed help from her! Was all my worrying pointless, as none of us know what's around the corner?

I now find myself back in that bubble of 25 years ago, only sometimes I am less optimistic. Our previous life as husband and wife has been replaced by a life with less. A life with less imagination, less adventure, dreams, kisses (yes, John can no longer kiss), hope, contentment, travel and high spirits. But on balance, it's a life with more time, thought, love and wellbeing. We are a stronger family team and proud of that - proud of just being us.

Enjoy every day and the world around you. Take a moment in your day to reminisce, be silent and be still. We must always be mindful and, as my dear mum always used to say, 'live every day like it's your birthday!'

A Brief Autobiography

The source of my personality and character
before cancer came knocking

18

GENES AND ROOTS

I think the first 49 years or so of my life have a lot of relevance to the cancer story. Not only does it explain some of the character and personality traits I was armed with when cancer reared its filthy, ugly head; it also might give some clues as to why the disease chose me, although my consultant said it was just very bad luck.

As I said before, when I was recovering from my first operation, a floodgate of memories washed over me. It may have been a typical 'life flashing before your eyes' kind of thing, a result of the shock, or just what an active mind does when it's forced to slow down. I think these memories were sent for a reason from the deep chambers of my mind, so I harnessed them and tried to make sense of why they'd surfaced.

Writing the stories down helped me understand the drivers of my own behaviour, something I'd never analysed before. I found the process quite therapeutic. The finished result in the following chapters also gives my kids some insight into my history that they've never been told, which is a gift. You never know, they might be surprised by some of this and understand why I may have been a little over-protective at times. My experiences determined the way I did things as a parent. Always with a good reason, but sometimes delivered clumsily. I've not been too bad a parent. My kids are fantastic young adolescents and are on track to become lovely people, but much of the credit deservedly goes to Jane because, at times, I have been a passing ship in the night.

Talking of parents, I am the product of two practical ones who, like me, found that life doesn't arm you with an instruction manual. You just put your head down, look what's in front of you, do what you think is best for the long run and hopefully cause minimal damage en route.

My mum, Noreen, was the second daughter of Watkin and Eva. Watkin suffered from epilepsy which lingered around from a motorcycle accident he'd had in his twenties. In those days, they used to fly around the lanes on their machines, with nothing more than a bobble hat and rain-coat for protection. Watkin was very lucky to survive the prang and the resulting bounce down the tarmac, but clearly the long-term effects following a knock to his head made family life less than straightforward. Watkin designed and built power stations for a living and the family was posted to the Middle East and Indian Subcontinent, courtesy of the British Empire.

Mum's sister, my Auntie Pat, was several years' older than her and enjoyed a 'maid and servants' upbringing. Mum's childhood was far more traditional.

I can only guess that her post-war upbringing drilled a fierce independent streak within my mum. She travelled to Germany on solo exchange trips for holidays (funny how things come round in families) and after leaving school, trained as a nurse at UCH in London, living in digs with some mates.

Anyhow, one night a friend invited Noreen to come with her to meet up at a bar. A visiting rugby club were there too and her friend was dating the hooker. Mum thought, sod it, I just passed my finals, why not? Let's give it a try (boom boom!). The evening started at The Bass House in Baker Street and it was there, across a smoky, mobbed bar, that she and her future husband's eyes first met.

Big Bad Bob from Basingstoke was in town, enjoying a post-match R & R session. I think he was fully-dressed and reasonably sober. His best mate Brian (who later became their best man) soon introduced the two coy lovebirds.

Dad was the second son of John (Jack) and Elsie May from Warrington. At 6 foot 4 inches, and weighing in at a sixteen stone-plus fighting weight, he enjoyed a wrecking ball style of rugby and the fun of the post-match frivolities. Basingstoke RFC provided a social life for him in his twenties and he went on to captain them in 1961-2. His name's carved on the list of captains at the clubhouse, which made my son and I proud when we saw it on display.

Elsie May was called Gran by me and my brother, Steve. A horn-rimmed bespectacled, loving gran who kept an immaculate front room where only 'visitors' were allowed (not grandchildren). Jack passed away before I met him and Gran did so when I was in my teens.

Jack was conscious of the status that the family had in town; his father had been a freemason of Warrington and was friends with the grand wizard of the marzipan lodge. Jack initially worked in the velvet industry at a factory, but later went into fleet sales of vans and cars at *Frank Ellison*. Elsie May worked at the *Liverpool Echo* for a time and together, they had two boys, Mick, then Bob. During the war, Jack was a special policeman and used to check up on Lancashire's farmers, as the amount of livestock they could rear was rationed. I'm told there was never a shortage of eggs in the house; his patch was very charitable.

It's said that dad nearly killed Gran in childbirth, being a very large baby compared to Mick, his elder brother. I imagine he was also one of the big 'uns in the early years of school (like my brother). Looking back now, dad thinks he might have been a little dyslexic, and unfortunately he failed his 11-plus exam. He's certainly not so mixed up nowadays as he's a demon cryptic crossword fan. The family went into a tailspin of shame on this news. There was no end of advice and counsel provided by close neighbours, nearby aunties and uncles. Dad affectionately refers to these nearby relatives and friends who lived in the neighbouring streets of Walton as the 'Northern Mafia.' Jack and Elsie decided to take drastic action and sent dad, aged eleven, to a private boarding school in Rhyll and later, Colwyn Bay in North Wales. He was literally dragged screaming through the school gates and despised the whole experience. Whilst these years had a profound effect on him, he found the fire in his belly, and escaped by sheer hard work. He was rewarded with some fine grades, but the experience still haunts him to this day.

After school, Jack took him under his wing again to find dad some gainful employment. It wasn't long before he was taken along to one of Jack's fleet customers, *Thorneycrofts*, where dad started in the stores as an odd job man. Similarities to my time after finishing school and ultimately my gaining employment with dad's advice are startling. Dad loved the fact that he was receiving a pay slip and got more interested in the craftsmanship of heavy metal, but in this case it meant gearboxes and axles. So when the opportunity came, he joined a proper apprenticeship and trained to be a mechanical engineer. Taking the role, miles away in Basingstoke, wasn't an issue - he was already very independent by then.

His elder brother, Mike, was naturally sharp and studious. He flew through school and accountancy exams with flying colours and eventually ran his own real estate business, William Tarr, in Warrington, which is now run by my cousins Edward and David. Clearly, there were long periods when the brothers hardly saw each other, but in later years, they became closer. Blood is thicker than water, they say, and dad later joined the family firm as an investor.

We all enjoyed some great times in the late 1990's when Mick and family invited the Southern Wilkos to a company bash and there, we introduced our extended families to each other.

Anyway, mum had bagged a solid second row catch and, as soon as she finished at UCH, they were planning their wedding and buying a home in what was then, but is no longer, the quaint market town of Basingstoke. Brian was in real estate, thanks to his father's business, so urged them to stretch their budgets and buy, which they did. Dad was serving his apprenticeship at *Thorneycrofts* in Basingstoke; he was handy with tools and enjoyed getting filthy with huge machinery, oil and dirt. They were lucky to leave 'Basingrad' in 1966, as Harold Wilson had just frozen the mortgage market to stem credit, given the state of Britain's vulnerable economy. Times were tough, cars were junk and jobs weren't easy to come by. To ease the housing pressure on central London, the London County Council emptied its tenants down the M3 (if it existed then), and sent in its town planners and builders with good intent to upgrade Basingstoke to a modern, new metropolis. But this was the late sixties, so the resultant architecture displayed the panache of a concrete-ridden Soviet block camp, full of monotonous roundabouts and housing projects. Quick pause here to say that since that explosion of grey vomit (take a look on Google Earth), more recent town planners of dear old 'Stoke, who clearly inherited this mess, rolled up their sleeves, got the wet wipes out and have tried very hard over subsequent decades to improve the town's allure. In the last twenty or so years, I've witnessed a welcome facelift. Well done, long overdue. Rome wasn't built in a day….carry on, there's plenty more to be done.

Back to the love story. Mum left her local job at Basingstoke County Hospital (there was no large general hospital facility like nowadays). Following his apprenticeship, dad was lured in by *Lancer Boss* near Luton, which offered more money and prospects. So he went off to Dunstable as an advance party to secure his new job, organise digs and set up the new home. Mum left her job at the local hospital and organised the house sale and removals. This modus operandi became their blue print for later moves in our lives, but naturally, having kids in tow only added to mum's burden.

They moved to a village called Toddington and were happy to afford a half decent family home. It wasn't long before the pitter-patter of tiny little feet beckoned and mum happily fell pregnant. Nine months later, she gave birth to their eldest son, Jonathon. You can imagine the elation and excitement they felt, but at the same time, the isolation, as they were miles away from family networks which were scattered across the country.

Sadly, Jonathon was not a healthy baby. He was born afflicted with multiple life-threatening disabilities. Given her nursing background, mum knew in her heart that there was little chance of survival. This came welling up many years later, when she painfully discussed these experiences with me and my brother when we were in our teens. As an act of 'apparent' compassion, the nursing staff simply wheeled the newborn away to another room to 'disconnect' and pass away in peace, which Jonathon did a few days later. It's not been discussed many times in our family's lifetime, but quite clearly, it's one of those seminal moments you can't simply brush over. Sitting here now, as a father of two healthy children, I find this period in my parents' lives difficult to comprehend. I also admire people I know who have raised children with disabilities to live as full and rich a life as possible. My parents were never given the chance. Brutal.

Thankfully, it wasn't long before mum fell pregnant again and I was born in the summer of 1968, enveloped in parental pride and love. They were on a roll and, before long, were joined in the house by the birth of Steven. Mum's early motherhood years were a bit of a blur as dad was asked to give his life and soul to *Lancer Boss*, who wanted their pound of flesh from him. There didn't appear to be any compassion in those days, certainly no paternity leave. My current employers provide a generous two weeks to new dads, vastly improved on the three days I got with my kids. And I hear that MPs are looking to bring in six months parental leave for themselves. Well I suppose, no surprise there. Let's face it, as a collective, they always seem to look after themselves when setting new rules, don't they? Mum coped by branching out with local friends in the same boat, despite doctors recommending that she start smoking to relax! She cracked on as a practical, young mum.

Some of the shared stories before my memory kicked in might cause children to be put in social care nowadays, but these were just simple, sensational moments that stuck in mum's mind. Every day would have been a hard, rewarding slog, and it doesn't sound like Steve and I were easy-going either (sorry mum).

Apparently, dad once broke my arm when he sat down on the sofa, coming home exhausted from work. I'd decided to play hide-and-seek, sitting upright beneath the cushions that lay on the sofa - nice. Also in excitement, no doubt over his big brother bringing him gifts of edible stones and slugs, Steve bounced his rocker chair off the top of the fridge. Splat! Face first on the floor. When mum dialled-up the surgery, the doctor asked,

" Is he crying Mrs Wilkinson? "
"Yes of course he is," said a nervous mum.
"Ahhhh, he'll be fine then. All good Mrs Wilkinson, relax, have a cigarette."

19

FIRST MEMORIES

I don't remember anything of Toddington, but the next house we moved to was in Leighton Buzzard. Dad was still racing around, working all hours for *Lancer Boss*, who were sucking the life force out of him. Being a little more local, the move was organised by mum and went pretty smoothly.

Our house, as I recollect, was in the middle of an estate, at the bottom of a hill on a crossroads. There were other children around and two in particular stand out in my memory. 'Goosey Lucy' was a bossy, prim and proper young madam who seemed to always be telling us off; we were very obedient and conformed with everything she demanded, to a point. I remember the visiting ice-cream van. To please her, I dashed up to dad's bedside table, found 2p and bought her a chocolate ice-cream. She wanted vanilla. So Steve and I shrugged our shoulders and noshed into it!

Full nappy

The other memorable child was a boy called Nigel who, looking back, seemed a little deranged. I'm told mum and dad watched in horror one day as Nigel revealed his demonic side. I was playing with a lovely, bright red, double-decker toy bus that dad had bought for me in London. Sitting on the pavement, I pretended I was driving down Regent Street or somewhere, and they observed Nigel quietly sitting down next to me, with great interest. After a while, being a generous soul, I let him have a go (probably somewhere near Marble Arch), but he had different ideas... I think his head was in a disaster movie set, which was being filmed along Embankment and he promptly dropped my new toy through the slots of a nearby drain cover. Paloooop! That was the end of that.

I also remember having a bright red, peddle racing car and would bomb down the hill on it whenever I could, probably when mum wasn't watching. It was by far the best vehicle, compared to the other kids' trikes and scooters. One day, I couldn't find it and asked all of the neighbours if they'd seen it. Nigel's family said they hadn't, but somehow I'd an inkling that they weren't being straight with me. So after the door politely closed behind me, I went around to the back of the house. Lo and behold, there was my car propped up against the wall. It didn't stay there for long! I promptly dragged it noisily out of the hiding place backwards, across their front lawn (probably through some prize tulips) and returned it to my dad's garage, and spilt the beans over tea. I didn't see much of dear old Nige after that, but I used to sit opposite their house on my car, like a stalker, giving them the hardest Paddington Bear stare I could muster (which was difficult for a baby-faced, curly blond-haired angel, I can tell you). So maybe even at an early age, I had inbuilt determination.

In Leighton Buzzard, Steve and I survived all the usual kiddy ailments of the time. We ploughed through mumps and chickenpox together, shipmates in our calamine lotion-soaked bunk beds, like sailors ridden with scurvy. I remember once, an adored neighbour's lovely golden retriever bit Steve on the inside of his thigh; apparently he got too close to her puppies. He still bears the scars (nothing compared to mine now!) but I think this was the first time I was genuinely worried about him. The curtains were drawn in our eerily silent bedroom and everyone spoke in hushed tones. Being a concerned brother, I searched for the best pick-me-up tonic I could lay my hands on: more stones, slugs and snails from the garden. Needless to say, this did the trick and he was right as rain within a week (made of strong stuff, our Steve).

Mine, hands off   Looking rather chuffed that my dietary
                                   supplements had assisted Steve's recovery

My only memories of nursery school are the smell of Playdoh and singing, "I'm a little teapot, short and stout," an interesting ditty where kids used to pretend to be a teapot, with a Larry Grayson-esque stance, for the benefit of doting mothers who thought an entertainment star had been born. More on my relationship with the stage later.

A final, lingering memory from Leighton Buzzard is fireworks night. There was a square pathway in a communal garden, set atop a hill where a bonfire was lit and fireworks were let off. Despite the seasonal advice from teachers and parents, I loved to be at the front of the crowd, feeling the warmth of the fire on my face and being close to the danger of sparklers, which burnt my fingers. I quickly skilled up though and learnt to bend the end, to create your own catherine wheel. I demonstrated this new-found skill to a semi-circle of fascinated, push-chaired babies, much to the horror of their retreating mothers. My fascination with fire developed arms and legs at our next home in Cheshire. Please do read on.

Lancer Boss were proving to be a nightmare employer. Dad was out all hours, called away at short notice and, when he secured a new job up in Lancashire, he was threatened with legal action over terminating his employment contract. My parents sought legal advice, then told his employers to do one, and prepared to move, using the now-established family M.O. Whilst moving houses, dad disappeared for weeks, staying with his parents. He settled into the role at *Rubery Owen* and found a house in nearby Kelsall, Cheshire, which became our home for over a dozen or so years. This left mum to organise the move and scoop up their two ragamuffins.

Kelsall was a hilly village, surrounded by fruit farms and flanked by the Delamere Forest. As kids, we spent a great deal of time with friends outdoors. There were fantastic natural playgrounds to explore, including quarries, ponds, large trees and farmers' dumps. It was cut in half by the winding A56 which took heavy traffic between Chester and Manchester and, typical of most villages its size, it had posh, ordinary and some rougher areas. We lived on a hilly road called the Old Coach Road, clearly the olden day A56 at some point. Whilst ordinary and modest, our cosy house had all that a five-year old needed: a front lawn on a slant for roly-polys, a triangular back garden with a perimeter of large evergreens which gave an endless supply for army camouflage, and a coal bunker at the back which later became a tennis practice net and hiding place for children on SAS black ops. At the end of the back garden, dad erected a swing that seemed to climb to the sky - this was our parachute hatch from the planes. The largest side of the house was converted to dad's veggie patch, where hedgerow warfare damaged many a crop of cauliflower and cabbage; I hated the stuff anyway.

Nan later joined us in the village when Watkin passed away and would help enormously with childcare. In the summer holidays, she'd set up residence at our house and tick us off for leaving our mugs of half-drunk tea in the bedroom, as we'd disappear out of the front door. After a full day's play, Steve and I would have a hot meal waiting for us, allowing mum to return later from her nursing job at Barrowmore Hospital. Nan's bungalow was within walking distance and we often stayed over when our parents went out partying. It was a very practical, two-bedroomed affair and rooms were guarded by her massive, vicious white and black moggy called Podgey. We used to try to play with him, but he had a deep mean streak. He'd bide his time with blackened eyes, a twitching tail, then swipe and scratch our bleeding fingers instead of the play mouse we'd made for half an hour. He then licked his paws, viewing us with disdain, as Steve and I would cry in pain; he was clearly king of his domain. It took us a year of agony and plasters to learn to leave him alone. Podgey didn't reserve his violence for children though: he took chunks out of all the family at some point. Despite Nan's small, demure frame, she was still ultimately in charge, and she'd lift the front of his body off the ground and walk him out of the back door, cursing him: "Bad Podgey, you naughty little beggar!".

Nan became an essential piece of the family fabric and a constant character at Christmas, which was great. "I think I'll have another sherry Bob, if I may," being one of her more frequent phrases. She'd obviously helped mum and dad a lot with babysitting. She'd also keep Steve and I in check and had developed a network of elderly spies from the village Women's Institute, who'd report back to HQ on our movements in the village. Later in life, she'd share stories with Jane and I, taking us back to her childhood and regaling us with yarns of her pre-marital run-ins with boys. It raised a few eyebrows, I can tell you. Great lady, sorely missed.

Mum and dad became deeply involved with Tarporley's Ladies Circle and Round Table and this brought with it wave after wave of parties, sleepovers and charity fundraising days. Steve and I, together with other kids, were always dragged along to get involved in setting up the events. It could be a bingo evening for the elderly or a pay-on-the-door family bonfire night. Drink driving hadn't been heard of back then and us kids used to slide about on the plastic seats in the back of British Leyland cars or inside trailers being towed by the cars, as parents bombed about the country lanes between houses or event sites. The club members were from all walks of life - butchers, landlords (very popular), solicitors, builders and farmers. We'd get to know every family and spent time bouncing from one house to the next at week-ends.

The annual Boxing Day party at Old Coach Road, Kelsall was legendary. Steve and I had to clear the lounge of presents, except the TCR set (Total Control Racing – better than Scalextrics, as the cars didn't fly off), to entertain the kids. Music would boom out and what seemed to be one hundred people drifted in and out throughout the day and night. At the end of the evening, it was only the hardcore left though. Lashed mums and dads were in full flow, dancing with Party 7s in tatty hats from left over crackers, whilst children were sent upstairs by eight o' clock, with the telly from the lounge as a treat.

We'd usually have a dozen or so kids in our bedroom overnight, sleeping under coats, as the party rocked on below. Mum and dad made lots of friends, some of whom still remain in contact. It was their time, they felt they belonged and raised loads of money with good mates.

Steve and I did a milk round once with a Tarporley round-tabler and milkman, Barnsey. I think it was meant to be a lesson in hard work, set up by dad. We were scraped out of bed very early one winter's morning and left knocking on Barnsey's front door. The day turned out to be a blast. We were allowed to drive the electric milkfloat whilst Barnsey darted between doorways; every now and then, he'd stop and have a natter with the oldies, who loved him. He was a cheeky chap too. We left a dead badger balanced over the welcome sign of a local stately home (Lord someone-or-other lived there). Steve and I tired easily and were exhausted by the halfway point. Barnsey gave us a decent wage that day and clearly had a giggle with us too. It taught us that you need to have some fun at work as well – what a legend.

We also holidayed with some of the families, very frequently with the Sims, and frankly, I don't remember many times when we didn't share holiday time with others. On a couple of occasions, we hired a fisherman's cottage in Boscastle, Cornwall, and immediately, we boys would get drenched in the stream that flowed through the middle of the village and into the sea. We'd pull as much of the white quartz out of the stream as we could - perhaps we were panning for gold - but the stream seemed magical. In fact, the whole village had a magical charm to it: there was a witches museum, a fairy cottage and an old curiosity shop within spitting distance of each other.

The witches museum was full of drawings, re-enactments and photographs of the occult, Satan worship and paganism. There were rooms dedicated to fascinating staged rituals, where fully-robed and half-naked mannequins displayed swords, baby sacrifices, pentangles and all the paraphernalia associated with *Hammer House of Horror* films of that era. The one abiding memory is a two-headed piglet in a jar of preservative. Steve and I would always forget where it was and search for it. Over the years, the jar yellowed - I wondered if was still about and Pru advised me that it was back at the museum, having been loaned out for safe-keeping, following the dreadful flooding of the village. We weren't the only kids to remember the two-headed pig!

As families, we'd visit all the little fishing villages between Boscastle and Padstow, spending whole days on beaches like Polzeath and Trebarwith Strand. We played cricket matches, football and went body surfing (no wet suits for us – sand rash – ouch!) and en route to various beaches, we'd stop off at Tintagel for a regular cuppa and cream meringue at Dot's Café, which was near to the amusement arcade. Steve and I used to deplete our holiday funds within hours of getting there, on ever so alluring video games, but Mark, the Sim's son, was Captain Sensible. He would budget his daily spend and store his funds within a little purse that he'd hang around his neck. "He's an example to you two," our parents would say as we begged for more money, on the promise that we wouldn't fritter it away again. We might have considered adopting some control on our spending, but couldn't bear the thought of having to adorn the obligatory fashion accessory of a purse, so blew the money again on Space Invaders.

Like most brothers, we were close, but had to be pulled apart now and then. Inevitably, Steve and I would enhance this bond with the animal instincts of play-fighting and general unpleasantries. Nothing too malicious, but just enough to make the other think twice before responding again. I remember an incident that occurred along the riverbank in Boscastle. We were walking with mum and dad back to the cottage, doing the usual tit for tat, sniping at each other. Out of the blue, we both went into Bruce Lee and Hong Kong Phooey-mode and somehow, I managed to throw Steve face-first into the tarmac. God knows how as he was much more thick set than me. His top row of baby teeth broke his fall and flew into the water. For the rest of the afternoon I sat in disgrace, on the back seat of the car, as the whole family scoured the countryside for an available dentist. Thankfully, he bears no scars (well, maybe mental ones), but what I hadn't reckoned was that Steve could hold a grudge like an elephant, and strike like a cobra when the opportunity arose.

He got his own back one bath time, a year or two later. I was standing up in the bath to get the shampoo or something and, whilst drying himself, he pulled my slippery, soapy legs away from underneath me. My front adult teeth broke my fall on the edge of the enamel bath, and 'ping' went a third of my front left incisor, as it hurtled across the floor towards the loo. A crown's still held in by a pin to this day. We stopped play-fighting around this time. Steve was getting even bigger and broader and I was getting taller and skinnier, so I worked out that, in future fights, there was only going to be one winner.

Cornwall provided wet, woolly, welly-clad summer holidays where the sun used to make the occasional appearance. The adults used to go to the pub on a nightly basis and we boys would entertain ourselves with pillow fights and *The Fall Guy* - a game dedicated to the Steve Majors TV series about an LA-based stuntman. This took place under the absent supervision of Julie, the Sims' daughter, who was far more sensible and older than the three of us. Not her fault, as looking after three boys must get boring for anybody. Initially, we took turns at the lead role, but in the end, there was only one of us fit for the job. I was tall and skinny, so couldn't curl up into a great ball and, given the high risk of limb damage, wasn't fit for purpose. Mark was the heaviest of us and likely to go through the staircase at some point, so he opted out too. This left Steve, who was the smallest and hewn from bouncy granite. He was also the only one who could fit into the equipment properly so naturally seemed an obvious choice for the job. The stunt involved pillows tied to Steve's arms, his body and head bound with dressing gown belts, then he was shoved into a giant pillowcase and rolled to the top of the staircase. With the hallway lights on, it was Lights…Camera…Action. We'd see how far Steve could bounce down the three quadrangle flights of stairs before Julie came out screaming blue murder from her room. Steve never complained and seemed to quite enjoy the notoriety.

Even the incessant rain didn't deter the fun. Instead of getting drenched outside, when the heavens opened for the day, we'd stay indoors and played mammoth games of Monopoly. I was the banker (early signs?) and was very charitable, slipping Steve and Mark the odd hundred or two. After all, we were up against two very competitive dads, so needed all the help we could get! This was probably the first time I understood the concept of finance; indeed, it's a game that teaches kids all about the basics of capitalism. Earning some sort of wage, paying out and receiving monies through chance, owning property, taking on a mortgage and over-extending your liquidity to the point of fire selling hotels at a fraction of the price. In true capitalist spirit, the best man wiped the board with the competition for at least a day. To be honest, we never got to the end of a game where all but the winner would be bankrupt, but it would be abundantly clear by day two who was going to win, so the others would insist we start again. After all, it was only a game.

To me, the coastline and countryside of north Cornwall still has an infectious ruggedness. I went on to revisit the area a few times as an adult and am now happily held hostage on Sunday nights when Jane and I watch Poldark, with 'Raaarsse and Demelza' trying to make their way through feudal family rows, ploughing all their hope into dilapidated tin mines.

20

EARLY SCHOOL DAZE

The Kelsall primary and junior schools were at the bottom of the village, so every morning, the school children would trudge downhill through the lanes. Kids from the northern side had to cross the busy A56 on a steel footbridge and walk a further half mile or so down past the shops, to the red-bricked, single storey school. It had a great wraparound playground and large, sprawling fields, surrounded by green, iron railings to hinder escapees.

Having made friends with a few kids on Old Coach Road, it was no problem tagging onto the daily procession which went past the bottom of our drive, so mum felt comfortable letting us walk to school. There were the sensible girls who kept an eye on the scallywags; I don't think I was a tearaway, but loved to peel off for a little adventure or two. We frequently stopped by the penny sweet shop to stock up on our sugar fix, and I remember once on the way home, we were caught by the goody-two-shoes girls, lighting a very controlled campfire amongst some trees. This would have spelt deep doo-doo with the headmaster if we had been snitched on, but Chris and I convinced the girls that this was our first and last such adventure involving fire. I kept my side of the story, in so much that I didn't have another pyromaniac adventure with Chris, but I certainly had other adventures, and fire continued to feature - more on that later. Chris was a bit of a tearaway and in me he had both a follower and an obedient stooge.

Chris lived in a rustic house offset from the Old Coach Road. His mum bred large, pointer-like dogs in the kennels behind the house. These silent, stalking canines used to spook me out as their heads were chest height to me. They'd just stare into my eyes, move forward towards me and I often found myself backing into a corner in fright, much to the amusement of Chris. Consequently, I insisted we play outdoors or in the surrounding countryside. At the back of his garden was a large damson tree that we used to climb, which allowed us to climb onto the roof of a store room belonging to a next door shop. Catapults at the ready, using squishy damsons as ammo, we'd wait for various targets walking in the road, out of sight. We were always pushing the boundaries for our age, I think driven by the fact that Chris had an elder brother, who was probably ten years his senior. Therefore it was Chris who took me to see his brother's stash of seventies porn and introduced me to a friend, Nick O'Teen.

He once gave me some money to buy us some cigarettes from the local VG Stores; we must have only been nine years old. I went in and asked for some for my mum, which was quite common in those days. "What brand, sonny?" I just pointed at the bottom row where the cheapest brands were, passed the guy the money and dashed out of the shop. We smoked them in the fruit fields until we were sick! When I got home, I faced the Spanish Inquisition. Mum had gone into the shop afterwards and the assistant innocently asked if she'd changed brands. Whoops. It was the start of the summer holidays and I still remember writing out my hundred lines of punishment. "I have been a bad boy and I will never smoke cigarettes again." I was allowed to do several lines a day then go out, but it was a heavy-laboured task for a kid yearning to get out and be free in the countryside all day. Lesson learned, don't do other's dirty work, unless you're paid.

Our whole year group, of say, 30 kids, all squeezed into a different classroom every year as we progressed through the school. Throughout the seven years, I don't recollect much turnover of faces. There were very intelligent, bright and articulate boys like Gareth, who was a nine-year old local genius and played the piano impeccably, and Peter, who was a very well-read, studious book worm.

Some boys were less bothered academically and saw school as a constant playground. I fitted in well here with local mates Darren (who lived just up the road) and Rob (who lived across the valley). Some boys were clearly far more interested in pushing the boundaries. 'Westy' was the class alpha male and I became one of his disciples for some time too. It was probably survival instinct to befriend the bad guys, so they left you alone. He also attracted others who were a little more mischievous than me, which got me into trouble now and then.

I just remember four teachers at the infant and junior schools. Mrs Warren, who was very patient and kind with all of the kids; Mrs Hood, who seemed to be constantly having a nervous break-down and classified me as trouble; Mr Barrett, a charming, sporty, musical bloke who taught our final year; and Mr Pugh, the Headmaster.

Mrs Warren was experienced, in control and seemed to bring out some of the best qualities in pupils, like me. We enjoyed school trips and the year in her class passed without major incident.

I can't remember what I did to offend Mrs Hood, but she seemed to have it in for me from day one. We were force-fed her constant accordion playing and my face probably reflected my horror as I drowned in weird hoots and blows from that voluminous bellowing instrument - I never did have much of a poker face. One school trip involved a day at a local nature resort,

Fox Howl. I was bored stiff with the other labelled naughty numpties, so we decided to try and wake up the badgers who were sleeping in their set during the middle of the day. Needless to say, our behaviour was seen as less than exemplary and upset the nature wardens, who were trying to quietly guide the school group through the forest. Fast forward a week later and a criminal trial by jury was played out in the Headmaster's Office.

Mrs Hood acted for the prosecution: she'd been looking forward to her day in court for a long time and excitedly showed the court the evidence. This was in the form of a letter written by the nature reserve wardens to the school. It listed what we scallywags had done in meticulous and logical order: the wardens were not happy badger fans. Apparently, we'd started causing a scene well before the incident, something we don't remember. Mankind had disturbed the peace that the badgers enjoyed that day and nature's fragile equilibrium - which the wardens very carefully tried to conserve - had been broken. Our fate was sealed when they recounted that an entrance to the badger set had part-collapsed.

Mr Pugh sat as judge and jury, whilst in the public gallery sat five very embarrassed, shame-faced mothers, who had been brought in to see their boys squirm in the dock. The fidgeting *Fox Howl Five* could only mutter their names as the charges were read out. As the evidence was examined, we stared at our shoes. You could feel the palpable glare of anger being emitted by the court beaming into our skulls. Despite tears being shed, mercy was in short supply that afternoon. We sensibly pleaded guilty to the crimes put before us and swiftly received sentencing there and then, delivered sternly by Mr Pugh. He had a booming voice and thumped his desk in disgust; the deafening sound seemed to ricochet off the walls of his office. Each of us had to write a one-page letter of apology, pick up litter for a couple of hours at the reserve over a week-end and stay in at break time for a week. Justice had been served and I'm sure this initial scrape with the law knocked me back on track for at least a month or two. In the next term, I was glad to leave Mrs Hood behind and went into the final year with a new teacher, Mr Barrett.

He was no fool and promptly separated the *Fox Howl Five*, sitting us next to more inspiring kids, including the girls. I remember a very bright, leggy girl called Helen and, shock-horror, she seemed to like that 'bit of rough' in me. We competed together in cycle proficiency, athletics and swimming, but in every way, she was better than me.

Delamere Forest sprawled for miles and miles around the northern end of the village and beyond. It was a magical place full of camouflage, bracken where me and friends would re-enact WWII guerrilla warfare, and we got to know parts of it like the back of our hands. We also 'scrambled' around on our bikes, years before BMX came along. We built tracks, curves and jumps in the dirt on a patch of forest called The Yell. Like most kids, I had a Raleigh racing bike, smelted and cast out of lead and wrought iron, which weighed a ton. Lightweight materials like aluminium were just coming of age and carbon fibre didn't exist. Darren had the coolest bike of the day for scrambling: a Grifter. This was like a 4x4 compared to other bikes, with spongy, knobbly tyres and short, flat handlebars. Darren lived only four doors away from me so I got to know him really well over the years. He was a kind kid and would give me a go on his Grifter every now and then, out of sympathy, whilst perusing my buckled-wheeled, often punctured, penny farthing equivalent.

In the final two years of junior school, our classes were subjected to an annual cross-country race around the forest. Unexpectedly, cross-country gave me some bragging rights, as I found that I was the fastest boy in my year when I first ran the race and didn't really try. I didn't exactly 'like' the exhausted breathing, panting, soggy feet and exertion, but being blessed with a light, skinny frame and large lungs, I seemed to excel at long distance. I couldn't believe it and enjoyed the little moment of playground fame. My parents were very proud and I knew I'd breeze the race in my final year.

Or at least that's what I thought. Unbeknown to me, quietly and industriously, a lad called Christian had been plotting my downfall. He enjoyed orienteering as a hobby and it hurt him to his core when I skipped across the finishing line the year before. He was the favourite to win that year: revenge is a dish best served cold. During the race, he thundered past me during a downhill section, weaving in and out of the path's obstacles – man, he was quick! Afterwards, we had a friendly chat; he'd been doing stamina training in the months leading up to the run and had completed the course a couple of times, leaving nothing to chance. I admired him for that and warmly congratulated him like Sebastian Coe did when he was beaten by Steve Ovett at the Olympics - through gritted teeth!

It taught me a lesson though. You need to plan well if you really want something and can't assume that others aren't doing so too. Looking back, this may have been my first hands-on experience of competition. You certainly couldn't call our school football team competitive, more like 'keenly spirited'. I was one of many left backs in the team (the old pun - would rather be 'left back' in the changing room), who randomly milled about in defence like zombies, making up the numbers, and desperately trying to hoof the ball up field to kids like Darren who had some skills.

I think my second lesson in the art of competition was dished out that year too. I desperately wanted to play a meaningful role in the end of year stage production, *Samson and Delilah*. It was obvious that most of the alpha males were going for the lead role and, looking at the script, I quickly worked out that the role of narrator, Phil O'Stein, had a good deal of involvement. Taking a leaf out of Christian's book, I took the script home, studied it, practised and drilled my performance to perfection in front of a surprised younger brother, mother and Nan. I was primed for the audition and was up against another boy in the class, Damon, who was bizarrely, Christian's next door neighbour.

Damon dallied with the arts and attended ballet, which wasn't lost on the other mickey-taking boys. Mr Barrett couldn't choose between the nice kid Damon and I, so held a head-to-head audition after school. After they'd finished, I saw his mum slither quietly into the classroom to talk to Mr Barrett alone, before taking Damon home. My mum picked me up and we left straight away. Lo and behold, Damon got the part. Clearly gutted, I vowed never to bother with the stage again, and stubbornly never did until my teen years in sixth form. I remember my parents nudging each other and giggling, as I sat through the whole of the play crossed-armed, turned away from the stage, with a bottom lip the size of a small sofa. I undertook my allocated understudy role well, but with attitude, and never got to play any of the parts. So, if there are any other budding luvvies out there who never made it past understudy, I'm with you, brothers and sisters. The second lesson? When you put your neck out and really want something, get sponsors and supporters involved too.

Despite the lack of a major role in the play, I did enjoy a bit of the limelight at the school's Queen's Jubilee celebrations in 1977, which took place on Saturday 18th June (at 2pm, to be precise), with an admission price of 10p – mum kept the programme. The school laid on a big party in the scorching sun and pupils of all ages adorned fancy dress in the 2.25pm parade. At the end, we were all asked on stage with Mr Pugh to introduce ourselves on the microphone. In my class, I noted that the boys were all pretty much the same. There was a handful of Robin Hoods, three superheroes like Batman and Robin, and a couple of soldiers. Only me and Peter and were different; he had actually personified his own character very well and came as a bookworm, trailing a stuffed sleeping-bag behind him for a maggoty abdomen. I was Dracula: I had black trousers, a black cape, cummerbund and a white shirt, with the final adornment being a set of false fangs which you could remove very quickly.

Little did they know, but I had actually come as two characters that day. It came to my turn and Mr Pugh announced my arrival on stage to the thronging crowd, in his deep booming voice: "Well parents, what do we have here? A horror-inspired vampire? But wait… I don't see any blood and where are your fangs?" It was time to reveal the other character. I piped up, "No Mr Pugh, you've got it wrong, I am the dreaded Phantom Raspberry Blower from *The Two Ronnies*." And with that, I filled my lungs and blew a fantastically long, reverberating raspberry whoopsie down the microphone, raising my cape like Zorro to give an air of mystique. Poor Mr Pugh didn't know where he was and froze. The parents burst out laughing and I was ushered off the stage in a gentle, but firm manner by the surrounding teachers, who muttered, "We should have checked it out. Did you know? I thought he was Dracula! Move along John, no you can't have another go."

Before I released the phantom on stage, next to the bookworm. See Christian the Viking. Also Darren, Rob, Damon, three Robin Hoods, on bottom row

I'd planned the character with my parents whilst watching the show. They were determined I was going to go as something current; it was fun and a little rebellious too, so I kept it under wraps. Mum might have looked the other way with a certain amount of pride at the fête, and dad was tickled pink by the story over tea. So when you're planning something a little risqué, it's better to seek forgiveness rather than permission.

Mr Barrett was impressed by a number of us who'd taken a shine to cross-country and devised the fantastic idea of an inaugural Kelsall Primary School Charity Cross-Country Run. A keen runner himself, he took time to practice and train the squad during lunch breaks. We wrote proudly of our exploits, knowing that they would be displayed at the end of year reviews in front of parents, and I remember drawing a route map showing our path. Mr Barrett was running the whole twenty or so miles, with the squad taking turns to run two mile stages with him. My stage was to run from a well-known car park near a hill called Rock of Ages, to deep within the Delamere Forest.

I remember waking up excitedly, prepared and enthused on the Saturday morning of the run. I'd laid out my kit the night before and was now pacing and warming up downstairs, pleading for my parents to hurry up and drop me off. Dad wasn't going anywhere without a shave; as a dark-haired ape, he generally looked like a caveman every morning and wasn't going to turn up like a scruff bag. Long story short, we rocked up probably two minutes late, only to find that the runners had already passed through: I'd missed the boat to the island of glory. I was absolutely gutted and was inconsolable all day. I can remember a thousand apologies from my parents, who were truly sorry. But this taught me another invaluable lesson – planning and punctuality. Mr Barrett was gracious enough to mention me in dispatches, reminding me how a team player doesn't necessarily turn up for each match, but it wasn't the same as participating in the actual event. In the future, if I wanted something badly enough I would ensure I had a contingency plan B.

I'm going to leave my memories of Kelsall School and my first dalliance with education here. It equipped me as best it could for senior school and taught me some valuable lessons. I left as a happy, semi-confident lad, thinking that the word 'mediocre' meant I was really good and destined for great things (this word featured heavily in my end of school report!).

21

TOUGHEN UP!

Cubs featured in my youth too; I remember participating in the annual fancy dress competition in the last two years. In the penultimate year, the theme was 'Indians'. I already possessed a great costume, complete with headdress and plastic tomahawk, but lied about some embroidery that I suggested I'd sewn, when it was clearly a printed pattern. Akela clearly knew I was fibbing and the prize was awarded to the kid who made the most effort in his costume, no matter how poor it looked. Another valuable lesson: in competitions, work out the scoring system and understand what they really want to see.

I kept this in mind for the following year's competition, which was comedian-themed. I asked my parents to help by cobbling some curtain cast-offs that they'd used at some previous event, and rustled up a home-made Indian headdress with feathers from some roadkill in the street, together with elements from an old costume in the play box. Dad scratched his head and wondered how this badly-dressed Indian was going to pull off the guise of a comedian and said that I ought to write a sign to explain my character. He convinced me that *The Last of the Mohicans* was a sketch from *The Two Ronnies* or something similar, so I scribbled it out on cardboard and dashed off to the fancy dress party at the scout hut.

I was so proud, clutching first prize on the way home, and mum and dad were stunned that I'd won. I don't think Darren was too pleased, as he trudged belligerently home in his beautiful, hand-crafted satin clown outfit with full make-up; his mum was a very gifted seamstress and had clearly spent days making it. Another lesson: learn from your mistakes!

Steve and I were by now fully-fledged scrappers and I experienced my first déjà vu moment on the back seat of the family car. Two boys are generally like this sometimes: one would want to break the boredom by flicking the ears of the other and, in the inevitable escalation, there were tears, usually of frustration from mum, as she pleaded with us to be quiet whilst she drove.

One day, as would occasionally occur, mum parked up on the steep hill in Quarry Lane whilst she popped into the shop to get a loaf of bread. At the bottom of the hill was a T-junction to the A56, with hurtling juggernauts, coaches and other fast, noisy vehicles. Kids avoided the road like the plague, after all, being run over is not good for your long-term health. Well, after waiting for about eight seconds or so, Steve and I reached our boredom threshold and a full-blown scrap ensued, whilst mum was innocently shopping in the store. Legs, arms, bundling – all the normal stuff.

It was a few seconds later that we both froze in horror as the scenery started to move and we felt the car creeping down the road towards the mayhem of the main road. By then, I'd kind of learnt that the steering wheel steered the car and there was something called brakes to slow the car down. I must have leapt screaming into the front seat to give every button and pedal a wiggle, in the hope that the car would stop, but nothing seemed to work. Despite the hill, the car didn't gain any momentum, it just slowly crept down the road, torturingly towards the traffic. As you can imagine, Steve and I went into meltdown and, no matter what levers I pressed, the car didn't stop. By luck, a lady walked out of the shop with a paper under her arm, and was met with a scene of a car on its way down the hill at less than walking pace, accompanied by the sound of muffled death throes from two rather excited boys. I managed to wind down the window and asked if she could help stop the car, which was continuing to inch down the road, and by now had travelled about ten feet. She calmly got in and pulled the handbrake fully up. "Did one of you take the brake off?", she enquired. "We don't quite remember doing it, but we might have done when we were playing. Could you stay until our mum returns? She's in the shop," we pleaded.

Thankfully, the lady could see the distress we were in and remained the Good Samaritan for the next few minutes. Mum came out of the shop and, as she turned the corner she instinctively looked up the hill to where the car should have been. It hadn't occurred to her that the car was now ten feet away from her, down the hill. No harm done, but lesson learnt: the handbrake is the big lever next to the driver's seat. Mum always parked the car in gear after that and said that should be a lesson to us, but knew it probably wasn't going to be (it wasn't). The funny thing was, in the months leading up to that point, I'd had a recurring dream about being in the back of a car and rolling backwards, out of control. After the event, I was convinced I had magical powers, but sadly, I wasn't a superhero from another planet.

In raising two boys, my parents set us boundaries but understood that we also needed to develop individually, so gave us some headroom. We still used to scrap and fight, but generally behaved within our set parameters, so were allowed a bit of free rein. I knew a pair of twins, Paul and Chris, who lived on the other side of the village. They didn't appear to have so much leeway. Paul was very effeminate, enjoying skipping and playing with the girls at school (which didn't exactly make him Mr Popular with the boys) and Chris stuck up for him. They just stood out as having a very different upbringing to everyone else.

The first time I met them was before they started at Kelsall Primary School. It had snowed heavily overnight and, on the walk to school, Darren and I were making snowballs and pelting each other with them. We'd take turns: one would walk in front, whilst the other built three balls and tried to aim at the back or head. The snow was perfect - its consistency was sticky so it would leave a circle of snow on our coats and making more snowballs to re-arm took no time at all. Darren was about ten feet in front of me and had already gone down one of the side roads alongside the vicarage wall. I threw my three balls in quick succession, rapid fire, machine gun-style. Unfortunately for me, a wayward ball landed smack in the middle of a car's windscreen, as it was pulling out of the junction. It carried on and came to an abrupt stop next to me. I peered into the back seat and pondered what to do.

There sat the twins, looking really worried. Before I could scarper, their huge, angry dad had got out. He came bounding around the car towards me and literally pushed me off my feet into the hedgerow, as he yelled something about the risk of snowballs. "But it's soft snow and...," I stammered. But he was having none of it - he towered threateningly over me whilst I was prostrate on the floor and bellowed at me some more. I looked at the two boys in the back seat, whose heads had appeared at the window. One looked like he was wincing and the other boy rolled his eyes as if to say, "Here we go again." So I decided to stay put until this oaf had vented his frustration. After a minute, he got back in the car and drove off, with the boys sitting perfectly silent, bolt up-right in the back. Darren came back after they'd gone and dusted me down. One can only imagine what sort of upbringing the twins had been given. Frankly, I'd rather put up with a bit of grief from my kids and allow them to exercise some character-building stuff; there's no point killing the life force within them.

Unfortunately, I came across their dad again and, if it wasn't for a kind lady, I reckon he'd have inflicted some physical damage on me. Mrs Thomas was in her sixties and lived with her husband in what looked like a Swiss chalet in the trees, high in the village in Quarry Lane. She wrote for the village magazine and also found energy to invite kids to archaeological digs in the woods during the summer holidays. This was a great cover for litter-picking as we generally left a dirty, unloved corner of the village in pristine condition. The same regular crowd of village kids used to attend which included me and a few boys I knew from Old Coach Road.

That year, the twins, Paul and Chris, had joined us for our junior Christmas party. The boredom thing came about quite quickly that evening and, before long, us boys were up to no good, play-fighting and ear-flicking. I think Chris' brother Paul was overwhelmed by excitement and got stuck into the thick of it, like a dog that had been let off the leash. Chris said he didn't like to have his ears flicked, which to us was like declaring, "Flick my ears until they bleed!" Well, boys will be boys, and within minutes, I think we all made sure that his ears were well and truly red raw, just as ours were. Unfortunately, we'd taken it too far for Chris and he went running home in tears, which didn't make us or our host, Mrs Thomas, feel great.

About half an hour later, after Mrs Thomas phoned his home to check he'd made it back OK (which he had), then five minutes later her doorbell chimed. Chris' big, furious dad was outside with him, twitching with anger. "I've come to put things right!" he boomed. "Who was it, Chris?", his dad asked. Chris sheepishly pointed at me - *just me* - as he clung on behind his dad's leg. Chris chose not to point out his brother and the other two culprits, for some reason. Well, in a split second, there seemed to be a receding tide of kids leaving my side as his dad squared up over me. I gulped what I thought was my last breath.

Out of nowhere, the little, frail frame of Mrs Thomas stepped in front of the ogre, sensing the likelihood of infanticide. She diplomatically suggested that all the boys had been doing the same things to each other and that in fact, one individual wasn't to blame. I think I managed to keep my undies clean and began to breathe again. It didn't stop him having a full-blown, hundred decibel barking rant at me though. I decided to take one for the team, behind my human shield, and just shut my ears and stood there, stoically. I felt a prize twat that afternoon, but the memory served me well for future years. If you're a relatively big bloke, your size alone can be quite oppressive when you're around kids. It's probably why I try really hard to disarm any fear in kids by trying to be funnier than I am and often speak with a high-pitched, smiling voice. I over-compensate sometimes.

Mrs Thomas was a legend. She took me aside to apologise to Chris, which I did, and made sure that I was OK after being quite shaken up. She very generously gave me an ornament from her house that I'd earlier been talking to her husband about; an ornately-painted, small, wooden elephant from India. I relayed that my grandad was in India too, like them, and they seemed to like that. It sits in our kitchen at home as a reminder.

As I wind up memories of this village, I wanted to give the Rock Of Ages another mention. This was a natural sledging hill during the winter months. People within a fifteen-mile radius would flock to it for the day when it snowed. It had a very long, steep section and a natural upward hill on the other side of the field, which would bring the sledges to a natural stop just before the A56. I remember annual deep, lasting snowfall in the village. To enjoy this to its full potential, dad bought Steve and I a cracking sledge that seemed to be the best one around. At a squeeze, we could fit four kids on the long metal and wood bomber and religiously waxed the runners the night before. Kids would beg us for a go, so in return, we asked them to pull it up the hill for us: Kings of the Hill, at least while the snow lasted.

One day, I spotted some skiers at the foot of the hill. I'd never seen anybody skiing before and remember being impressed how they seemed to create graceful curves in the snow with no effort. Annoyingly though, this carved up our precious toboggan run. It was getting late in the day and the iced run was very cold so the going was fast. We decided to try and go faster than ever before, so to help with the aerodynamics, we lay on top of each other and somebody gave us an almighty push start from the top of the run. I was driving, which meant holding on to the rope for dear life and daring to stick out your wellied leg to turn. After the initial twenty metres, the sledge was zooming, so I looked down the hill to see what lay in our path. We'd gone past the point of braking and steering would be nigh on impossible.

To my horror, one of skiers abruptly stopped at the bottom of the dip, right in our trajectory. He had no idea we were hurtling towards him. I yelled at him to get out of the way as we started to descend the steepest point of the hill, as did the other kids who were piled on top of me. But by the time he turned and saw us, it was too late. I witnessed how cumbersome skis can be when you try to go uphill from a standing start and saw the skier instinctively curl his upper body into a ball, crouching ready for the impact. I closed my eyes and braced. BANG! We hit him hard at shin-height on his boots and luckily, he completely flew over us, thankfully missing the laughing sandwich of kids, as we continued on with high momentum up the opposite slope. As we looked back, all we saw was his purple, one-piece ski-suited body crumpled and twisted in the snow and two halves of skis clamped to his bindings. He was conscious, but very dazed. Before he gained full consciousness and started to stir further, we quickly checked out how he was; his friends said he'd be fine so we returned up the hill, and noted that an ambulance had arrived for the first time at Rock of Ages. We walked away unscathed, but sadly the sledge adopted a slow lean to the right from that day onwards, thanks to some irreparable damage to one of its runners.

In transition between junior and senior school, I wore different hats for two sets of friends in the village, the 'nice' ones and the 'right little herberts', as my parents used to call them. My sensible group of friends were sporty, clever and had kind, warm, engaging and welcoming parents. Outstanding in this camp were Rob's mum and dad. Rob was a lovely kid: we played footy, climbed trees and even played a round of golf once. He was the middle of three brothers and seemed to enjoy my company. His parents welcomed our friendship and I was frequently there for tea and play days. He accepted me for who I was and I often found him saying I didn't need to lie to impress him, like I did with my other group of friends. I was just very grateful to be liked and wanted to impress him, like he impressed me. We'd hook up with others sometimes; Andy lived down the road at the bottom of the village near the school, he was also the middle of three brothers. We'd often meet up and traipse around the countryside and play in the fields and dumps that surrounded the village.

The high school we all attended was Helsby High School, an old grammar school on the southern edge of the Mersey estuary, miles away from the village. I think Kelsall must have had a baby boom because it seemed like we were the second year of kids to be bussed there daily. The much closer secondary school in Tarporley must have been full up.

School bus journeys were a baptism of fire, just like they are for kids nowadays, and Helsby High was absolutely enormous in comparison to junior school. There were nine classes in my year, three classes in each stream; top, middle and bottom. Being 'mediocre', I was lobbed in the middle stream, though was quickly promoted to the top stream when end of year marks were reviewed. Kids were basically left to fend for themselves in extremely large playgrounds during the long lunch break. Most kids came from some comparatively tougher areas around Merseyside, like Helsby, Ellesmere Port and Runcorn. I'm sure there are nice parts, but in the main, compared to sleepy Kelsall, they were the equivalent of Toxteth. Bullying during long lunch breaks was rife; it was a dog-eat-dog world and, as one of the weediest 'woolly backs' (Liverpudlian slang for an unsophisticated person from the countryside), I got my fair share of attention.

I didn't go out looking for trouble and actively tried to avoid it, but on a couple of occasions, it came and found me. Once, our school year enjoyed the thrills of a headbutting craze. Despite the warnings from the teachers, all the boys seemed to be at it, or certainly aware of it: everybody seemed to be bearing bruised temples. I'd managed to duck this new form of entertainment for weeks, until twenty or so kids surrounded me and at the centre of the throng, with the reigning headbutt champ, Michael, who pressed me into a competition. I really didn't fancy it, not least because he was taller than me and very brash. But equally, I didn't want to show that I was a complete pushover and be labelled as one for the rest of my days. So, as he lent back, I closed my eyes, bowed my head and at the last moment, gave my nut the smallest of nudges forward. He'd obviously expected me to remain square on. His nose erupted in a burst of claret and tears. Suddenly I was the champion and the egging crowd knew it was up to me to choose the next victim (as the rules dictated, the winner stays on). I decided to abdicate my crown and passed honours to the nearest kid, who was delighted. Michael never bothered me again thereafter.

I remember once, a huge Sea King rescue helicopter flew into the massive playground for a talk or display at the school. Ten of us, in identical, navy-blue snorkel coats (if you're my age, you might remember these came with a furry trim on the hood and bright orange inlay), thought it would be fun to run into the wind created by its rotor blades. With our unzipped jackets held like a sail above our heads, we went running into the down blast and were thrown backwards ten feet in the air. We quickly hid our faces and blended into the crowd of a hundred or so identically-dressed kids, much to the disgust of the teachers who tried to catch us.

For me, there was always an undercurrent of boredom-induced violence present at school. Every now and then, idle kids would roam menacingly in packs, looking for a fight. I was pretty free with my mouth and this is what, no doubt, got me in trouble now and then. I often fabricated stories to try and maintain 'street cred' with the thugs - probably a survival tactic, as I was late in coming of age. Some of the bigger kids in the top stream used to dish out random abuse too and bullying was indiscriminate. I remember being physically sick after being kneed in the goolies out of the blue by a big chump called Adrian. He was karate-trained and twice the size of the kids he'd victimise, which included me. Andy used to fight back and said I ought to as well. But all I saw was Andy getting more attention from Adrian, the knucklehead. I decided the best strategy was to keep a low profile where I could.

It didn't stop with the pupils though. I once got off the school bus in the bus park and yelled "See yer," in a loud-mouthed-cum-yobbish *On The Buses* manner to our regular bus driver. He had a giggle with us kids, often allowing us to lean out of the open doors of the double-decker, holding onto the pole in the entrance as we zoomed around fast corners. I was obviously enjoying being a mischievous, cocky gobshite at that time of my youth. As I turned to face the mundane, half-mile walk to the form class and registration, I was met by two looming teachers. The large-suited, Deputy Head of year and a female teacher were both staring down at me in disgust. In the low morning sun, I didn't see a raised arm bearing towards me.

WHABBAM! As the Deputy Head's open hand crashed across my head in a downward arc, I went out like a light onto my back, the fall to the tarmac only broken by my rucksack. The next thing I remember was the look of curious kids walking past and peering at me, whilst the female teacher tried to rouse me as I groaned. The Deputy Head moved the kids along: "Nothing to see here, move along, get to your classes." He was certainly one teacher you didn't mess with.

Bizarrely, I missed out on a lot of lessons when I moved up a stream. Given the large amount of children in the year, woodwork, metalwork and technical drawing classes were rotated between streams and I missed out on a whole term of metalwork and never once went to a technical drawing class. Shame, because it all looked pretty interesting. No-one seemed to care when I got 19% in a metalwork exam. Instead, I was flung into the second year of the top stream's Latin lessons, a year behind everyone else. The teacher suggested that I simply 'catch up', but it was all Greek to me, and I didn't see the point of the language anyway. So I offered to sit outside the class on a chair doing homework, which she agreed to - priceless.

Given that I was one of the youngest in the year, I carried a slight frame and wasn't expected to make any grade in sports. I surprised myself, and the whole rugby squad, when I decided to give it a go one lesson. I ran around like a madman and tackled whoever I knew. The teacher was blown away! He'd seen my shivering, dejected frame on the wing, week after week, and couldn't believe I was the same kid. As a result, I was picked for the school team the following week. Unfortunately, I hadn't a clue about the positions in the game, so when I found myself again on the wing and received the ball with the opposition closing in, I kicked it forward in the hope that our side would regain it. I didn't know that you had to run as fast as the wind. The teacher asked why I'd kicked and I mumbled something about territory, but that was the end of my school rugby days.

PE on the whole was OK, but again, looking back, the teachers could be pretty vicious if they wanted to. 'Zoneball' was the game we played in the gymnasium when the weather outside was too inclement. It was always teachers vs. boys (dressed in shorts only, so the balls would sting). There were three zones in the gym hall: the one in the middle remained empty, and there would be half a dozen plastic footballs thrown at high velocity by the teachers at the ducking, swirling mass of excited boys. If you got hit directly, or indirectly on a rebound, you were out and had to climb the monkey bars which flanked the two long sides of the hall, to cheer on the remaining boys. This brought out a competitive spirit in many of us and we were determined to beat the teachers, which never seemed to happen. However, one day, I found myself being the remaining boy and beat the teachers - the hall erupted with joy. The teachers asked me to stay behind with chump-cum-bullyboy, Adrian. They hooked the end of a long, wooden bench around some horizontal monkey bars and bench pressed it from their shoulders a couple of times. They then invited Adrian to do the same; to be fair, he struggled, but he managed to complete the task once. Then it was my turn. For all my grunting and effort, it didn't leave my shoulder. Not a word was spoken - it didn't need to be said. Their post-defeat ritual humiliation had been dished out and the PE teachers' egos had been restored. From that day, I didn't attempt any further sport whilst in education. Inspirational stuff being taught by poor losers.

At Helsby, I seemed to scrape by academically, but invariably achieved low grades at most subjects. I felt inadequate compared to the brain boxes of the top set, who seemed light years ahead of me. Rather than working harder, I gave up. Perhaps it wasn't the most inspiring of places, but equally, I was probably a lazy so-and-so, and was happy to hide my failures in the long grass.

22

LET THERE BE ROCK

In the start of my adolescence, I enjoyed the other set of friends in Kelsall. These were not the sensible, 'nice', sporty ones, but the tearaways, 'the little herberts'. Our meeting point once a week was the village youth club. I'd known these guys since primary school so didn't feel intimidated by them. To be honest, I loved the sense of mischief and excitement that ran through our veins when we got together, easily pleased.

Looking back, none of my other sensible friends ever went along to youth club; they had homework and perhaps their parents kept them on a tighter leash (or they were just disinterested).

Anyhow, at the youth club, we milled about with some older teenagers who we hero-worshiped. These guys were the equivalent of the local *Wild Ones*, the disaffected biker youth from the surrounding villages, who'd posse together on youth club night and descend on the village hall too. They rode the big, fast motorcycles of the day, dressed in denim and leather. Their evening's entertainment consisted of comparing bikes, girlfriends and head-banging to the throbbing music that was played by the DJ.

Some of these rockers had younger brothers in our ranks, which became our supply route to contraband. The collective bunch of snotty kids, that I was part of, idolised those guys. Hell, they seemed to possess bucketloads of attitude, swagger and independence that we could only dream of. After all, a number of our gang were still picked up from youth club by their parents!

The *Wild Ones* would drink beer on the sly, whilst smoking, and this became a benchmark that we aspired to. They started to supply us with fags and we bought shandy from the tuck shop. They didn't mind us darting in and out of their path and actually, a few of the older girls and younger bikers kind of adopted us for the Tuesday night. When the right music started to play, we'd unleash hell on the dance floor with our smouldering, pre-pubescent dance moves in front of the disco amps. We'd swear allegiance to the cause by sporting rock band patches on denim jackets and learnt to head-bang, play the air guitar and imitate other greebo dances, whilst being blasted by AC/DC, Motörhead, Rainbow and Status Quo, which broke up the monotony of 'Stars on 45' which was played on a loop. We must have looked hilarious with our bowl haircuts, but we were deadly serious thirteen-year olds.

Before long, on non-youth club nights, we'd wander aimlessly through the village with attitude, in our replica rocker uniforms. We didn't have a clue what we wanted, where we were going, or how we were going to get there and back before teatime. But we were bound together by bravado and a sense of comradeship, something like a band of medium-sized (and small) brothers.

Some of us started to collect a few records too. The music rubbed off on us and we went beyond being just plastic rockers. We genuinely got into the whole rock scene. Each of us would adopt a main band that we liked and tried to expand our record collection of that artist as best we could, within our pocket money limitations. When I say records - in my case - I meant tape cassettes. My dad had convinced me that vinyl wasn't as good as cassettes because of the scratches: clearly the wrong advice and, looking back, I regret this, but nevertheless, I was in business. I also procured two Pink Floyd albums that dad had hidden amongst his Abba collection - *The Wall* and *Dark Side of the Moon*. Absolute classics.

I remember being too shy to go into a record store at first, so I asked mum to help and, on a shopping trip to Chester, she purchased my first rock albums. Wow, I really was an early tearaway! Mum and the shop assistant came up trumps and I got what I asked for, eventually. AC/DC's *If you Want Blood*, an awesome live album, with some early years classics, and Motörhead's *No Sleep til Hammersmith* - another legendary live affair containing most of their early masterpieces. I also bought *Axe Attack*, a compilation album containing a dozen or so studio songs from other famous rock bands. I was the only muppet with cassettes, so I couldn't do swapsies with my mates, but undeterred, I started to grow my AC/DC collection. As far as I'm concerned, I'd hit the jackpot - the music was great and the music was loud.

Following the death of Bon Scott in 1980, AC/DC seemed to gain some mainstream notoriety with their new frontman, Brian Johnston. Some of their singles even made it on *Tiswas* and *Top of the Pops*. I loved *Tiswas*: it was a relatively wilder Saturday morning children's TV programme on ITV – *SwapShop* with Noel Edmonds seemed so boring and staged, in comparison. A lot of other rock groups like Motörhead and Status Quo were on *Tiswas* too. Clearly, there was a rock lover in the tent there and, like many adolescent boys, I remember Sally James in her infamous denim waistcoat.

It wasn't an extensive album collection, but it had enough depth to cover a spectrum of different rock genres. I took to the music as it provided a form of escape and fantasy, a glimpse of adult stories on life, rock, bikes, girls and all things that were hitherto out of reach. It's stayed with me to this day! I have a passion for an authentic core energy in music that can be a welcome release from the grinding reality of life or just make it more pleasurable. Clearly my musical palate has matured, deepened and widened with age, and my ears have now opened to other genres of music, but if you were ever to look at my top 100 playlist, it would contain far more rock tracks than anything else, much to the disappointment of my wife and kids.

This inevitably all rubbed off on Steve, who had to endure my din, thumping through the walls. We'd spend a little bit of time talking about music. At this point in time, music was pretty polarised beyond the edges of the mundane, banal, television-friendly 'pop' drivel. Punk was dying out, the new mod scene was emerging with ska, new romantics were in start-up mode, yet rock has endured and has always carried a loyal fan base.

Watching the new romantics filled us with a resolve to not succumb to spandex and hairspray (that came later with Bon Jovi and the hair rock days). *Top of The Pops* (and *The Young Ones*) were the staple diet of teenagers of the day. Crikey, we only had four channels on TV, and there was very little musical content, when compared to the endless universe you now find on other platforms. I wonder if there's a correlation between how music is treated by its fans nowadays and its availability across countless media channels? In the early nineties, music seemed to be nothing short of a nostalgic religion to the youth, whilst nowadays, it's seen as more of a disposable commodity.

Watching the rise of the new romantics on *Top of the Pops* in the early 1980's at our house was hilarious. A shiny, shoulder-padded drip of a bloke would sulk and moan into the camera and dad, Steve and I used to pass comment:

" Who the bloody hell does he think he is, someone's fairy godmother?"

" Christ alive, they've dug someone up from the eighteenth century and they're putting make-up on blokes nowadays."

" Is it singing of whining? Are they actual instruments or do they simply just press a button on their synthesisers and sit back?"

Despite all of our ranting disapproval, Canute's tide of cringeworthy New Romanticism could not be repelled, but now and then you'd get a gem on the telly. During the late seventies, the New Wave of British Heavy Metal was born from the ashes of punk, a reaction to the over-synthesised, exploratory prog rock as much as a response to the march of the new romantics and the boring shades of beige that filled our airwaves. In the early 1980's it gained much momentum and drove an upsurge in its fanbase, including yours truly.

We loved to witness a group growing in popularity in front of our eyes. Iron Maiden were brimming with electricity and a number of singles from their *Number of The Beast* album seemed to be over far too quickly when they played on *Top of the Pops*. Bruce Dickinson, their front man, blasted out vocals like an air raid siren, powerfully bellowing out song after song, whilst he and Steve Harris wrestled for position on his thumping bass line. Two lead guitarists would alternate rhythm with each other, in front of a drummer who kept an up-tempo beat. Everything was done with pace and power; it was fast for its time and pleasing to see their chart success. There was some representation on the radio - you had to forego a Friday night out and tune into Tommy Vance's *Rock Show*. Despite little early mainstream radio support, single after single would climb the charts and often sit at Number One for weeks. This was an endorsement to a movement of people out there, prepared to spend hard-earned pocket and paper round money on their heroes. To many, including me, rock music was a liberating, anti-establishment gift which said to the wall of mundanity, "Don't expect everyone to take the spoon-fed, musical drivel churned out on most airwaves - kids want more."

Steve decided he'd crack on and find his own band for him and his mates, something different and equally rocky. They got deeply into Kiss, which is an American glam rock band, famous for their make-up. Steve was Gene, Tim was Paul and Duncan was Peter. They used to apply face make-up to emulate their chosen band member and stick their tongues out, to the disgust of wagging tongues of nan's WI spies in the village.

Steve was a bit of a pack leader - always has been - so he and his close mates, Tim and Duncan, seemed to always get into trouble collectively. Once Tim's dad came over to relay that he'd found 'enough booze to kill a cow' stashed in their den: they'd been syphoning it from their parents' drinks cabinets for weeks. They were all grounded for a fortnight, then, on release from Alcatraz, they quickly re-stocked and found a better hideout.

One of the unsolved mysteries of 17, Old Coach Road started on a hot summer's day during the school holidays. This is a fable that still lives on to this day and is now being debated by the next generation of our family: *The Case of the Broken Utility Room Window*.

In short, the question is, who smashed the window? Little old me, or Steve and his mates? In my defence, Your Honour, I found the window smashed, after hearing a commotion, thinking that Steve and his mates had been re-enacting a Kiss concert in the utility room. I went looking for Steve and, out of the corner of my eye, I just happened to glance down the driveway to see the Turbo Trio making a quick getaway on their push bikes, tout de suite, in a familiar 'let's get the focaccia' fashion. Their individual defences were consistent, I'll give them that. It hinged on the known fact that "John was in all day, so it must have been him and he's pinning it on us, we never touched it …honest." Steve still swears blind to this day that they didn't break the window. One day he might let the truth emerge...remember the elephant.

Anyway, back to my wayward conduct at the youth club. Dad had got wind of my Tuesday nights of debauchery, as I'd always come home stinking of fags and booze, covered in sweat. Being a concerned parent, he volunteered as an adult helper at the youth club, for no other reason than to keep an eye on me. I protested as it was going to be profoundly embarrassing, but to no avail. I was snookered. If I had nothing to hide, I had nothing to worry about. The trouble for dad was that, in the dark, gloomy dance hall, he couldn't see anything, including me - hiding under the tables with the others, downing shandies, blowing bubblegum, smoking and sniggering as the biker teenagers groped and snogged their groupie girls all around us.

In other mid-week outings with the gang, we'd get up to nothing much more than smoking, hanging around shops or playing pranks on people. This might involve lining up on the steel footbridge that crossed the busy A56 and pulling moonies to lorries, who'd in turn blow their air horns. All innocent stuff really.

There was one occasion though, when things seemed to escalate and got a tad out of hand. Just down from the Rock of Ages, which was as far north in the village as you could go, there was a village pub. This historic, white-washed building had a huge car park at the back and put on an annual bonfire night for its customers. After the usual firework display, hot dogs and sausage rolls, when it started to get a bit nippy, the adults would go back inside, to the cosy fire and warm beer.

A gaggle of us decided to meet up at the pub to watch the fireworks, on the rumour that one of us was going to throw an aerosol on the embers for a laugh. We waited eagerly in anticipation as the adults peeled off back into the pub in dribs and drabs. Then we were alone with the burning embers of the fire. It resembled a roasting cauldron where you could feel your eyebrows singe from two metres away: perfectly positioned for Jonathon to place his aerosol can on, which he did. We hid in the car park behind cars and assorted stands where mulled wine and toffee apples had been dished out earlier. After about three minutes, the can started to expand loudly with the pressure and finally, there was a half decent Bang, Phut! Up it flew, three feet in the air. Was that it? We'd frozen our nuts off for that? It was then that someone had a groovy idea to up the ante.

The serving tables, now empty, had been assembled in haste by the pub staff. Some of these consisted of old, sealed oil drums with remnants of god-knows-what liquid swishing around in the bottom. Across these oil drums lay a few planks of wood to construct the makeshift surface. The drums were a fascinating proposition to put on the fire and it didn't take long before one was rolled into the pulsating embers of the fire. This clearly was going to be a little more dangerous, so it was decided that we'd take a bit more care in selecting cover, further away. We guessed that any explosion's trajectory would be upwards, so we lay flat, like plastic commando soldiers, behind logs where people had been sitting. Then it started.

Bong......bing...pip, pop, bong, pip, clunk. The material inside was being super-heated and the sealed drum was expanding quickly, the pressure building every second. At this point, I think a few of us (including me) realised that there was no going back and wished we hadn't been so reckless. But there was nothing for it now - we had to lie still, under cover, before the inevitable occurred. A few inquisitive heads peeked above and behind cover (including mine) of the hedgerow and cars parked well away from the fire, and then it happened.

There was one mighty, cataclysmic explosion of fire and metal: it didn't just go bang, the whole spewing barrel of flames seemed to lift out of the fire like a phoenix and with a colossal bang it split in mid-air. The main chunk flew into the next (empty) field, outside of the car park. The remaining fraction came back to rest in the embers and was camouflaged by various lumps of wood. It was an *A-Team* explosion in real life! To be honest, we couldn't believe what we had done and called out amongst ourselves to check that everyone was alright. Thank god, all present and correct.

♪ Burn (Deep Purple) ♪

This is the title track from this album - not the classic line-up, but still damn good. This fast-paced number featured two vocalists. I never figured out why Coverdale needed vocal cover, he's always packed a purring and growling voice, like a black panther. Jon Lord's organ is immense on this piece (!) as is the drumming. The song paints the picture in my mind of mischievous rioting, people being fuelled by the dirty deeds of others, with a raging fire in the middle.

At this point, we all fell silent. The fire and site didn't really show any scars of the explosion, but it was so loud that the inquisitive drinkers in the pub quickly emptied into the car park to find out who had ignited the mother of all bangers. We sat hidden, in the hedgerows, behind cars, full of an urge to punch the air and regale the story. Thankfully, before long, the drinkers went mumbling back into the pub, shrugging their shoulders.

High fives all round! A great sense of awe and relief, but a slowing realisation that we were lucky to live another day. Steve was up at firework night earlier that evening, but he left before all of the high jinx. He remembers hearing the explosion half a mile away when he was trudging home with a mate. I made my excuses there and then and walked home in a stupor of relief and excitement, leaving the rest of the groovy gang toying with the idea of loading another barrel on the fire. I don't think that anything else was discussed on the school bus for weeks - we had gained a certain type of reputation.

Looking back, I'm amazed how carefree, wasteful and blasé I was during my adolescence. The polar opposite to me now: the middle-aged, risk-averse, protective parent.

Unsurprisingly, my own parents' alarm bells began to chime and they paid a little more attention to some of the company I kept. Given the shock of the sights my father encountered down at the youth club, and a few unsubstantiated rumours of our gang's scrapes fed in from the W.I spy network, my parents clearly had an inkling that their eldest son was going a tad off the rails. My days with the 'right little herberts' - now affectionately called the 'rough-lot' - were numbered and I was told to re-acquaint myself with the other, far more sensible, set of 'nice' friends. Looking back, I resented my parent's intervention. I hadn't ignored my other friends at all, as I'd seen them on and off too, I just didn't like the arbitrary nature of my parents' command.

The rough lot didn't appreciate my growing absence either. I was rounded on by my old gang when I was playing football one Sunday morning. They were all clearly out to let it be known that no-one leaves without 'getting it'. I took the medicine and blurted out something along the lines of, "We can all be friends still." After all, we'd known each other since we were knee-high. But they didn't forgive me for leaving the clan - I was now an outsider.

All in all, despite my protests at the time, I reckon my parents stepped in at the right time. Six months later, it mattered not. We were moving again with dad's job. The delicate nature of 'boom and bust' UK economics came into play and I think *Rubery Owen* either laid him off or it folded. We would be off to Southern Poofterland within three months, somewhere called Newbury, so I'd have to leave the whole lot of them behind! My parents defaulted to the usual MO. Mum went into sell-pack-move mode and dad became the advance worker and house hunter.

I left with a warm feeling for Kelsall, but in antithesis to Steve, I couldn't wait to start afresh at a new school and make some new friends.

23

MOVE DOWN'T SOUTH

Whilst starting his new job, dad stayed at *The Enbourne Grange*, a hotel in Wash Common, just south of Newbury, which no longer exists. He quickly befriended the regular clientele, the likes of which included Bob Allison, an officer in the US Air Force who had just been posted to the Greenham Common airbase. We stayed there when we visited the area to see the new house we were moving to, and got to know the hotel owners. The Spencers were well-known in Newbury and their son Dudley was very welcoming to me and Steve. He said that most southern kids our age were into the New Romantic scene, as it attracted the girls. I certainly don't remember anybody declaring they were a New Romantic from Kelsall. They wouldn't last a day.

Clearly, this wasn't going to wash with me, but at the same time I liked the idea of attracting girls. I noted that, despite our different taste in music and fashion, Dudley and I shared similar mullet-styled haircuts, so perhaps I could slip in unnoticed at school? It wasn't until much later in life that I discovered Dudley was well-known to my wife, and the Spencers to Jane's family too, as they lived around the corner. He was known as a bit of a stud in Jane's year at school and was friends with Jane at that precise moment in time. Small world!

Mullet in all its glory   Mullet retained some years later

I think my parents found socialising in the south very different. In the north, strangers seemed to say hello and chat openly, but in the south, people seemed less approachable or disinterested if they didn't know you. It was a subtle difference. We kept in touch with the hotel and once went to a New Year's Eve party there. All of the kids, who ranged from six years old to late teens, were set up with a film. A lovely, gentle classic from Hollywood that most people would remember if they had watched it. As the opening titles ran and the film started, I remember an American pilot left the room and said, "Yep, based on a true story this, real classic." We were then fully plugged in to its authenticity; we hadn't a clue as to what was about to hit us, like lambs to the slaughter. I don't think I blinked or breathed once during *The Exorcist*.

When we got back home, Steve couldn't sleep alone, so came in to my bedroom. I remember at one point, his legs started to involuntarily jolt with shock under the covers and I played Jimi Hendrix on mum's ghetto blaster to take our mind off things. We probably got three hours' sleep that night and Steve kept a bible and crucifix by his bed for six months! The film remains one of my favourites, in terms of impact, but I wouldn't recommend it to children.

Living near the Greenham Common airbase was a little different. I loved aircraft and went to the last amazing Air Tattoo there, in 1983 I think. We got let in by Bob, who was waiting for us at a pre-arranged gate and were shown around the backstage areas and displays. It was great to see so many war-planes up close, behind the scenes and watch them take off. I think the loudest by far was the RAF Lightning, which was absolutely deafening as it hurtled down the runway and climbed into the sky.

In the early eighties, the Cold War heightened. Despite its obvious risks, we took some comfort, being in close proximity to the American airbase. At least we'd get to see an excellent firework display if the ICBMs ever took off and we'd be completely vaporised within seconds, thus missing out on a grim, post-apocalyptic world, as Greenham Common was surely on Russia's hit list. I remember the peace campers who took residence around the base too. In my late teens, I had a week's job experience at Newbury police station and, as part of one day's patrol, we navigated the airbase's perimeter fence. The constable who took us on his panda car beat told me and my friend Perrier (you'll meet him in a while) to sit back and enjoy the view, as the ladies of the camp were bound to put on a special show for us. Sure enough, after we pulled up kerbside at one of their backwater, tatty camps, the ladies clocked that the law was about, assembled en masse and proceeded to snog and grope each other in front of us. "Something memorable from your work experience, lads." Nowadays, not a big issue, but back in the late eighties, homosexuality was very discreet. This was a love-in protest by the peace campers, and they knew full well that they wouldn't be pulled up for it.

♪ Killer of Giants (Ozzy Osbourne) ♪

The Ultimate Sin album, released in 1986, seemed to come at the height of my consciousness about the Cold War. I wasn't even a twinkle in the old man's eye when the world faced the Cuban Crisis. TV was full of post-apocalyptic programmes and this track's a classic for me: a soft acoustic opening, building up to a strong chorus and then a guitar solo ripping it up to the end. "Mountains of madness" - the futile stockpiling of nuclear arms where nations can obliterate each other multiple times over. If you were an alien looking down at mankind, you'd wonder why a species is so hellbent on destroying itself so many times over.

The new house was in a modern estate in Woolton Hill: a peaceful, two pub (at the time), two shop (at the time) village, just south of Newbury. It was different, quiet and small, compared to Kelsall, but had some charm about it. It was dominated by the Gainsborough Stud, one of the breeding stables for a sheikh of the Emirates. Not knowing what to expect, we plodded off to catch the school bus on our first day. My Ian Botham curls waved in the wind and I was conscious that I might sound a little different with my near-Scouse accent. Do you think I stuck out like a sore thumb in an easy-going, leafy school comprehensive, The Clere School, set in deep Hampshire countryside? You bet I did!

The school took one look at me and asked a sensible lad, Mark (who I nicknamed Perrier), to look after me for the first week or so, for my own protection. We instantly hit it off and I knew I'd made a life-long friend, there and then. Perrier had the gift of the gab; he was very presentable to the adults, but actually loved having a laugh. In fact, we had a scream and got into a few scrapes of our own. He was well-liked by my family and his family were welcoming, not just to me, but to my parents too. Mike and Anne were members of the local Round table and Ladies Circle, so tried to help my parents integrate. Perrier and I have renewed contact once more, thanks to the abundance of time that cancer has gifted me. He stuck fast to his love of design and now runs a successful wood furniture design business, *Plank Design*.

Another friend I instantly made at school was Chris, the same chap you read about in the cancer story who helped us out with Max's football and shopping, over 35 years later. He had always had a good work ethic and earned money whilst at school from various gardening jobs dotted around the village. To be honest, I was a lazy toad when it came to any sort of manual work, but eventually decided I needed to earn a little crust for myself. Chris rubbed off on me at an early age in that regard.

He helped by passing a gardening referral to me, but this didn't work out as I had no idea what I was doing. All I seemed to do was shuffle my spade in the dirt and make a mess. I was soon creosoting a very long fence in the blistering sunshine one summer holiday. The trouble was, I hadn't a clue when it came to Health and Safety, and burnt my arms with the wood stainer during the week. The client came to our house to check if I was alright and was horrified when I showed her my injuries. In hindsight, I was seeing the early signs of being a DIY disaster.

Back at the Clere School, it wasn't long before I was on the radar of some hard men. One of those was Tim, a real force of nature. He was a fully-developed, barrel-chested adult in school clothes who would dwarf some teachers. Bizarrely, he established a friendship with me and was good company; he shared some of my interests in music and introduced me to some of the roots of the rock genre, especially Jimi Hendrix. He seemed to look out for me and my younger brother in the early months and, in return, we fed him Fray Bentos pies at home when he visited on school nights. Tim too was well-liked by all at my home. He spoke on the same level with my parents, which frustrated the hell out of me because I couldn't seem to communicate with them at all. The pressures of being a surly, miserable git of a teenager, I suppose.

Tim lived in the local children's home in the village, though I never asked why he found himself there; he seemed very sensitive about it and I didn't want to risk spoiling the growing friendship. The home seemed pleasant enough - everyone stayed out of Tim's way when we walked around the corridors and, after gaining his trust, he led me to areas in the gardens to show me how mixed-up kids sometimes vented their frustration.

Littered amongst the rhododendron bushes, out of sight, were plastic bags with solvent or glue stuck to the bottom. I was so naive and couldn't work out why so many kids felt they needed to do this. Tim and I chatted it through. I was too young to appreciate the difference in our upbringings and hadn't realised how lucky I was, despite thinking I had the worst parents around. Once, Tim took me to a drinking den where some of the kids 'obtained' a barrel of ale from the back of a pub and rolled it down the hill into the undergrowth. It had been there for a few weeks and tasted foul as it had clearly gone off, so I wisely spat it out. The other kids continued to drink it for a further week or so after that - stomachs of steel! Whilst writing this book, I also reconnected with Tim. He found his biological mum ten years ago and now has contact with his siblings too; he's still searching for his dad.

Drugs, well - recreational ones at least - have never really featured in my life. I've experimented in a number of mild class B drugs but they did very little for me, even after inhaling. Instead, I concentrated my teenage addictions on wildly available cigarettes and alcohol.

♪ Cigarettes & Alcohol (Oasis) ♪

This BritPop band might not be everyone's cup of tea in the purest sense of rock, but the song's got loose attitude and sums up a lot of youthful frustration. I loved it then and still do now.

My wildest night on alcohol around this time was an exploratory solo effort which earned me a day off school and a week-end hangover. I was left 'babysitting' Steve one Thursday night, a phrase he detested, however I was left in charge of the house when my parents went out. This gave me free access to a well-stocked drinks cabinet, which grabbed my attention. Curiosity got the better of me and I wondered what cocktails I could muster up with the brightly-coloured liquors that adorned the shelves. My parents had always returned from holidays abroad with different-shaped bottles, full of strangely-coloured concoctions, including a wide array of flavoured brandies. I couldn't find a cocktail shaker that most barmen worth their salt would use, so I concluded that all I needed to do was drink them individually, as they'd mix in my stomach.

Moderation (or sensibility) wasn't a word I understood back then, so I started to pour third pints of each bottle down my neck. Fast forward an hour or so, and Steve found me comatose at the foot of the stairs, and our roles quickly reversed. I think he phoned my parents at the party they'd gone to and they came back to take over nursing duties. *The Exorcist* had a memorable, projectile-vomiting scene and this clearly motivated me to give it a go. I couldn't smell brandy without my stomach churning for decades afterwards.

One sunny afternoon after school, I was walking down a road with Bruce, another local mate of mine from school. We were probably debating the latest Iron Maiden album, as he was another rock fan too. I gravitated to him to compare albums and tracks, as I'd done with other friends in Kelsall. Bruce lived around the corner and had a chirpy, loud disposition which I loved. He had the voice of a foghorn and a legendary party trick: he was famous for stuffing three Mars bars in his mouth sideways, an awesome life skill if ever there was one. No wonder his workmates affectionately nicknamed him 'Zippy'. I'm in touch with Bruce once more now and he's still hilarious.

Whilst walking, Bruce and I spotted a squirrel at the side of the road and sadly, its back legs didn't work. It had probably been hit by a car or had fallen from one of the large oak trees that swayed overhead. We were genuinely gutted for the poor creature and wanted to help it. We decided to scoop it up, take it to his house, pop it in a box and convince his mum to take it to a vet, so Bruce picked it up. Well, Mr Squirrel didn't understand that we had heart-felt, kind intentions and promptly locked its jaw onto the end of Bruce's index finger.

The intense pain was clear to see; Bruce's face turned red and I watched in awe as he danced about, screaming blue murder. It was like watching a gymnastic floor display as Bruce ran up and down the road with his fully-locked arm doing windmill movements, as the squirrel's tail swooshed gracefully like a ribbon. Thankfully, the rodent released its grip mid arc and flew safely into the vegetation. Bruce ran home screaming in shock to get patched up and left me on guard over the animal, wondering what to do. He returned within ten minutes with a bandaged hand. He said his mum wasn't prepared to take it to a vet so we decided that the only humane thing we could do was to put the poor thing out of its misery. Neither of us had the heart to do this, but who should come yomping down the road on the way to the shops, but Tim. We relayed the story to him and after agreeing with our plan, in a flash, he did the deed with a large log. The rodent was sent merrily on his way to acorn heaven. It was for the best.

Before long, I was happily and deeply embedded within the Clere School. I was probably a curiosity to most of my friends and maybe the teachers too, who I noted were far less 'hands-on' than at Helsby. Their approach was, 'If you don't do the work, you're going to fail and that's your problem.' Leaving little in the way of me having an uninterrupted easy time. I relaxed further and breezed along, doing little beyond the bare minimum amount of work to stay out of trouble. I certainly don't see myself as one of the bright ones, rather, I had a fair bit left in the tank which was never ignited. I was capable of much more than I achieved and comments like 'could have tried harder' littered my school reports. My parents genuinely tried to make me study, but I kicked back and moodily resented further paternal intervention. In simple terms, I still hadn't grown up by the time I sat my final exams and my weak results reflected this.

Whilst I didn't apply myself to school work, I found a steady week-end job in the last couple of years at Clere School. I got a summer holiday job initially by literally cycling around lots of small businesses within a mile radius and knocking on doors. One of those was *Bally's Garage* in Ball Hill. The garage had one workshop, an MOT bay, one petrol pump and a cabin.

It was a small and local affair, but was clearly busy with work. I remember speaking with the owner, and was honest about my lack of any mechanical experience, and maybe he thought it would be good to have an extra pair of hands about, sweeping up, clearing mess and handing tools over. Perhaps he thought I might take to it and become an apprentice. I got used to handling the air tools, helped with some heavy lifting, filled petrol, fetched doughnuts from the local bakery up the road and read the garage's back catalogue of *Razzle* - every fifteen-year old boy's dream. I was nicknamed 'Junior' and fitted in. I knew my place.

I managed to negotiate a monstrous weekly salary of £18 during the holidays, but the real money was earned with Saturday morning MOTs. Ray, the chief mechanic, would do all the hard stuff, inspecting and checking, whilst I sat in the driver's seat playing with the instruments when instructed. Horn, brakes, steering: all very technical. I got to know Ray well; he literally lived opposite the garage with his parents and had joined the garage since leaving school, ten years or so before me. Around the back of the garage was a car body repair shop and that's where I first met Ron. Ron and Ray were good to me and we later became friends again, when we met up to help Ron with his ballooning business. More on this later.

Back at school, I slunk into some re-takes and A-levels at sixth form college - St Bartholomew's in Newbury - and envied friends who'd chosen to get a job and earn some hard cash. Thankfully, I wasn't the only minimalist worker in our year and met some more kindred spirits at St Barts. Perrier came away from Clere School with a handful of grades like me; we were brothers in arms.

At St Barts, to mix it up a bit, I joined the Combined Cadet Force and spent time in the RAF section there. I always fancied being a pilot, but knew that I couldn't join up because of my colour blindness. Shame really, as my uncle and cousin were both Harrier squadron leaders in their time. As a sixth former, I was soon a low-ranked officer and we took charge of about twenty younger kids in lower years. I enjoyed marching around the countryside, map reading, and the Friday afternoon away from class. But the best experience by far was my introduction to flying.

We were all packed into a bus in the morning and sent to an airfield near Abingdon in Oxfordshire, where we were met by our flying instructors. These were all very experienced RAF pilots and trainers. The students all took turns to fly in the aircraft, one-to-one with an instructor. There were half a dozen Chipmunks at the airfield. These aircraft were the mono-winged, single propeller, two-seater, safe, reliable plodding learner vehicles of the skies. Throughout school, given my surname began with a 'W,' I'd become accustomed to being one of the last names read out on any list or register, and this day was no exception. I witnessed lots of the younger kids coming back from their flights, some looked decidedly sick (some had *been* sick), but most were full of buzz about their flight, how they'd steered left then right, up then down - it was one hell of a memory for them.

Soon enough, it was my turn and the instructor introduced himself. "First flight, is it?". I confirmed that it was and said that I'd be happy for him to simply fly me about. By then, I'd become a little nervous, as everything in the old, glass-domed cockpit seemed to rattle and looked like it might have been used in the First World War. The instructor was having none of it. He was also in a 'Gung-ho, let's put the frighteners up him' kind of mood. Mine was one of the last flights, and he'd taken up several younger kids that day with hardly any excitement, so he wanted to liven it up a bit. "You're up for that, aren't you?". Well, I could hardly say no, could I?

So after take-off, we climbed to a decent altitude and performed some acrobatics. He explained every manoeuvre before he executed them, just so I knew why it felt like my arse and stomach were coming through my mouth at times. We did an inside loop-the-loop, an outside loop-the-loop and a barrel roll – stunts that every schoolboy dreams of when thinking of Spitfires. It was staggering! I couldn't escape and during the second trick, I began to really enjoy it. I recognised that I was in very experienced hands and logically thought it through: he's done it a thousand times and the statistics of plummeting to the ground must be negligible. Instead of looking at the inside of the cockpit, I began to look into the turns and through the clouds and lived in the moment. The huge, blue sky was enormous and I was astounded to see the horizon appear and disappear with such regularity. Everything began to feel ever so smooth too; when the speed increased, things stopped rattling. To top it all, the instructor turned the engine off and glided the plane in to land. He said, "We need to do this once in a while to show that we don't drop out of the sky - it's usually OK."

I couldn't stop beaming when we landed. I thanked him enormously and his face lit up when he saw that I'd had such a great time. "Nice flight?", his NCO asked, passing him on the tarmac. "Ah, you know, pointed it left, then right - lovely weather, though." What a naughty cad!

Another friend I made at Clere School and who also went to St Barts, was Johnny. He lived in Woolton Hill and I got to know him whilst his parents were going through an acrimonious separation. His mum was left at home during the week, looking after Johnny and his younger brother Richard, whilst his dad visited less frequently. She was a lovely lady and well-liked by all of us, but was clearly hurt by all the pain of the separation. She could see that her kids were disturbed by it too so was happy for friends to visit the boys whilst she went out.

Johnny's house became a meeting place for several teenagers every night. Most of us would sport the obligatory denim or leather jackets, with our long hair, and just doss about, race around and have a laugh. We hilariously named ourselves the *Woolton Hill Well Hards* (WHWH), knowing full well that, in truth, we couldn't punch our way out of a paper bag! It was more a case of herd mentality - protection in numbers. I rediscovered a love of painting, and dutifully adorned some of our jackets with colourful works of art. My own became a masterpiece, with pictures of dead rock stars, but regrettably, it rotted away into a smelly mulch of mould when I lived in a damp caravan later in life (covered later in the book). I can vaguely remember doing a couple of commissions for others which earned me a bit of money; this all helped, since my parents had stopped providing pocket money (they were unwilling to fund my smoking habit). I also ventured into my first experiences of week-end 'student' employment.

To fund our lives of regular rock concerts, debauchery, fags and the occasional four pack of beer, the WHWH's all got jobs in the retail sector. I initially worked with Johnny at *Bejams*. I worked on the Fish & Veg section and the name of the game was to keep the freezers full up with frozen produce ahead of the hordes of shoppers on Friday night and Saturday. It was kind of fun and the store manager was actually a nice bloke who, despite knowing what he was letting himself in for, gave us a job. As you can imagine, a -22° freezer, complete with industrial blowers, can be a world of adventure for teenagers, not just a great place to scoff plenty of ice lollies.

One day, I performed a challenge in the freezers that I won't forget. I was dared to put my tongue onto a frozen shelf whilst I was mucking about with the lads, which obviously got stuck fast, very quickly. I was there for a few minutes and a small crowd of staff gathered to view my predicament. At the time, it seemed that the only way to free myself was to rip myself away from the shelf, which I did to screams of anguish and hilarity. The middle of my tongue bled and hurt for weeks afterwards! It wasn't until just after everyone had stopped wetting themselves, that I was advised the best way to free my tongue would have been to pour warm water onto the shelf and my tongue. We left *Bejams* when the management had had enough of us and went down the road to *Tesco* for employment.

At *Tesco*, most part-time workers stacked shelves. I don't know why, but I was given a white overall, cream trilby and sent to the deli counter, for my sins. It seemed better fun than shelf-stacking and I quickly got the hang of busily working a long queue, whilst scoffing discarded, out-of-date scotch eggs under the counter.

We rubbed shoulders with some of the permanent workers, and probably rubbed some up the wrong way too at both stores. They could see that we weren't going to be there forever, so probably had a care-free attitude to a number of things. You could sense their resentful realisation that they were there for the longer term.

Back at Johnny's house, amongst the gang, I made another notable friend, Corgi. We're still in contact after all these years. Legend has it that he was born on a full moon and dogs howled for several miles around. Some of the tales from his school days still make me chuckle; they certainly earned my kids' respect when I told them a few of them. There is no way my kids would be able to replicate some of the jaunts nowadays, even if they wanted to.

Here are a few Corgi-isms. He presented his school report to his mum, who was naturally delighted to read that he was an A-star pupil. She rushed straight to the local shop to show her friend how well Corgi had done. It was only then that the shopkeeper pointed out that 'A' meant 'absent' at his exams.

Corgi's favourite subject was woodwork, which involved sharp instruments and an element of danger. He took some time choosing what to construct for his final project and, after pondering for a while, came up with a stunning idea. His coffin. He wanted it to be coloured black, so to save the workshop, the woodwork teacher sent Corgi to the school greenhouse to spray paint his work of art. He finished the paint job, including the window panes and most of the plants inside the greenhouse. Corgi liked black. He was definitely a 'hands on' creative spirit, not an artist, as he drew a stick man in his Art Exam.

To the outsider, Corgi's rock'n'roll lifestyle had no limits, but the inner circle knew better. He had to make sure that he was back home by a certain time so he was often the first to leave Johnny's house, which always got some laughs.

He loved motorbikes and bought an old 'rat bike', a chopper style 250cc, from one of the guys in the village. He rode around the village on this for a month before it went on to die on his lawn. Corgi later developed an unhealthy love for Harley Davidsons. Don't get me wrong, these bikes are classic hogs and he loved their image, but the earlier models seemed to lack reliability.

Later in life, one of his first bikes was an imported Harley; it looked fantastic and Corgi cherished it dearly. It had cost him a fortune to ship it across from the US. Whilst out and about on my Kawasaki, I bumped into him a couple of times. He was never riding it, mind you: invariably, he'd be pushing his hog home as it had conked out. Undeterred, he'd defend their reputation to the end – you've got to admire his tenacity and loyalty. Corgi still constructs chopper bikes and has shown his prize winners in bike magazines. He's compromised on certain things though to improve reliability, and now uses Japanese engines.

Corgi introduced a friend to the fold called 'Nosher', who lived around the corner from me. I never got to understand how he came about his nickname, as his real name was James. Nosher had a 125cc bike which you could hear coming for miles, on account of there being no baffles in the exhaust. It didn't go very fast, but at least Nosher looked like he had a practical use for his leather jacket - the rest of us only had bicycles. Nosher seemed to have an S & M fetish which would surface occasionally in Johnny's lounge. At one point, he asked us to attach crocodile clips (from jump leads) to his nipples. He'd scream in pain, but at the same time, loved it. Bit weird that one, even for the WHWHs.

I had a lot of fun with my mate Corgi - he was truly the joker of the pack, making us all laugh at his ways. He modelled his image on Lemmy from Motörhead, right down to a chrome bullet belt and white cowboy boots. Fair play though, he eventually settled down and pursued a printing career, which allowed him to get on in life. This was surprising, given that he'd been sacked on the first day of work experience at *Bayer*; apparently he destroyed their very expensive postage machine after mucking about. Corgi's passion for woodwork still burns strong within and he uses his experiences of youth to help kids at a local school. Hats off to him.

During this time, I met my first girlfriend in a whirlwind romance which lasted all of eighteen months. Unfortunately for me, I didn't see the warning signs, as she was well on the way to building an insatiable appetite for the opposite sex. Her numerous indiscretions broke my heart and one of her first off-piste adventures was with Johnny, which meant that our friendship fizzled out. I certainly wasn't the perfect boyfriend by any stretch of the imagination, but was a bit of a lamb to the slaughter in terms of my naivety. Looking back we were both far too young to try and settle down but good friendships survive the years. Johnny and I subsequently met up, reacquainted and buried the hatchet a long time ago.

♪ Back off Bitch (Guns & Roses) ♪

I would have probably chosen this cracking track in my maelstrom of hurt, angry adolescent youth, a cracking venomous song about being cheated on, turning into hate for the pain caused. Months later though I was much more mellow about it so I chose the following track too, which says it all:

♪ Love is Blind (Uriah Heep) ♪

Some of this band's earlier material is quite 'out there' but, for a period, the band seemed to swing a little more mainstream. Their Head First album was great and probably didn't get the accolades it deserved.

Unsurprisingly, when I sat my A-levels, given the lack of preparation, the distractions and my lack of focus, I found them challenging. I was just glad to get out of the exam hall. I quickly came to the conclusion (to my parents' relief) that I wasn't cut out for further education.

I recognised then that I didn't have the right work ethic and commitment to make a successful student and I thought there'd be no point pissing money and two or three years of my life up a wall. In all honesty, I was also gagging to start earning money and get on with ' real life'. I wanted a steady job, a car and eventually hoped to buy a property of my own so I could leave home. I wanted to undertake a vocational route, but hadn't a clue what jobs to apply for. All I knew was that I wanted to be in 'business' - whatever that meant. Businessmen looked like they all had cars, houses and families. A million and one things more than I had at the time, so that was something to aim for. Good enough for me!

Back in 1987, it seemed that there were jobs everywhere for anyone who wanted one. Newbury was described as 'Thatcher-Town', after the then Prime Minister. I don't know why it got the name, perhaps because it was a typical growing town, slap bang in the Tory heartland and some politicians wanted to show how 'dynamic' it was. Newbury didn't feel dynamic to me though, it seemed to be an ordinary market town, with a number of industrial estates around its perimeter, but didn't seem anything special. The traffic of the A34, a main arterial North-South route, flowed slowly drudged through the town and was, more often than not, in gridlock. Its train services were slam-door, old wooden carriages, not the slick, automatic-doored trains you'd see in towns closer to London. It wasn't a bad town to grow up in though; it had its fair share of amenities and plenty of pubs and restaurants to enjoy in the evening. As soon as I'd finished my A-levels, I took a job as a delivery van assistant for *Currys*, the electrical shop. I was very honest with the manager who interviewed me and let him know that I was looking for something permanent elsewhere.

Most of my evenings were spent at *The Rampant Cat* and this soon became a place where most of my friends were. I enjoyed having a little bit of money in my pocket and felt proud that I'd truly earned the cash. The only A-level entrant vacancies advertised in *The Newbury Weekly News* seemed to be for banks; they were certainly businesses, so I applied for a few.

At *Currys*, my driver was a kind bloke in his fifties and I was determined to enjoy the summer. I don't know what he suffered from but he had two permanent corks of snot up each nostril that used to go up and down as he breathed: talk about being put off your sandwiches! To quell the boredom he didn't mind if I took turns behind the wheel and we zoomed about Berkshire and Hampshire. I got to know the roads really well, in fact I still wind Jane up when I suddenly declare "I delivered a TV to that house". I have three memorable 'Confessions of a delivery man' stories to tell you, but looking back, it's hard to imagine how these all occurred in such a short period of time: it was classic Laurel and Hardy.

One of the most annoying things a delivery man encounters on his rounds is being told that the guy in the shop had said we would fit the item the customer had bought. We delivered a washing machine to a house in Lambourn. It was perched on a hill and had at least three split levels descending down from the kitchen, where the washing machine was going. The owner had already removed a very old washing machine from its fittings and we found that the new fittings didn't fit straight on to the old piping. When we tried to tell her that we couldn't do the job, the lady started to kick up a fuss and got very angry. She was adamant that we had to give it a go and wouldn't let us leave without applying some brute strength to the pipe's fittings. Unfortunately, they were so old, they started to come off in our hands and the pipes started to leak profusely. A stream of water flowed out of the kitchen, down the hallway and into the lounge, the lowest level of the house. There, a pool started to form in the middle of her carpet. We panicked a bit, but eventually turned the water off, rescued the carpet as best we could with towels and made sure that an emergency plumber was called, leaving the owner stranded, as we had many more deliveries that day. This taught us, going forward, that we would refuse to touch dodgy old piping or wiring, point blank.

I wish we'd learnt that lesson by the time we pulled up to a little old lady's house in Kingsclere. She'd bought an electric oven and, guess what? The lovely, young man on the shop floor had said that we'd fit it for her! Her neighbour had already removed the old oven for us, leaving the live wires dangling from the bottom of the wall. Unfortunately, the wiring was so decrepit that none of the fittings seemed to reach the power input area of the oven, which was hip height. We tried to find a solution but, given the potential dangers, we felt it best that she turn the electricity off and call in a qualified electrician to install the oven. It wasn't until later in the day, when we phoned in to the store on our rounds, that we heard the neighbour had fiercely complained. We'd left a vulnerable old lady alone, with live wiring coming out of the wall, like he had. The lady couldn't have heard us and at worse we'd simply left it as we found it!

But one of the funniest events at *Currys* was when we went to Basingstoke town centre for a pick-up. It was unfamiliar territory for us and, as previously mentioned, the roads in the centre of a town can be an alien maze of roundabouts and inter-connecting roads to the uninitiated. I directed us under a low flyover, and with a juddering thud, scrape and crunch, we managed to get the van wedged fast under the bridge. The rail inside the back of the van, where we fixed the new and discarded goods, abruptly snapped under the pressure of the abrupt stop. But the van lurched forward again, wedging us further in. All the heavy washing machines, TVs and dishwashers had flown into the front end of the van and the momentum of this had caused us to shunt forward more.

We must have looked hilarious, stuck under that flyover, unsuccessfully trying to reverse the van out. It was wedged firmly against the concrete roof. As the traffic behind us built up, someone yelled, "Let the tyres down!". Sure enough, that was the solution. As you can imagine, the area director was not too pleased about the damage to the van, the destroyed goods and customer complaints that day, but I chirpily said, "At least no-one got injured." My helpful comment was only met with a tirade of verbal abuse as he vented off and gave us the hairdryer treatment; clearly this unfortunate oversight had affected his bonus that month.

One memory of this era was a real ground-shaker, but wasn't in the slightest bit funny. During my time at *Currys*, mum was a district nurse in Hungerford. On a hot summer's day, whilst zooming around in the van in Reading, we heard on the radio that a nutter named Michael Ryan had gone on a shooting spree in Hungerford. The connection didn't initially compute, but then I started to think that my mum might have been caught up in the shootings somehow. When we got to the store, I phoned home as Steve was there studying. He was anxious and started to become very concerned when the Hungerford surgery kept calling the home line to ask whether mum had got home OK: she was clearly missing.

Dad heard the news at work too and, like me, came home early. Back in those days, there were no mobile phones, so all we could do was call her office at the surgery, but it was constantly engaged. We spent most of the evening pacing the floor and waiting for a call which never came - it was a very tense time.

To our huge relief, mum thankfully walked in later that night. She was very shaken up and had been caught up in the day's events. Although she doesn't talk about it much, as I understand it, she had been shot at and took shelter behind some cars. Unfortunately, others weren't so lucky. That day, mum witnessed a few sights that you don't expect on your average district nursing rounds in a quaint Berkshire market town. She wasn't allowed to leave Hungerford until all of the police witness statements had been taken, and the police had created a physical and virtual perimeter around the town. Nobody could get in or out, and all calls had been barred.

The whole episode had understandably shaken Mum, but I have to say that she seemed to deal with it very well. She went straight back to work because there were still patients to see, and life seemed to bounce back into normality very quickly, despite avoiding a major disaster in our lives. I now wonder how well she truly coped.

My search for more permanent, gainful employment was not in vain and, after two offers, I plumped for the *Midland Bank*. My decision was based wholly around the person who'd interviewed me; I'd liked his friendly and welcoming manner, far more than the other stuffy one who seemed to hail from the Dad's Army era. He became my first boss, a down-to-earth chap who happened to live in the village. To this day, I'm grateful that he gave me the opportunity. Probably best he did too, before I killed someone with *Currys*!

24

FIRST RUNGS

Mum was so proud that the eldest of her brood had finally conformed, grown up and joined what was deemed to be a steady, respectable employer. Dad had already worked out what rent to charge me, and I was looking forward to earning some steady cash. Mum made her last clothing investment in me and bought my first suit: a thick, slate-grey number off the peg at *M & S*. On 14th September 1987, day one, I turned up, not quite knowing what to expect.

I was led around the branch in Newbury and my initial impression was one of surprise: how could you squeeze that many people into a back office? The building was a bit of a rabbit warren, and housed over 40 staff who busied themselves with lots of paper, lists, scrolls of adding-up and confusing dockets. All of this baffling, manual paperwork was then stuffed into lots of bags that would be collected overnight and sent to a central site, where I've no doubt, it would once again get manually re-listed, summarised, added up and sent on again. I could see that the managers were held in high regard and each had their own office space and a secretary. They'd only just stopped the ritual of standing up whenever the branch manager walked in the room. Here in front of me was the iconic bank manager I'd wanted to become - a friend of society, a pillar of the community and a business facilitator.

Back then, banking was a respectable industry to be associated with. However, it was quite antiquated and it felt like I worked in the public sector. As a result, customer service could have been better. In the early nineties, more nimble lenders and organisations gave the industry the kick up the arse it sorely needed and it faced huge change: it was a case of do or die. Over the next decade there was a wave of cost-cutting, centralisation, offshoring, investment in IT platforms, as well as a core focus on sales. Suddenly, employees were given targets to achieve and unfortunately, over time, its leadership lost its way, starting to care more about squeezing profit from a relationship than servicing it.

The industry sprouted many departments dedicated to providing 'other' financial services, such as insurance and investments. I didn't meet anybody who went to work with the intention of hoodwinking the customer base, but the culture became a tad warped. Leaders chased targets at all costs, and pressure to achieve these was applied to the frontline staff which, in turn, drove some misguided moral decision-making. Many within the industry today remain embarrassed about past behaviours and the press never seems to be short of a story where a bank is fined huge sums for past misdemeanours.

The banking industry is now, quite rightly, trying to rebuild the trust it once had with its loyal customers. Targets are far less product-specific and customer satisfaction is keenly observed because, at the end of the day, customers have lots of alternative choices. It's a tough gig though: with the advent of technology, customers' needs, demands and expectations of their bank are constantly changing and accelerating in frequency, so the industry needs to continue to reinvest and, at the same time, monitor behaviour.

The A-level entrant 'MDP Scheme' was hailed as a fast-track programme to management. I expected that I'd sail through the clerical roles in months, dipping in like a swallow over a pool, to get a taste of what happened on the way up a career ladder. To my horror, I soon realised that in reality, things were a little more glacial. I would need to spend months in each role and would only move on when I'd mastered said role. I didn't know it then, but this was a proper apprenticeship where, by the end, you would be expected to be master of all trades. En route, my employer would in turn get the measure of me. Throughout the scheme, I recognised that I would need to bite my lip, no matter how boring the task was. And boy, at times it was frustrating! It often seemed mind-numbingly pointless and futile.

My starting salary was a disgraceful pittance, so to boost my meagre wages, I decided to work at *The Rampant Cat* during busy evenings. I figured that it would be where I'd be some evenings anyhow, so it was better to receive an income from it and fund my social life. The landlords, Anita and Roger, were good fun and had created a loyal bunch of regulars, with my friends making up half of the pub most nights. This enabled me to save enough money to buy my first car, a bright-blue, T-reg Mini. If you've ever watched the movie *Police Academy*, there's a scene where a very large cop, Hightower, sits in the back seat to drive his very small car. I didn't have the forethought to make this adjustment, so would steer away with my knees around my ears, dancing on the tiny pedals.

Around this time, my indiscreet girlfriend had taken on her last indiscretion with a local at the pub, right under my gullible, naive nose. It took a friend to point out what was obvious to everyone else, and I felt so stupid. Despite her lies and pleading, we finally split up for good, but it seemed to take an eternity to truly escape, as she continued to write to me for months. I decided the best strategy was to ignore it all and pay no attention to the letter bombing, despite the hurt inside. It was hard for me and I became quite cold-hearted about it; but I was fed up being the victim. Despite the intensity of my first true relationship, I was conscious that it had still lasted a relatively short period, and was likely to be the first of a few. I began to develop a focus on the long game to deal with the day-to-day drama.

At the new job, most of the clerical staff were women, as was the norm in those days. My colleagues were often very patient with me, some more than others. I don't think I was the best student at times and, like at school, my strategy was to put in just enough effort to stay off the naughty list. I didn't see the point in becoming an ace at adding up or writing out dockets. I just wanted to learn the big picture, understand how it all fitted together and enjoy myself as much as possible outside of work. I wasn't very ambitious.

I was appallingly bad at most branch roles that involved mundane listing and paperwork and when I got a chance to go on the counter and meet real customers, I was equally poor at the paperwork. I couldn't balance my till for toffee. It seems bizarre nowadays, but back then, the banking hall had a length of rope for the customers to queue against and the cashiers used to smoke and drink mugs of tea in front of customers.

I was better-suited to roles that involved a bit of initiative and freedom, which were in short supply at my grade. After a year or so, I was transferred to the area office in Reading, where some of the branch roles had started to be centralised. At least someone showed some faith in me, I thought. In retrospect, I think they wanted me out of the way as they could see that I was going to have a massive fall out with someone!

♪ Keep the Faith (Bon Jovi) ♪

These guys remain the best known hair-rock hairband to this day. But sadly, at times, their material is sometimes deemed to be quite beige, but Messrs Sambora and Bon Jovi didn't half pen some classics! This track is one of my favourites and a real crowd pleaser.

Outside of work, I met up again with old friends Ron and Ray from *Bally's Garage*, who had started to regularly frequent the pub where I'd worked. By now, it had a great reputation and people seemed to flock from miles around to go there.

Ron had always had an interest in flying. I first met him when he worked in the paint shop behind the garage; he was a keen hang glider then. Now he'd gone up a league and owned a hot air balloon. It wasn't long before he followed his passion, started a business flying customers and began to make a good living out of it. This was a great experience for a few of us down at the pub, who he happily recruited as his ground team. Ron needed us too as he soon owned the largest balloon by far in the vicinity. The basket held a dozen or so passengers and weighed a ton, taking at least four of us to get it off its huge trailer. When the weather was flyable, I would race home from work and be available for an early pick-up to get the balloon airborne at the take-off site, just outside Hungerford. Ron was extremely well-known amongst the ballooning enthusiasts and had taught most of them how to fly over the years. We were all allocated specific roles and I tended to lift the envelope near the burners on inflation, as I was relatively tall. It was extremely noisy and hot, but the best part was when I was asked to jump into the basket to provide some ballast. I must have flown two dozen times over a couple of years and unlike some, declined to be paid, instead opting for a couple of pints back at the pub after the flight. Apart from taking my mum on a trip across the stunning, rolling Hampshire countryside, there was one very memorable trip that sticks in my mind.

It was New Year's Day and a light, persistent, cold drizzle had stubbornly settled in overhead. The mood was no better down the pub, so Ron checked the weather and said, "Let's go ballooning." We'd had a few by then, but undeterred, unravelled the canopy in a field and inflated. In no time at all, we were climbing through the drizzle and, as we popped out above the cloud, I was taken aback by the view. As far as the eye could see, large, billowy clouds glittered and bubbled in the bright sun which sat above us in the picture-perfect, blue sky. Around us, water crystals played with the light and formed rainbows and jewels against the clouds - everybody's spirits were instantly lifted. Eventually, the gas canisters emptied and we had to find a landing site. Below us, the clouds seemed to be consumed by a black hole; the cotton-puffed shapes were being sucked into some sort of vortex and it looked like we were heading for the eye of the storm, although it was very calm. Sure enough, we sank into the engulfing, swirling hole and when we popped out on the other side, we discovered that it had been caused by the heat of a bonfire, some 1,000 feet below. It turned out that we were still above the take-off field and had only travelled horizontally 500 yards or so; all we had to do was lower a rope and get led across the field to deflate, next to the trailer. I was buzzing all day from that experience and was amazed what an effect getting taken somewhere completely different from your humble surroundings could have on you. It made me think, sometimes our own mood can be set by a constant environment; if you change scenery or place, you can have a different, sometimes better time. That memory served me well later in my career and general life. If you're not happy with your lot and nothing around you looks like it's going to change, perhaps it's better to move on.

Ron and I have recently reconnected too and he still flies, but now for fun. He has a one-man clodhopper he built himself and went on to marry Alison, a well-loved local from the pub. She became his ground crew and enjoys the occasional trip in his light aircraft. Yes, he's certainly got the passion for flying still and is now a successful businessman in his own right. I remembered having conversations about his ambitions outside of ballooning. He respected my work ambitions and drive over the years, as I did his. To me, we were in some way kindred spirits in that respect.

On a refreshing balloon retrieval with Ron

Back to the story… I'd been to the Reading Area Office once before on a training day and remembered it vividly, for one reason: the course had to be cancelled and we were sent home. Halfway through that afternoon, the wind picked up and we watched in surprise as road signs and bins hurtled past the first-floor window. This was to be the night of the famous 1987 hurricane and, after battling across town to get to the railway station, I hunkered down in *The Three Guineas* at Reading station, waiting for a train to Newbury. I eventually walked in just after 9pm as the wind was really picking up again. Getting into work the next day was a challenge, as there were at least three trees down across the lanes I commuted down, but get into work I did, unlike some.

I joined the Foreign team in Reading. There were only four of us and the day consisted of calculating, adding and listing - all the monotonous tasks I hated. My concentration wandered and soon my mistakes stuck out like a sore thumb. The boss was a no-nonsense type of guy and unfortunately, I felt little was done to welcome or train me. In fact, within a couple of months, I was ambushed by him, out of the blue.

He asked me to pop into a room for a quick meeting and an HR representative was there too: I was receiving a verbal warning! But soon, the tables seemed to turn on the boss, when the HR person inferred that my boss and his 'favourite' could have made more of an effort in training me and making the environment more welcoming. It was clear that the boss had a bit of a history with the HR bod. At the end of the meeting, I was encouraged to take up a grievance to alleviate my predicament, but to me, the choice was a simple one. There was no way I wanted to have the reputation as a troublemaker at this early stage; I wanted to move on to other jobs in the area office. Instead, I accepted that the whole incident was maybe the wake-up call I'd needed and decided to just take the medicine and knuckle down. This, in turn, had a great effect on my relationship with the boss, who seemed relieved and eased up on me. He gave me some input, I put in more effort and my work standards improved. In leadership, it's very important to create the right environment to get the best out of individuals. It's about improving and investing in others, not making it easier for yourself. If you want people to grow, nurture them during their mistakes: these are learning opportunities and people shouldn't be punished for them.

By now, I'd managed to move out of my parents' home and bought my first house with a new girlfriend. It was a tiny, one-bed house in Newbury and, looking back, it was an incredibly stupid move. We bought at a peak in the market, could barely afford to keep the house running and made a binding financial and emotional commitment before initially renting and trialling our relationship. We were both impetuous for different reasons. I wanted to become independent and move out of my parents' house at the first opportunity and she didn't have a great relationship with her mother, who lived in Ecchinswell, a village surrounded by countryside, halfway between Newbury and Kingsclere.

In investment, often timing is everything. Macro events are beyond your control and can wipe you out. Within six months, the UK was in the grip of a deep recession, so we were locked in negative equity and outgrowing the two-up-two-down rabbit hutch. My girlfriend initially worked as a nanny in the evenings, but then started to work in a nearby factory in Newbury, to earn a bit more money and free up her evenings. Not at all what a country girl had envisaged doing: she was used to horses and mucking out, not factory life and clocking in.

Around this time, I hooked up again with my mate from school, Chris, and his crowd, who all had motorbikes. In fact, one summer, we all travelled on bikes to the Paul Ricard Bol d'Or circuit in southern France to go to the 24-hour motorcycle race. I rode pillion on my friend Max's bright red GSXR1000. It felt great, thundering through ancient French towns and whizzing around the breath-taking scenery that central France provided. It was during this trip that I made a pact with myself to buy a bike, when I could afford it. This was going to be some time away as my wages made up the vast majority of the household income.

We arrived at the foot of the hill on our bikes and the race circuit was situated on its summit. I couldn't work out why so many ambulances had parked on the roadside. As we ascended up the hair-pinned road in single file, it soon became clear. A few of the European bikers rode like absolute nutters, overtaking on blind bends, with a mountain gorge over the curb. We saw a couple of crashes, so took it easy all the way to the gates of the circuit, where we headed to the campsite. It was very interesting to see how the different nationalities organised themselves.

The French bikers were well-equipped, had support vehicles parked up and claimed pitching rights next to the utilities. After all, it was their country. The Germans arranged themselves in strict, linear order with rows of BMW bikes in straight lines. You could tell where the Brits were: we got the lousiest pitches which were already lit up by numerous large, random campfires. Beer cans were stacked proudly in mountain shapes and music blared across the field. I don't remember seeing much of the race itself - it was more about the experience of the journey. However, one vivid memory at the event was saving another friend Dave's arse, literally.

On the final night, the race circuit put on a concert and Dave got completely drunk, to the point where he was being dragged and carried around by us. A group of huge, leather-clad, openly homosexual European bikers took a fancy to Dave as their play thing for the night. They danced with him and kissed him and, as the party got going, wanted to take him back to their tents for a game of pass the parcel. I looked in horror as my group of friends turned a blind eye: they'd clearly got so fed up with Dave that they thought he needed to be taught a lesson. It took some convincing, but I got my mates to grab Dave from their clutches and we took him back to the safety of our tents. The lesson there was watch your back and try not to completely lose control: you can't always rely on others to watch out for you, despite them claiming to be your friends.

At the Bol d'Or

Back at work, I moved from the Foreign department to a larger team of twenty who made up the Securities department. This was far more interesting as it brought to life some of the elements of my night school studying, where the lender would take a charge over an asset owned by the borrower as collateral for a loan - this was 'business'. I was still attending Reading College in the evening to study for my professional exams. To kill time after work, my mate David and I went to the local casino with a £5 budget. It was just a bit of fun, before heading off for boring lessons; fortunately, neither of us ended up in heavy debt.

The economic climate began to grip our industry hard and recruitment dried up. A lot of cost-saving initiatives were introduced at the office and I could see the writing on the wall for those local, specialised teams. I figured they were going to be nationalised or off-shored eventually so I decided to make the most of what was on offer, and move on.

The Securities team was an eclectic bunch of experienced personnel, plucked from various branches in the area. There were some very eccentric characters who'd spent a decade or two perfecting the craft of hand writing ledgers (at that time, none of our records had been computerised). Some of these were works of art - the calligraphy skills used were only matched by Benedictine monks. At the end of the day, the ledgers followed the same pattern of information and that was the important part. I was put under the wing of Tim, who quite rightly pointed out that I needed to get more experience before going for promotion: this was sage advice.

I knuckled down, learnt how to do the role properly and got to understand how the work fitted in with the corporate lending side of customer relationships, the area in which I wanted to move towards. We had some fun times in the team, working and playing hard. One of the other jovial characters was Marcel and he spoke with a slight impediment where he didn't pronounce his R's. He and Tim would urge me to do a rendition of Lenny Henry's David Bellamy impression. 'Gwapple me Gwapenuts' was Marcel's nickname from therein. Tim and I got to see each other when I later returned to the local office after leaving London, but more on that later.

During this period, I could sense some traction in my career at last. I began to sense some sort of realistic direction and, looking back at the end of my time with the Securities department, as far as I was concerned, I had finished my formal apprenticeship.

Steve, my brother, had known what he wanted to be since he was young. Mum and dad were rightly very proud of his achievements at school, university and later, when he practised as an architect. In contrast, I felt that I'd let the side down a bit and had been in his shadow. It felt like I'd just been left to 'get on with it'. You might say that there was a bit of sibling rivalry that got me fired up, but I also think I wanted to make my parents proud. At this point in my career, I recognised that I'd been a late developer, compared to Steve, and decided there and then to stop pissing about at the coalface, put my back into it and take some control of my own destiny.

I dropped off the MDP scheme as I didn't want to work locally any more. I also detested the HR manager, who seemed to exercise far too much control on everybody's career path. It didn't matter anyway because, within months, the scheme was dropped by the bank due to cost-cutting. By now, some of my peers were disillusioned with the bank and started to leave in droves. I figured out that if I stayed with my employer and made the best of it, more opportunities might arise as the competition within my generation was thinning out. The bank had ceased recruiting heavily a number of years ago, to enable the efficiencies to be made, so I recognised that somebody of a certain age, with a wide skill set, might be a good candidate for future roles. But the local area didn't have anything further for me; everyone seemed happy to work in their roles for ages.

When the time was right, I applied for a role in London, and off I went to experience my first major commute. The office was in Pall Mall so I had to trudge across London from Paddington station. It was a long, tiring journey, but I quickly adapted and learnt to 'switch off', just like many commuters do. Although it was a promotion, any financial benefit was absorbed by the season ticket, so I consoled myself with the hope that putting myself in this temporary position would provide further opportunities. It was an investment. Mind you, I had to keep reminding myself why I was doing it. I sacrificed a lot of social time at home: not only was I commuting, but I was also attending night school in London.

The offices were within a huge building near the Commonwealth Offices and the Agriculture HQ, operating out of the two top floors. With the windows open, you could hear the Changing of the Guard down the Mall and look into St James's Park. I would sometimes catch glimpses of minor royalties and VIPs as they'd be zoomed about in their chauffeur-driven limousines around St James's Palace. My career had reached new heights: I was now Head of Stapling.

Large, computerised lending applications came in for approval by the directors and it was my role to pull these tree-wasting reams of paper together and make comment on the request. I got to understand the lending systems inside out; I also got a taste of how to present an argument in my recommendations. One of the directors, Graham, was an experienced career banker, who smoked a cigar each afternoon at precisely 3pm. He did his best to explain to me how things worked. Graham used to compare his first tentative career years in Yorkshire with mine. When he started out, he had to "get coal in and stoke t'boiler." It sounded a bit like a Hovis advert, but I appreciated a lot of his sanguine advice. He was generous with his time and genuinely cared that I didn't get too settled in the Pall Mall job.

I had some fun with the staff there too. Each director had a secretary and Graham's was Kath; I used to jump out of cupboards to spook her as she wandered around the corridors. She often returned the favour and once, accidentally jumped out on the unsuspecting Graham, armed with a brush. The poor guy nearly died of shock on the spot, whilst I was curled up in a ball, screaming in silence with laughter next door. "Let's say no more on the matter Kath and put this tomfoolery to bed - this is no place for frivolity," he purred, in an authoritative tone.

It wasn't too long before I saw a managerial role advertised at the agriculture office in Worthing, on the south coast, so I applied. I knew full well that I had a good chance of being offered the role as I'd got to know the boss there, Ken, and liked him. I felt I had to grab the first opportunity of a managerial appointment, given the economic climate and various re-organisations going on. Again, any pay rise was superficial as I had to fund all accommodation and travel costs myself. It was also costly to my social life as I'd need to spend the week away in digs, returning home at the week-ends. It was certainly not ideal, but again, I saw this as an investment for the future.

Clearly my girlfriend wasn't keen on staying put in Newbury on her own, but instead of taking a leap of faith and moving to the south coast with me, she decided to move back to her mother's smallholding. There, she lived in a caravan, whilst we let the house out. The office in Woking could never understand why I smelt of bonfires when I rocked up on a Monday morning. The fact was, the wood burner was the only heating in the musty caravan, so you can safely say that I've experienced some humble beginnings. In hindsight, this was the beginning of the end for us as a couple - time away and absence of hearts meant we started to grow apart.

I grabbed some great week-ends at the smallholding and learnt to ride a scramble bike, shoot, split logs and also owned a dog, who I took beating for pheasants now and then. It was paid employment and exercise for the mad mutt and I. Mattie was a beautiful springer spaniel who'd been passed to us when the first owner couldn't provide the outdoor life she required. Whilst I certainly wasn't the best of trainers, I tried my best and genuinely felt I'd got somewhere with her.

Coming back to live in the dilapidated caravan during the week-ends was never going to be a permanent lifestyle for me and, after a while, I inevitably split up from my girlfriend. Whilst this was a sad experience, we were already miles apart in spirit by the time we admitted to each other that it was over. Reluctantly, I realised I couldn't keep Mattie (the dog), as she was a 100% genuine working breed and couldn't be cooped up during the day, so we gifted her to Lee, a gamekeeper we knew. She turned out to be one of his best bitches and gun dogs - I was very pleased.

Despite my best efforts, I never really felt settled in Worthing, and lodged with three different landlords before finally renting a flat of my own. During this period, I think my personality worsened. I didn't feel like I was rooted anywhere and wasn't suited to a nomadic lifestyle. Frankly, it was very lonely too, but I began to get to know myself better. I began to question why I'd bothered to seemingly sacrifice so much to better my career. Perhaps I had a masochistic streak in me? But thinking it through, I was determined to stick at it for the long game and at work, kept a beady eye out for a new role which might well take me back to familiar ground. If I wanted to make something of myself, I felt that this was an early sacrifice I had to make. If relationships weren't strong enough to last the tests of time, they couldn't have been that great in the first place.

One of the complications to unwind was the now, let-out, jointly-owned rabbit hutch in Newbury. While in Worthing, I'd survived Black Wednesday, when interest rates hit 15%. Despite us paying off a little of the joint mortgage, the house was still deeply in negative equity. Neither my ex-girlfriend or I felt like selling up, as this would only crystallise a loss, so to me, the only logical solution was for me to take on the paper loss of the mortgage in my sole name.

Funnily enough, a role came up back in Newbury and, after eighteen months on the south coast, I was over the moon to be heading back home to friends and surroundings I knew well. Unsurprisingly, my ex wanted to get back together, but that ship had sailed a long time ago, when she'd shown her true colours. In response to this rejection, I think she decided to make life more interesting and said she didn't want me to take on the house alone. It felt like she just wanted to frustrate things as much as possible. The crazy thing was, I was happy for her to take it on, but we both knew she couldn't raise a mortgage on her own.

As annoying as this was, I had to remain calmly focussed on the long game and decided to detach myself from the emotion of the situation as best I could. In a few heated exchanges, we got ourselves into a stalemate position that felt like it could go on for an eternity, so to raise the stakes, I refused to re-let the house out when the tenancy came up for renewal. The last thing I wanted was to be in some way attached to her forever and a day, so I needed to make it as hard as possible for her. Both of us continued to pay for half of the mortgage on an unoccupied property for about a year. My logic was that it would hurt her financially more than me and I hoped that the reality of watching vast sums of her earnings going up in smoke might make her see sense. I wrote off the cost in my head; it was another investment and, thanks to reduced travel costs, it wasn't stretching me. I became bloody-minded about it and stubbornly dug in.

The only downside to moving back to the area was moving back to my parents' house until I could get the house sorted. My old mate, Ron, helped me move out of the smoky caravan and we trundled off with half a trailer load of meagre possessions. Mum and dad had begun to enjoy semi-retirement together with an empty nest and started to take numerous holidays. But soon, both sons had returned to shatter their peace and tranquility, as Steve had returned from university around the same time.

I know I've focussed on this negative period of my life for a while, but at the time, it felt like I had a real millstone around my neck. I certainly don't bear any grudges and totally appreciate that we were young, foolish and both did things we weren't proud of. For me now, the interesting part is looking back on my mindset at the time. I kept an eye on the long game and shut the emotion of the situation out, as it was only a financial tie from my perspective. I just concentrated on enjoying the many positives around me. There are some parallels with the mindset I've adopted with cancer.

In no time at all, I was happily back with the crowd at the local pub, helping out with ballooning trips once again in the summer months. It was a magical time and, for a couple of years, I found I had a little more cash on the hip, despite the mortgage payment. With my social life buzzing again and my finances in check, I committed to pass my test and get a motorbike.

To pass the test, I enrolled at a learner school in Bristol and spent five wet and windy days bombing around the lanes and streets of Avon, in a convoy of 125cc bikes. I came away with a pass certificate and piles, thanks to the wet conditions and leaky waterproofs! Unfortunately, these didn't emerge until the following week when I was on holiday with my mates in Corfu. I knew something wasn't right when my anus started to resemble an angry bunch of grapes. Trying to keep my plight a secret, I snuck out to the pharmacy in the town where we were staying. I was embarrassed as hell to ask for some medication and, as the shop floor was full of people, I whispered to the local male pharmacist whether he had any cream for haemorrhoids. I think he must have been hard of hearing and, to my horror, boomed in his Greekaccented English, "Are your piles internal or external?" At the same time, demonstrating to me (and the whole shop floor, who had all turned around by now) the difference between the two types, using an elastic band for an anus and his thumbs for the haemorrhoids. Mortified, I hoarsely whispered the answer, then tried to slip unnoticed out of the shop and raced back to the room to apply the medicine. When my mates found out, they were in stitches.

Back home, I soon purchased my first bike from Chris' brother, who was emigrating to New Zealand and wanted to raise some funds, so it seemed like it was meant to be. It was a big, ugly, heavy, shaft-driven silver Yamaha XJ650. I rode it around until the novelty wore off and soon realised that I'd still got a lot of learning to do: I wasn't anywhere near road-safe. The country roads I travelled on were generally covered in loose gravel, mud, animal droppings and all sorts of hazards that are worth avoiding. I had a few hair-raising moments but, to my amazement, didn't fall off or drop the bike once. Lady luck was looking over me for sure! In talking to Ron and Corgi, who'd each been riding for years, I needed to slow down, sort my road positioning out, smooth the ride and put some miles in. After a few months, I began to feel more confident.

I worked at the Corporate Office in Newbury and supported the boss there, Gordon. He was very experienced, polished off some of my rough edges and helped me develop my credit skills. He also urged me to spend time finishing my exams, knowing full well that completing them would help in the long run. To be fair, I knew this too, so invested a little time in studying. I didn't want my social life to suffer as I was having too much fun, so I opted to do this slowly, rather than cram a number in over my years there.

After returning to Newbury for a year or so, my ex eventually smelt the coffee and got fed up of blowing most of her wages on an unused property, month after month. We agreed to switch the house into my sole name – finally, we could both move on.

At this point, the house was slightly in negative equity, but I was happy to stomach it: a small price to pay for freedom. In no time, I got the keys and rocked up to the house on the bike to check that all was well, as the house had been dormant for over a year. I knocked at the house next door in the dead of night to explain why it had been left empty, and introduced myself to Jo and Kev, my new next door neighbours.

They were over the moon that somebody was going to finally move in and when I did, with the few valuables I had, they looked out for me and we became close friends. Over the next couple of years, I enjoyed the single

Sharing habits with the girls from the Newbury branch on a charity float

life there. There's something to be said for living on your own for a while and I got to know myself even more than I'd done before. This gave me insight into what I did and didn't want in any future long-term relationship. I continued to garage my bike at my parents' house as mine didn't have one. It would have probably been stolen if I'd left it outside (it wasn't the safest part of town). The house wasn't in the best of areas and sometimes the scally-wags from the neighbouring estate would torch their stolen cars in the parking spaces around the house. Still, great to see the fire service in action.

I decided to upgrade the bike and purchased a modern ZZR600. Kev dropped me off in Swindon to collect the bike one night and I raced home along the M4 at a horrendous speed. I couldn't believe how responsive it was; it was like an extension of my limbs and the suspension was so smooth compared to the spring loaded XJ650, it was like floating on air. I spent six happy evenings whizzing around the countryside and flying around the A-roads on that bike; I felt immortal and that nothing could stop me.

Unfortunately I wasn't. I misjudged a fast corner in the middle of the beautiful Hampshire countryside near Watership Down and, as I flew through the air, I counted my blessings that I'd missed the trees and a signpost. The bike disintegrated behind me and cartwheeled nose to tail umpteen times down the tarmac, before the smouldering pile of alloy and plastic came to rest in a field. I had ploughed a furrow through a grass bank with my helmet and came to a halt, face down. I opened my eyes, checked that I still had all my limbs and stood up with a lot of pain in my left ankle. Thankfully, someone took me to The Royal Hampshire County Hospital in Winchester and I called Ron, who quickly and helpfully scooped the wreckage up for me and took it to his lockup for the insurance company to inspect later. Yet again, Ron had bailed me out and picked up the pieces.

In Winchester A & E, where Steve met me, after taking as much morphine as possible, the nurses eventually opted to give me an epidural to pop my dislocated ankle bone back in place. Later, on the ward, it dawned on me how lucky I'd been. I remember cursing myself, "You still haven't learnt your lesson, have you? You got too cocky, you plonker." Out of the twelve beds in that hospital ward, seven others were occupied by bike accidents. Six had multiple broken bones and there was one paraplegic case; it was quite an eye-opener for me and I made a pact with myself to be much more sensible.

When I returned home with a leg in plaster, mum couldn't talk to me for a few days and work were none too happy either as I couldn't get into the office. Not to worry though, ingeniously, they bussed some of the paperwork to me via the secretaries, so I could do it at home.

Once recovered, I bought another ZZR 600 out of the insurance proceeds, and found the older model a lot more suited to my size. I'd grown over the last year or so as I'd started going to the gym regularly. Before I could organise a garage (I knew that having it parked up at my parents' would finish off my mum), I parked it in my lounge. The smell of petrol in the morning was a little strange whilst eating breakfast and watching telly perched on it was also a bit odd.

I'd been going to the gym for a couple of years, initially with some mates at the pub who, like me, had got a little bored of the monotony, cost and aimlessness of smoking. After a while, some of the weight decided to stick around my body and, on a night out in town, I was apprehended by a crack ninja recruitment squad from Hungerford Rugby Club, in the shape of Simon and Charter. "Oooh, you look like you could play second row, have a beer. What's the point of a physique like that if you don't use it, have a beer. You look like a natural rugby player, have a beer." Simon and I already knew each other, as our parents had been neighbours in Woolton Hill and he was a year above me in school.

And so it started. A reacquaintance with a game in my mid twenties which I was never quite big enough to play well at as a child. At around the same time, something else very positive occurred.

It was 12.15pm on 25th September 1995, and the Newbury branch's downstairs team phoned my line. "John, we're sending up a young lady to your interview room who wants to transfer her parents' business accounts to us." I was a little miffed as I was literally grabbing my jacket to pop out for a sandwich, but business beckoned, so I dutifully prepared for the meeting and went to the room.

Waiting for me was Jane. A slim, attractive, effervescent young lady who beamed the most fantastic smile at me as I walked into the room. This wasn't a time for a tired line like, "Have I met you somewhere?". But there was something familiar about Jane that I couldn't put my finger on. I don't remember much about the business side of things we discussed, as all I did was get drawn more and more into her company. Within the formal discussions of the application, we established that we were both single, and paused pregnantly upon that.

When Jane left, I knew that I'd fallen head over heels in love with her there and then, and said to myself, "I'm going to marry that girl." Jane later relayed that she rang her mum, as she was running an errand for her, and said that she'd fallen in love too.

♪ Love Walked In (Thunder) ♪

When "Back Street Symphony" was released as their debut album, it was packed with some great new material and was a breath of refreshing air. Authentic, riff-led British rock where other bands seemed bloated and too corporate. You could sense the band members were a good bunch, determined to work hard and have some fun. This ballad is a beautiful powerful, piece of art. I including it on a compilation tape I put together for Jane - romance isn't dead!

It wasn't long before Jane was visiting me at the branch regularly for an update on the account opening and, despite the glaringly obvious interest on her part, it took me a while to pluck up the courage to ask her for a date. I'd quickly worked out that I had to ask for her mum, Beryl's, approval for a date first as she was the matriarch. The last thing I needed was a complaint levied against me about some unethical behaviour!

We worked out that, although I didn't directly know Jane, my mum had met her whilst undergoing hydrotherapy in Highclere for rheumatoid arthritis. Looking back, mum had spoken about a girl she'd met who'd endured a near-fatal car crash at a local black spot called the Penwood Crossroads, breaking all her limbs in the process. Mum had later met Jane's parents, who were tenderly nursing her, and went on to befriend Beryl through a mutual friend. They had clearly both nattered about their children in the process. I remember the night before I had gone on holiday with my friends to Corfu being down the pub, hearing that there had been a horrific crash there, involving a local girl and later reading about it in the paper. Spooky.

I nervously made my case to Beryl over the telephone from the office and didn't quite know how this was going to play out. She quite quickly

Leather clad couple

said, "Bloody hell love, you took your time, we were starting to give up hope." I took that as a seal of approval. Jane seemed to like keeping fit, rugby players, motorbike owners and my weird sense of humour, so our first date was spent whizzing around the country roads on the bike. We went to the stone circle at Avebury, then zoomed on to Hungerford and Newbury in the drizzle. Jane was understandably nervous about riding pillion so we kept our first ride quiet from Beryl and worked on the premise that if we got back in one piece, all would be forgiven.

Spookily again, Jane's car crash occurred precisely two years before she first met me. Beryl relayed that the phone call Jane made to her about meeting me was at exactly the same time that the emergency services had called her two years earlier, telling her that Jane was in Basingstoke Hospital with life-threatening injuries. Two years later, when Beryl picked up the phone to Jane in very different circumstances, she only hoped that this relationship wasn't going to be a car crash too!

25

NOT JONNY WILKINSON

As some readers will know, there's nothing quite like being part of a sport's team or club. You take the piss out of each other mercilessly, but at the same time, on the field of play, you look out for each other as a band of brothers.

Rugby is such a sport and Hungerford, like other clubs throughout the country, is such a club. When I first joined, I was warmly welcomed by all: they were pleased to get some new blood into the team. I played one game for the second team, *The Surfers*, but thereafter was a permanent fixture in the first team, which I was surprised about, given I was still learning the game.

The club was initially a modest affair, with little in the way of its own facilities. Before we played home games, we had to shoo away the cows, as the pitch was located near the common where the beasts would roam, graze and defecate. After clearing most of the cowpats off the field of play, we'd mark the pitch out. The nearby changing rooms were kindly provided by the cricket club, who had a single dribble shower in their hut, and we used a pub as an impromptu clubhouse. The latter seemed to change a few times in the season: I thought it was about spreading trade around the town's hostelries, but it was more about moving on to another venue before we were barred!

Simon introduced me to the club. As he lived in Newbury, we took turns driving up to Hungerford for training and matches. He was engaged to marry Debbie, a girl who I'd known from St Barts, and coincidentally, Debbie's parents were once neighbours with Jane's parents. Simon and Debbie helped us integrate with the members, players and whole social scene. We had lots of fun.

Mid-week training facilities in the early days weren't much either. We stomped about Barry Wiggins' farm under the security lights of his chicken field, trying to avoid the ankle-deep pot holes where the birds had tried to nest. We played at a basic entry level in the lowest division of Berks, Wilts and Dorset, and initially were just happy to simply be playing. Post-training, we gathered at *The Green Door*, which was owned by Sarah, a sympathetic bar owner. Socialising was a core element of the club.

Then, one year, we seemed to get a little more serious about our aspirations. The committee had played a blinder and the National Lottery part-funded the building of the club's first own facilities, consisting of a kitchen and changing rooms at the Triangle field, where two huge pitches were marked out. Hungerford was well-placed for such funding, not least on account of its past history (mentioned in previous chapters). From then on, things took off. Bob, a gregarious Cornishman and local thatcher, became the first team coach when he returned from New Zealand, the club acquired a set of generator lights which gave us a little pocket of illumination to train in at night, and we recruited players, who all had talent by the bucketful. The theory being that a rising tide lifts all boats.

Sadly, funding didn't extend to a permanent clubhouse bar, but undeterred, the club started to throw many a fundraising barbecue as this acquisition was the next club's goal. At the makeshift bar, drink was often supplied by Cat Weasel, aka Pricey (RIP), who worked at the local *Butts Brewery*. He preferred a simple lifestyle of promoting the ale around local pubs, using his motorcycle and sidecar as transport for the taster barrel.

Members and players came from all different walks of life: office workers like me played alongside farmers and servicemen. Most people were from the town itself or surrounding villages and were deeply rooted in the neighbourhood, but this didn't stop me feeling part of the community. In fact, a few people would nod and say hello to me every time I walked down the high street, for the fact of playing for their town.

Simon and I made a formidable second row partnership; some said the best the club had produced and the tight five was always a solid, consistent platform. We dominated most opposition and supplied ball for those more nimble glory boys, our backs, so they could muck it up in front of our disappointed eyes. The front row regulars included Darren, the owner of the coach company in Newbury, that transported us on many an away fixture. The trouble was, at that time, Darren's buses had a habit of breaking down, as I experienced on my stag do, so the club's transport provider was nicknamed *Voodoo Tours*.

Ralph always seemed to play hooker and, after meeting up recently, he relayed that he played rugby into his mid-fifties and has just had a hip replacement. Wayne played tight head prop most matches and had the job of lifting all sixteen stone of me in the line out; he, for one, was glad I could jump, but not so pleased when I'd occasionally land on his toes when returning to earth. He also lived in Newbury, so we'd often share lifts after Simon moved to Hungerford. This helped me in another way as he was also a mechanic and sorted out my car a few times - a chipped, ex-racer Peugeot 205 1.9 GTi - which had a habit of pinking all too often.

The games were sometimes a tad brutal. It wasn't just blatant violence - there were rules to abide by and both teams left as friends. It was controlled, hard aggression, played on the edge. I loved the fact that anger from the week could be saved and channelled into the week-end's game. Now and then, things would happen in the midst of battle that would stick in your memory vividly, which still make me chuckle. I remember playing a team in a friendly and in the scrum, a boot from the opposition kept swinging towards my face, attempting to connect. This happened a few times before I decided to sort it out, find the culprit and teach him a lesson. I told Simon and the flanker what was happening and told them to bind me in tightly, which kept me in place enough to free up one arm when we packed down. Sure enough, the guilty boot came into view once more, but this time I grabbed it, yanked it and bit the toes of the owner's foot. There was, of course, a scream of agony, given their hooker was now precariously doing the splits with one foot in the mouth of an opponent. When the scrum collapsed, I hid his boot down my shorts and he spent the next five minutes limping about looking for it. It was dog eat dog, but funnily enough, he didn't try it on again. After the match I confessed, bought him a pint and he roared with laughter, admitting it was the first time someone had managed to outfox him. Classic!

Back row, second left, sporting a bandana like Simon

As a novice, my initial tackle technique was poor and often self-harming. In the first season, I sustained a number of injuries and regularly broke my nose from going in face first and too high, meeting an elbow or hand off for my stupidity. I quite often got black eyes, grazes and a swollen, broken hooter. My sinuses took a frequent battering and would empty, with clear, yellowish fluid draining from my nasal cavity when heavily knocked, but I seemed to heal up OK.

Often I would carry the hallmarks of a pub brawl when I turned up at work, freshly suited, on Monday, but they seemed happy for me to explain to customers that I played rugby. As Gordon used to play himself, I was cut some slack. He still remained keen for me to continue studying for the exams and get them finished. He continued to do what he could to encourage me but I stuck with the slow study approach. I was having so much fun and the demands on my time now involved lots more socialising with Jane. In the end, he said I reminded him of himself when he was younger, so surrendered to a lost cause.

One of the most memorable matches was one of my last for the club. We gained promotion to a higher league, thanks mainly to a number of high quality players who had joined our ranks. Two *Voodoo Tours* coaches were dispatched to Warminster, one full of spectators and one with players. It felt like a home fixture, given the support we had that afternoon, and boy, we needed it. We narrowly won the match, even though we were down to fourteen men at one point. I felt awful about conceding a penalty, but redeemed myself making a try-saving tackle late in the second half. We persevered and ground out a win, just. With promotion gained, the next season was all-important as we needed to try and stay up a division higher. The club seemed to be taking shape on the back of it.

On my first tour, which took the club to Italy, I roomed with Pricey, and boy, he could drink. The club's president, Millsy, was forever the diplomat. He calmed the team down in the changing room when we arrived at our first match in Este, at a huge stadium where 2,000 locals had turned up; we wondered why there were so many people. Hungerford had been wrongly billed as Division Two champions of England in the run-up to the match and posters were everywhere in the town, emblazoned with our incorrect status. In reality, the first XV was still playing at the foot of Berks, Wilts and Dorset leagues, Division Three.

Este had taken the fixture very seriously: to them, it was a matter of national pride. They wanted to put out a strong side against the Division Two champions, so peppered their side with ex-international and county ringers. Hungerford was touring with a handful of First team players but the rest of the side were veterans of the game or mates who fancied a laugh, came along and borrowed some boots.

After we'd lined up in front of the townsfolk for the obligatory national anthems, we took a deep breath and prepared for Armageddon. Given that we'd been on the lash since breakfast, we were all feeling a little worse for wear at the 7pm kick off. The score line wasn't pleasant to look at and reflected one-way traffic.

Our hosts were in hysterics after the match. They truly believed that they were going to play a formidable squad, but admitted to elaborating about our position in order to sell more tickets in town. Millsy had to think on his feet that night as he sat down next to the Italian Minister of Sport, who had come along to support his provincial side. In his speech, he paid homage to the growing quality of Italy's rugby and looked forward to the day when the Five Nations would become Six. We also went to play Udinese, who produced the familiar mixture of ringers. They didn't try as hard the next time round - they didn't have to. All day long, we'd been plied with lots of food and drink until you could have rolled us onto the pitch. True to form, we were thoroughly beaten again.

We didn't let the rugby get in the way of a good tour and got to see a little of beautiful Venice. Naturally, it wasn't long before we found a suitable bar in a side street off St Mark's Square. I don't think Venice had seen many visiting rugby teams and weren't used to large groups of men harmlessly drinking and singing. We were soon picked up on the radar and tracked by the local plain-clothed police, who stayed a little behind us on their radios. They must have been concerned that we were football hooligans but didn't need to worry at all: rugby crowds aren't like that. Anyway, we finally got fed up with our trailing spies, so on a count of ten, we split up and made a dash for the ferry, in different directions. We sprinted through the narrow back streets, over bridges and met up on the ferry back to the hotel.

My time at the rugby club gave me self-confidence and also taught me humility. As mentioned previously, I struggled with sport at school as I was physically less-developed than my peers. I was always on the back foot. Later, I realised that everyone ends up as a fully-grown adult and as such, huge advantages in physicality can disappear. From a personal perspective, I think the sport enhanced my character enormously, enabling me to exorcise the childhood demon of inadequacy.

One of our team, a fantastic young lad named Lyle, was tragically killed in a farming accident. This occurred when he and his best mate, another player nicknamed Shag, worked together. At the time, it was a real leveller for the whole club, and affected Shag hugely - he and Lyle had been inseparable. In a small way, the club honours Lyle's memory at an annual memorial match.

Then there's Simon. He'd built a successful career selling computer stuff he didn't understand and forged a happy family life too. Just after their third child was born, Debbie found Simon on the landing, after he'd returned from watching an Autumn International at Twickenham. She thought he was just sleeping off a hangover as he'd had a few shandies. But he was in a coma and was rushed to A & E. He was later diagnosed with ADEM (acute disseminated encephalomyelitis), an inflammation of his brain and spinal cord. After several months of rehabilitation, he was still unable to walk and now mainly uses a wheelchair and endures a number of other medical complications. He and his wife separated around this time and, very sadly, they lost their eldest child in 2010 to a long, protracted fight against leukemia. Life has thrown him some huge, dark challenges and yet he still radiates positive energy, which has given me perspective during my life, especially over the last year or so. Most recently, he's become very altruistic and is driven by a burning desire to share the pleasure of his newfound music with the world. He learnt to play guitar and formed a rock group with our old half back Sparky. The band is called *The Unwashed Commoners* and they'll probably be selling out Wembley Arena in a few years… maybe. Some people don't get to meet their heroes - I'm delighted to say I'm good friends with one of mine.

With the old rascal, Simon

Back to my playing days. I was surrounded by individuals with far more experience than me on the field of play, but I eventually started to contribute more and more as my skills grew. Parallels could be drawn with my career.

Life was being enjoyed at full throttle. I had a fantastic girlfriend, rugby provided us with a superb social life on a plate and we were contemplating moving to Hungerford and settling down there.

Then, after a year or so of Nirvana, the merry-go-round stopped. At work I was told I had to go and report to the Bracknell branch, doing exactly the same job as in Newbury, but just for the hell of it, with an added daily round trip of 65 miles through the highly-infested traffic routes of the M4 and A329. Gordon tried his best to sell it to me, but he couldn't polish a turd, so I initially refused to go.

The area director wasn't mucking about and told me that I should take the new role or leave the bank. To say that the ultimatum was less than motivating would be an understatement. In an instant, it summed up the culture of our leadership at the time. Up until that point, I'd had a lot of respect for him but that evaporated in an instant. Reputations are built over years, but disappear in a nanosecond. There were other, more local candidates who would learn from the role, but he seemed set on reducing the headcount at the Newbury office too.

I pondered on resigning and getting another local job, which would have been very easy, as Vodafone's head office was booming and yearning for suitable candidates; the salaries were a fair bit higher too. I would have thoroughly enjoyed the sheer satisfaction of saying 'screw you' and a number of people (from within his own team) egged me on to stand up to him, out of principle. But when it came down to it, I thought about the ten-year investment of time and effort I'd already ploughed into my career to that point. I again focussed on the long game. It wasn't about the next year or so, but more about where that might take me and Jane in the future. So with a nod to the long term, I tried to get the best deal I could. Little old me vs. Big Boss.

I begrudgingly agreed to serve a maximum of eighteen months in Bracknell and negotiated a pay rise to cover some of the fuel and transport costs I now had to endure (none being offered up by the area office originally). He clearly underestimated my resolve, probably not even knowing that I'd ventured out of his clutches to London and Worthing a year or two earlier.

After sulking through the first morning at the Bracknell office, I decided to get stuck in. I was determined to enjoy my time there, ensuring that time would pass quickly, whilst keeping a beady eye on the eighteen-month leaving date.

The branch was in the centre of the town - a hideous, concrete shopping precinct at the time that was probably built in the 1950's. I nicknamed the branch 'the bunker' and found it was full of some cracking people who quickly became friends. It was smaller than Newbury and, as everyone was on the same ground floor, the team seemed more tight-knit. The fall-outs between staff were also spectacular, as everyone got a ring side seat. The team seemed to enjoy my humour as I quickly gave nicknames to some of its colourful characters - Captain Chaos and Vlad the Impaler - to name a few. We had fun; I'd made the best of a bad situation and some friends to boot. I didn't learn anything new in particular, apart from changing the codes on a safe door, which was a hugely fiddly job. As soon as the eighteen month timeline started to appear on the horizon, I began to look for new roles, pointedly searching in alternative locations. I had no wish to remain in the area, so Jane encouraged me to try London. After all, that's where most of the interesting jobs were being advertised. The shame was, it ultimately meant a move away from my beloved rugby club, but my future married life with Jane came first.

Jane and I were married in May 1998, locally at Highclere Castle, where Jane had always dreamt of getting wed. It was a stunning, local backdrop to a magical day and the kids still can't believe that we got hitched in Downton Abbey! In some ways, it was a farewell to a number of close friends we'd made living in Newbury and socialising in Hungerford. The rugby season was over and we partied hard with friends during the summer. In no time at all, I was offered a job and promotion at the London Head Office branch at Poultry and Princes Street. So, off to the bright lights of the big city I went.

Married at Highclere Castle, the 7th Earl of Canarvon in shot too

Before we move onto the next chapter, I think it's worth sharing details of the last rugby tour I played in, so let's fast forward to Hungerford's Veteran's Tour to Tavistock in 2016. I think it's connected to the cancer story and worth a mention.

Transport was again laid on by Darren's coach firm. No longer were we allowed to mention *Voodoo Tours*. Now our carriage was a posh, state-of-the-art executive coach, one of many in their growing fleet. On the Friday morning, after joining the bus at Newbury with Simon, we picked up the bulk of the players at Hungerford's Town Hall. The fixture had been organised by our old training coach, Bob, who by now was living in the South West.

Simon and I had been planning to go for some time and typically, missed one of the most important details. We didn't realise there was a fancy dress code for the journey there. On the bus, quite a few had made the effort. We had Rowley (tourist extraordinaire) dressed as a buxom lady pirate and Matt as God himself, with full beard, sandals and a monk's habit. Luckily, we weren't the only ones without costume, so Fordy, one of the club's less legendary second rows, acquired various ladies' frocks and wigs from a charity shop on the high street.

The coach pulled away at 11am, we got changed into our frocks and the port started to flow. It was getting messy by the time we stopped at the Forest of Dene motorway service station on the M4. We got plenty of looks and requests from travellers who wanted to have their photo taken with us.

At Tavistock, half of the team took residence in a comfortable B & B and I roomed with another good mate Fordy. The other half selected rooms above a pub up in town. This was to become our club HQ for the week-end.

Match day was predictably tough. Getting mustered after our first night on the town was always going to be a challenge in itself. Following a full English breakfast, accompanied by a few pints of Guinness at the pub, we walked up to the club and were met in the bar by the opposition, who bought us a few more rounds. They played regularly as a vets team and their squad consisted of 25 burly Devon boys who had put many a visiting scratch team on the sword.

Let's assess the quality and depth of our team for a moment. Some were drawing a pension and 90% of us, like me, were lumbering ex-forwards. I was surprised when they said, "Wilko, ever played outside centre? It'll only be for ten or so minutes." I don't mind saying, I was relatively fit, strong and mobile for my 48 years of age, but this was my first game for about eighteen years. Every tackle I missed or made hurt a lot and I was very rusty. You're never match fit unless you play regularly.

After fifteen minutes of concerted, defensive effort, the Tavistock Vets carved their way through our slow back line and, 25-0 down, we eagerly trudged behind the uprights to quench our thirst at half time. Refreshments were kindly laid on by the hosts who supplied a couple of buckets of scrumpy, to stop us sobering up.

Early in the second half, I was handed off in the face, sustaining another hit to my nose. As usual, my sinuses emptied their yellowish liquid in front of me. Aha! Freeze that picture and fast forward a couple of years. When I started to research spindle cell sarcomas, I found that they were synonymous with repetitive injuries. Spindle cells are a naturally occurring part of the body's result to injury. My godfather (mentioned before as an awesome eye patch craftsman) also told me that he knew a boxer who didn't have a great guard and, consequently, his nose received regular injuries from jabbing opponents. He contracted the cancer in his nose and had to have it amputated. I'm no medical expert, but maybe, just maybe, I've pinpointed the cause of my cancer…my incredibly crap tackle technique.

Back to the veterans game. Despite the injury and my protests, I ended up playing the whole 80 minutes. We lost heavily and I didn't know that my body could hurt so much, but true to form, we did our club proud. We didn't let the rugby get in the way of enjoying the tour. Tavistock were fantastic hosts and we all drank and sang our way through that Bank Holiday week-end, which culminated in a usual court case on the last day. Fordy was the barrister for the prosecution and I was in the dock for damaging Simon's property.

As Simon was in a wheelchair, I felt it was my duty, as a friend, to get this prepared when we got off the coach and pushed him up Tavistock's steep, cobbled streets. He warmly referred to me as his 'week-end bitch'. Unfortunately, I was a little too exuberant one time putting the 'easy fit' wheels on and he accused me of irreparably damaging the bearings of the axle. In my defence, I claimed that it might have had something to do with a couple of the burly lads 'having a go' on the wheelchair around town whilst Simon was sitting in the pub. Naturally, I was found guilty and can't quite remember what I drank and ate as punishment, or even whether I remained clothed. Another sign of a good tour.

Once you've been a player and member of a very sociable rugby team, you're always able to walk into its bar and pick off from where you've left, even many years later. It might initially cost you a round, but that's not the point, you feel instantly rooted. In any case, you're always remembered and invariably someone says, "Hi mate, let me get this," or you get plenty bought back. It's great to see how embedded some team mates who remained local became and on the back on their hard work, drive and goodwill, the club has blossomed. A lot of my team mates now volunteer in the echelons of the club's committee, refereeing and coaching. If I had stayed locally, I've no doubt I'd have followed a similar path. The club continues to be the epicentre of its members' social lives and the clubhouse has increased its footprint. It boasts an excellent number of senior teams and hundreds of juniors are coached at the week-ends.

I coached at Basingstoke RFC for a handful of years and thoroughly enjoyed the experience. But although I could see it remained dad's club, which he occasionally visited, it was never mine. Again it 'belonged' to those who had played and lived there too.

Over the years, I kept in touch which wasn't easy from afar. More recently, I've revisited Hungerford RFC and its new, bustling clubhouse with a little more regularity. Cancer's gift of time has helped. I'm a very small part of the club's history and proud that I'm in a few photos on the wall and that my name is etched on some bricks, recognising donations I made to its construction. I re-connected with many of my ex-team mates and made new friends as well. Hungerford RFC and my friends there will always have a special place in my heart and invariably my liver too.

26

LONDON CALLING

Back to 1998. Poultry & Princes Street Head Office was very different to any market town branch I'd frequented. The branch itself stretched out on the very large ground floor area of the iconic building, with several floors of offices housing thousands of staff, including the senior executives of the bank. Consequently, we were always under the watchful gaze of the top brass who habitually rang the branch manager if they felt something wasn't quite right, and a large number of them had accounts with us too.

Designed in 1924 by the famous Sir Edwin Lutyens, it was a stunning, Grade 1 listed masterpiece. Steeped in history, a monument to an era of commerce and banking, when the city was full of gentlemen who wore top hats to work. Antique, wooden hat storage boxes lined the corridors of the upper floors that encircled the grand director's board room. This was adorned with a tapestry and the largest table I'd ever seen; it must have weighed a few tons. Along these long walkways hung portraits of past chairmen on high walls. They all seemed to look down their noses at you, sitting perfectly, demanding respect, having achieved their ambition. Dotted about the corridors were small dining rooms which were frequently used to entertain customers. They were of course heavily utilised by all of the local teams, including ourselves. More than three courses, restaurant-style food and fine wines for lunch - better than sandwiches at your desk!

Enormous, beautiful, yet tired and a little dysfunctional. The building worked in its own unique way for the modern day too - just. Working on the ground floor reminded me of going to the swimming pool as a child: the permanent din of peoples' voices reverberated around the 30 feet-tall, green Italian marble columns surrounding the work areas, which were hidden by tall, wooden walls. Its famous banking hall and huge, steel safe door and strong room had been used in film sets (*Mary Poppins* and *James Bond*), and deep in its subterranean basement lay an artesian well. It was also a bit of a nature reserve too: the whole ground floor was ridden with mice. It was hilarious to hear the daily shriek of female cashiers and clerks when a rodent or two dashed over their feet.

The branch manager, Yvonne, was growing her personal banking team and clearly had seen something deep inside the raw slab of talent sitting in front of her at the interview. I was quickly introduced to the rest of the team and we got to know one another by going for a drink - shame not to, after all. This was something that continued to occur frequently and there were plenty of historic hostelries within walking distance, one of the unforeseen benefits I thoroughly enjoyed. Some taverns were famous and centuries old, tucked away down ancient alleyways; it all added to the nostalgia of the area. It was clearly very different from the Bracknell bunker situated within its Luftwaffe-inspired concrete precinct. I knew very quickly that I was going to enjoy myself there.

Charity costume day at Poultry. Return of the phantom?

Effectively, my role was to look after very important, often wealthy, customers who might be CEOs or leaders of industry within the Square Mile. Often we'd help in a small way to ensure new executives of corporate customers were treated well when they joined their UK offices from overseas, so we frequently mixed with the global corporate teams upstairs. It was a great insight to meet some incredibly high-flying, über clever people and celebrities. On the face of it, a few seemed to be blessed with no more than good fortune and luck, but most were highly intelligent, extremely well-polished and very hard-working. They didn't expect you to bow, but needed you to be on top of your game. Making things easy and seamless would engender loyalty and they would refer friends at work, which grew the business.

I was surprised to find that a few of my new colleagues were initially quite wary of me and I wasn't initially taken into everybody's confidence. I wanted to get to the bottom of it and, when I asked why, they relayed that I'd appeared too keen. I initially found this bizarre but I guess it takes a while to build up trust. They felt I may have been a mole but they clearly didn't know me at all, for I'd shown team loyalty many times in the past. However, there was no avoiding it: I was the new kid on the block. I was simply fired up and hell-bent on working hard for someone who had plucked me from obscurity. Some saw this in me and took me into their confidence; they were similarly minded and I was content with their friendship and support. Fired up with ambition, I vowed to complete my professional exams, despite the fact that some of the syllabus harked back to a bygone era of banking, which was fast becoming irrelevant.

After a while, I got the hump with the naysayers in the team and chose to ignore them. As far as I was concerned, if I showed others up by coming into the role with no baggage, then sod 'em. I was there to get on, not make friends with peculiar people. Some of the more vocal ones had clearly been around the block a few times and weren't there by choice. This was the last role for a few, so I took their grumbles with a pinch of salt. At the same time, it made me reflect; I was still relatively young in career and hadn't really spent long enough in one place to establish a good reputation. As I wanted to stay in London for the long haul, I consciously observed that everything I did from hereon in would influence this.

From my point of view, it wouldn't have been too difficult for one or two of my peers to be a little more welcoming and open. It's what I'd have done: treat others how you would like to be treated, I thought. But the longer the playground behaviour went on, the more bloody-minded I became and just got on with the job in hand.

Contemporaneously, I could understand some of the frustrations about our role - some things didn't make sense to me. What I found particularly odd was the lack of portfolio financial information. There was no focus on how much a manager's portfolio was contributing, or whether it was growing. We also lacked a robust way of independently measuring how well our service was received by the very people who pay the bills - the customers. Surely if you ran a business with portfolios of customers, this information should be key? All that seemed to matter was the amount of commission generated by financial planning referrals.

It wasn't my branch manager's decision to focus on this specific area of services (here we go again). It was the directive of top executives, who set the strategy, later underpinned by divisional and regional leaders who set the culture. Before you know it, those on the frontline are whipped up in a frenzy with the view that the only thing that matters is making commission for a select few.

I noted that team members moved on to other roles more rapidly in London. It seemed far more fluid and, within a year, 50% of the team had already turned over. Suddenly I was one of the longest-serving staff members. If I worked hard, kept my nose clean and got results, then I could move on and be in a completely different role within say, three years.

In late 1998, Jane and I moved to Beckenham, where the bank's sports club was based, and it was a half decent commute into the centre of London. Back in the day when gentlemen wore top hats, all of the large domestic banks chose to have their sports and social clubs in the same vicinity because a lot of the senior executives lived there. So they built a station there too, allowing for a convenient commute and letting the hoi polloi come to the clubs too.

We initially rented a small, one-bedroom flat in a block of flats, to get a lay of the land, but quickly tired of listening to humping neighbours. The other bone of contention was parking. One night, we parked our dilapidated Peugeot 505 estate outside our flat window and it got stolen by a pick-up truck. When a neighbour mentioned that he'd watched it being towed away whilst walking his dog in the early hours, it made my blood boil. When I reported the crime, the police reckoned it was already on a ship out of Folkestone to live another life in Africa as a taxi. Apparently, these type of vehicles had been heavily targeted by thieves. Within six months, we'd had enough and bought a little Victorian, two-bed end of terrace, just off the high street.

I joined the rugby club at the sports and social club as it was on the doorstep, and what amazing facilities it had. A 1920's pavilion, surrounded by sports pitches of different types and a great bar. It was fantastic to be playing again, but the club atmosphere was nothing like Hungerford. I tried to integrate, but found that it lacked a galvanising spirit of fun. I trained hard and played a few times but soon lost interest.

Coming to our rescue, someone arrived in a neighbouring office at Poultry who became great friends with us. Paul (aka Viper) was a sharp-suited snake who loved the City lifestyle, especially slithering into wine bars with his Café Creme cigars, ordering Laurent Perrier Rose champagne with his 'bugger the consequences' attitude. He lived in Beckenham too and happily showed us about, taking me and Jane under his wing. Vipes had also come to London to seek a better career and was full of character. Thanks to him, we were soon woven into a network of close friends in Beckenham and 'settled in' for the long haul.

Our group centred around three local girls who'd known each other since childhood. One by one, they got married in quick succession. Jane and I fitted in nicely, despite already being married, and Clair, John, Jo, Gary, Paula and Tom were great company. The girls loved Jane. The boys found similar interests in beer and sport, had a craic and tried not to get into too much trouble. We spent a lot of time together, partying hard in local bars and going on trips down to the coast at week-ends. It was hilarious to see Paula's recurring travel sickness on these journeys. She was a hard-nosed detective in the Met and had clearly seen a few stomach-churning things in her career. Tom announced that she'd once kept a head in the fridge as evidence - don't know if I believed him though!

Given the frequency of trains to the City and West End, Beckenham was a great base to live. I'd often get back late from work and hook up with Jane in one of the two dozen or so pubs or restaurants on the high street. Jane took on some local office work and made friends of her own too. Our house became party central for a while and we travelled on a few far-flung holidays when we could. We were proper DINKYs!

Party central. An 'EastEnders'-inspired fancy dress party - I'm Pat

As the three years at Poultry started to loom, I completed my professional exams and converted them to a First Class BSc degree. Look at me, the under-achieving late developer who'd sensibly chosen the apprentice route, finally getting an academic accolade to hang on the wall. One in the eye for the early developers! I was pleased as punch and so happy to finally put the burden of studying after work and at week-ends behind me. Passing this milestone also seemed to stir up a positive wave of interest at work and I was eager for a change.

I was approached to join the institutional banking team, which essentially managed relationships with other banks around the world and in the past had been referred to as 'correspondent banking'. I was lucky enough to have the pick of two jobs and, after consulting with a mentor, Malcolm, chose the one on the Middle East & Africa desk, as the likely foreign travel to these regions sounded far more exciting. "I don't see you making a long career here, so you might as well grab the experience of doing business in far-flung places," Malcolm advised. I wasn't disappointed.

The first trip I took was to Nigeria, the only country where company policy dictated employees travel in twos for safety reasons. At the time, the security advice was such that we needed to travel with a designated 'fixer' too, who I think was armed in the front seat of the car, next to the driver. I didn't ask him to get out his pistol.

Some of the sights I witnessed are seared into my memory forever. "I have a feeling we're not in Kansas anymore," I said to Brian, my boss, whilst looking out of the back seat of the car at the Lagos skyline. It was Brian's first visit there too and he commented, "You know what? I set up our offices in India where there was abject poverty all around, like here, but at least there was something nice to look at, like a temple or two. This place is the worst shit-hole I've ever been to." Sobering words from an experienced colleague who'd travelled to most parts of the world for over 20 years.

Brian must have been in various roles across many regions in his 30-plus year career and was very experienced. He was quite a character and was happiest when he was out of the office and travelling. He filled up dozens of passports during his time and didn't abate on travelling himself. His boss, Quentin, was similarly experienced and his office was adorned with many trophies from his travels, such as African head masks, shields and trinkets.

Lagos offered chaos in abundance: it had a beach but this was overrun with a shanty town. Stepping outside of the high security-fenced hotel was a no-no and, although it had a modern airport, a customs official made me very aware that he fancied taking my suit for his own wardrobe. Flying to Abuja with the local operator, *Chinga Chinga Airways*, gave us a taste of the local service standards. The stewardess couldn't reach me in the window seat so threw me the lunch to catch, a wrapped meat pie. This made Brian spit out his coffee in disgust - he didn't get this on *British Airways* club class! I didn't get to ask what type of meat it was but it had a picture of a monkey on the wrapper. By then, the stewardess was in her stride, already several aisles down the plane, lobbing pies at other passengers.

Another memory was the traffic. Given the precarious nature of government spending, three-lane carriageways and flyovers were often left unfinished when the project's cash was depleted. So all of the traffic would converge into one lane where the concrete ran out at the end of the highway, in a hot maelstrom of parping horns, raised fists and hot fumes. Once cars were trapped in this bottleneck, they were besieged by fruit sellers, beggars and sadly, crippled children, who dragged themselves around on makeshift skateboards. "Probably crippled by their gang leader to bring in more money," said the fixer. This really hit home as the eldest of the ragged, wheeled kids could only have been ten years old.

At that point, there was a shrieking of sirens behind us in the chaotic triangle of traffic and we could see a blue Peugeot security van which was apparently transporting cash or bullion between the banks. Two guards hanging out of the back doors were in some sort of uniform, shouting abuse and brandishing their AK47s in the air, kicking any cars in their path. The front passenger guard was even more menacing: he looked very drugged up and dangerous as he stood on a side plate and used a bullwhip on cars in front of the van to get them to part and let the van through. Miraculously, the surrounding cars found some space and got out of its way. It must have been a frequent occurrence. The bullion van passed slowly but surely through the metal scrum of smoking vehicles and our driver had the foresight to follow it. Nigeria was a baptism of fire for me, the uninitiated lamb to the slaughter. I survived and made it home.

Funnily enough, I had a couple of very minor medical episodes around that time. When I got back from Nigeria, I developed a swelling around my gums and went to the doctor's. It was a little surreal: when I started to explain that I'd been abroad and thought I might have a virus, they automatically thought I'd contracted a little STD downstairs. They almost referred me to a clinic and believed I wanted to surreptitiously get it sorted, without my wife knowing. Thankfully, the swelling turned out to be an innocent reaction to the very powerful anti-malaria tablets I'd been taking. Beckenham must have been a hotbed of promiscuity.

The other episode still makes Jane and I laugh. I'd been going to the gym, weight-training, and felt a hernia pop in my groin area. I knew straight away that I'd overdone it and, as I was now in my thirties, I noted that I needed to ease up in the future. Anyway, I eventually ended up going to hospital for a very small procedure to fix it. Jane was adamant that I help the nursing staff as much as possible, and Beryl, her mum, was on at me too. She'd been surviving cancer for decades by then and was all for helping out the NHS. Given that I am rather hairy, they suggested I help by shaving the area myself in preparation. I don't think Jane could bear the thought of someone shaving my downstairs region for me. I saw the logic, gingerly got the razor to work and buffed up.

When I was admitted, we proudly told the nurse that I'd helped her out, so to speak, and explained why. She wet herself laughing. Nobody had advised us that the whole thing was to be done via keyhole surgery so there was no need to have shaved at all! As well as a bit of soreness from surgery, I was itching for weeks afterwards and vowed to let the experts do their job in future.

The role lived up to the promise of more international travel and it's clear why some colleagues stayed in the department for many years. They'd literally seen most, if not all, of the world, courtesy of the bank; they found the air miles very useful too.

Travelling was pretty safe and, despite its obvious cost, was seen as an integral part of keeping overseas relationships strong. Once I'd got a couple of trips under my belt, I was allowed to fly solo and enjoyed the responsibility and freedom. As anyone will tell you though, foreign travel with work isn't a stroll in the park and can be exhausting. We were expected to conduct five meetings a day, write up reports and get back to work that had piled up in our absence. You had to conserve energy. But I knew I was in a pretty special job and could see why colleagues stuck, rather than twisted for another role.

Jane and I would snatch time together between trips and made the most of being back home, spending the majority of time in Beckenham. We occasionally went back to visit Berkshire, so as not to lose touch with some friends completely. When I was overseas, Jane's parents would often pop up and stay, which was great for Jane and me, as the house would often need a little bit of tender loving care. My father-in-law, Bob, was a dab hand with all the household DIY jobs and loved getting stuck in. I wasn't allowed to lift a brush!

We continued to have lots of fun at week-ends when I was home and visited a few villages in Kent with friends. One of them being Chilham, a historical, quintessentially English village. At the top of a hill sat the village square, with the church and pristinely-kept listed buildings, dating back to the fifteenth century. At the bottom of the hill was a cosy pub, *The Woolpack Inn*, where we stayed. We'd gone to celebrate Jane's birthday around Halloween and, after getting rather inebriated, the boys decided we ought to dress up as ghosts with the bedsheets from our rooms and race around the graveyard. This had all the chilling charm of a *Hammer House of Horror* opening scene; there was even mist rolling across the ivy-infested tombstones. We caused a few curtains to twitch in neighbouring houses, but when the vicar came out of the church, we had to hurriedly hide behind the gravestones and remove the garments quickly without being seen. He just walked merrily past us without a murmur, as if we weren't there. It was all rather deflating, so we just went back to our rooms. The next morning at breakfast, we were told that the graveyard was reputed to be one of the most haunted in England. We didn't see any ghosts and had probably frightened them away.

On my travels to other countries like Jordan and Egypt, I found myself more confidently participating in hospitality, mixing with the natives a little and getting royally ripped off.

Gary was a colleague who worked alongside the relationship managers and was an expert on payments, a big part of mutual business between banks. He and I arrived in Amman for a two-day visit and, on the last night, as we'd got to know our taxi driver during the day, we asked him to take us out to see some sights – "Somewhere where we can mix with the locals and see how Jordanians let their hair down," we requested. In no time at all, we were at a multi-restaurant, fast food complex which was extremely busy. Everyone stared at the two mad Englishmen who looked very much out of place. We didn't feel at all like we were in any danger, we just didn't fit in. Then our driver said he'd organised some drinks at a bar he knew, owned by a relative. "That's more like it!", said Gary. We were thirsty and in need of a cool beer after the hot, dry meal we'd tried to scoff. In a matter of minutes, we pulled up on a dusty road outside a two-storey, flat-roofed building, which had a single bar sign above its narrow, dark doorway. Inside was a tiny ticket office then upstairs, the bar, where Arabic music was already blaring out.

"No problem gentlemen, you are most welcome, just go upstairs and take a table, make yourselves at home - we have a dancing girl tonight." The driver had surpassed the mandate. Drinks, entertainment and culture. Excitedly, we climbed the stairs and turned the corner.

The room was completely empty. We had the pick of many tables so the two of us settled at a table large enough for ten, with a beer in hand, and tried to talk over the din of the wailing music. Then out from behind a stage rushed a plump Arabic lady in local costume, who started to take layers of clothing off. Gary and I weren't sure if this was a strip joint and settled for the theory that it was a belly dancing palace, and thankfully, the lady stopped taking off her several veils and started to gyrate around, between, over and in front of us.

You couldn't miss her large, bejewelled moving belly. At first glance, you wouldn't have expected her ample mid-riff to be able to roll and cavort to the fast rhythm of the Bedouin beats, but it did, rather well we thought. Anyhow, after half an hour, we'd had enough; we'd consumed a few beers and the tiredness of the day had caught up with us. We were clearly there way before any local customers were due to arrive so we signalled that we wanted to leave and asked for the bill. Gary was great at one thing and that was arguing, so I volunteered him to sort out the $500 bill that had landed on our table.

After half an hour of heated haggling at the box office, Gary had managed to attract the attention of a couple of large henchmen who lurked menacingly in the shadows, to back up the owner. He got the bill down to $100 though. I suggested we pay it, given we had to pay for the entertainment, as well as the imported beer that had been ice cold: it was a fair price. Luckily, the owner was happy with this mediation. We avoided a diplomatic incident or being bundled into the boot of a car to become landfill. We went outside to get back to the hotel for a nightcap. The driver wasn't too happy though: he'd been charged $20 parking for bringing two stingy Englishman to the nightclub without enough money.

Another trip took me to Cairo which was a chaotic city. By my reckoning, you can generally tell how mad a city is by the amount of car horns you hear from the traffic. Cairo was another crazy place where drivers used their horns as a declaration of territory, whilst driving in what looked like a demolition derby. It was incessant!

I met up with Nigel there to see the customers. Nigel had previously worked in the London office before taking a secondment in Dubai. He was very experienced in international trade and took the lead role on many of our global relationships. I managed the business that our London office did with the customers. He was good fun on trips and we got on well.

The working day started early, due to the rising heat. Our five daily visits were completed by 2.30pm, so Nigel and I decided that we ought to take in a few sites on our second night, rather than just blob out at the swimming pool with a large, cool beer again (although this was very tempting).

When we got back to the hotel, we were changed in five minutes and jumped in a taxi to see the Great Pyramids. It's amazing how well-connected taxi drivers are around the world! This one apparently had a brother who owned two camels next to the pyramids and he could happily arrange a tour of a recently-excavated tomb. We said we'd love to meet his brother and gave him the thumbs up. I sensed that he was rubbing his hands together all the way to Giza.

Camel riding is an art form. Swaying like curtains in a breeze, I got my hips into action as the ships of the desert took us through some dodgy backstreets up a hill, to the foot of the pyramids. "I can't get the hang of this sodding thing. You look like John Wayne up there, you bugger, how d'you do it?", Nigel complained. "All in the hip action mate, at one with the beast," I replied.

I don't think our beasts were in prime condition and I dare say they weren't the best kept in the world. They just about managed to carry us and, whilst groaning and grunting, seemed to be bitterly complaining. Thanks to their dropping-infested back legs, we were soon enveloped by the halo of flies which seemed to follow the beasts and now us, everywhere. My shorts and tee-shirt were going to stink for weeks.

Although I'd spent a day exploring the pyramids on holiday before, this experience was a new one to me. Nigel and I sat atop a hill, on our majestic beasts, swatting and spitting out insects, as we watched the tourist buses load up and scuttle home. It was amazing to see the Sphinx and the Great Pyramid in this manner, as the sun began to fall. Less Lawrence of Arabia, more Laurel & Hardy on tour.

"Meester, we've prepared a tomb for you, so we'll lead you there." Off I swayed, getting more and more adept at absorbing the swinging motion of the travel. Poor old Nigel was less flexible: I heard his cries and curses behind me. After we'd visited the tomb of a Pharaoh's architect and said goodbye to our camels, we were asked to take a seat inside a building, knowing that this type of hospitality doesn't come free, even if your taxi driver has a kind brother. Yet again, the initial bargaining started in the mid hundred dollars, but Nigel was canny enough to tell me to only take $50 out that night, which we put on the table and showed our empty wallets. Our hosts were clearly a little disappointed to have not ripped us off further, but accepted our fair payment.

Working on the Middle East desk was interesting to say the least, during September 2001. I was working at my London desk when the images of 9/11 started to unfold. We didn't have internet or mobile telephony, so went to the boardroom to look at the TV there. I called Jane and asked her to tune in and watch. Looking back, this was our equivalent of the JFK moment for our parents. That night, I went home early, reading *The Evening Standard*. Jane and I got home and were glued to the set as the whole drama unfolded, including the collapse of both towers. I think the BBC aired a *Question Time* debate on screen with US embassy officials, who were clearly in a state of shock. When asked why anyone would do this, there was a small element of the room who suggested that US foreign policy over the years, in promoting puppet corrupt dictators and clear assassination programmes, had brought it on themselves. I don't like the hypocrisy of Western governments that seem to show little or no action when genocides or other atrocities occur around the world because it isn't in their country's interests to control puppet dictators in countries far weaker than them. But the logic of 'deserving it' didn't, and doesn't, sit well with me at all. It was a calculated, cold-blooded, inhumane, murderous act of innocent civilians. It was not a protest of US foreign policy.

Over the next year or so after 9/11, there was a palpable call to arms by the US and a rally of support drew the UK shoulder to shoulder. Before long, our country instructed its very brave, loyal armed forces to launch headfirst (and sometimes ill-prepared) into an unplanned, long war of retribution which seemed to have the effect of throwing fuel on the flames of the Jihadists. This wasn't a war in reaction to an invasion of our own sovereign land, like the Falklands for instance, this was blatant, ill sighted revenge. Many, many further innocent lives were either lost or affected by what seemed a lashing out at a rogue dictator (who is said to have been put in power by the West some years earlier). It seemed a total misreading of the tea leaves by Number 10, but some might say leaders like to have the chance of war as it is the ultimate power. The UK government instructed our brave forces into a war where the evidence of weapons of mass destruction didn't actually exist. They ignored the common man's gut feel and the marching of a million or so people in protest.

♪ War Pigs (Black Sabbath) ♪

One of the old classics. It conjures up images of bloated, out-of-touch politicians and generals driven on by a lust of negative emotions such as revenge, power and control, ordering the horrific fate of the suffering common man on the front line and resulting in the loss of innocent lives.

As we now know, 9/11 and the response of the UK and USA, in the shape of an ill-thought out invasion of Iraq and Afghanistan, set the scene for diplomatic relations with many parts of the region for future generations.

You'd be right to conclude that all this had a major impact at the office, especially on the Middle East desk where I worked. I remember being in Turkey when tanks rolled into Iraq and many meetings with customers were spent discussing foreign policy. It's all we talked about. We soon realised that we were the only bank travelling in the region and loved that badge of honour. But in my view, we were rather myopic to the changing environment around us.

The cosy world of correspondent banking that was built on an old boy's network of trust was not a great fit with the rise of modernity and alongside it, tighter compliance and regulation brought on by the Patriot Act that came about after 9/11.

Jane naturally became a little more worried about me travelling, but an even bigger worry arose when our offices moved from Poultry to the 32nd floor of the brand new global HQ in Canary Wharf. I remember an induction meeting got quite heated when the audience kept pressing the presenters about the safety of the building if it were to become the target of airborne terrorism. They fessed up the glaringly obvious: you can't design a building to withstand an impact of that magnitude. Windows were sealed and the only alternative way down was 42 floors of stairs for 8,500 staff. My desk faced east and, in the first few weeks, I was obsessed by the planes taking off from City Airport, which would head towards the building on take-off, then bank away to their destination.

After a couple of years, we had other things to think about when Jane fell pregnant with Max. In the last few weeks before his birth, I went to Hong Kong on a training course and travelled with a good friend, Rossy, who worked in an adjoining office. He vowed to look after me and noted that I intended to fill my boots and absorb as much of the culture as possible, given that I had many sleepless nights ahead.

The training centre was a 30-minute tube journey from our hotel in Kowloon and, one night, we hooked up for heavy drinks and dinner with another friend who'd been posted there, Arjan. By now, Arjan had got to know all the back street drinking dens and restaurants, so we knew we were in for a great time. The strangest meal I came across was called *Hot Pot* - please skip the next paragraph if you're a vegan.

Hong Kong Hot Pot was nothing like the Lancashire variety my mum occasionally made. Here, diners were presented with a boiling pot of fish stew surrounded by a pile of ice, upon which your food, fish and crustaceans, were placed. The trouble was, some of the food was clearly still alive. Some more mobile and alert specimens (usually nimble-legged large shrimps) tried to make a dash for safety, like a scene out of *The Great Escape*, so you had to deal with those first. Think of a fondue, but with shrimps instead of meat or cheese. It was pretty barbaric as you'd need to hold on to the spear whilst the poor creature carried out its last death throes in the boiling pot. It's probably not a cuisine style that would catch on in London, but a real insight as to how other cultures view food sources. Some of the restaurants kept animals and poultry outside in small cages and diners would pick which one they fancied. Brutal, or just culturally different?

Drinking was very much more Western-influenced and Wan Chai had plenty of bars to choose from. On our last night, I believe Rossy and I visited most of them. I discovered a taste for the tequila that night and remember swaying underneath a scantily-clad waitress who was dancing on the bar, holding a huge bottle of spirits under each arm, most of it directed at my awaiting open mouth. That was my last memory of the evening.

The next thing I remember was finding myself naked, sitting upright on the edge of my bed, feeling a little shabby, back at the hotel I may add. Then I noticed the time. I'd already missed the start of the day's lesson and needed to pack, check out and haul myself and the luggage to the classroom if I was going to catch the flight home. Painfully, with a heavy head, I made it in for the morning's coffee break. Thank goodness Rossy had made up a few excuses for me as I slipped in amongst the other students. I apologised to the tutor and was relieved that I'd made him aware of my presence as he was just about to call my line manager in London to see if he knew where I was. Talk about dodging a bullet!

Jane and I enjoyed some fantastic holidays throughout this time, but better than great photos and memories, we made some life-long friends too. We met one couple, Grant and Shelley, in a hot tub at a hotel in Whistler and hit it off in an instant. Two bottles of wine and a few North American tourist disapproving tuts later, we were singing songs and the best of mates. This initial meeting was made more memorable because Shelley's hair turned green due to the chlorine in the hot tub. It was probably also reacting to the spilled wine being sloshed in with the bubbles.

On a rest day during our trip to Whistler, we went downtown to Vancouver on the Greyhound bus to check out the city, a couple of hours' drive away.

On the way there, we were driven through some of the most breath-taking scenery on this planet, where the pines bled into the still waters of the Howe Sound. We passed through and stopped at various townships; I remember Squamish and a peculiarly-named Furry Creek! Once we'd gone through the outskirts of Stanley Park, we entered the financial district and planned to visit the Lookout Tower for the views across the harbour.

As we drove along the road in between the skyscrapers, I noticed lots of people had started to congregate outside office buildings, clutching their coffees and smoking. Was this a daily 11 o'clock ritual in Canada? Every building seemed to have 50 or so people outside. Anyway, we got off the bus and made our way to the tower. We'd been told to expect a queue, but there wasn't one, so we went straight up to the observation deck. Being heated, we soon got too hot in our ski jackets, so I went to find a cloakroom, where I found a bell. I rang it, but no answer. I rang it again and a sheepish-looking teenager nervously took my coat and said, "What are you guys doing up here?". A little confused, I said, "Checking out the views… it is the observation tower, isn't it?". He then went on to relay that Vancouver had just experienced a rare earthquake. We must have missed the whole thing whilst sitting on the bouncy bus and this explained the crowds outside the building. Needless to say, we kept our coats, had a quick butcher's at the view, then moved down to the safety of terra firma as quickly as we could.

We've been blissfully acquainted with Grant and Shelley since the beginning of our children journey. Their first-born, Aaron, is five days older than Max, and their second child, Ben, is in the same school year as Lois. Despite living 150 miles apart, we ensure that we hook up periodically and, when we do, it's like going on laughter boot camp. Our jaws always ache for days afterwards - it's an absolute tonic.

Maybe it's always been there, but during our baby years, Jane and I met a handful of couples who were still trying or coming out of various fertility procedures. Come to think of it, I got to know plenty of childless adults at work, probably a generation ahead of me. It may have been their choice, but it sure feels like modern fertility treatment has come on leaps and bounds. Maybe that's a great news story for medicine.

I remember how sensitive we felt about telling Grant and Shelley when Jane was pregnant because they'd been trying for a while. We clearly felt quite apprehensive, but it didn't matter, they wet themselves laughing and told us their happy news too. We ended up planning a boating holiday on the Norfolk broads, as you do - one last blast before we all went to Nappyland. What a scream that was: two heavily pregnant, very hormonal women, who weren't allowed near the technical end or ropes, accompanied by two drunken landlubbers, who'd never even commandeered a canoe, let alone a big 40-foot river cruiser.

Grant and I were in charge of food and transport. My role was galley boy extraordinaire whilst Grant drove, masterfully taking out the surrounding fauna, wildlife and fishing lines in his epic sixteen-point turn parking manoeuvres. I think we quickly built a bit of a reputation that week in Norfolk. As it wore on, I sensed that lock keepers had forewarned their colleagues of our impending arrival and we got a number of disapproving grunts. When we rocked up to moor in the afternoons, regular boaters could be seen dashing on deck to fix more fenders to protect their cherished paintwork.

After a few bruising encounters, mooring soon became a well-oiled naval routine. I would take the bow, looking cool and serious with ropes in hand, trying to hold it together. Grant would be at the wheel with an air of Admiral Nelson about him. The girls were below deck with the curtains closed, holding their crotches for fear of literally wetting themselves with laughter. It didn't take too long for them to break into absolute hysterics and they were crying with laughter as the boys manned up to some nautical challenges. All they could hear was, "(bump) Sorry! (shudder) Sorry! Not so fast, Grant, BE CAREFUL. We're only here for one night." It's a wonder that neither Aaron nor Max were born prematurely that week-end.

I remember we were one of the first to receive a call from Grant at the hospital when Aaron was born. I put him on loud speaker, so my heavily pregnant Jane could feel the pride and admiration for Shelley flow down the phone line. We needed to hear it as Max was due any day.

He launched straight into it: "Johnny, it's like the fucking trenches, the Somme, blood, guts everywhere. Jesus, it's a horror show, really!". Jane and I roared out laughing.

"Oh my god! Didn't realise you were there, Jane. Shelley was fantastic, awesome, it was an amazing experience, I feel so honoured. Oh… sorry Jane, you'll be fine girl, be a hero like my Shel, better go, been phoning people for hours and I can hear Shelley yelling for me, doing her twisty turny thing."

Max was born in December 2002 and this was a truly magical time. I got to witness it all and cut the umbilical cord, which was an amazing privilege. Suddenly having the responsibility of a child was a huge change to our circumstances, as I'm sure most parents will concur. To be sent home after the birth, with your frail little bundle of joy, was a jaw-dropping experience. Then the reality hit home. Squeaky bum time.

Looking back, we were overly attentive first-time parents. At home, I tried to get stuck into as many baby duties as possible. Jane always took the lead as she was the one at home during the week, but I did some changes, clumsily. Max used to come down on my shoulder with an oversized nappy hanging off his legs. Truth be known, I didn't want to break him whilst he screamed and thrashed about on the mat.

Naturally, my perspective changed at work. Being away for weeks on end wasn't conducive to my new home life and I also wanted to move on up the ladder. Additionally, there'd been a few 'restructurings' at the office which got up my nose, so I began to think on.

27

FAMILY INFLUENCE

The last country I visited was Iran, again with Nigel. It was an interesting backdrop, following events in New York; the US Government had started to ramp up rhetoric on the country, referring frequently to it as an 'Axis of Evil'. We were naively surprised that our newly-formed, one-man compliance team and US colleagues over the pond had started to become interested in certain relationships. In London, the culture seemed to be 'carry on until told otherwise', so we got the green light and planned the trip.

There wasn't much said in preparation, in terms of how politically sensitive the trip might be, as we were to be accompanied by our local representative in Tehran. Nigel and I flew in and picked up our luggage at Tehran's airport. We marched out of the baggage collection area, a little wearily. As we walked through the door into the main airport hall, at the opposite end, a large bearded cleric, dressed in black robes, entered with a military entourage. I couldn't stop looking at this scene; it was something out of a movie. My glance turned into a stare, I caught his gaze and our eyes locked on.

It might have been wind, but he had a menacing look about him. It looked like disgust was written all over his face and he seemed to be making a beeline directly in my direction. You could sense the whole room noting his presence; he was plainly a man of importance. Before him, the sea of people parted for Moses. I stupidly carried on staring at him as I walked in the opposite direction. I'd had a lousy flight and refused to be intimidated.

Thankfully, there wasn't any confrontation and, as we passed, we both looked back on each other and finally lost eye contact. It was a surreal near-encounter. I felt quite relieved that it passed without incident and a bit of a numpty for playing chicken. I then noticed that most people in the crowd now seemed to be looking quizzically at me and Nigel, who had caught up with me by now. He was still lame for many months after from the camel riding. He whispered, "What do you think you're doing, John? I thought you were going to be taken away for questioning at one point. I don't fancy telling Jane you've been jailed, let's skedaddle."

From that time on, it felt like our presence was as clandestine as possible. We were delighted to be there, but at the same time, didn't want to appear on any unwanted radar. Nasser, the local rep, explained that following the US's declaration, things were politically on a turn for the worse, with a hard-line government soon to be formed.

Despite this knowledge, we were well-received by our customers and, on a night off, decided to go to the historic Grand Bazaar with Nasser. He wanted to take us to an antique carpet seller… apparently he was a close relative! We arrived in the early evening after a two-hour journey, having left the hotel less than ten miles away. Yes, Iran was top of the tragic traffic charts for sure. Nasser showed me and Nigel around the outskirts of the ancient and beautiful Shah Mosque and the bazaar's stunning historic corridors. Vendors of certain goods would congregate in the same areas of the bazaar, so we were taken to the Persian rug area in the cloisters.

By the look of passers-by, the bazaar didn't receive many Western visitors; we didn't want to hang about for fear of a crowd gathering. Thankfully, the shop was tucked away on the first floor of an open square, literally two chaps in a couple of well-lit rooms, piled high with rugs. Nasser enabled the exchange of pleasantries and said it was best for the vendors to give us a brief overview of what was available in their stock, and then for us to think about what pattern we wanted to purchase. The process was well-rehearsed and he'd obviously brought visiting executives there many times before.

We looked through many carpets and I became fixated on what looked like a really old one that you might say had seen better days. But its design instantly meant something to me; it had a non-symmetrical picture of an anciently-dressed, beautiful maiden with a deer on it. Max is a Capricorn and it reminded me of Jane looking after him. Guess what? The rug happened to be one of the most expensive ones in their collection - of course it was! Haggling started in the range of several thousand dollars. I kept a poker face and declared that I was happy to walk away with nothing, as I didn't really need a rug. Nasser could see that I was digging in my heels and eventually we agreed on what I thought was a fair price, which equated to about £600 at the prevailing exchange rate.

As I walked through a beautifully gardened square towards the car with the rug over my shoulder, Nigel said I'd picked up a bargain and Nasser was more forthcoming. He said, "I've brought many of your colleagues here, right up to the chief executive, and nobody negotiated as hard as you, John."

"It's easier for me Nasser," I said. "I can't afford to pay silly money."

"You should be very pleased with your purchase, you got it at an amazing price," Nasser volunteered.

Perhaps I hadn't overpaid for the triple-knotted, 50-year old, 100% silk Persian rug from Qom, if you believe the details on the hand-written receipt. Perhaps the vendors were scoffing into their coffee having fleeced another gullible Westerner. I'll never know, but the rug represented a lot for me. The end of an era and the start of a new one - I love it.

At the end of the exhausting trip to Tehran, I was bound for home and felt a sense of something exciting coming to an end. Foreign travel was certainly hard work and, at times, very chaotic and frustrating, but there wasn't anything like it to get the adrenaline running. A lot of the time, many things were out of your control, so it taught me to chill out and enjoy the ride. What will be, will be, so avoid stressing out where possible, especially as it doesn't change anything. All I had to do was to remember this at times.

On the plane back home, I ordered a second G & T when we got out of Iranian airspace and smiled as I witnessed a few Iranian women emerge from the toilets, one by on. It was like a seeing a supermarket dash in the changing rooms of a clothes boutique. Wholly transformed, women emerged invigorated by the removal of their niqabs and burkhas. Hair flowing, with full make-up and a great abundance of perfume, ladies openly expressing their femininity with full force. They were probably going to spend the summer in their London homes, where certain freedoms were not forbidden.

I had a growing suspicion that the Institutional Banking department wasn't going to be around for much longer, at least in its current size and format. A number of longer-serving managers were retiring around me but their roles weren't being advertised. I was glad that I'd ploughed a wide enough furrow in my earlier years and decided to try and find something else in London. I had always been a poor networker and hoped that I'd built a sufficient reputation for people to remember me.

When I got back to the office, we looked into extending our long running US$ clearing solution for the Iranian banks. There was clearly a demand building and we didn't seem to question why other clearers had started to pull out. It didn't seem to have the support we were looking for, which we were genuinely surprised about. I got the sense that we'd stirred up a bit of a hornet's nest. It wasn't until much later that these enquiries came back to bite me on the bum. I'll cover this later.

In the meantime, I kept my eyes peeled on the internal job journals and found one with a promotion in the Holborn area office, next to the City. I was interviewed by a friend, James, a great guy who I admired. He couldn't understand why I'd want to come back into the 'ordinary' part of banking, until I mentioned my new family. Then it all made sense to him and I was lucky to be offered the role.

But a week before I started, I chanced on a stroke of luck which could have equally been a disaster. The bank decided to have a little restructure and the Holborn area was to be absorbed into its two adjoining areas, enlarging each. Rather than plummeting down a snake all the way back to square one again, in the City, I was asked to join the West End area team, for the same role. What a result! Instead of starting in a new area, I was back in familiar territory. Back to Pall Mall, collect £200 on passing Go, in Monopoly terms. I'd gone full circle again, so to speak, and was a tad dizzy.

Working for my new area director, Roy, was nothing short of a pleasure. He was also very experienced and had a canny knack of being well-respected by his whole team and all personnel. He had what I describe as a bit of a magical touch with people and the culture was very different from the previous working environment. There, it had seemed comparably cold at times, less about relationships and more dog eat dog. I was also delighted to be working again with a familiar face in Andy, who had worked at Poultry with me. He'd spent time with Roy for a couple of years and loved it - he too was liked by all.

I initially felt like an outsider and it was clear that I'd need to adjust to the new environment. I'd inherited some sharp-elbowed culture from my previous role and I was carrying some bad traits. These were rightly pointed out. Thankfully, those who wielded the most power, the branch managers, could see a diamond in the rough, and knocked a few edges off me, for my own good.

One afternoon, Peter, a future boss of mine, recommended that I should "Get to know the branch managers a little better, stay on for a drink or two after the meeting." He was already back at the office when he received a call warning him that I was on my way back. I'd enjoyed their hospitality a bit too much and was returning, a little worse for wear. As I weaved my way back to the office, he kindly met me at the steps of the office with my belongings and persuaded me to go home. Nobody would have appreciated me wandering back to my desk in my current state. "Honestly John, it's all fine, you've been Sallyed." My staying power had evidently fallen way short of one of the branch managers, who'd been plying me with wine. I knew that afternoon that I'd finally been accepted: people were looking out for me. This did my confidence the world of good, despite the hangover and feeling very sheepish and apologetic the following day.

Roy would often send me home too, if I was working late. "Your young family needs you John, you've put in some hard yards and you will again, but it should be family first during baby times." Roy wasn't wrong.

This, however, caught me off guard. It was completely at odds to what I thought I'd experienced in my career to date. Perhaps it was my own stupid self-doing. At times, I was daft enough to believe that grinding out an extended daily shift showed commitment, some macho rubbish. I have to say that, nowadays, you might argue that it shows that you're ineffective, not being able to organise your tasks within decent working hours. It's certainly not good for wellbeing in the long run.

Maybe working extended hours was necessary at times because there were so many inefficiencies. Mind you, some of my inefficiencies may have been self-inflicted and of a liquid lunch variety, so to speak. Work hard, play hard has always been an ethos of mine; perhaps I just needed to keep the two separate. I sense that generations to come aren't willing to sacrifice their personal time so easily: sounds healthier to me.

At home, Max suffered from colic and was proving to be quite a handful in his first year. He still slept sporadically and was a bundle of boundless energy as a toddler. Jane won't mind me saying that she found the experience very tough-going. I'd been away a lot with work and crucially, we were miles from family support, in the shape of Jane's parents. Thank goodness they were more than willing to pop over regularly to help out and would also take her away on week-ends, to ease the burden of what I likened to Gulag: hard labour and sleep deprivation.

At some point in Max's first year, we observed how much our lives had changed. We hadn't lost complete touch with our Beckenham friends, but whilst they continued to party we'd hunker down in either shock, sheer exhaustion or both. Over time, Jane and I felt that we needed to move closer to Newbury, to maintain our sanity, so in 2004, we did.

We were determined that we'd try to purchase a house that could accommodate a growing family and I signed up for a monster mortgage, which stretched us. Yes, despite the recent, raw, tender mental scars from our lovely first born, we were hoping to provide Max with a sibling.

We looked at options along the Waterloo train line as I wanted to avoid commuting in from Paddington, having done it before. I'd still have to commute into London and wanted to be able to travel easily to the West End, Canary Wharf or the City. We eventually focussed on the village of

Hook, about half an hour's drive from the parents and an hour to London on the train. It also had four pubs.

After viewing 21 properties, we set our hearts on one that was still in the process of being built. Max didn't seem too enamoured with the idea though, as he screamed blue murder all the way around the site. But he settled down when he saw the diggers and plenty of Bob the Builders.

It was fun settling into the new house and we initially felt that we, and our meagre possessions, were rattling around it as it was much bigger. Over time though, which will resonate with most parents, we started to collect all sorts of junk and became plastic magnets.

Now and then, Jane and Max would pop up to see me in London and we'd meet in St James's Park or somewhere else nearby the office for lunch. Jane loved coming back to London and still gets a buzz returning there: it broke down the monotony of raising a toddler. I remember we once met outside Hamleys, the world-famous toy store. Max was so excited to see me, he came running down Regent's Street, dodging people like a heat-seeking missile into my open arms. It was a magical moment and everyone there seemed to stop and watch as I lifted him up into the sky, as he giggled excitedly. The shop was an Aladdin's cave of toys and, on the top floor, there was a large Scalextrics track with two racing cars, which we played on through my extended lunch break. Somehow I knew this had Roy's blessing.

Only nine months passed before we faced another restructure at work and I ended up as the manager of the Chinatown branch in Gerrard Street. The business was determined to start a retail revolution in banking and in different ways, Andy (who was asked to manage the illustrious branch of Pall Mall) and I faced a similar dilemma.

For different reasons, our branches weren't suited for this change. Pall Mall was a historic, high cache branch where most of its customers would not walk in off the street like they might in Chipping Sodbury. The Chinatown branch had been opened to service the many people who'd emigrated from Hong Kong when Britain handed over the region to the Chinese in 1997. It was a very busy branch, often full of tourists, where the mother tongue of its customers and staff was Cantonese.

Some of the personal products and services were used well by our customer base, but the high profile, insurance-type ones were often inappropriate. Our customers were very often ineligible so we refused to sell, for instance, PPI when it wasn't appropriate. Our performance, in the eyes of some excitable members of the regional team, was put under the microscope, but I refused to budge.

The July 2015 London tube and bus bombings occurred whilst I was working at Chinatown: it was a bit of an eye-opener. News filtered in during the day and our regional office told us to close up and go into lockdown. After making calls to family, the staff soon got hungry so something had to be done. There was nothing else for it, so we phoned out for a takeaway delivery. Let's just say there were a few restaurants around Chinatown.

The enormity of that terrorist attack didn't hit me until I got home to a heavily-pregnant Jane as I hadn't seen any TV all day. Some things that you remember are very personal and where you were on this particular day was a common thread with some customers. A partner of an accountancy firm who I knew was in a car behind the bus that exploded in Berkeley Square. He saw it happen in front of his eyes. It had a profound effect on him and he wandered around the streets in a daze for the rest of the day.

One of the perks of the role was to visit our offices and customers in Hong Kong, Beijing and Shanghai. Roy was adamant that I should go early on before it got clamped down. He probably selected me for the branch given my international experience. We had a successful trip in terms of business subsequently routed through the branch and, in that year, we were one of the best-performing branches in the country, alongside Pall Mall. Even though the performance of our team was great, it was still my first leadership role and, as such, I made a few glaring errors of judgement.

One memorable error was organising the movement of some desks together, to build some momentum when calling out to customers, without consulting the staff. This landed like a lead balloon with some, but eventually they agreed to give it a go.

Another had been to mischievously question the work output, openly in front of staff, in an attempt to show that I was 'keeping an eye on things'. It was meant to be a bit of a ribbing and I hoped it might put the cat amongst the pigeons, but it spectacularly backfired on me and almost caused a mutiny. This taught me that it pays to be tactful and respectful when trying to make changes that involve people - talk about missing the obvious.

To make amends, I chose to own up. I openly admitted that I'd made mistakes, but the intentions were genuinely well-meant. This leadership lark was still new to me and I needed their help for us all to succeed. This was a bit at odds with the history of the branch, which seemed to be about reserving respect at all costs and not discussing mistakes. In the end, on balance, I think this went down well with the staff and I gained their trust, eventually. It taught me a lesson: there's a hard way and an easier way to effect change. Win over the people's hearts and minds first, and don't go in like a bull in a china shop (no pun intended).

Some changes were welcomed though. I stalked a contact I knew in the marketing department and provided the branch with its own up-to-date, traditional, Chinese-worded branch posters and livery, which was a first.

We also reignited our ties with the local Chinese Language School which ran at week-ends, attended by a few children of staff and surrounding businesses. I secured an investment from the bank to update some of its tired facilities. The elderly headmaster made the point of thanking me in front of as many influential people as possible, which helped our standing enormously.

In learning from my mistakes, when the opportunity for a culturally acceptable branch refurbishment came along, I passed the important decisions to those who mattered - the staff - knowing that they would give a nod to Feng Shui.

As time rolled on though, it was apparent that the branch would be far better managed by someone who spoke Cantonese and I asked for a transfer into the Commercial Centre at Pall Mall, where I worked under the leadership of Peter again. Third time back to the building: maybe this time I might stay a little longer.

At home, Max was joined by a second bundle of joy when Jane gave birth to our daughter, Lois. She was a totally different baby and happily slept through the night in no time at all. We found that we were far more relaxed the second time around, compared to the whirlwind journey of our first-born. I guess this must have rubbed off on the baby too. Moving to Hook was a great idea as it was easily accessible to Jane's parents, who came over whenever they could, so we were far happier than being isolated miles down the road. Commuting daily was a costly, time-consuming, boring, but necessary affair and I was happy to do it for the good of our family. Although it was 90 minutes each way, door to door, the journey went in no time at all when you 'got in the zone'. Commuting kept me reasonably fit too as I cycled ten minutes each way to the station, uphill and exhilarating in the morning, downhill and unwinding in the evening.

In my eleven years of commuting up to London, I went through three bicycles and two suits when I skidded off on black ice. To aid stability, I finally settled on adorning the back wheel with saddle bags, where I'd house my waterproof gear, trousers and shoe covers, as well as a high-vis jacket. Some days, I looked like a deep-sea trawler man, cycling down to the quayside to haul in his nets, but it kept me dry-ish and the costs down. I couldn't believe that some commuters I knew, who lived nearer to the station than me, parked a car there all day: it seemed so expensive. It was glaringly obvious why, when it rained hard!

My role in the Commercial Centre meant that I was one of Peter's few deputies and looked after some high-profile relationships. He was a great boss to work for and believed strongly in empowerment. We were left to account for our own actions yet there was an open door policy if we ever wanted to discuss anything.

One memorable account I looked after was a very large, foreign embassy in Mayfair and its supporting offices throughout the West End. As I passed through the security gate, I was immediately transported back to my time travelling in the Middle East. I loved immersing myself with the key people and built great, deep relationships and grew the business considerably. On a couple of occasions, I was summoned to meet the ambassador who was a member of the country's royal family and was made to feel very special. You had to pinch yourself that this was part of the role sometimes.

My colleagues and I were a successful team. We all acted individually, enjoying the autonomy and responsibility of delivering great service and growth. I made a mental note for the future; if I were to lead a team again one day, having worked in this culture could prove useful. The boss wouldn't question us if we needed to let our hair down a bit. I'd only have a wobbly cycle ride home to contend with and just needed to ensure that I didn't nod off on the train and end up in Bournemouth!

Then came the global economic crash of 2007. I won't cover it fully here as I won't do it justice. Suffice to say, in my view, a small 'creative' part of the banking industry was given too much capital to play with. Regulation wasn't what it is today and markets started to operate on thin air; when the merry-go-round stopped, the bubble exploded.

My colleagues and I operated in an area of banking which had always looked after people's money, not gambled it away. We looked after it on their behalf and funded growth of businesses, which in turn helped society and the general economy. Overnight though, we had become social pariahs. It became very embarrassing to say that you worked in a bank. We were all tarred with the same brush by the media and, understandably, a very hacked-off general public. I get the anger and frustration though, I really do. It had a cataclysmic effect on many innocent people. Livelihoods and homes were lost, countries - including the UK - faced years of austerity and all because of a period of greed, capitalism gone mad and a lack of control. Talk about a few bad apples spoiling the barrel: it clearly should never have been allowed to happen.

Given their geography and business purpose, the crash didn't seem to hit my customers that hard, but in speaking to colleagues, I knew it affected a lot of businesses worldwide. Unsurprisingly, this caused a lot of navel-gazing internally and the climate became far more cost-conscious. I counted my blessings. I still had a paying job, a great family and my health. I'd also been given the green light to move on.

Thanks to taking the advice of the new regional director, six months before the crash I withdrew my application for a six-month job swap in New York. She'd built up my hopes of getting a full secondment overseas sorted out, something a number of more canny, networking savvy friends had managed to muster. The timing would have been perfect. My CV, credentials and reputation were all strong enough and our children wouldn't have missed out on any key schooling.

It never transpired. It felt like I'd been strung a line to keep me there but, in reality, the world had changed. In the scheme of things, it wasn't a big issue; I still counted my blessings. If any-thing, it reaffirmed that I'd have been better off seizing the opportunity when it presented itself, a bird in the hand is worth two in the bush. Don't ever rely on jam tomorrow.

Despite the uncertain times, London never seemed to sleep and jobs became available. I applied to join the City Corporate team as there didn't appear to be a vacancy in the West End Corporate team in Pall Mall downstairs, but was invited in for a chat anyhow.

Martin was the long-standing boss of the West End Corporate Team who'd built its presence over decades. It rightfully enjoyed a first-class reputation in the market and internally too. Martin was very patient with people and always kept an eye out for individuals to join the West End team. "Why didn't you come and see me?", he asked, clearly highlighting my crap networking skills. "I'll see if I can make a space for you, you'll fit in well here." So that was decided and, true to his word, he did just that. I joined within a month.

I started with an eclectic mix of customers to learn some corporate skills as the product suite was more complex than I was used to. I also decided to help the situation by studying for my corporate finance professional qualifications, so as to fast track some learning. As far as I was aware, nobody had ever done this before and I soon found out why. It was a very tough gig: the studying and revision was intense, at MBA Level I was told. I learnt many things which helped me accelerate my understanding of the fiscal world, but also some weird things, such as how to manually value a bond, were not exactly useful in my role!

Martin was very supportive and I knuckled down hard in my studies every week-end for three months, coupled with studying reams of text books on the commute. This wasn't fully appreciated at home as I became a secret week-end visitor at home tucked away in his study, after the long hours of the overall commuting week. Understandably, Jane and the kids got fed up. There I was again, doing what I felt needed to do to climb the ladder. Short-term sacrifice for long-term gain. Jane was prepared to support me but told me that was the end of it. Never again was I to consider undertaking a sacrifice of family time, so I'd better bloody well pass the bloody thing first time! No pressure then. I thought I'd bitten off more than I could chew as the exam was extremely tough.

I was convinced I'd failed, so sheepishly advised Martin that I wasn't likely to re-sit, for the sake of my marriage. Hedging my bets. When the result came in the post, I took a huge gulp as I opened the envelope. I'd passed. Thank chuff. Only 25% of students had obtained a pass in that sitting, and back at the office, I bought drinks at *The Golden Lion* to celebrate. I enjoyed a few pints with mates that day and they still remember it fondly. The bar bill wasn't shabby either. At one point, I leaned on Martin, who was of a smaller build, and gave him a hug. He bristled, but gracefully accepted my beer-infused appreciation. Or was that relief? Maybe a career-defining moment.

As I suspected, all of my colleagues certainly worked hard and played hard too. It wasn't uncommon to down tools in an impromptu fashion and go for a few drinks - it built legendary team spirit. Martin had the utmost loyalty from all of his team and if transactions were completing, people would work whatever hours were necessary to get them over the line.

I got the affectionate nickname of 'Lenny' from the team (from *Of Mice and Men*). This paid homage to my large frame and hands, as well as, perhaps, my slow uptake on certain things, given the depth of experience around me. I wasn't offended though, as core friends looked out for me. I remember on a karaoke night out one of the bosses, strangely another Martin, turned to me wetting himself at my rendition of 'Living on a Prayer'. He said, "You know what Len? You make me smile, you're just happy being yourself. You love rock, rugby and good times. You'll fit in here no problem and I'm sure you'll leave a legacy of stories." I took the compliment, knowing full well that I wouldn't be remembered as a guru in Corporate Finance.

I attended one of the legendary West End office off-sites, in Dublin. In a way, it was like going on tour with friends. As our plane attempted to land, you could feel the nose and tail pitch and sway in the high wind from a storm that had blown in; it was like being in a giant dodgem on a roller-coaster ride. I was sitting in the aisle and, in the seats next to me, in the middle of the plane, sat three nuns. They had their eyes closed and were grasping their rosary beads, praying for a safe landing. I think we eventually did so on our third attempt and my hand cramped up from grasping the headrest on the seat in front of me so hard. The sisters' plea for divine intervention did us no harm!

I roomed with my colleague Hutch, a good buddy who was up for the craic, and it wasn't long before we were strategising in Temple Bar, *St James's Gate*, *The Old Jamesons Distillery* and other great examples of Dublin's beverage and leisure sector that needed serious study. The highlight for me was rescuing a damsel in distress, a bubbly lady called Nicola, who couldn't get across the cobbled sections of streets on Temple Bar because of her high heels. Nicola wasn't the lightest of ladies, and was a larger-than-life, lovely character who roared out laughing whilst I tried to provide a piggy-back service. Everyone was in stitches.

Back in the office, I loved reading about customers in the broadsheets and, if I was involved, knowing what was truly going on behind the scenes. England's best-known tennis club in south west London was a customer and I looked after this like a precious jewel. There were many internal, more senior stakeholders wrapped up in the overall relationship, given our sponsorship. You didn't want to leave any stone unturned and I tried to plan for every eventuality.

In return, the club was generous to its custodians and provided me with tickets to its annual championship competition. Jane and I thoroughly enjoyed seeing friends there, after the business meeting had been conducted. Spending the day wandering around the courts and viewing world-class players was one of the highlights of my career. Again, you had to pinch yourself as it seemed surreal. It almost got much better too as we attempted to woo a certain large national rugby union, again in south west London, but alas, we were outbid on the sponsorship deal by a nationally-owned bank. Our marketing team had wrongly speculated that they wouldn't be able to muster a competitive bid as it was the taxpayer's money being spent. If we'd have won that relationship, I don't think I'd have ever wanted to move on. Ever.

One ordinary day in the office, I had another career-defining moment. I received a call from Tudor, a dear friend who worked in the branch below the offices in Pall Mall. Our paths had previously crossed when he audited the Bracknell bunker when I was there; he was a thoughtful, experienced, genuine guy. His role now was very much related to compliance matters and he was a bit of an expert in his field.

"John, I don't want to alarm you, but you know that the group is being prosecuted by the US Government's Department of Justice in New York?", he opened. I confirmed that I had read something internally about it. "I've just read an enormous document called the Deferred Prosecution Document and your name appears in it about ten times, something to do with Iranian payments. It's public knowledge and on the internet." At this point, I stopped mid-sandwich and swallowed slowly in my instantly dry mouth. I felt the pit of my stomach disappear through my arse and hit the floor of the branch, three stories below.

"Thanks for the heads up mate, I'd better have a look, would you be able to send it over to me?". As soon as it arrived, I spent the rest of the afternoon reviewing its contents. The document was over 900 pages long and essentially the prosecutor had listed in its view a number of compliance failings our bank had made over the last ten years or so. Amongst these was the knowing act of altering payment details to avoid US OFAC sanctions. Yours truly's emails dated 2002 were quoted verbatim and suggested to the reader that this was written evidence that the offices in the UK disregarded their duties concerning USD payments.

To be honest, this whole story didn't come as a complete surprise as I'd already met with the legal counsel of the bank in that year to discuss the contents of the historic emails. I felt frustrated that they'd asked me to recollect what was going on when I was working in Institutional Banking. I explained that I was no payments expert, had stumbled across the well-known practice which had been in place for years and was exploring an opportunity with others to widen the availability of these services to new customers. I also stated plainly that all of this took place several years ago, so I could only provide a rough sketch of what certain emails were trying to achieve. I thought it wasn't going to come to anything much.

It was laughable. I'd gone to London to build a credible, solid reputation that I might be able to leverage later in my career, and ended up feeling that I was one of the people responsible for legal action taken against my employer. Perhaps not something to mention on a CV.

Instead of shouting for help from the rooftops, I decided to share the story with only Jane and a few very close friends away from the office. There was no appetite on my part to start informing others, including my reporting line. I'd have the piss ripped out of me mercilessly, for a start.

Whilst my mind was racing, I tried to calmly and logically think it through. As I hadn't been asked to go into anybody's office to explain myself, I surmised that my employer had rightfully come to the conclusion that I'd done nothing wrong. If anything, I might be seen as a bit of an accidental whistleblower. Good then, me and my employer were on the same page. I hoped the United States of America was too.

Coping calmly with that initial shock like I did certainly helped me later in life, not least through the process of cancer diagnosis and treatments. It taught me to, if possible, remove emotion from the situation and focus on the facts alone.

The enormity of my name going public in such a way hit me a week or so later though. We'd just booked a US holiday with the kids. I endured a few sleepless nights with worry as I had visions of handing our passports over in Orlando and being led away in front of my family, chained up in an orange boiler suit and sent off to Guantanamo Bay. I'd rather visit Mickey Mouse if it's all the same.

Only time became a healer and the longer it passed by without incident, the more comfortable with the situation I became. Senior executives named within the same legal papers had long since retired or left the bank. I was clearly too low down the food chain for anyone to pursue.

An overdue action of the business was to ramp up its compliance awareness in all areas of its operations and I remember attending a training course at Heathrow, about six months after the bank made a settlement with the legal prosecution. Each delegate was asked to relay something interesting about themselves over dinner. I felt emboldened with a couple of glasses of red inside me and decided to relay the story, warts and all, as there were no links back to the office. There were a few dropped knives and forks on plates and you could've heard a pin drop. Everyone was stunned and wanted to know more, but there really wasn't any more to say. In deciding to put this skeleton away to the back of my closet, I'd inadvertently stored a unique experience. We shall cover this later on.

Back at the office, my portfolio wasn't exactly brimming with active corporate clients and, in retrospect, I got quite complacent in the role. I should have pressed closer to others who were active, to learn some further transactional skills. I didn't complain though as I was having a great time with some fantastic customers and colleagues. I also tried to see as much of the family as possible, which was difficult, given the distance of the commute. However, this purple patch seemed to last a year or so.

Then the inevitable winds of change once again stirred up with yet another restructure. Our West End office was merged with the City office. On paper, it looked an obvious move, however it was a clash of different cultures. Martin retired happily with a number of business interests to keep him going and the prevailing culture changed overnight. We were crammed into a relatively small office in the City - some joked that we'd become 'Highly Stressed Battery Chickens'.

The enlarged London office was now run by a very different regime and over time, everyone seemed to be put under the microscope. After a year or so, it was deemed that I was better suited to a role I didn't want, so I became an unhappy bunny for a six-month period. In fact, I became quite snappy at home and withdrawn. Looking back, I was probably a tad depressed, stressed or a combination of both.

For the first time, I began to dread going into work each day. I'd rarely felt like this before in my career and tried as best I could to keep my head down. Working from home was out of the question as I needed to see London-based customers and it was bedlam with the kids there. I just put my head down, got on with the job in hand and thought about planning for the long game.

Ultimately, I knew that I needed to take control, before decisions were made for me, and seriously contemplated leaving the bank. Again, I was unwilling to throw many years of my career away at the first sign of trouble, so I held my nerve and looked at a number of advertised leadership roles elsewhere. I asked for a meeting with the top boss. He seemed a little embarrassed and tried his best to polish the turd of the other role on offer. But I got what I wanted: his blessing to apply for a number of other roles.

The regime held the cards to one of the jobs being advertised. I thoroughly prepared for the interview and aced it; the feedback I received confirmed that

I was the successful candidate. But then the criteria mysteriously changed and one of my colleagues got the role instead. He'd worked for the new boss for years, no hard feelings against him. I couldn't quite believe what was happening and it felt like I was being snookered. This just wasn't cricket.

♪ No Class (Motörhead) ♪

You always got thumping tracks from this lot. It's not my favourite track, but one that encourages you to stay high when things go low. "I can't believe you exist, I crossed you right off my list."

My old colleagues were thinning out by now and leaving for other roles. I wondered how much better the larger team might have been if we had truly merged as one, in spirit and culture. Leadership is about winning over hearts and minds and building followership. Managing by numbers and moving around the chess pieces as you see fit, without buy-in, is at best, management, not leadership.

I applied for another role and felt it was a far better fit, for two reasons. Firstly, it was based near to home and secondly, because of its geography, it was outside the regime's influence. I gave what I thought was a good interview and came away reasonably confident. When I was offered the role, I felt electricity pulse through my body and was charged up with excitement. As well as gaining a great, local role in leadership, it felt like I'd just picked up a Get Out of Jail Free card.

28

COMING HOME

The new role was the biggest responsibility I'd been given so far. The team was about 50-strong and spread across three centres in three counties. The incumbent leadership team of three had held the fort well on their own for a few months but I could sense they were a bit frazzled. They were glad to hear that I was joining, together with two new deputies, to relieve the pressure. One of the best parts of the role was its locality; I was now living 'on patch' and, although I hadn't worked in the Thames Valley for years, I knew it was a great location to reacquaint myself with. I also knew a number of people from when I'd left the area, some fifteen years ago.

This was the first leadership role since the Chinatown branch and looking back, I was pretty ill-equipped then and had to grow in the role. The regional team had faith in their new appointment and supported me. The performance of the area had been flatlining at best since the last area director left and, given it was one of the largest centres in the region, they naturally wanted to see it fly high again as quickly as possible.

In what seemed like no time at all, a lot of key people, who had served in their role for a while, decided it was to move on. Perhaps they took one look at me and thought 'Let's get out of here'. Unfortunately, this included one leadership member, who'd been plotting his exit for a while. He wasn't at all happy with the way he'd been supported whilst waiting for the cavalry and it had deeply affected him. Regrettably, there wasn't anything I could say to persuade him to stay: such a shame, as he left spitting feathers six months later, feeling bitter, rather than on a high which he deserved. We were in the middle of a very challenging time and I found recruiting frustratingly difficult. The sector of business we were in didn't enjoy the same cache as others, so there were too few suitable internal candidates applying.

I found the role all-consuming and Jane often joked that she saw much less of me than when I was working in central London! The trouble was, she wasn't wrong. She also hit home with a few truths that hurt. I was much less pleasant to be around, which was a result of never really feeling off-duty. My work-life balance was clearly off the rails. I was conscious of never feeling in control. Sure, like an oil tanker, the performance slowly turned around, but it felt like we were fire-fighting on a daily basis. This was admittedly a big job, but at the end of the day, home wasn't a happy bunny as I kept on telling Jane, like a broken record, "Don't worry, it'll all calm down soon," knowing full well that it was unlikely to do so.

After eighteen months or so, once again the business shook the can and undertook the mother-of-all restructures to date. This would see half of the current team split away to merge with a few local corporate colleagues and the other half to remain in business banking. Thankfully, the leadership team had sensibly decided to divvy up and allocate individuals to roles, rather than put everyone on notice and ask people to reapply for their jobs. I was allocated a heavily back office, risk-orientated role in the new corporate area team, one of two leaders.

Having never done anything like this type of role before, I found it a strange choice. I thought my strengths lay in front of customers, with the relationship directors, and initially my hackles bristled. Looking back, my ego was now probably self-inflated beyond any useful purpose. I had to get over myself as there was plenty to do. My unhealthy ego took another major knock when I wasn't successful in getting the top leadership job, but it was probably a blessing in disguise, in retrospect.

My new boss, Nick, and I worked extremely well together as a double act and we went on to become good friends. I was the more grounded one to his Zebedee-style enthusiasm: a good, complementary balance for the team. We truly merged the best elements from both of the constituent previous teams and built a tangible ethic. Some were doggedly never going to change and sometimes left when the opportunity arose, but the vast majority who stayed on enjoyed their time and forged a great team spirit.

During this period of adjustment, I took time to reflect on my leadership style and work-life balance which still needed to improve. Throughout my career, I'd undergone many psychometric assessments and, at times, I'd chosen to ignore feedback, thinking mistakenly that sticking tenaciously to a hard line was a badge of honour. But this time I felt different. I felt safe enough to open up to the team and ask for their help. I wanted to wipe the slate clean, change and, as a result, have a more pleasant home life and rewarding work life. I yearned to become a better human being.

Somewhere on my career path, I'd lost my way a bit. I wasn't a psychotic axe murderer and felt inherently good at heart. I just needed to reconnect with the authentic me.

♪ The Real Me (The Who) ♪

An old classic, fast beat track with a great bass line running throughout the storyline of the song and a thumping chorus too.

This didn't just mean some initial tweaks, only to fall back into my old ways. It required a deep-rooted, permanent shift in behaviour. In short, I wanted to be fondly respected at the office and more loved at home. By now, home had begun to enjoy a new, less stressed animal. I came to realise that my career stock had peaked and I was still enjoying contributing massively to the team.

So ahead of a forthcoming training course, I apprehensively asked everyone to participate in providing some anonymous feedback, seizing the opportunity to get the most out of the exercise. I received plenty of uplifting comments, which was reassuring (thank god!) and, whilst it was painful to read some criticism, it came straight from the horse's mouth. In general, the team had the utmost respect for me, but some had found me unapproachable. I needed to land better with them and chill out. Funnily enough, Jane had been saying the same all along.

It's a challenge for some to ask for authentic feedback. You've got to be prepared for some knocks and bruises to your precious ego. It's another to truly listen and even more difficult to effectively act upon it.

Throughout my career, I've been led by many different styles, some great and some not so good. I've only been asked to provide feedback a handful of times and, unless it's done anonymously by line reports, it's a waste of time. Some leaders seem to happily adopt a fearful reputation and plough on regardless or just pay lip service to their faults. Maybe they're incapable of changing, or maybe the organisation decides it needs this kind of style now and then. Perhaps it's a quirk of capitalism. Businesses are heavily judged on short-term performance and profit whilst relatively little attention is paid to the culture and feeling - which is more long term.

It may have taken a swift kick in the balls to bring me back down to earth but, despite the worry and angst, I was truly happier for it and felt far more comfortable with myself. I decided to go the whole hog for impact and openly shared the feedback with everyone at a team meeting. It was nerve-wracking and you could see some of them squirm in discomfort as I bared all and asked the team for further help down the road. To some, it probably looked like I'd smoked some herbal cigarettes and perhaps in their eyes I looked weak. But I saw grasping the nettle as a strength. From that point on, it took the pressure off maintaining a false persona that just wasn't me: I chilled out and became happier.

A good number of the audience came up to me afterwards and said how brave I'd been, as they'd never seen anything like it in their careers. The point was, I felt liberated in a way and wanted them all to take a leaf out of my book and be honest with themselves - I've no doubt that I set a few minds whirring that night. I'm confident that I did change over time, as the team and Jane said so, and the kids too! It showed me that I was capable of changing my modus operandi and resetting my hardwiring as a human being. This lesson filled me with confident when I dealt with my change in health.

It took three decades of grit and determination to find the Nirvana of an appropriate work-life balance. The opportunity may have arisen by pure accident or luck, but I'm glad I seized it when I did. I've reflected on why this took me so long over the last couple of years or so, with cancer. I believe I made so many personal sacrifices throughout the early stages of my career because I felt I needed to catch up with my alleged potential. As you've read, I didn't give myself a great start: perhaps it's a typical late developer trait. This went on to build tenacity and resilience - an in-built belief in the long game, something out there in the distance to aim for. I was running a marathon, not a sprint. Again, something I needed to use in a medical capacity later in life.

Without formally visualising and mapping out a future, I had enough strength of character to believe that, if I put in the hard work and presented luck with the option to fall into my lap if it chose to, there was every chance something great might occur. I'm not just talking about my career, but finding Jane too. Yes, luck has played a huge role here, but if you don't build yourself a net and hold it out, you'll never catch a star.

Sometimes I wonder whether I'd have reached this point in my career had I achieved 'contentment' earlier. Would I have pushed myself to apply for more challenging roles? I think the answer is, I wouldn't have been content until I had experienced certain things: love, marriage, family, nice holidays and the recognition from my parents that I'd overcome the odds and made something of myself. I defaulted to a hungry breadwinner and, in a caveman sense, became a half-decent hunter gatherer. In the modern office world in which I operated, this meant do well, get new job, get paid, enjoy nice times and repeat - at a higher level.

I believe you can only be truly happy when you are satisfied with your lot on both sides of the coin, when work and home are aligned and in harmony. Inevitably, after being more at peace with myself, I adjusted my focus and became far more interested in the softer areas of leadership, such as supporting, developing, training and mentoring people.

When Nick left the area for a new role, my workload increased significantly. It would take nine months for his replacement to start. In times like these, you've got to allow the scales of the work-life balance to tip in one direction, which they inevitably did.

You will probably have realised that this is the point of the story where the end of this tale starts to complete the circle with the beginning of my first - the cancer story. Like the picture of a snake, eating its own tail. I don't want to repeat part of the story unnecessarily, but I think there's merit in revealing something that happened, as it was a bit of closure for me.

In addition, I was asked to undertake a significant amount of risk training at numerous sites around the country. Initially, I was very sceptical about taking time away from the team, given the pressures at the office. But the importance of the bigger picture later dawned on me. It just meant that I had to steal even more time from home, temporarily.

Jane was unbelievably supportive and in truth, I felt guilty asking, as Jane's mother had recently passed away. We both saw the long term-potential in me learning a new craft and not getting bogged down in the office. We also knew that with me out of the way for a while, so to speak, it would allow my father-in-law to come over and spend time at our house, which he needed. Besides, I tended to get under Jane's feet with my well-intentioned 'special' attention. With her endorsement, I decided to throw everything into learning a new skill.

The training subject matter was very much compliance-orientated and, in order to get a license to facilitate the courses, I needed to pass the daunting test of an assessed presentation, in front of my peers and external professionals who did it for a living. I already bore the scars from a few scrapes within the subject, so I was in familiar territory. It also became apparent that a certain personal work drama I'd endured would fit in nicely. It could become my own unique, powerful story - I just needed to find the balls to use it.

I started to research the 'Deferred Prosecution Agreement' on the internet - you remember - the one about the Iranian payments saga. Seeing my name appear just once in this document instantly regurgitated fears and paranoia that I thought I'd buried a long time ago, it was there ten times! The rising angst from the pit of my stomach felt like I'd just downed a litre of very fizzy beer. I was handling gelignite.

I weighed up the pros and cons and reckoned it was the right time and the right place to exorcise the demon once and for all. It was my dirty little secret's Martini moment. I decided to use the story as an ace card, a centre piece. It would be either be a great victory or a fantastic failure. Either way, I'd go down in a blaze of glory.

Thankfully, it went down very well indeed and I got top marks. Using this material provided me with instant gravitas. Not just because I was a named individual in a huge milestone in the business' history, but also being open and honest with my feelings won some hearts. I felt electricity run through every fibre of my body as I delivered my presentation. It was therapy!

The training team were inspiring, the material was excellent, and it involved rubbing shoulders with interesting experts in the field. Although the work was a very tall order, on top of everything else in the office, I threw myself into it and became familiar with the content. I loved being involved; I was told that I was a 'natural' (the first time in my 30-year career that anyone had said that, even though I'd been called a lot of other things...) and was asked to facilitate several two-day sessions around the UK.

Delegates on the course included other peers and senior managers up through the chain of leadership and they gave me great feedback. My co-facilitators, who were external to the business, said I was a natural, and the training department asked me to take the course overseas to our Armenian office. I wasn't used to receiving such gushing accolades and once again enjoyed the buzz of international travel.

My reborn spirit energised me at home too. It was lovely for us to have some good news for a change. We were adjusting to life without Beryl and Jane was delighted to see me happier. We'd gone through a lot in a year, with Jane's surgery, then her mum's passing. As time became even more precious together, we focussed on enjoying the kids. They were growing into their teenage years and striking a different relationship with us. After the year we'd had, we felt that the family had earned a 'sod the expense' luxury summer holiday, so booked one to Cyprus.

It was very busy back in the office as our new boss wasn't now due to start until September. I thought it might slow down a few months after he'd joined and I wondered how I might make more use of my new-found skill set, so I signed up to run some different courses in 2018. Perhaps this might take my career in a different direction. Who knows, lady luck might still be smiling on me?

As I approached 30 years in service, I started to feel excited about what the future might hold. I just needed to get the weird numbness in my upper jaw re-examined by my dentist. We'd been so wrapped up in life, I hadn't had it checked out again...

THE END (OF MY BRIEF AUTOBIOGRAPHY)

THE PLAYLIST

The following might not include my favourite tracks that the quoted bands have penned, nor do they include all of the bands I love. But they sprang to mind and played in my head as I went through the experience and wrote.

♪ I Want To Break Free (Queen) ♪

♪ Breakdown (Guns & Roses) ♪

♪ Holiday (Scorpions) ♪

♪ In My Time of Dying (Led Zeppelin) ♪

♪ Damage inc (Metallica) ♪

♪ Comfortably Numb (Pink Floyd) ♪

♪ Sweet Home Alabama (Lynyrd Skynyrd) ♪

♪ Get In The Ring (Guns & Roses) ♪

♪ I Just Can't Slow Down (Joe Satriani) ♪

♪ Sweet Emotion (Aerosmith) ♪

♪ Kickstart My Heart (Mötley Crüe) ♪

♪ Kicked In The Teeth Again (AC/DC) ♪

♪ Burnin' Alive (AC/DC) ♪

♪ Breath (Pink Floyd) ♪

♪ Purple Sky (Kid Rock) ♪

♪ Ronnie Rising Medley (Metallica - a tribute to Ronnie James Dio) ♪

♪ Burn (Deep Purple) ♪

♪ Killer of Giants (Ozzy Osbourne) ♪

♪ Cigarettes & Alcohol (Oasis) ♪

♪ Back Off Bitch (Guns & Roses) ♪

♪ Love is Blind (Uriah Heep) ♪

♪ Keep the Faith (Bon Jovi) ♪

♪ Love Walked in (Thunder) ♪

♪ War Pigs (Black Sabbath) ♪

♪ No Class (Motörhead) ♪

♪ The Real Me (The Who) ♪

GLOSSARY OF SENT MESSAGES

Hopefully these reflect some of the humour and mindset I employed. I'm convinced that, by setting the tone of communication, I ensured positive responses, which I fed upon.

Chapter 2: First message -'setting the tone' during diagnosis stage.

Firstly a big thank you for all of your kind thoughts over the last few weeks, it's very humbling.

I thought I might save myself a load of hassle by giving everybody an update at once, hope you don't mind and think this too impersonal.

The bad news - unfortunately I've been told that I have a malignant tumour in my right maxillary sinus, not great news, but apparently it's not one of the worst types. Samples have been sent to the Royal Marsden for further investigation to pin down which type of strain it is and this will determine the medical pathway forward – this is likely to involve radiotherapy/chemotherapy and surgery. They are likely to test further for spreading. I get the further results back in 1-4 weeks' time.

I've got a great doctor and a fantastic support network around me, which I'll need. The doctor feels I should do what I think I need to do to keep positive and, as it's not going to be much fun moping around at home, I'd still like to come in where I can and contribute. I enjoy time with all of the team, but this will have to be limited to Reading as I've been advised to no longer drive.

I would like to ask you all to still to have a laugh with me as usual, BAU please. I know you all care, but let's all talk about stuff that will make me smile.

Chapter 3: Second message outlining our first meeting at The Royal Marsden hospital.

Just a brief update email.

As some of you will know, I went to the Royal Marsden on Friday for a first consultation. Not much to report, and as expected, they are going to re-scan and undertake full body scanning to measure the speed and extent of spreading early next week.

They confirmed that it was a malignant tumour called a spindle cell sarcoma (undifferentiated), a nasty blighter by all accounts that attacks bone/soft tissue. Contrary to earlier advice, treatment is likely to start with surgery, rather than chemotherapy or radiotherapy. The outcome of the imminent tests will determine whether it's operable (hope so!) and the extent of any surgery. This I should know at a follow-up consultation next Friday. Goes without saying that I'm likely to lose some of my film star good looks. On the plus side, the Royal

Marsden is the centre of excellence for these rare cancers, so I don't think I could be in better hands.

Again, many thanks for your ongoing kind messages of support, they really do keep me in a healthy frame of mind.

Chapter 3: Message following initial meeting with surgeon.

As many of you know I visited the surgeon yesterday.

I'm pleased to report that we will shortly start to unleash hell on the cancer.

I'd originally understood this would entail a single, v long operation, but in order to maintain the possibility of retaining my eye, the surgeon wishes to split the operation into 2 stages.

The first procedure will be on October 17th, a 2-3 hour operation, removing a relatively large amount of tissue from my upper jaw area and some from within the eye socket. I will be patched up, given a temporary plate for the roof of my mouth and sent home within a few days. If pathology confirms that a sufficient level of tissue has been taken (especially around the eye), then we will move onto the second procedure a couple of weeks later. This entails a 6-7hr reconstruction operation, taking tissue from other parts of my body (I've offered up a tummy tuck) to form the upper jaw area once again. I should then be sent home after a week or so and move on to physiotherapy.

Whilst there's still some bullets to dodge down the road, I'm delighted that we still have a chance to keep my eye and it's great to finally see a plan unfolding in front of me (hopefully in double vision).

Many thanks for all of your continued kind messages of support, it means so much to have great people fighting for me in my corner.

Chapter 6: An update on my condition and describing the Eureka moment.

Morning Campers!

Just a quick update from me to bring a further dash of colour to your sunny Monday.

Well blow me, wasn't expecting the healing process to be such a drama and having said that Operation No1 seems to have gone OK, pathology reports over the next few weeks should hopefully confirm that my poisonous squatter has been fully evicted by the bailiffs. Next op pencilled in for 21 Nov, it's a reconstruction all-dayer, taking material from my lower left leg to fill in bone, flesh, muscle and the roof of the mouth. I have a hairy inside of the mouth to look forward to, better start waxing!!

Stitches came out Friday, and I turned a corner. Half of my face currently resemble a cross between Marty Feldman and a rabid, dribbling Bulldog on heat, definitely an improvement given the 25 stitch scar (cool!). There's a temporary plate at the roof of the mouth above which lies on packing material. Got rods inside and holes that shouldn't be inside my mouth, so last night's Bacon and Eggs was fun (solids at last, sick of soup); and the eye (post trauma) is probably working at 20%, but I'll take that, beats a gaping hole. Also now grasped talking again, so all looking good.

Anyhow, in a good space, in fact last Wednesday morning at 2am I had a bit of a moment. You know how your mind races at work and before you know it, flying around at 150mph is the norm? Well my noggin has refused to be shoved in a lay-by and fed umpteen episodes of pain-distracting films and TV (highly recommend Narcos). Suddenly woke up with an urge to help the magical Royal Marsden, so have started to pen a book. Started off as "Experiences of Virgin Cancer Tackler", with a view to helping others who may be starting the journey in the future, Lord knows we've done a lot of planning for it. Now it's grown arms and legs and is prologued with a full blown autobiography to date, filled with stories, observations on life, work (say now if you'd rather keep anonymity or are hyper-sensitive) and play. Needless to say, this was a little left field for a bloke who scraped English O-level on his second attempt, but hey, let's go for it. At this point, I want to stress that I'm drug-free and only taking a handful of painkillers - building resistance up. Still it's enriching so far, and I'm conscious that there's a long way to go in my recovery.

Once again many thanks for being in my corner, it's a stable platform that I build from.

PS: If there's anyone out there who's media savvy or has any ideas of where or how to push this masterpiece out into the wide world, I'd appreciate some advice. It wasn't too long ago when I thought a tablet was something Moses wrote the commandments on and Tweet was bird food. I'd rather not blog, so as to contain the material in the hope that some people may wish to donate and receive something in return.

Chapter 9: Preparation for radiotherapy.

Happy New Year from Home on this murky, but dry Friday

Just a quick update to relay that my recovery seems to be going well. I've been whizzing back and forth to the Royal Marsden in the build-up to the next treatment which will be 6 weeks of Radiotherapy starting 29th Jan.

Hilariously they built for what I would term a death mask, by stretching warm, malleable plastic over my head and shoulders and allowing it to cool and harden. This will be bolted to the table in the 30 sessions to prevent me *from escaping from the James Bond Goldfinger-esque set up. A barrel of laughs awaits.*

I've taken full advantage of Christmas and thanks to mince pies, chocolate and lots of other abundant calories have put on some weight in readiness. I've also been building strength up by walking and going to the gym as my left leg still resembles a patchwork quilt.

Over the next week I'll get to see an eye surgeon, who'll give me an indication of the chances of getting more sight in my right eye and I'm also undertaking Manual Lymphatic Drainage sessions to try to take some of the swelling away from my balloon head.

If anyone fancies a bit of an insight to the surgical procedure, a very similar Maxillofacial operation was shown last Sunday by the BBC on Surgeons: The Cutting Edge, it was on BBC 2 and is on iPlayer. The only difference I could see was that the female patient lost her eye and she had the tumour and reconstruction done in a single 8 hour surgery. My procedures were staged in 2 operations to save the right eye and lasted a total of 24hours if you include the third unexpected one. Well, you've got to maintain some bragging rights.

Anyhow, I hope that you're all fantastically well and I hope to catch up with you later this year.

Chapter 11: Half way through radiotherapy.

Just a quick update from me.

Spirits are high and I'm feeling relatively ok as I pass the halfway mark of 6 weeks of radiotherapy. YAY!

I do feel like a bit of a lab rat on the slab, strapped down with the death mask, as my head is zapped; but I'm still smiling and recognise I'm lucky compared to some.

Some of the side effects from radiotherapy are starting to occur and these will heighten as it continues. The right hand side of my face carries a lovely beetroot-rouge tone (no need to buy make-up now), my beard is thinning thanks to hair loss, the inside of my mouth is sore, I've lost the sense of taste and I'm getting more fatigued. On the upside though, I can't taste the hideous vegetable-based concoctions I'm drinking, the hair from the roof of my mouth (which was courtesy of reconstruction) has disappeared and I'm focussing on keeping my weight and fitness in good shape. I'm also attending Manual Lymphatic Drainage sessions locally where the swelling is massaged away from my face. This helps enormously and for homework, I've had a nylon compression full head mask made for me (I call it my Mexican wrestler mask), which I wear around the house and in bed. I've been given strict instructions to avoid wearing it outside given I'd be mistaken for an armed robber or terrorist.

Whilst the sight in right eye will not return (damaged optic nerve) I still get to keep it, which is a bonus. It will hopefully follow the good eye in terms of direction and not go wondering off at 90 degrees. This hasn't deterred me from phoning the DVLA, who are more than happy to allow me to get back driving, my blind spot is naturally a lot bigger than most people's though. Perhaps the local radio station ought to put a traffic alert out when I'm on the roads, judging distances is a little tricky. Some good news on the golf ball sized lump under my bad eye picked up on a recent MRI, looks like it's not another sarcoma and is likely to be a bruise, hopefully it will dissipate later.

Chapter 11: Completing radiotherapy and introducing the Mexican wrestler.

Just a quick update from me, apologies for being off air for a while...

I finished radiotherapy mid-March, but before we could get the bunting out, we discovered that the side effects continued to heighten well past the finish date. Interestingly my noggin resembled a microwave meal as it continued to cook well after the oven had been turned off. Despite his medium to well-done head, in week 9, my alter ego, Mexican Wrestler 'Gonzalez the Gimp' got the radiotherapy in a headlock and symptoms have slowly started to improve.

When things settle down more, I will start to plan the next stages of reconstruction. I've got to sort out some teeth for the right hand side of my upper jaw, organise some further surgery on the droopy eye-lid and get the Frankenstein bolt removed from the side of my head. I might also ask for a tap to be installed on my nostrils, given the gallons of stuff that comes down them at the moment, but hopefully this might be temporary.

Some hot news just in from the Royal Marsden Hospital - on Friday, I had a further MRI scan and saw my oncologist, to check the progress of the unknown blob under my dodgy eye (fell asleep again in the machine). I'm pleased to report that initial analysis has revealed it's reduced slightly, further suggesting that it might not be cancerous.

My energy now seems to be seeping back, just in time for spring, which is providing us with some long-awaited sunshine :). I'm continuing with lots of Manual Lymphatic Drainage sessions, and alongside the gimp mask, these are keeping the face swelling at bay. I anticipate getting back to the book project soon and am looking to building a Facebook profile, to promote the birth of this literary masterpiece. Watch this space - I might be reaching out to friends.

Chapter 12: Taking on the pirate look.

Fantastic Friday Felicitations

Roll on the great weather for the bank holiday, looks like it's going to be a hot one. Just a quick update from cancer corner.

I've now gone live on Facebook and am using this and LinkedIn as mediums to provide photos and updates. If you're not already a victim of my posts, then please search my name and Face Cancer Book on Facebook, 'befriend' me and share the articles to spread the word. I have to confess I feel like a bit of a dinosaur in the headlights of social media, but hopefully haven't yet caused any of-fence. To my utter surprise, I set up a JustGiving page to bank some cash donations I'd received and the total shot up to just shy of £1,500 for the Royal Marsden Cancer Charity in under two weeks, amazing generosity.

The medics have advised me to wear an eye patch when I'm out now, as droopy drawers (my right bottom eyelid) seems determined to travel to my chin. So quite aptly, Hook (the village I live in) now has its own resident pirate. A swashbuckler by day and a Mexican Wrestler by night, who said cancer was boring?

Anyhow not much news on the medical front to speak of, my recovery from radiotherapy is a slow grinding rollercoaster ride. I've been told to ease up and took a bit of a backward step, but hopefully am now on a steady course. Will be seeing my oncologist and surgeon to discuss some further surgery for Droopy Drawers and to remove a Frankenstein nut from the side of my head which is irritating. Talking of backward steps, if I'm fit enough, I'll be abseiling down the Arcellor Mittal Orbit at the Olympic Park with the Thames Tower Team in July, it'll be just like walking the plank!

Have a great Bank Holiday and many thanks again for your enduring support.

Chapter 12: 3 month scans.

Quick update from me on this record Farenheit Friday.

The recent MRI & CT three-monthly check-ups are clear.

I'm finding some new side effects along the glacial path of recovery which are a tad amusing:

- *I currently sound like John Hurt's character in Elephant Man thanks to holes in the roof of my mouth, hopefully these might be plugged if I get some denture teeth on a plate fitted soon.*

- *My dodgy lower eyelid has disappeared from view, so the Pugwash eyepatch will be a summer fashion item, at least 'til the next surgery.*

· *Hairs are returning to the cooked areas of my noggin, nice to see some symmetry returning to my beard now, not so great to have hairs back in the roof of my mouth though.*

Unfortunately the abseil off the Orbit was postponed due to high wind (I hadn't eaten anything odd?) and the new date is now early September.

Finally I spoke (sounding like I had pencils up my nose) at a recent Ability call, this is an internal wellbeing support community. It was great for me to relay parts of my story and answer a few questions, I later got a call from someone who wanted to independently ask me some questions, it felt really great to help them.

I'll sign off for now and wish you all a fantastic break over the sizzling summer. Once again, a heartfelt thanks for your encouraging words of support.

Chapter 12: Glacial plod of radiotherapy, surviving to 50 and charity abseil.

Quick update from Cancer Corner

I hope everyone enjoyed a fantastic holiday, whizzed by for me with both kids at home, peaceful now they're back at school – YAY!!!

The glacial plod of radiotherapy recovery continues and whilst I still sound like John Merrick (Elephant Man) thanks to holes in the roof of my mouth, I've detected a little progress around my eye. Over the last week, I've decided to discard the eye patch now and then - to see what happens. Scabs the size of cornflakes form and when they drop off I think there's a tiny more bit more skin left. It may be wishful thinking and it's certainly a painful long process, but hopefully a worthwhile one.

I saw the passing of my 50th year in August whilst spending a week in France with family around me. It was lovely to get a change of scenery and enjoy some of the local produce ;-), age is only a number.

Eight other nutters from the Reading office and I finally completed our charity 262 feet abseil from the Arcellor Mittal Orbit in the Olympic Park last Sunday in aid of the Royal Marsden Cancer Charity. I usually get jelly legs watching elevated images on TV, especially at the edge of buildings. For some reason I didn't experience any of this at all and as I leant out (see photo), I felt very confident and strong. I reckon it's something to do with what I've endured so far, it just didn't seem a big deal, I even turned into a navy seal on the way down (albeit a one-eyed slow veteran).

Face Cancer book is nearing its completion, 98,000 words written, so I'll be going into proof reading-publishing mode soon. With my three month all-clear given in late July, I expect my medical team will soon be in touch with further appointments etc. Can't wait to see if they notice any change, hopefully I'll continue to recover well with the cornflake strategy.

Chapter 13: Dodgy Scans.

Happy New Year from Cancer Corner!

Hope you had a great festive break with family and friends, I did.

Santa came early and gifted me a load of infections during December…nice. This kept me off the pop during a couple of courses of antibiotics and thanks to my clean living, I seem to have kicked these down into the opposition's 22 and am now looking forward to surgery this Saturday. If all goes to plan, the holes in the roof of my mouth will be sealed, I'll get implants embedded into my new jaw bone (taken from my lower leg) and a very irritating nut taken out of my eyebrow, which plays havoc with my eye patch. Maybe further down the road, we'll look ('scuse the pun) at surgery to build a lower eyelid, blinking hope so (sorry couldn't resist).

Unfortunately, I didn't get the all-clear from my last quarterly scans in mid-December which is a bit of shame. They're concerned about some new swelling in the back of my skull around my cranial nerves (a junction box where 13 nerves feed into your brain), but we're all hoping it's another infection. Time will tell and I'll get rescanned at the end of January to see if there's any change. Wondered why I was getting thumping hangover symptoms whilst 'dry'.

I'm still tinkering with the finished book 'Face Cancer' and am genuinely pleased with it, looking to publish in the next month or two, watch this space.

Anyhow, looking forward to getting a new and improved mouth and taking it for a test drive with a few pints at some point soon.

Chapter 13: Discharged from Operation No.4.

Happy Monday from Cancer Corner

Just a quickie to say I got discharged (sounds disgusting) from hospital on Saturday night. Early signs - the operation appears to have gone well. The scary anaesthetic process was overcome well- I can now add injections to my vocal chords as a new experience (some would love to shut me up I'm sure).

Now recuperating after surgery No. 4, takes my tally to 330 stitches. Face swollen like I've been in the ring with Anthony Joshua as expected, but I'm kind of smiling. Dribbling like a rabid St Bernard again, need a drip tray under my chin.

Next up is to organise a set of scans to check out the sinister-looking cranial nerve swelling, funnily enough, can't feel the thumping headaches at the moment…

Many thanks again for the warm wishes of luck, took them all in with me, your support is very up-lifting.

Chapter 14: 'Recurring Nightmare' going public with bad news again.

Morning (or evening if you're picking this up tonight in the UK).

I didn't think I'd be writing this email, but here goes.

Unfortunately the filthy little squatter has made a reappearance. It's in small patches behind my dodgy eye, in my cranial nerves and surrounding areas.

They can't give me further radiotherapy as they'll melt my head and it's inoperable. Therefore chemotherapy starts next week... well I might as well get the complete set of treatments!!

This means the book 'Face Cancer' is now being rushed to completion (cover completed — copywriting done on 50%) . I'm currently penning the last chapters, giving me something to get my teeth into.

I hate giving out bad news, but I know I've got many supporters in my corner rooting for me. I've found further strength and resolve I'd thought I'd already used up... so bring it on!!

SOME NOTABLE RESPONSES:

Rugby Humour

Si: Afternoon mucka, I have in my diary we're coming to yours on bank holiday Monday 28th. Is that right? Are you available?

Me: Yes, but may be subject to possible change as might be going in for a bit of surgery. All good with you buddy boy?

Si: Having a brain fitted? All good here mate, off on hols Friday. How's you and yours?

Me: Had a gr8 holiday, surgery is dick reduction, need to get it under 14inches :)

Si: Oh right, so you're having your fantasy world removed.

Me: When u coming over with grapes?

Si: I don't know who grapes is? How about Tuesday or Wednesday this week?

Me: Appt good, more tests due early next week, see if spread elsewhere and also assess how fast it's growing. Then likely to be surgery early doors, invasive and probably lose an eye with a lot of face, I knew my looks would improve with this!

Giff: John, I would normally be a bloke and reply taking the piss but I just can't. I am so sorry. If there is anything we can do to help in any way (kids sleepover, pick up from Hook after school for dinner etc.) before/during/after just ask. Happy to sink a quick beer tomorrow if you fancy a chat but understand if not. Hope whatever needs doing starts ASAP. Thoughts with all the Wilkos.

Me: Go on Mark, be a bloke, keep the banter up, need my spirits kept high.

Giff: Ok Nelson!

Hey, I heard it went really well and you're back home early so that's terrific.....I'll come round with the old sponge and bucket and some vaz when you're ready... so just let me know...take care, Rhyds.

John. Your text is much appreciated especially so soon after the op. Amazing to be home so soon and a trick or treat reality show awaits the neighbours' kids. Let's be honest, top man you are, the days of film and stage had passed many moons ago.

Top tip. Don't watch Casualty, cubicle 3 is a departure lounge.

Keep that amazing positive attitude up and eviction of all evidence of your unwelcome squatter should soon be a thing of the past. Nick & Jo

Ski Buddies:

We are all in your corner mate. I can't imagine anyone who has had the pleasure to get to know you even a little wouldn't be standing beside you through this situation. Sounds like you will come out the other side stronger.

Good idea with the book, you hear how cathartic doing just that can be to those facing challenging times. Great idea. Can't wait for Ski Dad piss-taking a few chapters in!

You are an inspiration John and I am looking forward to raising a glass with you next year.

I would love to think of a rousing quote or even settle for a cliché but I am not that guy. For me signing off I can only say - remember you have a formidable network of people who care a great deal for you. Keep that strength with you and tell misfortune to fuck right off! D

Friends:

We're thinking of you a lot and wishing you well. In particular we missed you at the DAD meeting last week, which was quieter and more serious without your levity and your occasional hilarious comment!

M: If you need any more tissue, I can supply a Goodyear tyre size – just let me know - always happy to share:)

Me: Thanks M, I could then be a hybrid in the LGBT community as I'd have lady cells in me

M: OMG, LOL!!!

As you requested, I have deliberately ignored this issue and not raised it with you at all - or provided any support when you have been in the office! However this made me feel very awkward – because I just wanted to give you a hug! I can resist no more! :) So please know that since I heard this news, you have been in my thoughts (a lot). You have my full support and whilst there is little I can do to help, I will try to keep up the banter, fun and laughter, G

Oh Lord, you have made me laugh and cry at the same time.....sounds like they've given you a humour implant at the same time, not that you weren't funny before, but this email has tickled me. As for the description of how you are looking, you might want to stay in on Halloween :)

It's so lovely to hear an update, we do all think about you a lot.

Keep up the good work with the jokes, book and more importantly getting better, can't wait to see your new rugged good looks.

:) :) :) :)It is truly wonderful to hear your positivity and I have huge admiration for you and how you are facing up (sorry, didn't mean the pun, but as it is out there............!!) to dealing with 'the squatter'.

Not so sure I was comfortable with the mouth hair............dealing with the nasal variety is bad enough :)

Looking forward to the first edition of the memoirs - will it include before, during and after photos?...........we can then all decide which was the best version of you!!

Great to hear from you John and to know that the first stage has been positive. Hopefully the Autumn internationals will give you a break from the film/box set viewing (clearly talking about Scotland just now!!).

Having returned from leave today and with all the emails I received this is the best one !!...

Oh and btw – welcome to the world of waxing ! LOL – now you can feel a woman's pain outside of their mood swings and nagging that I'm sure most men have become accustomed to with their good ladies. Selective hearing won't help you out with that one I'm afraid. Take care and I look forward to hearing from you again in due course.

Jane, words usually come easy to me - but this is already my 6th or 7th effort to answer your message concerning John. We are all deeply touched and thoroughly upset to hear about the diagnosis John is confronted with (more precisely: all of you are confronted with). It calls to mind my condition when I was diagnosed with the same disease less than three years ago. I remember well how radically, all of a sudden, all other things get less important and how burdensome the uncertainty about the exact outcome of biopsies and other examinations feels. You will need a lot of patience. In retrospect I think Klaus - and probably Jonathan and Benjamin as well - were so concerned about me that they suffered more than me.

We feel deeply attached to all of you and realise once again what close ties have established between us in the relatively short time we've known each other.

We're thinking of you and looking forward very much to welcome our dear Max here in October! Anja, Klaus and Benny

---

Me: Thanks Jo, back to the gym today with my personal trainer Jane, who thankfully reined me in when I need to, so I enjoyed a 45 min gentle work out. The Sunshine milf looks delicious and will get a mention in my book :). John

Jo: sunshine milf you wrote - made me laugh because that was what you were to John's flirting surgeon last week!!! hahahahah xxx Jo

ACKNOWLEDGEMENTS

A huge heartfelt thank you to everyone listed here for their deep support. You have made my path easier to navigate, filled my tank with resolve and generally kept me in check. *Face Cancer* is a testament to you all.

My wife Jane and children, Max and Lois, there all the way, constantly by my side.

My wider family.

All of my friends and supporters: the longstanding, renewed and new friendships I've made are gold dust. Peter for his fantastic company and safe passage!

A special mention to Liam Ryan, fellow author and face cancer survivor - you rock, even more than the Smashing Pumpkins!

The many amazing, caring staff at various hospitals I attended including The Royal Marsden, The Chelsea & Westminster, Basingstoke and North Hampshire, The Royal Surrey, Clare Park, The Hampshire Clinic and the Hampshire Lymphoedema Clinic.

My team of medical experts: Dr Aisha Miah - Consultant Oncologist Consultant , Cyrus Kerawala - Maxillofacial and Oral Consultant, my first consultant Jacob D'Souza, Richard Scawn - Consultant Ophthalmic Plastic Surgeon, Rodger Whitelocke (retired).

Dr Kate McKenna at the local doctor's surgery, Dawn Heal & Sue Barnes - my MLD team, Louise Sanders - Osteopath. Jo Abbott at *Body MOT Systems*, Eva Tanner and GP at *The O Lab Practice*, Jamie at *The Guinea Court Dental Surgery*.

With particular support to the publication of *Face Cancer*:

My initial proof readers - Gabi, Jane, Steve, Mum, Nick, Ewan and Jess in my employer's regulatory compliance team.

Contributors to the 'Glossary of Sent Messages' and all of those who responded to my messages. I asked for the banter to continue, you didn't disappoint.

Pru Gayton at *PAC Copywriting*, who went over and above.

My publisher Paul, at *The Self Publishing Studio*, who took the idea to market with Pru and me.

The superb design, web and photography team at *Clere Group Ltd*, especially Sarah and Paul for your personal support and advice on the project.

Heather Mason for your sterling medical research.

Phil Tufnell, Matt Dawson and Dr Miah for very kindly agreeing to lend a hand with the foreword and the book's success.